AN INTRODUCTION TO ENGLISH LANGUAGE

Consultant Editors: Noël Burton-Roberts, *University of Newcastle* and
Andrew Spencer, *University of Essex*

An Introduction to English Language

Word, Sound and Sentence

3rd Edition

Koenraad Kuiper

AND

W. Scott Allan

palgrave
macmillan

© Koenraad Kuiper and W. Scott Allan, 1996, 2004
© Koenraad Kuiper and Harriet Allan, 2010

First published 1996 by Palgrave Macmillan
Second edition published 2004 by Palgrave Macmillan
Third edition published 2010 by
PALGRAVE MACMILLAN

Palgrave Macmillan in the UK is an imprint of Macmillan Publishers Limited, registered in England, company number 785998, of Houndmills, Basingstoke, Hampshire RG21 6XS.

Palgrave Macmillan in the US is a division of St Martin's Press LLC, 175 Fifth Avenue, New York, NY 10010.

Palgrave Macmillan is the global academic imprint of the above companies and has companies and representatives throughout the world.

Palgrave® and Macmillan® are registered trademarks in the United States, the United Kingdom, Europe and other countries.

ISBN: 978–0–230–20800–1 hardback
ISBN: 978–0–230–20801–8 paperback

This book is printed on paper suitable for recycling and made from fully managed and sustained forest sources. Logging, pulping and manufacturing processes are expected to conform to the environmental regulations of the country of origin.

A catalogue record for this book is available from the British Library.

A catalog record for this book is available from the Library of Congress.

10 9 8 7 6 5 4 3 2 1
19 18 17 16 15 14 13 12 11 10

Printed in China

Dedicated to the memory of W. Scott Allan

Never despise grammar; a fascinating machine, full of cunning tricks and clever devices.

Fleur Adcock

Contents

part two   Sounds   113

Preface to the Third Edition

This edition was produced without the inspirational collaboration of Scott Allan, who died before he could contribute to it. I miss his keen sense of how to teach something, his great sense of humour and his passion for linguistics. I hope, in preparing this edition without him, that none of the essence of his contribution has been lost.

This third edition has become more than a book. It now has a set of on-line supports which have been trialled for the last five years. These can be seen as part of the book but in electronic form. In providing these additional learning resources, the aim has been to give users of the book additional learning pathways. These do not replace the book but supplement it. They include a set of movies, each of which consists of a PowerPoint presentation with voiceover. Each covers and refers to a section of the book. They can be viewed before the section of the book is read as a way into the exposition or they can be used for revision at any time. The PowerPoint slides themselves are downloadable as a way of gaining some structure for note taking when reading the book. While the textbook contains a number of exercises, the on-line site contains a large number of quizzes to facilitate gaining mastery of the concepts and analytic processes outlined in the book. Each quiz is short and can be attempted many times, often with different individual questions being randomly assigned so that readers can get better at simple things like recognizing parts of speech and doing simple phonetic description. Each section ends with quizzes which test knowledge of terminology in the section and the general contents of the section. These aim to provide useful revision before a test. The site also contains a set of audio files which introduce small extension topics such as applications which are interesting, observations about language and anything that seemed worth people having on their ipods, however briefly. Reference to the web-based resources that go with the book is given at the end of each of the sections. The site is: http://www.palgrave.com/language/kuiperandallan/

In harmony with the burgeoning web, this edition also makes reference to web sites that readers might find interesting or helpful. For example, readers may want to download an IPA font or they might want to hear how Nigerian speakers of English sound or to see what the vocal cords look like when they vibrate. There are references to URLs to facilitate this. The disadvantage of doing this is the URLs do not always remain constant. Most students, are, however, savvy enough to find their way on the web.

Though the bones of the book remain much the same, it has further extended its focus throughout with more material on new and other Englishes. These offer readers examples of linguistic variation and illustrate how different English is in different parts of the world. At the suggestion of reviewers, I have also included a new section (1.1.7) on variation and change raising the interesting question of what the core attributes of a language might be when there is such a great deal of variation and when languages can change beyond recognition in a millennium.

Although previous editions were tacitly also introductions to linguistics, again at the suggestion of a reviewer, I have included in the introductory chapter a section on linguistics, its interaction with related disciplines and some of its applications (1.2). The sound files often refer back to these applications which, although not central to the book are, nevertheless, worthwhile and stimulating.

To make way for the new material, most of Chapter 5.7 has been dropped. I have found, and so did Scott, that this section was a little too advanced for introductory students. Instead, a shorter more introductory approach has been taken to phonological features.

One of our reviewers has also suggested that we have not addressed ourselves earlier to users of the book who are training to be teachers. That is true and so the question is, why should you, if your are training to be a schoolteacher, want to know something of the English language? The answer is not far to seek. All teachers for whom English is the medium of instruction, at whatever level, but particularly at elementary school level, are teaching English. They do that often without an understanding of the language that is being taught. For example, when a teacher teaches reading early on in elementary school, the complex nature of the skills that children acquire as they learn to read is easy to underestimate. The diagnosis of dyslexia in the case of children who are having trouble to read has to be taken on trust if the nature of reading skills is uniformed by a basic understanding of the nature of language. Without a preliminary appreciation that language varies and changes, it is easy for teachers of elementary school-aged children to come to believe that children who do not speak and write prestige varieties of a language are deficient in some way. This book attempts to provide a backdrop to a more informed pedagogy in such domains.

For various forms of help with this edition I have to thank Georgie Columbus and Joan Smith/Kocamahhul who wrote some of the quizzes and quiz items, Gregor Ronald for help with setting the web site up at the University of Canterbury, Teaching and Learning Services at the University of Canterbury for grants to build the web site and my students who each year provide the encouragement to have me widen and upgrade the avenues by which they can learn (and find typos and infelicities of expression).

KOENRAAD KUIPER
Christchurch

Preface to the Second Edition

We are pleased that so many people have read and used this book that a second edition has been made possible. We have benefited from the comments of many people, particularly our own students who have shown us in various ways which parts of the book they found difficult. We are pleased to be able to have another attempt at making things better for them.

At the suggestion of a number of readers we have transferred the Words section to the beginning since it contains material that is more familiar to many students.

We are aware that this book is being used world-wide. Colleagues have seen it in Helsinki, Kuala Lumpur and Amsterdam. This places us under an obligation to make it clear that English is not homogeneous. Thus, in this edition, we pay more attention to regional and social dialect variation with examples drawn from the Englishes of various parts of the world.

We have ensured more attention is paid to the student of literature who is using this book, by paying greater attention to the terminology used in textual analysis. This includes giving attention to figures of speech in the Words section and, in the Sounds section, to form in poetry including rhyme schemes, meter and traditional verse forms.

We have included a grading notation for the exercises at the end of the chapters, starting with elementary ones (identified by •) and concluding with some more taxing ones (labelled •••) for those who are better able to cope with them. We have also made numerous changes in wording, corrected errors in the first edition and generally tried to improve the pedagogical flow of the exposition. We hope this edition will continue to be useful to teachers and students alike.

Our thanks go to those of our students who have made suggestions, found mistakes and infelicities, and those who have tutored in our courses, for drawing their suggestions to our attention, and to those who have enjoyed using the first edition and said so. We are also grateful to our respective institutions for periods of study leave which have made working on the book easier, and the first author wishes to acknowledge the assistance of the Netherlands Institute for Advanced Studies for a Fellowship during which the finishing touches were put to this edition. For the preparation of the second edition we also have the following individuals to thank for helpful comments, new materials, or for finding infelicities and errors: Peter Cragg, Carolyn Davies, Alison Kuiper, Heidi Quinn, Lee Stanton and Jeroen van de Weijer.

KOENRAAD KUIPER   W. SCOTT ALLAN
Christchurch   *Auckland*

Preface to the First Edition

This book is written for students of English and their teachers. Its aim is to introduce you, our readers, to the English language: to its sounds, its words and its sentences. We have supposed that you know little about these topics but are willing to learn. We also suppose that the best way to learn is through a combination of listening and doing. We have made our exposition relatively simple, trying always to present the essential nature of the phenomena rather than getting too caught up in the details. This book may therefore be seen (and hopefully used) both as a stand-alone introduction or as precursor to more advanced treatments of linguistic phenomena elsewhere.

In order to help beginners in the study of language we have included extensive glossaries at the end of each section (that is, at the end of the Introduction, and Parts One, Two and Three) where students can use them for reference and for revision. Professional linguists might take issue with some of our definitions of specialist terms. Our excuse is that we have tried to keep our definitions as simple as possible so that students may go on later to come to a deeper understanding of the theories that lie behind the terms.

At the end of each of the three parts of the book we also provide some additional reading and references dealing with the areas we covered in that particular part.

A large part of this book consists of exercises, which we hope you will do, rather than skim over. We have put stop signs in the form of a row of dots at the end of many exercises to suggest that you do not go on until you have actually tried the exercise.

The exercises are of three kinds. The first are expository exercises, which ask questions so as to set the scene for an expository section. These are indicated in the text by a shaded box. The answers to these exercises often follow directly in the text. The second are practice exercises, which should be done at the point where they appear in the book so that some skill in analytic technique is acquired at the appropriate time. The third type are applied exercises, which enable you to use some of the material you have learned to explore texts. There are more of both the latter types at the end of chapters. Most exercises, other than open-ended ones, have answers provided at the end of the book. Readers should, of course, work through the questions for themselves before looking at our answers. A disagreement with our answer does not always mean that the student is wrong. Sometimes differences of opinion are the beginning of new understanding.

We wish also to justify creating a new textbook of this kind. It is our belief that a great many students of English around the world take introductory courses dealing with the English language. We have in mind a one-semester or full-year course taken as a requirement or option for undergraduate students of English or trainee teachers. We believe that there are few purpose-built texts for such courses. Students of English tend to make do with books which are introductions to linguistics and which make use of data from languages other than English. Such books often include a variety of topics of interest to students of linguistics such as how children acquire languages and whether animals have languages. Although all these topics are of interest, we believe that such an approach is not the best one for students of English.

The courses for which this book is intended were in the past promoted as a way of learning to speak and write more effectively. It seems, however, that people learn to speak and write better not by studying the structure of the language they already speak, but by writing and speaking more, and with appropriate audiences in mind and appropriate feedback.

It does not follow that it is not valuable for those who already know a language or are learning to speak it to know something about it. Students and teachers of English often need an informed way to talk about English. An agreed terminology and understanding of its use can be useful in pointing out particular problems in a student's writing, or in clarifying a complex passage. In addition, an ability to analyse language contributes significantly to the conscious appreciation of literary form and style. Since many students of English devote most of their studies to the reading and analysis of literature this seems a valuable ability to foster. Finally, and most importantly, an understanding of human language is essential to understanding what it means to be human. The acquisition of a human language is a major intellectual accomplishment, however effortlessly this acquisition comes about. So much else that we learn or accomplish throughout our lives depends on our ability to speak, write, read and understand a language.

We believe that this book aims clearly at these particular ends.

Both authors have developed the material in this book in the first-year courses in English which they teach at the Universities of Auckland and Canterbury. The students in these courses are usually correctly presumed to have little or no knowledge of the nature of the English language and its structure. The great majority of them take these courses as their only course in English language. We are grateful to them and their candid comments on our teaching material. This book is written therefore for students of English and their teachers in the hope that they find their language as interesting as we do.

It is impossible properly to acknowledge the help of all the very many people, among them John Andreae, Mary Clark, Derek Davy and Doug Haggo, who have used and commented on this text and its precursors through their long and variable geneses. To all the many friends, colleagues and students who have used and commented on this material, our profound thanks.

We are grateful to Harriet Allan, Alison Kuiper, Francesca Hickey, Linda Whybrew and the Macmillan editors for many helpful suggestions during the drafting of the final versions. For those errors and infelicities that remain we take sole responsibility.

Both authors are grateful to their respective institutions for a period of study-leave during which this book went through its last revisions. The first author also gratefully acknowledges the assistance of the Research Institute for Language and Speech of Utrecht University and the Netherlands Scientific Organisation (NWO).

We would value any comments and suggestions for the book's future improvement.

KOENRAAD KUIPER   W. SCOTT ALLAN
Christchurch   *Auckland*

Acknowledgements

Section 6 of Chapter 1 draws on D. Crystal and D. Davy, *Investigating English Style* (London: Longman, 1969).

The examples of loan word vocabulary in South Africa in Chapter 3 are drawn from P. Silva, 'The lexis of South African English: Reflections of a multilingual society', in *Englishes around the World 2: Caribbean, Africa, Asia, Australasia. Studies in Honour of Manfred Görlach*, ed. E. W. Schneider (Amsterdam/ Philadelphia: John Benjamins, 1997).

The examples of loan word vocabulary in the Antarctic in Chapter 3 are drawn from B. Hince, *The Antarctic Dictionary: A Complete Guide to Antarctic English* (Collingwood: CSIRO Publishing, 2000).

The section dealing with phonological differences between dialects, in Chapter 5, draws on J. D. O'Connor, *Phonetics* (Harmondsworth: Pelican, 1973), and I. C. Wells, *Accents of English* (Cambridge: Cambridge University Press, 1982).

Data for Exercise 5.9 are from H. A. Gleason, *A Workbook in Linguistics* (New York: Holt, Rinehart & Winston, 1955).

The model of syllable structure in Chapter 6 is taken from that introduced in R. Lass, *Phonology: An Introduction to Basic Concepts* (Cambridge: Cambridge University Press, 1984). The discussion of stress placement is based on that found in P. Roach, *English Phonetics and Phonology: A Practical Course* (Cambridge: Cambridge University Press, 1983).

The terms tone, tone group, tonic relating to intonation are taken from D. Crystal, *The English Tone of Voice* (London: Edward Arnold, 1975), and M. A. K. Halliday, *A Course in Spoken English Intonation* (Oxford: Oxford University Press, 1970).

The authors and publisher wish to thank the following for permission to use copyright material:

John Benjamins Publishing Company for Tables 5.4, 5.5 adapted from W S Allan and D Starks, 'No-one sounds like us?' from *New Zealand English*, ed. A Bell and K Kuiper (2000) Tables 2, 3;

Carlton Publishing Group and Curtis Brown Ltd, New York, on behalf of the Estate of the author for Ogdon Nash, 'The Cuckoo' from *Candy is Dandy* by Ogdon Nash (1953), Andre Deutsch, first published in *The New Yorker* (1950). Copyright © 1950 by Ogdon Nash;

Curtis Brown (Aust) Pty Ltd on behalf of the author for Albert Wendt, 'Conversation' from *Inside Us the Dead* by Albert Wendt, Longman Paul (1976);

Faber and Faber Ltd and Random House, Inc for an extract from W H Auden, 'Night Mail' from *Collected Poems* by W H Auden (1976). Copyright © 1938 by W H Auden;

The International Phonetic Association for the International Phonetic Alphabet and extracts from IPA charts. Copyright © International Phonetic Association;

W W Norton & Company for e. e. cummings, 'love is more thicker than forget' from *Complete Poems, 1904-1962* by e. e. cummings, edited by George J Firmage. Copyright © 1991 by the Trustees for the E. E. Cummings Trust and George James Firmage;

Oxford University Press for the entry 'freight' from *Oxford Concise English Dictionary*, 9th edn (1955), p. 450; entry for 'freight' from *Oxford English Dictionary*, 1st edn, vol. 4 (1933) pp. 529–30; and entry for 'sept' from *Pocket Oxford Dictionary of Current English*, 4th edn, p.751;

Every effort has been made to trace the copyright holders but if any have been inadvertently overlooked the publishers will be pleased to make the necessary arrangement at the first opportunity.

Abbreviations and Symbols

#	word boundary
*	indicates that the following is an ungrammatical form
/ /	slash brackets surrounding phonemic symbols
[]	brackets surrounding phonetic symbols or constituents of complex structures in morphology and syntax
A	adjective, adverb, numeral
ADJ	adjective
AP	adjective phrase, adverb phrase
AuxV	auxiliary verb
C	consonant
CD	compact disc
CD ROM	compact disc read-only memory
Co	coda
CONJ	conjunction
DEG	degree adverb
DET	determiner
IPA	International Phonetic Alphabet
LexV	lexical verb
N	noun
NP	noun phrase
Nu	nucleus
OED	*Oxford English Dictionary*
On	onset
P	preposition
POSS	possessive phrase
PP	prepositional phrase
PRON	pronoun
Rh	rhyme

S	clause or sentence
S'	embedded clause
Σ	syllable
V	vowel
V	verb
VP	verb phrase
|	tone unit boundary

THE INTERNATIONAL PHONETIC ALPHABET (revised to 2005)

CONSONANTS (PULMONIC)

© 2005 IPA

	Bilabial	Labiodental	Dental	Alveolar	Postalveolar	Retroflex	Palatal	Velar	Uvular	Pharyngeal	Glottal
Plosive	p b			t d		ʈ ɖ	c ɟ	k g	q ɢ		ʔ
Nasal	m	ɱ		n		ɳ	ɲ	ŋ	N		
Trill	B			r					R		
Tap or Flap				ɾ		ɽ					
Fricative	ɸ β	f v	θ ð	s z	ʃ ʒ	ʂ ʐ	ç ʝ	x ɣ	χ ʁ	ħ ʕ	h ɦ
Lateral fricative				ɬ ɮ							
Approximant		ʋ		ɹ		ɻ	j	ɰ			
Lateral approximant				l		ɭ	ʎ	L			

Where symbols appear in pairs, the one to the right represents a voiced consonant. Shaded areas denote articulations judged impossible.

CONSONANTS (NON-PULMONIC)

Clicks		Voiced implosives		Ejectives	
ʘ	Bilabial	ɓ	Bilabial	ʼ	Examples:
ǀ	Dental	ɗ	Dental/alveolar	pʼ	Bilabial
ǃ	(Post)alveolar	ʄ	Palatal	tʼ	Dental/alveolar
ǂ	Palatoalveolar	ɠ	Velar	kʼ	Velar
ǁ	Alveolar lateral	ʛ	Uvular	sʼ	Alveolar fricative

OTHER SYMBOLS

ʍ Voiceless labial-velar fricative

w Voiced labial-velar approximant

ɥ Voiced labial-palatal approximant

ʜ Voiceless epiglottal fricative

ʢ Voiced epiglottal fricative

ʡ Epiglottal plosive

ɕ ʑ Alveolo-palatal fricatives

ɺ Voiced alveolar lateral flap

ɧ Simultaneous ʃ and x

Affricates and double articulations can be represented by two symbols joined by a tie bar if necessary.

k͡p t͡s

VOWELS

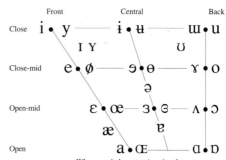

Where symbols appear in pairs, the one to the right represents a rounded vowel.

SUPRASEGMENTALS

	Primary stress	foʊnəˈtɪʃən
	Secondary stress	
ː	Long	eː
ˑ	Half-long	eˑ
̆	Extra-short	ĕ
	Minor (foot) group	
‖	Major (intonation) group	
.	Syllable break	ɹi.ækt
‿	Linking (absence of a break)	

TONES AND WORD ACCENTS

LEVEL			CONTOUR		
e̋ or ˥	Extra high		ě or ˩˥	Rising
é ˦	High		ê ˥˩	Falling
ē ˧	Mid		e᷄ ˦˥	High rising
è ˨	Low		e᷅ ˩˨	Low rising
ȅ ˩	Extra low		e᷈	Rising-falling
↓	Downstep		↗	Global rise
↑	Upstep		↘	Global fall

DIACRITICS Diatrics may be placed above a symbol with a descender, e.g. ŋ̊

Voiceless	n̥ d̥		Breathy voiced	b̤ a̤		Dental	t̪ d̪
Voiced	s̬ t̬		Creaky voiced	b̰ a̰		Apical	t̺ d̺
Aspirated	tʰ dʰ		Linguolabial	t̼ d̼		Laminal	t̻ d̻
More rounded	ɔ̹	w	Labialized	tʷ dʷ	~	Nasalized	ẽ
Less rounded	ɔ̜	j	Palatalized	tʲ dʲ	n	Nasal release	dⁿ
Advanced	u̟	ɣ	Velarized	tˠ dˠ	l	Lateral release	dˡ
Retracted	e̠	ˤ	Pharyngealized	tˤ dˤ	̚	No audible release	d̚
Centralized	ë	~	Velarized or Pharyngealized	ɫ			
Mid-centralized	e̽		Raised	e̝	(ɹ̝ = voiced alveolar fricative)		
Syllabic	n̩		Lowered	e̞	(β̞ = voiced bilabial approximant)		
Non-syllabic	e̯		Advanced Tongue Root	e̘			
Rhoticity	ɚ a˞		Retracted Tongue Root	e̙			

Introduction: What is a Language?

1.1 PROPERTIES OF HUMAN LANGUAGE

This book is written for students who are embarking on the study of the English language and so we will be looking at knowledge which people who speak English have already acquired. Since most of you who are looking at these words can read this book, you will already 'know' its content. You could not read English if you did not know English. This knowledge you have is unconscious and this book's aim is to bring it to your conscious awareness.

However, if you are studying English formally in a classroom, the subject usually focuses on the use people make of the language. This can take the form of helping students to improve their reading, writing, speaking and listening, or studying the use other people, such as writers, have made of the English language. In order to understand how you, writers, and others, have used language in particular ways and situations it is necessary first to know something about what language is; that is, what people know when they know it rather than what people do when they use it. So there is a practical as well as an intellectual point to knowing about the language you speak and write.

So what do people know when they know a language? You would think that this is an easy question to answer since, as speakers of it, we all use our language frequently. The situation is rather like driving a car. Many people drive a car perfectly well without knowing how the car works. In the case of languages, the situation is more difficult in that languages are not physical objects like cars. They exist only within the minds of speakers. There are many theories about how language works, but the more language is studied the more complex it seems to become.

When people know a language, they must know how speech sounds relate to meanings. When speaking, we produce sounds and our hearers hear sound. Speech sounds are the medium we use to represent what it is we are saying, that is, they represent content or meaning, and both the speaker and hearer normally know the meanings which are conveyed by the sounds produced by a speaker (always provided that both the speaker and hearer speak the same language). But sounds convey meaning only indirectly. Speech sounds do not themselves have meaning. Words (and some other units to be studied later) have meanings. Words, when we use them, come from our mouths as sounds. But not necessarily. In writing they take the form of marks on paper and in the case of some people who are deaf, words can take the form of signs made by the person's hands and face. However, for most speakers, a language is a complex relationship between speech sounds and the meanings which they indirectly convey.

By way of contrast, whales and porpoises produce a large range of sounds: grunts, squeaks, whistles, among other things. If you were a marine biologist and following a school of whales, recording their sounds, what would you be able to say about whale language on the basis of your observations of the whales' behaviour and the sounds they made? The answer must be 'very little'. You might be able to relate particular sounds to particular activities, such as feeding. However, this would not prove much since the sounds could indicate pleasure, or the type of food being consumed, or call signs that food was available, and any number of other things. The problem is that as a marine biologist you cannot crack the code because you know nothing about how the code is organized or indeed if there is a code at all. It seems, in fact, that it is a kind of sonar to locate friends and relatives a long way apart in the ocean.

1.1.1 LANGUAGE IS A CODE

code
symbol

A language can be regarded as a code for conveying a great variety of information. The linguistic code uses symbols – signals which mean or convey something other than themselves. Think, for example, of traffic lights. What are the symbols in the traffic-light code, and what meaning does each convey? In the traffic-light code, each of a set of three, vertically arranged, coloured lights is associated with a particular instruction to the motorist. A red light conveys the instruction 'Stop'. A yellow light conveys the instruction 'Prepare to stop'. A green light conveys the instruction 'Proceed'. The relationship between a particular colour and the instruction it conveys is established by convention. It is quite easy to imagine a society which used different colours, or different signals, for the same instructions. In some countries a yellow light comes on to tell you the light is going to turn to green. There are relationships between what one light conveys and what the others convey. Unless the lights are not working, one of them is always on but they are never all on at once. The red light and the green light convey conflicting messages, and it would be contradictory to have them both on at the same time.

This simple example has some useful analogies with human languages. A language uses sounds as its basic medium rather than lights, but it too has a set of symbols. Each word of a language is a symbol, a sequence of sounds or letters, or hand and face signs in the case of signing for the deaf, which is related by convention to a particular meaning. As in the example of the lights, this relationship is arbitrary; the living creature which is represented in English by the sound sequence *horse* might just as easily be called *cheval, paard* or *caballo* – as it is in other languages. Also there are relationships between symbols. For example, it is sometimes said that no two words of a language have exactly the same meaning. Stop for a moment and decide whether you think this is true.

1.1.2 LINGUISTIC SYMBOLS HAVE FUNCTION AND FORM

Not only does a language contain the set of symbols called words, but words are also put together to make phrases and sentences. The phrases and sentences of **phrase** a language (and, indeed, as we will see, the words themselves) have structure. **sentence** What is a structure? Look, for example, at a building, a flower, a scaffolding, a **structure** book. The structured things are organized according to some kind of principle or pattern. For instance, they may consist of sequences of similar items. Various parts may relate to each other in fixed ways. There may appear to be an overall plan to the thing.

One of the most fundamental facts about language is that it has structure. To illustrate this, think of a simple sentence such as *Mary swims*. Say it out loud and listen to its sound. Just listening for sound, this sentence seems to be a totally unstructured sequence of noises, one merging into the next, like a whale melody. But as a sentence in a human language and one that we know, we can ask: what structure is there in this simple sentence, *Mary swims*?

The following features of the sentence appear to have structure:

1   Although the sound of the sentence *Mary swims* is continuous (we do not stop between letters) it is heard as a *sequence of sounds*. The first sound is a *m*, the second an *e,* as in *red* (or for some speakers as in *hairy*), and the third an *r*, and so on. There are nine sounds altogether.

2   The nine sounds of this sentence are grouped into two words, the word *Mary* and the word *swims*. The word *Mary* is the name of a person or animal; *swims* designates an action. You may know that *Mary* is a noun and *swims* is a verb and that the *s* on the end of *swims* tells us that the swimming is not taking place in the past.

3   We may also perceive that during the saying of the sequence of individual sounds, emphasis is placed in some places more than it is in others, and that there are, in fact, two main places where emphasis can be placed: either on the *a* of *Mary* or on the *i* of *swims*.

4   We might also perceive that the pitch of the speaker's voice rises and falls during the speaking. Normally it would fall at the end of *swims*.

In the structure of this sentence, a sequence of units is built up from others. A sequence of nine sounds make up a sequence of two words. The first four sounds make up the first word while the rest make up the second word. We are simplifying here since it is not just sounds which make a word into a word. We suggested above that words also have meanings and grammatical properties such as, for example, being nouns.

constituent
linear
hierarchical
level

The words in turn are the constituent parts (or constituents) of the sentence. Notwithstanding this, we can see that the structure is linear, that is, a particular set of units in a particular order, and it is hierarchical, that is, one unit is made up of units lower down on the hierarchy. So the units are on different levels.

Such a hierarchy can be represented as a tree or box diagram.

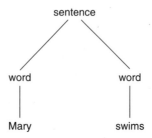

Figure 1.1   Tree diagram

sentence	
word	word
Mary	swims

Figure 1.2   Box diagram

To gain an understanding of structures like this we can suppose sentences to be rather like some trains. Let us look at a train which consists of two engines at the front, a freight section, first- and second-class passenger cars, and a caboose or guard's van. Diagrams of such a train might look something like this:

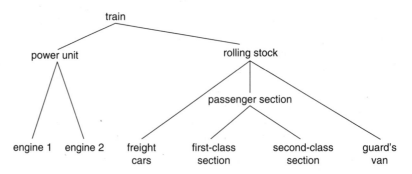

Figure 1.3   Tree diagram

train						
power unit			rolling stock			
engine 1	engine 2	freight cars	passenger cars		guard's van	
			first class	second class		

Figure 1.4 Box diagram

Why choose a train as an analogy? Think of a train appearing out of a tunnel. You first see the engine and then various carriages until finally you see the guard's van or caboose. When a sentence comes from your mouth it is rather like the train emerging from the tunnel, first one word, then another and so on until the sentence reaches its end. We can only recognize words after they have started to appear from someone's mouth, just as we can only recognize carriages when they have at least partially appeared from the tunnel. Furthermore we do not know the structure of the sentence until the last word has been uttered, just as we do not know the train is completely out of the tunnel until the guard's van has appeared.

In describing the structure of a train or a sentence, each unit can be looked at in two ways. First, we can describe the function of the unit by seeing what part it plays in the structure of the next highest unit. The power unit functions as the first unit of the train. Secondly, we can describe the form of the unit by examining its internal structure. The power unit of the train has the form of two engines coupled one behind the other. **function**

form

At the top level of the hierarchy units have no function because they do not play a role in higher structures. Trains as such are not parts of other units larger than trains. In the case of sentences it depends what one wishes to study. For people who study the grammatical structure of a language, the sentence can be regarded as the top level. It therefore has no function, not being part of a larger structure. But if one were studying people's writing, then sentences would function in larger units. In essays, sentences have a function in paragraphs, as topic sentences or as sentences that expand the topic in some way. Paragraphs have a function in the essay. There are introductory paragraphs, intermediate paragraphs, and concluding paragraphs, all of which have particular functions. However, because sentences have a special kind of structure that is different from that of an essay, grammatical analyses generally stop at the level of the sentence.

Classify each of the following units according to its *form*, that is, its internal structure, and its *function*, that is, the role the unit plays in another:

eraser on a pencil, a semicolon, a newspaper headline

The *form* of an eraser is a cylindrical piece of rubber about the same diameter as the pencil. The eraser *functions* as the element on the other end of a pencil from the point.

A semicolon has the *form* of a full stop over a comma. It *functions* as a mark of punctuation between two independent sections of a sentence.

A newspaper headline has the *form* of a rather telegraphic phrase or sentence in much larger type than the body of the article. It *functions* as the line(s) at the top of an article in the newspaper.

Music is structured in a similar hierarchical fashion. A pop song might start with a few introductory chords, followed by the first melody, then the chorus, a repeat of the first melody, then the chorus again. Then a second melody appears, after which there is a chorus and then the first melody reappears, and the final chorus. But each melody has its own structure; a particular sequence of notes organized into bars.

1.1.3 LINGUISTIC UNITS ARE CONSTRUCTED ACCORDING TO RULES

rule

As we have seen, units of a language have a hierarchical organization; that is, they are made up of a series of units, each of which may have an internal structure. Some linguistic units (for example, the words of a language) usually have to be learned one by one. However, larger units of the language are often put together in a systematic way by means of rules that combine or rearrange smaller units to form larger ones, and which assign a meaning to the result.

Make a sentence out of each of the following sets of words. What does this tell you about word order in English sentences?

(a)   sleeps, a, baby, newborn

(b)   in, house, live, green, the, a, people

(c)   the, kicked, boy, ball, a

You will see that only a few word orders actually give acceptable English sentences. All other orders (including the original ones in the question) are contrary to the rules of English sentence construction.

What is the exact nature of the rules that determine how units in English may be combined? This is a difficult question but we can get some idea of the diversity of such rules by looking at how they operate in particular instances. There are rules, for example, which determine the sequencing possibilities of larger units within words. Whereas both the word *sanity* and the word *saneness* are possible, the word *bleakness* is possible but the word *bleakity* is not. The rules which determine these possibilities will be looked at in Part One.

Other rules determine which sequences of sound are permitted to be words in English. For example, of the words *blick* and *bnick*: only *blick* is a potential English word. Speakers of English can also locate which sequence is not permitted. In the case of *bnick,* it is the *bn* sequence. In the first instance it might seem that the sequence is not allowed because it is more difficult to pronounce. However, that cannot be so because it occurs in places other than initially in a word, for instance in the word *hobnailed,* as in *hobnailed boots,* and when it does, speakers of English have no difficulty pronouncing it. This shows that this rule is a linguistic one and not a purely biological one. We shall have more to discover about such restrictions in Part Two.

Then there are rules which determine how words fit into sentences. For example, the sentence *Mary wheeled* is somehow unfinished because the word *wheel* (and not the word *Mary*) requires additional constituents to play a role in this sentence. We also know that there are related questions which correspond to the following statements: *John is eating his breakfast, John won't eat his breakfast, John should eat his breakfast, John ate his breakfast.* These questions are: *Is John eating his breakfast? Won't John eat his breakfast? Should John eat his breakfast?* and *Did John eat his breakfast?* Regardless of the particular form of the statement and regardless of whether you or any other speaker of English has ever come across the statement before, you will be able to form the related question. This suggests that there must be rules for relating statements to questions and there must be rules determining how sentences may be formed. They form the subject matter of Part Three.

The important thing to realize at this point is that the knowledge you have just exhibited is knowledge of the rules by which smaller units of English must form larger ones. You were never taught these rules directly, either at school or by your parents. Somehow they have come to exist unconsciously in your mind. You use them almost without error whenever you speak, read, write or listen to English. In a real way we have just tapped into your unconscious mind because that is where your language is.

Notice that we are using the word *rule* here in a different sense from that which it ordinarily carries. The rules we are concerned with here are not of the sort *Keep off the grass* or *Skirt hems must be no higher than two inches above the knee.* Our rules are descriptive, not prescriptive; this means they describe regularities in the structure of language, they do not tell you what to do.

descriptive, prescriptive rule

We are now ready to return to our earlier questions: What is language? and What do we know when we know a language? Language is a code that allows us to represent thoughts and ideas by means of sounds (or letters). A special property of this code is that its symbols are complex; that is, they have internal structure. This means that the sounds do not directly convey meanings in the way that a scream of pain might convey directly that the person who screamed is in pain. Units have a structure which is rule-governed. As we have suggested, speakers of the language know these rules intuitively, although they are not able to say what they are or how they work. The rules are of many different kinds. Some of them are concerned with the combination of sounds, some with the formation of phrases and sentences, and some with the assignment of meaning. Some of these latter rules are extremely subtle. For example:

Whose dressing is under consideration in each of the following sentences?

(a)   Jill appealed to Mary to dress herself.

(b)   Jill appeared to Mary to dress herself.

In (a) it is Mary's dressing that is under consideration; in (b) it is Jill's. This switch in the identity of the person who is dressing is created by a change of just one letter in the written version of the sentence. Let us examine in more detail just what is going on in this example. The difference in the way these two sentences are understood by you, the speakers of English, rests not on the difference in the sounds 'l' and 'r' but in the words *appeal* and *appear,* which happen to differ in form by just this one sound. Furthermore, the difference in meaning is not signalled by any difference in the order of the words in the two sentences. The order is exactly the same. It must therefore be that on the basis of important differences in the linguistic properties of *appear* and *appeal,* differences that are not apparent on the page, speakers of English understand the identical sequence of the other words in these two sentences quite differently. This suggests that the internalized rules we have been looking at are complex. It also shows that they are in the speaker's head and not on the page, since what is on the page is virtually identical. There is certainly nothing on the page which tells us who is getting dressed, Jill or Mary.

1.1.4   LANGUAGE IS SPECIFICALLY HUMAN

Imagine that you are an anthropologist entering a remote area of South America to study the language of a tribe of people whose existence has only recently been discovered. Assuming that the people are friendly and co-operative, how might you go about cracking the code that is their language?

However you proceed, the task is easier than your task with dolphins and whales because you know even before beginning that the language these people use will be organized in certain ways. That will be so because the people you are dealing with are human beings and you will rightly assume that their language and yours will have many common properties. (Of course if you are not trained in this task you might well be thoroughly mistaken about what those common properties are.) If, when you hold up a leaf and say 'leaf' in English, your new companions respond with the utterance *rogan,* you may suspect that this is the word for 'leaf' in their language. If you jump up and down or pretend to sleep, they may give you their words for 'jump' and 'sleep'. However wrong you may be in these guesses, throughout your investigation you can assume that the language you are studying uses *sound* to encode meaning, and that meaning is attached to something like the sound *sequences* that we call words. Furthermore, you can safely assume that the words you hear will belong to grammatical classes, such as *noun* and *verb,* and that these grammatical classes can be combined into phrases and sentences. There will be ways of making statements, asking questions, giving commands, and making negative assertions. All these properties are true of every human language, a fact that will help you enormously in cracking the code of your new language.

1.1.5 LANGUAGE USE IS CREATIVE

Make up ten sentences you have never said before.

   (a)   Was it difficult?

   (b)   Did you feel creative?

   (c)   Were you, in fact, being creative?

Answers:

   (a)   No.

   (b)   Probably not.

   (c)   Undoubtedly.

The reason you can perform this task so easily is that there are many words in English, and the rules of English permit these words to be combined in many different ways.

How many times a day do you say the same sentence? How many times in a year/lifetime?

There are phrases and sentences that we repeat often. *How are you? Nice weather we're having,* might be two of them. But by and large we do not repeat whole sentences exactly. Most of the sentences we utter are put together on the spot.

What is the longest English sentence?

There isn't one. You can keep adding to a sentence ad infinitum by using the little word *and*. Whenever you think you have reached the last sentence in the language, it is always possible to produce another by taking the last sentence, adding *and* to it and joining another sentence after the *and*. That way you get a new sentence. This means that there is no limit to the number of sentences which can be constructed in accordance with the rules of English.

The fact that we can create new sentences at will by adding on to old ones is by itself of little importance. What is more important is the fact that the rules of language allow us to put words together in *new ways* to create symbols for objects and ideas that have no pre-established symbols in the language. Lack of vocabulary is only a minor inconvenience. If you do not know the name of a student in your class, you can create one by specifying as many of their characteristics as are necessary to distinguish them from other students in the class. You can say 'that tall person with wavy blond hair and glasses and a long nose who sits in the second row near the window', continuing as long as is necessary to distinguish this one student from all others in the class. The same device is available for objects and concepts that have no conventional names. The four-year-old who says *I do it the way Mummy bakes a cake* has created a name for a way of doing things that has no name in English (or, presumably, any other language) – the way Mummy bakes a cake. Similarly, when the Bible was translated into African and Native American languages that had no word for *snow*, the translators easily constructed phrases in each language that would convey the crucial properties of this substance.

We might reflect a moment at this point on just what we are, in fact, doing with language. We have seen that language is a code for linking speech sounds with meaning. If that code allows for the creation of new meanings because it allows for speakers to be creative, then just what are these meanings? In effect sentences are ways of representing not just the world outside us, but the worlds which we create in our minds. Look, for a moment, at what must happen when a pigmy from the African rain forest learns to read and reads about snow. In the process of coming to understand what snow is, such a reader is changing his or her mental representation of the world. It contains a new substance with a variety of properties. Yet the reader has never actually seen, felt or tasted it.

So language provides a key to open the door to possible worlds, worlds which differ from the one we currently live in in any way which we might imagine. By rearranging words into new sequences we can imagine the future, plan a space telescope or journeys to the moon, reconstruct the age of the dinosaurs, as well as write letters to friends.

1.1.6 LANGUAGE USE IS CONSTRAINED

While the rules of a language allow us a great deal of freedom to say whatever we like, external circumstances often place constraints on this freedom. While visiting grandparents, joining in a class discussion, or conversing with someone we think may not like us, we may find it necessary to exercise caution in our use of words.

List five situations you have been in where you were restricted as to what you could say or how you could say it? What was it that restricted you?

In all probability most of the situations you have listed are ones in which you were not at ease. You were the inferior party; you had not met the other person before; you were in a strange place. Notice that these factors have nothing to do with the English language; they have to do with the situation in which you *use* language.

Do a brief parody of a variety of English that you are familiar with: for example, a radio commentary, a TV weather report, a sermon, a political speech, a disc jockey's patter, a supermarket checkout exchange. What aspects of your language have you had to restrict, and how?

Each variety of a language restricts a speaker's choices in its own way. A minister or priest giving a sermon cannot use swear words. A person reading the news cannot address the viewers as 'Dearly beloved brethren'. Words, sounds, sentences and meaning are all potentially restricted.   **utterance**

Below are a number of utterances.
  What factors in the situation have influenced the choice of pronunciation, vocabulary, and grammar in each utterance? (You will have to use your imagination in describing the pronunciation.)

(a) My friends and fellow Americans, I speak to you tonight on one of the gravest issues facing our great nation, and at this time I want to make one thing perfectly clear ...

(b) Canada is 3.3 million square miles in area. It is the second largest country in the world, covering more than half the North American continent.

(c) Johnson waits for the pitch. Here it comes ... Swung at and missed! One down. That brings up Thomas.

(d) Tonight it appears that all the 247 passengers are dead. Search and rescue teams are making their way to the scene in order to start a full search at daybreak.

(e) The earth is the Lord's, and the fullness thereof; the world, and they that dwell therein: For he hath founded it upon the seas, and established it upon the floods.

(f) That's a good boy. Now you promise your grandpappy you won't do that again.

(g) My husband and I are pleased again to be visiting your beautiful country.

Answers:

(a)   The speaker seems to be a politician. He or she is probably speaking on radio or TV. The audience therefore cannot reply; and the message sounds as though the speaker wants to persuade the audience about something.

(b)   This text is probably from a geography book or tourist brochure. The author is anonymous, is not giving a personal view but merely trying to convey factual information.

(c)   This is a commentary on a baseball or softball game. The speaker is a sports commentator. The purpose of the commentary is to tell the audience what is going on in the field and to hold their interest in the game.

(d)   Here a radio or TV news reader is reading a news item.

(e)   This sounds like a passage from the Bible. It also appears to have been written at an earlier period than our own.

(f)   The speaker appears to be talking to a child or perhaps a dog.

(g)   The speaker appears to be Queen Elizabeth II of England, using one of the introductions she often uses in a public speech (or someone imitating her).

Here are some general headings for the kinds of factors we have discovered:

1   The speaker or writer is always a factor. Each speaker has his or her own identifying features. For example, in (a) the phrase 'I want to make one thing perfectly clear' is one that was memorably used by Richard M. Nixon, a former President of the USA. In (h) the phrase 'My husband and I' is particularly the 'property' of Queen Elizabeth II of England.

dialect   2   Other aspects of a speaker's language reflect his or her dialect. In (f), for example, we have the word 'grandpappy', which is used particularly in certain regions of the USA. This is therefore a reflection of the place the person comes from. A person's social position can also be reflected in their language. For example, the sentence in (d) is being spoken in a middle-class social dialect. There are therefore at least two kinds of dialects, regional and social, reflecting a person's place of origin geographically and socially.

3   The time at which the person is speaking or writing also influences their range of choices. This can be seen clearly in (e) with its old-fashioned words and expressions.

4   The speaker's purpose can also have an effect. They may be trying to persuade, explain, inform or entertain their audience. Each purpose involves choosing certain features of language over others.

mode   5   The mode the speaker chooses to communicate in also influences how something can be said. If they are writing, as in (b) and (e), they can think about what they are doing and change it if necessary. If they are speaking, other options are available: the spoken rhetorical flourishes that would accompany (a), the slow, measured speed of (d), and so on.

6   Speech or writing can be conveyed by different media. A medium can be thought of as a channel of communication. Writing can appear on a television screen, in a book, in lights on a building. Speech can come direct from speaker to hearer, over the radio, in a film. Each medium places its own limitations on language. Only so much writing can fit on a TV screen; the screen then has to be wiped to display more writing. Speech on television, however, can come across in the normal way. **medium**

7   The audience also plays a part. It may be that they are passive, or absent altogether, in which case the speaker produces a monologue. Or it may be that they are present and actively involved in a dialogue.

8   The relationship of speaker and audience is conveyed linguistically. A US President speaking to American citizens can use an expression like 'My friends and fellow Americans' since Presidents are expected to speak in an elevated way and to have the interests of all Americans at heart. A street sweeper at the local shops could not seriously address shoppers this way. One important factor in such a relationship is the relative status of the two parties. Teachers talk differently when speaking to each other than they do when talking to students. Status often influences style. This can, for example, involve differences in the choice of words and grammatical constructions. The more familiar the participants are, the more likely they are to use a colloquial, informal style. The less well they know each other, the more formal will be the style that they will tend to adopt.

9   Particular occupations and tasks also place restrictions on the language of the speaker. Doctors, news readers, politicians, when they are being doctors, news readers, or politicians, speak in the register appropriate to their occupation. Of course, when the news reader gets home she does not tell her husband about her day's activities in the same way as she reads the news. Registers are restricted to particular uses and often to particular situations. **register**

Language itself allows speakers to create new utterances whenever they choose. But this creativity is circumscribed by the social forces that influence the speaker. The rest of this book will largely be concerned with the linguistic resources that we have as speakers of English, and to a lesser extent with how our choice of them is influenced by the situations in which our language is used.

1.1.7   LANGUAGE CHANGE AND VARIATION

If language use is constrained, as we suggested in the previous section, what about a language itself? We tend to think that we, who speak it, must all speak English, just as most people who live in China think they speak Chinese. This may be a comfortable belief but a moment's reflection will show that this belief is difficult to sustain.

Below are a number of sentences. Are they English?

(a)   Lēofan men, gecnāwath þæt sōþ is: ðēos woruld is on ofste, and hit nēalæcð þām ende.

(b)   Micel hadde Henri king gadered gold and syluer, and na god ne dide me for his saule thar-of.

(c)   In Ethiope ben many dyuerse folk, and Ethiope is clept 'Cusis'. In þat countree ben folk þat han but o foot; and they gon so blyue þat it is meruaylle.

All these are English. The first is from a sermon preached in the north of England in 1014. There is the odd word that you might be able to pick as English such as *men*, *is* and *and*, but otherwise it is unintelligible. Word by word is reads, 'Dear men, know that true is: this world is in haste, and it approaches the end.' (Sound familiar? Who said that the world being in haste is a modern phenomenon?)

The second was written in a monastery in Peterborough a century or so later. This is a bit clearer when you take some of the spelling into account. Gadered = gathered, syluer = silver, sauwle = soul, god = good. 'Much had Henry king gathered of gold and silver and no good no did it for his soul thereof.' That's kind of English but not your and my English.

The third was written about 1350 and this is getting to the point where we can read it with a little help. 'In Ethiopia there are many different people, and Ethiopia is called "Cusis". In that country there are people that have only one foot; and they have gone so blue that it is marvellous.' The author goes on to say that the big foot is useful when you are lying down in the sun since it can be used as parasol. (This text shows that you shouldn't believe all you read even in the fourteenth century.)

But all three texts show something more important, namely, that language changes through time, sometimes quite radically. Such changes should make us think about what a language is. If we cannot understand what is being said but only recognize the odd word, as with the passages from Old and Early Middle English above, is this still English? Is it necessary to be able to understand everything another speaker says for us to say that we speak the same language?

Let us suppose that you were able to sit down with Sir John Maundeville, who purportedly wrote the last passage, for a month or two and listen to him discussing his 'travels' with other people, how long would it take before you understood most of what he said? Probably a few months would see you not doing badly.

After a year in his household, you might be able to produce quite acceptable late Middle English. Is this any different from arriving in a working-class Glasgow neighbourhood now? Probably not. You would understand little to start with and pick it up after a month or two. Here we have contemporary variation rather than historical variation. While Sir John Maundeville lived around 1350, your new friend Jemma who supports the Glasgow Celtic football team (and so wears a green and white striped scarf) is your contemporary.

Is it any different landing in Ethiopia now and hearing what is spoken there? The answer is, yes it is. In Ethiopia you can rely on the local languages being human languages and having words, sounds and sentences. You can't rely on the words of, say Orono, having any relationship to the words you already know as you can with earlier and other contemporary varieties of English. While the words, sounds and sentences of English may have changed over time, there are commonalities underneath these changes which you can use as handholds into the different varieties of English.

So how do languages change? Changes in a language over time are built on variation in a language at a particular time, that is, many changes that become established in a language were originally variations within a language. It may be that some of Jemma's variations on the English theme might become features of English in the UK as a whole.

Language contact also often results in language change. English changed a good deal from the time that the Norman invaders brought their form of French with them in 1066. They settled and English changed in various complex ways. Many of its grammatical endings, for example, disappeared in this period. New Englishes, such as those spoken in Africa, the Caribbean and Asia, are influenced by the first languages people speak, as we will see later.

What are these variations and what is the theme, that is, how much of English stays unchanged and how much varies? If we go back far enough by reconstructing the parent language from which English is descended, then there will certainly have been a time a few thousand years ago when English didn't exist. Instead some language from which English, German, Dutch, Icelandic, Norwegian, Swedish and Danish all descended was being spoken in northern Europe. We have good reason to think this because there is a good example of this happening to neighbouring languages. If we look at French, Portuguese, Spanish, Italian and Romanian, then these can all be traced back to Latin. The reason for us being able to do this is that Latin was written more than 2000 years ago and we can trace the process of one language becoming more than one over that period. As you would expect, all the descendant languages and dialects still carry something of Latin in many aspects of their vocabulary, sound system and grammar. English, however, was only written from about 700 AD on and the language from which it is descended was never written down. We can, therefore, only reconstruct what it was like.

So languages vary and change. We have outlined some of the factors involved in creating variation in the section 1.1.6. We now turn to variation itself.

In section 1.1.4, we suggested that there were universal features of human languages. Clearly those cannot change.

Below are some suggested changes that a language might undergo. Which ones do you think are plausible and which of them do you think would violate the basic properties of human languages?

(a)   Language X has added 20,000 words to its vocabulary in the last century.

(b)   Language Y has lost one of its distinctive sounds.

(c)   Language Z, which used to form questions by adding a particle *ma* at the end of the sentences, now reverses the linear order of words to form questions.

The first two possibilities do not seem unnatural but the last does. We would not expect any human language to take a sentence like *Jemma enjoys going to see Celtic play Rangers at the Ibrox ground* into *Ground Ibrox the at Rangers play Celtic see to going enjoys Jemma*?

linguistic variable

The natural bounds of variation are signalled by points where a language can vary. These are often called linguistic variables. In Charles Dickens' novel *Great Expectations* Philip Pirrip, a village boy, is invited to play cards with Estella who lives in a mysterious manor house. When they are playing, Estella makes the following observation: ' "He calls the knaves, Jacks, this boy!" said Estella with disdain, before our first game was out. "And what coarse hands he has! And what thick boots!" ' Estella has noticed a linguistic variable. As far as English goes, it doesn't matter whether you call a card a knave or a jack but it does matter socially to Estella. Most of us now would call the court cards: *ace, king, queen, jack*, but Estella associates called them *jacks* with coarse hands and thick boots, that is, with working people. In section 1.1.6 terms, *jacks* indicates a speaker of a lower social dialect while *knaves* indicates that the speaker speaks a higher social dialect.

Linguistic variables like this are to be found in every language and in every part of a language. *Knaves* vs. *jacks* is a lexical variable, that is, to do with words. Variation in sound is also obvious since we all have accents. (Yes, all of us.) Variables here are of a number of different kinds at which we will look more closely in Chapter 5.1.5, but to give you an idea, the middle vowel in the word *man* is often pronounced rather like the vowel in *mon* in Jamaica.

Languages also have grammatical variables. In the north of England people sometimes form syntactic tags that go like this. Take a sentence like *Our Brian is getting too big for his boots*. The sentence with the tag on the end might be, *He is getting too big for his boots, is our Brian*. They might also say, *Our Brian's getting too big for his boots, he is*.

So what is a linguistic variable? The easiest way to think of this is in terms of a language having a system. Sometimes the language makes available choices to speakers which make no difference to the central meaning of what they are saying.

What is the difference between saying each of the following of sentences?

(a)   I have not done it.

(b)   I haven't done it.

(c)   I ain't done it.

The answer is that there isn't any difference in what is actually said. The choice among *have not*, *haven't* and *ain't* is a variable choice. It is also clear that this choice bears a relation to the kinds of factors we looked at in section 1.1.6, factors like formality, social class, situation and gender. It might be that *ain't* is more commonly used by working men in informal situations than by professional men in informal situations.

This, however, raises another issue. The choice of variable is seldom an all-or-nothing choice. Alf may use *ain't* more frequently than Ted, although both are working men and both have been recorded in informal situations. It may be that Alf and Ted use *ain't* more frequently than their wives do in informal situations. It may be that neither uses *ain't* as frequently in formal situations, for example, in giving a wedding speech when their daughters were married, as they would at work over lunch. In other words, variables are often linked to their social context in a complex and probabilistic way. Teasing these choices and their associated factors apart is a job for the statistically literate. Since we are not supposing you to be statistically literate (and will do nothing to help you become statistically literate), we will leave it there. What we will do, throughout Parts One, Two and Three of this book, is illustrate the variability of English from time to time, particularly to show how different English is in different parts of the world. English can thus be seen as a family of dialects, something which has been implicit in much of what we have seen in the last two sections of this chapter.

1.2 LINGUISTICS, ITS NEIGHBOURS AND ITS APPLICATIONS

This concluding section of our introduction will outline from where we got the tools which will be used to present the English language to you. No domain can be thoroughly examined without a discipline within which the phenomena of that domain are explained. Language is no different in this regard from the nature of the atom, the origins of the universe or the habitat of the orangutan. Sub-atomic particle physicists take care of atoms; cosmologists are responsible for the universe (and what a heavy responsibility that is); ecologists study the habitat of the great apes while linguists study language and languages. Each area of study has its own way of dividing up the territory, and each has its own theoretical baggage to explain how things work. In this section we will first look at the way in which linguistics divides up the work of understanding languages and then we will look at some of the ways in which this descriptive function interacts with associated areas and applications.

syntax

We have seen that languages are codes which connect speech sound to meaning. We shall see later in this book that we need syntax to connect the two (which is not to say that syntax is independent of either phonology or semantics). Syntax deals with the structure of sentences and the meaning of a sentence depends in part on its grammatical structure and in part on the meaning of the words in it.

In miniature, words connect speech sounds with meanings. When we speak, we utter words so that the sounds of the words are conveyed to others who, on hearing that sound, associate it with the meaning(s) they have in their heads, just as when we spoke the word ourselves, we also had in our head the sound associated with its meaning. Also in miniature, words often have more than one meaning-bearing element within them. For example, *parental* consists of the meaning-bearing element *parent* and another one, *-al*, which is added to the meaning of *parent* to make up the meaning of the whole word. Lexis is the field

lexicology
lexis
morphology

which deals with words and lexicology is the study of lexis while morphology is the field that deals with the properties of complex words like *parental* and *parenthood*.

phonetics

The science of phonetics deals with speech sounds. If we look at sounds as a physicist might, that is, as sound waves and their properties as they travel from

acoustic phonetics

a mouth to an ear, then we would be studying acoustic phonetics. For that we would need recording equipment which collects the sound in the air and analytic equipment which tells us about sounds waves and their physical properties. Or we could look at how speech sounds are produced by the human vocal apparatus: the lungs, voice box, tongue and lips (among other organs of speech). If

articulatory phonetics

we did that we would be studying articulatory phonetics. If we turned instead to the ear and how it reacts to the sound waves that impinge upon the eardrum and are then transferred to the small bones of the inner ear, the tiny hairs within the snail-like organ of the cochlea and finally excite the auditory nerve, we would be

auditory phonetics

studying auditory phonetics.

You can see that each of these areas has its special problems. How do you get inside the human head to observe what happens when the tiny bones inside your skull are being vibrated by the air drum? You can't do that without doing serious surgery for which you would not get the owner of the ear's permission. What kinds of equipment would you need to observe human speech in the ear and how would you process it? Looking at the equipment in the human head which makes the sounds is rather easier and that is what we will be doing in Chapter 4. Not withstanding their potential difficulties, the other two branches of phonetics are also important. For example, to help those with hearing loss, an understanding of auditory phonetics is essential. If we want to manufacture telephones and high-fidelity musical equipment we also need to understand what humans can and cannot hear. Hearing aids and audio amplifiers need to take human hearing and the quality of the signal into account.

Think for a moment of what you might need to know to help people with either partial or total hearing loss to be able to understand people who are speaking.

If the hearing loss is partial, it is vital to know what elements of the speech sounds are inaudible to the hearer and then to design hearing aids which amplify what is partially missing. You also need electronic engineers who know about speech acoustics to do this. If someone is completely deaf, is there some way of converting speech sounds into some other medium than sound? Lip reading is a partial answer but many deaf people learn a form of sign language which allows vision to take over from hearing when communicating.

If speech sounds could be made in an unrestricted way, then words would never sound the same. In order to recognize that we are dealing with the same word, some features of the sound of a word must remain constant. For that reason every language uses systems of sound segments which sound the same to the speakers of that language. For example, most speakers of English hear the difference between the words *tea* and *thee* as significant, the significant difference being in the first segment of the word. But in some dialects of English that difference is not heard and is not made. The study of such differences and the systems in which they are organized in languages is called phonology.   **phonology**

We saw earlier that the language code makes use of words which link speech sounds to meanings just as traffic lights connect the colour of the lights to instructions. The meanings that language can convey, even if we only look at the total number of words and all their meanings, is much larger than three traffic lights. The sub-discipline of linguistics that deals with word meaning is lexical seman-   **lexical semantics** tics. There is more to meaning than just the meaning of words, however. Words are put into sentences and have their meanings combined to form composite meanings. This branch of semantics we can call formal semantics since it relates   **formal semantics** to the grammatical form of the sentence. We can tell that formal semantics exists just by performing a small thought experiment.

Examine the following sentences:

   (a)   Wugs tremmed sigs.

   (b)   Sigs tremmed wugs.

Whatever the lexical meanings of the three words in them might be, the two sentences have different meanings because the three words come in two different grammatical orders. Formal semantics studies the effect that the order in which words come has on the meaning of sentences. It is now clear that syntax, the way in which words can be ordered in sentences, is significant not just for itself, but also for the contribution it makes to the meaning of the sentence.

But the meanings of words and the meaning of syntax are not all that there is to the meanings that speakers convey to hearers. The context in which things are said also plays a role. Look, for example, at the words *I* and *tomorrow* in *I am coming tomorrow*. In this sentence *I* is the speaker. That is clear from the dictionary meaning of the word and *tomorrow* is the day after today. But let us suppose that you said this sentence on the 25 August 2011. Then, if your hearer knew you, your hearer would know not just that *I* was the speaker but would know the exact person who was speaking. They would also know exactly that tomorrow was the 26 August 2011. They would get these additional elements of the meaning of what you had said, not from the meaning of the sentence but from its having been uttered in a particular place, at a particular time by a particular person, that is, these aspects of the meaning come from the context. The study of the way in **pragmatics** which the context contributes to meaning is pragmatics.

If you were to continue with the study of linguistics, then each of these sub-disciplines would play a crucial role in understanding how language works. In many departments of linguistics in universities, these subjects have whole courses devoted to them and at various levels.

1.2.1 INTER- AND APPLIED LINGUISTICS

Language and languages are fascinating in their own right but language does not exist in a vacuum. It exists inside a human body, is used for human communication, and for a wide variety of intellectual and social ends. So linguistics has a rich set of associations with other disciplines. These associations have led to the formation of a number of inter-disciplines. Two well-established ones are sociolinguistics and psycholinguistics. As you might have guessed, sociolinguistics deals with the roles language plays socially and psycholinguistics looks at language as a psychological phenomenon.

sociolinguistics Sociolinguistics has various ways of looking at the relationship of social and linguistic phenomena. There is variationist sociolinguistics which looks at the kinds of variation outlined in section 1.7 and relates it to the kinds of factors outlined in section 1.6. This involves collecting texts of various kinds, written and spoken, finding linguistic variables and counting them. These statistics can then be related to social variables. Its methods are quantitative. Qualitative sociolinguistics often uses participant observation where a linguist joins a particular group and looks at how it is organized and the kinds of work which language does within the group. Macro-sociolinguists look at how language fits into society from a broader perspective. For example, there are nation-states which have more than one official language. Most modern states have speakers of many languages within their borders. How do nation-states deal with this linguistic and social fact? What linguistic human rights do people have? What part does education play in maintaining minority languages? You can see that such topics are relevant and significant.

psycholinguistics
speech production
speech perception
developmental
**   psycholinguistics**
Psycholinguists tries to answer three main questions: how do humans acquire languages, how do they produce speech, how do they perceive speech? The first domain is developmental psycholinguistics. One is tempted to think that small children just imitate their parents and siblings. But that is clearly not true. When a parent says, 'Eat your vegetables' a child seldom replies, 'Eat your vegetables.' They may say, 'No.' In many respects, language develops within its own trajectory. Small children learn words and then start putting them together in ways that sometimes approximate the ways adults do. At other times they make up

sentences in their own ways. Even when children follow adult ways of making sentences, the results can be creative.

The next question is, how do we construct speech in real time at the rate of about five syllables a second? That is also not an easy question to answer since all the processes by which we do so are unconscious. In the time it takes, just thousandths of a second, you have to think of what to say, find the words to say it, string them into the right order, and then get them out of your mouth and on to the airwaves. All this is done effortlessly.

How does your hearer take the sound that you have just blown into the air and (filtering out the background noise) find out what you meant by these sounds. How does your hearer do that fast enough to get what you mean just after you have meant it? These are very complex and entirely involuntary processes, that is, you can't stop yourself from understanding what others are saying.

Somewhere all this is happening in real time in a real brain. Real neurons are being fired. Neurolinguistics looks at that. It has been helped in the last few **neurolinguistics** years by the growth in sophistication of neural imaging. Machines can now take pictures of the activation of the nerves in your brain by looking, for example, at how the blood supply to those nerves changes over time. When your neurons are not firing they do not need much oxygen because they are not doing much, but when they are firing they do need oxygen and that is delivered by means of blood vessels, with which the brain is richly endowed. By tracking where there is more oxygen being used, neurologists can infer where in the brain the tasks the brain is currently performing are taking place.

You can see that sociolinguistics, psycholinguistics and neurolinguistics are at the interface between different ways of looking at the same phenomena. In all cases the two areas can talk to each other giving a richer understanding of language and its use.

Whatever our understandings of language may be, they have practical repercussions and so there is a wide spectrum of domains within which linguistics may be applied. A traditional area is the construction of descriptions of languages which have not been described before. This is termed field linguistics **field linguistics** since it takes place in the field. Many of the roughly 6000 languages of the world have been only partly or poorly described. Some have received no attention at all from linguists. When field linguists describe previously unstudied languages, applications soon follow. Usually such languages have no writing system. When linguists understand the phonology of a previously undescribed language, they can create an alphabet for it since alphabets tend to rest on an understanding of the phonemes of the language. Governments are keen for this to happen since literacy enables a government to communicate with its citizens. In parts of the world this does not happen because all the people in a region are illiterate. Once there is an alphabet, dictionaries can be produced and thus assist in the teaching of reading and in translating. Many linguists are involved in this work. It is not without its ethical problems. Social changes happen when illiterate people gain a written language and become literate. Some of these changes may not be to the benefit of the people concerned while others may be.

Behind everyone who teaches a language as a first, second or foreign language there lies an application of linguistics. Let us suppose that you are teaching reading in an elementary school. English spelling is difficult, as we will see in Chapter 4. How you teach it will have a lot to do with how sophisticated your understanding of language is. Teachers of English as a foreign language are also in an interesting situation. Suppose you are a Chinese speaker who knows English as a foreign language and you are teaching students of English in a university in China. In that situation you will be partly dependent on grammar books, dictionaries, usage manuals and maybe videos made by native speakers. Since there are now more non-native speakers of English in the world than native speakers, **applied linguistics** applied linguistics of this kind is an important industry with many associated areas such as text book writing, dictionary production, and even the writing of this book, which is being used in many parts of the world by people studying English.

We have already seen that an understanding of language is vital in aiding the deaf. But there are other forms of disorder for which an understanding of language is also important. Many people suffer strokes or brain injury through accidents. Often, this results in disordered language and disordered speech, sometimes in people not being able to speak at all, at least for a while. Speech pathologists and speech and language therapists provide interventions to try and help restore a brain injury patient's speech. This is difficult and important work. Sometimes speech production does not take its normal developmental course for various reasons. Both diagnosing developmentally disordered speech and therapeutic interventions require specialized applications of linguistics.

Some of our close friends, computers, also need the attention of linguists. In their early days, their minders needed to talk as the computers talked, in a machine language of zeros and ones. But gradually computers are beginning to deceive us by how lifelike they sound. They can read and then speak back to us using speech synthesis systems. They can understand us in a limited way by utilizing speech recognition systems. Progress has even been made with machine translation where one feeds sentences from one language in and translations (sometimes looking rather like the indecipherable instructions for a video recorder) come out the other end of the machine. Natural language interfaces can make a big difference to people with physical disabilities. Suppose that you can instruct your computer to tell your robot to turn a light on, make a cup of tea and turn the pages of a book you are reading. This is not important if you can do this yourself but some people cannot, and so such systems can make a big difference to the lives of disabled people.

Finally, and again just as illustrations, there are significant areas of national and international policy where linguistics plays a role. International interaction often makes use of international languages. Supra-national organizations such as the European Union and the United Nations need to decide which languages are going to be used for international communication within these large organizations. There are nation-states which need standard languages and a language policy because so many languages are spoken within their borders. Language planners are often used in such situations. Translators also become important in such contexts. In many European cities there are translation bureaus to enable people who do not speak one of the European Union's official languages to communicate with people who do speak that language. Home appliances in Europe often have instructions written in a large number of languages so that if you buy a washing machine in France you may get a manual in German, which you can't read, as well as the one in French which you can read. Someone has translated these manuals.

As you can see from this brief sketch, linguistics, the provider of the toolbox from which we are going to select the tools to describe the English language in the rest of this book, has many parts and many applications. So, if anyone asks you why you are studying a subject which has such a funny name, you now have a few answers to their question.

Glossary •

Acoustic phonetics   The physical properties of speech sounds.

Applied linguistics   The application of linguistics to the teaching of languages.

Articulatory phonetics   The way in which speech sounds are produced.

Auditory phonetics   The way in which speech sounds are perceived.

Box diagram   Box diagrams are a way to picture hierarchies by representing lower levels on a hierarchy as being enclosed within boxes which are then enclosed within boxes representing higher levels on the hierarchy. This can be paraphrased as 'what is in the outer box has as constituents what is in the inner boxes'.

Code   A code is a system of symbols that allows things to represent others for the purpose of communicating. Morse code, for example, uses sounds of only two different lengths to represent all the different letters of the alphabet.

Constituent   Any grammatically coherent component part of a sentence or word. *See* Chapters 7 and 8.

Descriptive rule   A descriptive rule is a statement of a regular pattern that actually exists; unlike a **prescriptive rule**, where someone attempts to prescribe that people should follow a rule which they actually do not follow (at least some of the time).

Developmental psycholinguistics   The study of language acquisition.

Dialect   Regional or social variety of a language.

Field linguistics   Studying languages (usually not yet fully recorded in the field, e.g., in Vanuatu where there are many only partially documented languages).

Form   The form of a unit is what it looks like, particularly on the basis of its internal structure.

Formal semantics   The study of the contribution that syntax makes to sentence meaning though models which employ logics.

Function   The function of a unit is the role the unit plays in another unit.

Hierarchical   Having the form of a hierarchy. In the description of languages, the hierarchies that are used usually represent units which consist of sub-units. The sub-units are lower on the hierarchy.

Level   When linguists describe languages the description is usually sub-divided into different levels. Each level of description deals with different kinds of units, all of which together go to make up the way the language works.

Lexical semantics   The study of word meanings.

Lexicology   The study of words.

Linear   In the form of a line.

Linguistic variable   A feature of a language or dialect which can be optionally changed without affecting the meaning of a sentence, that is, different ways of saying the same thing, e.g., using the word *couch* instead of *sofa* or saying 'I aint done it' as compared with 'I haven't done it.'

Medium   The channel through which an utterance is conveyed, e.g., telephone, television.

Mode of an utterance   Whether the person producing the utterance is speaking or writing.

Morphology   The structure of words and the study of the structure of words.

Phonology   Phonology is the study of the function and organization of sounds in a particular language, or in language in general.

Phonetics   Phonetics is the scientific study of the production and perception of speech sounds.

Phrase   Grammatically coherent constituent part of a sentence. *See* Chapter 7.

Pragmatics   That part of the meaning of an utterance which is inferred on the basis of what a text (written or spoken) says and the context in which it appears.

Psycholinguistics   The study of the psychology of language.

Register   Variation of a language according to the use that speakers make of it. For example, occupational varieties of a language such as the speech of market criers.

Rule   A rule is a statement of a regular pattern.

Sentence A sequence of words having a structure which is grammatically independent of that of other sentences. *See* Chapters 7 and 8.

Sociolinguistics   The study of language in its social context.

Speech perception   The psychological processes which begin with speech sounds hitting the eardrum and end with the hearer understanding what the speaker has said.

Speech production   The psychological processes that begin with speakers wanting to say something and end with speech sounds coming from their mouths.

Structure   A structure consists of parts that are organized in some way. For example, a bridge is a structure that has many parts, all of which are organized to make the whole.

Symbol   Symbols have two aspects: a form and a meaning. The two are arbitrarily linked. For example, the symbol of the Campaign for Nuclear Disarmament consists of a circle with a letter Y upside down with a line down the middle of it, inside the circle. Although most people who are familiar with this symbol don't know it, it is based on the letters N and D as they would be signalled in semaphore. (That doesn't change its being an arbitrary symbol, of course.)

Syntax   The organizational principles that determine the order of words in a sentence.

Tree diagram   Tree diagrams are a way to picture hierarchies. Tree diagrams are so called because they look like trees turned upside down. Tree-diagram representations can be paraphrased as 'what is given higher up in the tree has as constituents what is connected to it lower in the tree'.

Utterance   What a speaker says or a writer writes at a particular point in time.

Further reading •

Bauer, L., Holmes, J. and Warren, P., *Language Matters* (Basingstoke: Palgrave Macmillan, 2006).

Bolinger, D., *Aspects of Language,* 2nd edn (New York: Harcourt Brace Jovanovich, 1975).

Burridge, K. and Kortmann, B. (eds.), *Varieties of English: The Pacific and Australasia* (Berlin: Mouton de Gruyter, 2008).

Cheshire, J. (ed.) *English around the World: Sociolinguistic Perspectives* (Cambridge: Cambridge University Press, 1991).

Crystal, D. and Davy, D., *Investigating English Style* (London: Longman, 1969).

Falk, J. S., *Linguistics and Language: A Survey of Basic Concepts and Applications* (Lexington, MA: Xerox College Publishing, 1973).

Finegan, E., *Language: Its Structure and Use,* 2nd edn (New York: Harcourt Brace Jovanovich, 1994).

Fromkin, V., Rodman. R. and Hyams, N., *An Introduction to Language,* 7th edn (Boston, MA: Heinle, 2003).

Kortmann, B. and Upton, C. (ed.), *Varieties of English: The British Isles* (Berlin: Mouton de Gruyter, 2008).

Mesthrie, R. (ed.), *Varieties of English: Africa, South and Southeast Asia* (Berlin: Mouton de Gruyter. 2008).

Miller, G. A., *Language and Speech* (San Francisco, CA: W. H. Freeman, 1981).

Pinker, S., *The Language Instinct: How the Mind Creates Language* (New York: Perennial Classics, 2000).

Schneider, E. W. (ed.), *Varieties of English: The Americas and the Caribbean* (Berlin: Mouton de Gruyter).

Traugott, E. C. and Pratt, M. L., *Linguistics for Students of Literature* (New York: Harcourt Brace Jovanovich, 1980).

Electronic resources •

http://www.palgrave.com/language/kuiperandallan/
All the web-based resources for this book are to be found on this site.

http://www.palgrave.com/language/freeborn/site/index.htm
This site has a number of downloadable readings taken from the texts from the whole history of English including a section from the Peterborough Chronicle.

http://www.linguistlist.org/
This site contains a great range of material of interest to linguists including directories of expertise and a neat place to ask a linguist a question to which you want an informed answer.

http://linguistics.online.uni-marburg.de/
On-line university courses in linguistics.

http://web.ku.edu/idea/
This site has people from various places reading an English text so that you can hear accents from all over the world.

http://www.ucl.ac.uk/english-usage/ice/index.htm
The ICE is a collection of corpora, collections of systematically organized texts (oral and written) from various regional varieties of English.

part one

Words

In this section you will be introduced to the formal properties of words, that is, their grammatical category and their internal structure. You will then look at:

- the meanings of words;
- various ways in which groups of words form vocabularies through being used by different speakers and for different uses;
- how vocabularies may have words added to them, or lose words.

By the end of this section you should be able to:

- recognize the major syntactic categories: noun, verb, adjective, adverb and preposition;
- determine the internal structure of words belonging to these categories; and
- draw tree diagrams of their structure.

The Form and Function of Words

When people think of what is central to their language, they often turn to its dictionary, the written repository of its words. This is, in part, because there is a widespread belief that words *are* the language. Although this is a half-truth it is certainly the case that one of the major tasks anyone has in learning a language is acquiring their own lexicon, their personal internalized store of words (as opposed to the store of words written in a dictionary).

lexicon

We can get an initial idea of what knowing a word involves by looking at a dictionary entry. Dictionaries attempt to represent what a literate native speaker of a language knows about words. Since you will be familiar with dictionaries, they are a useful place to start.

Examine the following simple dictionary entry taken from the *Oxford Dictionary of Current English*:

Sept, *n.* Clan, esp. in Ireland.

First comes the spelling of the word. In some dictionary entries the written spelling of the word is followed by a representation of its pronunciation in some form of phonetic script. (We will see examples of this later in this section.) These two forms of spelling, orthographic and phonetic, represent the word's *phonological form*. To be able to be said, a word must have a phonological form since this represents, in the abstract, what is going to come out of your mouth when you say the word. There are no 'silent' words.

orthography
phonological form

While a word may have just one phonological form, this is not always the case. Look, for example, at *go* and *went*. Native speakers of English know that these are different forms of the same word. Because of cases such as this it is necessary to distinguish between the abstract item of vocabulary GO and the shapes which it can take in sound or spelling. We can think of these shapes as the abstract vocabulary item's realizations (in sound or print). Linguists term such an abstract vocabulary word a lexeme, on analogy with phonemes, which you will meet in Chapter 5. It follows that a single lexeme can have a variety of

lexeme

part of speech

grammatical category
syntactic category

word-form realizations. You can think of this as being rather like the concept of a face, and actual faces. A face has two eyes, a mouth, and a nose in the middle, but an actual face 'realizes' this in particular ways. The eyes may be blue and the nose previously broken.

Next in the dictionary entry for *sept* comes its part of speech label. For example, in the above word the letter n. is an abbreviation for *noun*. Virtually every word in the dictionary has one of these labels. What it represents is the word's grammatical or syntactic category, indicated by a syntactic category label. The syntactic category label of a word is a kind of summary of its grammatical properties. In essence these properties determine the locations which the word can occupy in phrases. We will explore this facet of words in section 2.1 and Chapter 7.1. All words belong to a grammatical category, with a very small number of exceptions. These are words which are never part of a phrase or sentence. The word *yes* is a case in point. If you think of where the word *yes* is used in a sentence, then you will find that it is never part of a phrase or a sentence. For example, *yes* is not a word that can function in phrases like **the old yes*, **has been yessing the grass*, **yes the lawns*. (Asterisks here indicate that these are ungrammatical phrases.) In fact it seems that *yes* is a one-word sentence. Therefore, it cannot have a syntactic category label, as it never functions as a constituent part of a phrase or sentence.

Third in the above dictionary entry comes a gloss for the meaning of the word. Most words have meanings which speakers can readily identify, such as the meaning of the word *horse*. So if you want to know the meaning of the word *sept* you look at this section of the dictionary entry, where you find a phrase or sentence or two which gives you the meaning of the word but expressed in different words. It should be noted, however, that just as *yes* does not have a grammatical category, not all words have easily definable meanings. This is clear when one looks at the meaning of a word like *of* in a phrase such as *the pursuit of happiness*. Other words, such as *this* and *a*, have important grammatical roles to play. However difficult it may be to pin down exactly what their meaning is, they clearly are not meaningless. But the word *of* in the *pursuit of happiness* seems only to have a phonological form and grammatical category, but is otherwise meaningless.

sense
semantic representation

We can call the representation of the meanings or senses of a lexeme its semantic representation.

So a word, or, as we can now say, a lexeme, generally speaking, is a three-part symbol. It has a form or a number of forms, grammatical category, and meaning, the link between the form and meaning being arbitrary. The link between the syntactic category and the meaning of a word is less arbitrary. For example, it is clear that for breathing to be happening, some biological organism with lungs must be doing it. This semantic fact about the lexeme *breathe* has grammatical repercussions. In looking at lexemes in this part of the book we will be looking at all three of these aspects in turn.

The properties of lexemes we have just glanced at are strictly linguistic, that is, they form part of the knowledge which speakers have of their language. However, when we examine how words are used, they also appear to have a social aspect. Again using a dictionary for illustration, one sometimes finds words listed with indications as to how they should be used. For example, the abbreviation *vulg.,* short for *vulgar,* is often used to indicate that one should be careful about using such a word in polite company.

Furthermore, sets of words are often used by members of particular groups. This can be seen through the large number of specialist dictionaries which exist. There are dictionaries for foreign-language learners, for biologists, dictionaries of slang, dictionaries of the vocabulary of the criminal underworld and bilingual English–Greek dictionaries sold at airports for tourists going on holiday to Crete. Later, in Chapter 3, we will look at how words are used for specialized purposes.

2.1 WORDS AND THEIR GRAMMATICAL CATEGORIES: SYNTACTIC CATEGORIES AND INFLECTION

2.1.1 INTRODUCTION

As we saw above, in a dictionary the words of a language are classified by grammatical category. In this section we will look at grammatical categories and how words may be assigned to particular categories. The reason for examining this property of words first is that the later section in this chapter, where we look at the internal structure of words, depends on being able to identify a word's grammatical category.

The speakers of a language recognize not only the words of their language, but also that words fit in different places in phrases and sentences. On the basis of where they fit, words can be classed into different categories. Speakers of English may not know the names of these categories or the principles by which words are assigned to categories, but they are aware that, for example, *wombat* and *stupid* are different in a rather basic way. If you are uncertain about this, try inserting each in turn in the following frame: *a... idea.* We will find that this difference is because they belong to different syntactic categories.

At this stage in our exploration of syntactic categories we have said only that syntactic categories indicate the function which words have in phrases and sentences. However, we have not said anything in detail about phrases and sentences themselves, and will not be looking at phrases and sentences seriously until Part Three. Fortunately this does not prevent us from looking at syntactic categories in a preliminary way. It happens that particular syntactic categories of words often have characteristic grammatical endings which change the form of the word. We can use these as a partial way to identify at least some syntactic categories. We can also look at some of the functions of lexical categories as a way of supporting the analysis based on the word's grammatical endings.

Before looking at the grammatical categories of English lexemes we need to look in a little more detail at the way lexemes change their form. Look, for example, at the lexeme TRY. Depending on how it is functioning it can take any of the following forms: *try, tries, tried, trying,* as in the following sentences: *The horse must try, The horse tries, The horse tried, The horse is trying.* We can call each

grammatical word form

inflection
stem

morphology

morphosyntactic category
morphosyntactic property

noun

of these forms a grammatical word form of the lexeme, since it is the grammar of English which requires the lexeme TRY to have these different forms in different contexts. The grammatical endings which create these different grammatical word forms are termed inflections. The form of the lexeme to which they are attached is termed its stem.

The processes whereby words come to have internal structure such as a stem and inflection are morphological processes, the morphology of words having to do with their internal structure, just as geomorphology has to do with the structure of the earth. Since inflections are associated with both the morphological structure of words and the syntactic functions of words, the categories for which words inflect are often called morphosyntactic categories. Tense, which accounts for the past-tense inflection -ed in tried, is an example of a morphosyntactic category. Properties such as present tense or past tense are therefore morphosyntactic properties.

The categories which we will look at in this section are five major lexical categories: nouns, adjectives, adverbs, verbs and prepositions. We will be looking at the morphosyntactic categories for which the first four inflect. At the section's conclusion we will briefly look at prepositions, although these do not have any characteristic grammatical endings.

2.1.2 NOUNS

Traditionally, a noun is a naming word; typically the name of a person, place, or thing. For example:

> snake, rat, alligator, Fred, chainsaw, lawnmower

are all nouns. For each of the above words we can find a set of objects to which the word is normally used to refer (although the name of a particular snake, rat, or alligator may be *Fred* or *Freda* for those with whom the animal is on intimate terms).

Consider the following nouns. Do they pose any problems for our definition of a noun?

anger, fame, cyclops, Zeus, Hamlet, Lilliput, furniture

It is impossible to point to an object in the physical world to which these words refer. Anger is a feeling and fame is an abstract quality; cyclops, and Zeus are both mythical beings; Hamlet is a fictional character, while Lilliput is a fictitious place. Furniture is not a person or a place or a thing either, or even a set of objects. In fact it isn't any particular thing but a class of things. Unlike alligators, where we can say of a particular alligator, 'That's an alligator,' we cannot say when pointing to a chair, 'That's a furniture.' So although sometimes when identifying nouns their meaning may be useful, we must look elsewhere for some supporting facts about nouns if we are to become more familiar with them and be able to tell whether a particular word is a noun. To do that we will look at the inflections which nouns characteristically take.

Many nouns inflect for the morphosyntactic category of number and, as such, **number** have a plural form like -s or -es. These are the regular (also termed weak) forms. **plural** For example:

snapper	snappers
bee	bees
rosella	rosellas
box	boxes

The uninflected form is the singular form. Some nouns mark their plural in other, **singular** irregular ways, often termed strong forms, for example:

foot	feet
mouse	mice
louse	lice
child	children
ox	oxen

Other nouns never mark their plurals overtly:

sheep	sheep
deer	deer

while some nouns never occur without the plural marker, for example *scissors* and *trousers*. These are facts about the form of nouns. If a word has a plural form, then it belongs to the category *noun*. (Note that the reverse does not follow: namely, that if a word has no plural form then it is not a noun.)

Notice that although words like *sheep* and *deer* do not take an ending to indicate that they are plural, they do have a plural form. It happens to be identical to their singular form. On the basis of this, we can see the necessity to make a distinction between a lexeme and a grammatical word form. There are two grammatical words with the word form *sheep*. One is the singular form of the lexeme SHEEP and the other the plural form. So SHEEP is a noun because it has a plural form.

We can also identify nouns by looking at the words that typically appear with them in a sentence or phrase. (Let us suppose for the time being that a phrase is a grammatically complete part of a sentence. We'll look at phrases in Part Three.)

Most nouns appear with either *a(n)* or *the*, or denote things that can be counted, for example:

a wombat   the wombat   three wombats

a barbecue   the barbecue   one barbecue

Consider the following list of nouns, and divide them into the following groups: nouns that can take *a(n)*, nouns that can take *the*, nouns that have a plural form, and nouns that refer to things that can be counted. Some nouns will appear in more than one group,

   alligator, wombat, Pittsburg, video, lawnmower, butter, Fred.

Which nouns fit into which categories?

Your answer should look as in Table 2.1.

Table 2.1

	a(n)	*the*	plural	count
alligator	✓	✓	✓	✓
wombat	✓	✓	✓	✓
Pittsburg	✕	✕	✕	✕
video	✓	✓	✓	✓
lawnmover	✓	✓	✓	✓
butter	✕	✓	✕	✕
Fred	✕	✕	✕	✕

count noun
non-count noun
proper noun

common noun

Notice that these nouns fall into three groups: those which appear in all four groups, those which appear in one group, and those which appear in none of the groups. The set which appear in all four groups are called count nouns, those that appear in only one group are called non-count nouns, while those that appear in none of the groups are proper nouns. In English, proper nouns, typically the names of people and places, always begin with a capital letter. The nouns that appeared in all four groups, together with those that appeared in only one group, are called common nouns.

In English, *a(n)* does not occur with mass nouns (that is, non-count nouns which refer to uncountable substances such as *putty*), and mass nouns do not have plurals.

The properties of nouns we have just looked at determine the way nouns are arranged in grammatical sequences with other categories of word. In other words, nouns are nouns because of their distribution, that is, where they come in grammatical sequences relative to where other words come. **distribution**

So we have looked at nouns now from the perspective of both their form and a little of their function.

Find the nouns in the following poem:

EXERCISE 2.1

The Sick Rose

Oh rose, thou art sick!
The invisible worm,
That flies in the night
In the howling storm,

Has found out thy bed
Of crimson joy:
And his dark secret love
Does thy life destroy.

William Blake

. . . .

2.1.3 ADJECTIVES

Traditionally adjectives ascribe a property or quality to an object, for example: **adjective**

the *ripe* apple   the *evil* alligator

Adjectives may take two different inflectional endings, giving three forms, for example:

big   bigger   biggest

tall   taller   tallest

The adjective without the ending is called the standard form and represents the positive degree of comparison. The one with the *-er* ending is the comparative, and is used when we compare two objects for the same property. For example: **standard form** **positive** **comparative**

My dad is taller than your dad.

The *-est* ending is called the superlative. It is used when we are comparing three or more objects for the same property. For example: **superlative**

Your dad may be taller than my dad but Raewyn's dad is the tallest.

Not all adjectives take the *-er* and *-est* endings; some use *more* and *most*. For example:

evil	more evil	most evil
incredible	more incredible	most incredible

comparison

The morphosyntactic category which has the morphosyntactic properties of comparative and superlative is called comparison. Adjectives which show comparison therefore show it in three forms: the uninflected positive form, the comparative form, and the superlative form.

Consider the following list of adjectives, and divide them into three groups: those which take the *-er* and *-est* endings, those which take *more* and *most,* and those which take neither of the above.

high, wide, dead, red, medical, ugly, narrow, absolute, painful, final

Your answers should look as in Table 2.2.

Table 2.2

	-er, -est	more, most	neither
high	✓	✕	✕
wide	✓	✕	✕
dead	✕	✕	✓
red	✓	✕	✕
medical	✕	✕	✓
ugly	✓	✓	✕
narrow	✓	✕	✕
absolute	✕	✕	✓
painful	✕	✓	✕
final	✕	✕	✓

gradable adjective
non-gradable
adjectives

Those adjectives that have comparative and superlative forms are called gradable adjectives, while those that do not are called non-gradable adjectives. What we mean by 'gradable' is that there are degrees of the particular property rather than just the presence or absence of it. A medical bill cannot be more or less medical, at least as far as the English language is concerned. As to their function,

English adjectives may appear either before a noun or after a form of the verb *to be* (*am*, *is*, *are*, *was*, *were*, *being*, or *been*), for example:

    the ripe apple   the apple is ripe

    the evil alligator   the alligator is evil

Not all adjectives may appear in both of these positions. Some may only appear before nouns, while others may only appear after a form of the verb *to be*. (There is some licence in these restrictions where poetry is concerned, as you will see in Exercise 2.2.)

> Consider the following list of adjectives. Which may appear only before a noun, which may appear only after the verb *to be*, and which may appear in both positions?
>
>   older, elder, hungry, ill, red, ugly, afraid, utter, incredible, loath.

Your answer might look as in Table 2.3.

Table 2.3

	Before nouns	After *to be*	Both
older	✓	✓	✓
elder	✓	✗	✗
hungry	✓	✓	✓
ill	✗	✓	✗
red	✓	✓	✓
ugly	✓	✓	✓
afraid	✗	✓	✗
utter	✓	✗	✗
incredible	✓	✓	✓
loath	✗	✓	✗

Find the adjectives in the following poem: **EXERCISE 2.2**

The Lily

The modest Rose puts forth a thorn,
The humble Sheep a threat'ning horn;

> While the Lily white shall in love delight,
> Nor a thorn nor a threat stain her beauty bright.
>
> (William Blake)

- -

APPLICATION

Below is a portion of a short story with its adjectives in italics. What would the description be like without the adjectives?

His name described him better than I can. He looked like a *great, stupid, smiling* bear. His *black, matted* head bobbed forward and his *long* arms hung out as though he should have been on all fours and was only standing upright as a trick. His legs were *short* and *bowed*, ending in *strange, square* feet. He was dressed in *dark blue* denim, but his feet were *bare*; they didn't seem to be *crippled* or *deformed* in any way, but they were *square*, just as *wide* as they were *long*.

John Steinbeck, 'Johnny Bear'

If you remove the adjectives which come after forms of *be* such as *is, was, were,* the sentences become ungrammatical. When you remove all the adjectives which come before nouns as well, there is virtually no description left.

2.1.4 ADVERBS

adverb

Traditionally, adverbs tell us how (manner), where (place), or when (time) the action denoted by a verb occurs but this is problematic since not only adverbs perform this function. For the meantime let us suppose that these are adverbs:

She runs *quickly*.	how
The cat sat *here*.	where
They left *yesterday*.	when

Adverbs have no inflected forms, although many do, like adjectives, take comparison, but using the *more* and *most* forms, for example *more quickly, most quickly*.

The class of adverbs may be divided into two groups: degree, and general adverbs. Degree adverbs are a small group of words like *very, more* and *most*. They must always appear with either an adjective or a general adverb, for example:

She runs very quickly.   *She runs very.

This sculpture is more beautiful.   *This sculpture is more.

General adverbs are a large class, and may appear without a degree adverb. For example:

She runs quickly.

Many adverbs end with *-ly,* for example:

quickly, quietly, properly, instantly, seemingly, stupidly.

The sharp-eyed reader will notice that the *-ly* ending which forms adverbs is attached to adjectives. It is not an inflection since it does not relate to any morphosyntactic categories such as tense or number. We shall have more to say about such word-forming endings in the next section.

We will not provide an exercise for hunting adverbs. The easy cases all end in *-ly,* which makes such an exercise hardly worth doing. In other cases adjectives and adverbs behave in rather similar ways and so they are often hard to tell apart, which makes such an exercise difficult.

2.1.5 VERBS

The grammatical class of verbs may be divided into two groups: auxiliary verbs and lexical verbs. The class of auxiliaries is quite small, and contains the following: *has, had, have, be, am, is, are, was, were, do, does, did, can, could, shall, should, will, would, may, might* and *must.* We will look at these verbs in more detail in Part Three. In this section we will concentrate on the class of lexical verbs.

auxiliary verb
lexical verb

Traditionally lexical verbs are defined as denoting actions or states, for example *eat, drink, run, speak, forgive, understand, hate.* The first four of these verbs denote actions: that is, in doing these things we perform some physical action; while the final three denote states: that is, we can 'do' these things without performing any physical action.

English verb lexemes have more grammatical word forms associated with them than with either nouns or adjectives. Each verb lexeme has five associated grammatical words. The changes in form associated with each grammatical word form, listed below, are brought about by adding an inflection to the verb. (The oddity of the form *called* being placed under *-en* will be explained later.)

V-stem	V-*s*	V-*ed*	V-*ing*	V-*en*
call	calls	called	calling	called

Let us look at the morphosyntactic categories that give rise to these different grammatical words and word forms. The first category is tense. All English verbs can take tense and there are two tenses: past and present. The present tense form of CALL is *call* and the past tense form is *called.* You may ask what happens to the future in English. The future is not indicated by a grammatical word form but can be indicated by other means, such as the auxiliary verb *will* as in *will call.* So it is not the case that English has no future; it just has no future tense inflection. Future is not a morphosyntactic property of English verbs.

The next inflected form, the one ending in *-s*, indicates a number of morphosyntactic properties. It is found only if the verb to which it is attached is in the present tense, the noun in front of it in a simple two-word sentence must be singular and can be substituted for by *he, she* or *it*, for example:

he / she / it / the postman / Mary calls in the morning.

person
first person
second person
third person
agreement

Such nouns are the third person nouns: not the speaker, who is the first person, or the person being addressed, the second person, but the person or thing spoken about, the third person. So here we have an inflection which indicates the state of not one morphosyntactic category but three: tense, number and person. It also illustrates a process called agreement. Notice that only the tense is a morphosyntactic property of the verb itself while the number and person categories are a result of the morphosyntactic properties of something else with which the verb must 'agree'.

This is a very complicated set of arrangements to keep in mind when you are speaking. Perhaps that is why the *-s* ending is not used in many parts of the English-speaking world. For example, it is often not used in Singapore and Malaysian English. Singapore speakers will say, *She lock that door every day* rather than *She locks that door every day.* Since almost all Singaporeans are at least bilingual it is worth mentioning that the other languages which Singaporeans speak do not show third person singular present tense agreement. Official attitudes to this lack of agreement are not positive. The National University of Singapore, for example, requires its students to use 'standard English', including showing this agreement.

participle
progressive
  participle
perfect participle
infinitive

The V-*ing* and V-*en* forms are called participles. The V-*ing* form is the progressive participle and the V-*en* form is the perfect participle. We discuss the function of these participles in Part Three. The simple form of verbs, without any endings, is called the infinitive. It is often introduced by the word *to,* for example, *to call.*

Verbs like *call* are regular, and regular verbs form the majority of verbs in English. For regular verbs, the past tense form and the perfect participle form are identical. So how can we tell that these identical forms represent different grammatical words? In part because they have different functions in phrases and sentences, but also because, in the case of irregular verbs, the forms are different. There are about 200 irregular verbs in English. Some are given in Table 2.4.

Table 2.4

V-stem	V-*s*	V-*ed*	V-*ing*	V-*en*
meet	meets	met	meeting	met
put	puts	put	putting	put
write	writes	wrote	writing	written
bring	brings	brought	bringing	brought

These verbs are all irregular in one way or another. All the verbs above and in Table 2.4, both regular and irregular, have regular V-*s* and progressive participle forms. The differences occur in the past tense and perfect participle.

Each of the verbs in Table 2.4 has its own way of being irregular. In the case of *meet*, a different vowel sound is used in the stem of the word for the past tense form. Other verbs that follow this pattern include *bleed* (*bled*) and *feed* (*fed*). *Write* and *bring* similarly change their stem vowels in the past tense (*wrote* and *brought*) and perfect participle forms (*written* and *brought*). Other verbs that also do this include: *sing, ring, ride*, and *strive*.

Put does not change at all in its past tense and perfect participle forms. *Hit* is another verb that follows this pattern.

Morphemes can, as we have now illustrated repeatedly, have variant forms (allomorphs). Just like variant pronunciations these can sometimes tell us where a speaker comes from. In English almost everywhere you go there are two allo- morphs of the -*ing* progressive participle inflection. The -*ing* ending is one of the most studied morphological variables in sociolinguistics. These appear in many different varieties of English. In the American South -*in* is more common. Men, the English-speaking world over, seem to use -*in* more frequently than women in the same region. And almost everywhere you go, the -*ing* pronun- ciation is more socially prestigious than the -*in* pronunciation. Some regional, social and ethnic dialects with low prestige, such as some working-class London dialects and African American Vernacular English, characteristically use the -*in* pronunciation, as in *I am goin*. In Irish English the -*in* form is more generally used so is an indicator of regional dialect. The perfective participle of GOT is *got* in England and in all the Southern Hemisphere Englishes but is usually *gotten* in the USA.

allomorph

We can now note again that not all changes of word form are by way of inflec- tion, that is, the addition of an ending. Some morphosyntactic categories are realized in particular lexemes by changes to the stem of the lexeme. We have seen this earlier in the case of nouns some of which also have strong forms of the plural.

If the verb *to concorde,* meaning 'to fly at supersonic speed', or *to potato*, meaning 'turn something into a potato', were to be added to the language, would they follow the regular pat- tern or one of the irregular patterns? If there were more groups of irregular verbs, and these groups were larger, would this cause any problems for someone trying to learn English?

Any new verb would follow the regular pattern. In fact the classes of irregular verbs have been getting smaller over the centuries. If the irregular classes were more numerous, and larger, then this would make learning English more difficult. Rather than learning that the past tense and perfect participle forms of most verbs are formed by adding -*ed* to a stem, we would have to remember which class a verb belonged to and how that class formed its past tense and perfect participle forms. It is interesting that young children frequently show how the regular form is used by using it on an irregular verb. For example, a child may say *I bringed my doggy*. For them, the regular forms allow them to use the past tense, while later, as they grow up, they can and do learn all the exceptions.

<table>
<tr><td>

EXERCISE 2.3

</td><td>

Find the lexical verbs in the following poem:

</td></tr>
</table>

Nurse's Song

When the voices of children are heard on the green
And whisp'rings are in the dale
The days of my youth rise fresh in my mind,
My face turns green and pale.

Then come home my children, the sun is gone down,
And the dews of night arise,
Your spring and your day are wasted in play,
And your winter and night in disguise.

William Blake

. . . .

2.1.6 PREPOSITIONS

preposition

The last major syntactic category we will look at in this chapter is the preposition. Prepositions are words such as *in, out, on, by,* which often indicate relationships involving locations in time or space, or direction. These locations can be of actions or things, for example, *Jean sat in a chair, the umbrella in the hall.*

open class
closed class

While nouns, adjectives, adverbs and verbs are members of open classes because the classes they belong to are large, and because it is possible to add new items to them, prepositions are members of a small closed class.

Try to make up a new preposition by compounding two existing prepositions.

You will see that plausible options like *in under* and *out from* seem fine when you put them together as individual words but not when you try to make a new preposition out of the sequence as in *inunder* and *outfrom*. These seem impossible, suggesting that the class of prepositions is closed.

conjunction
determiner

Other closed classes of words are conjunctions, for example: *and, but, because;* or determiners, for example: *a, an, the, these, those;* and the class of auxiliary verbs we looked at earlier in this chapter. It is not possible to add new members to the closed classes. In fact, there is no record of anyone ever adding a new conjunction to the language. Because the function of these words requires us to look more closely at the grammar of sentences, we will leave discussing them until Part Three, where we look at sentence structure.

The morphosyntactic categories and properties of English lexemes and how they relate to inflections in English are summarized in Table 2.5. If you speak a variety of English that does not inflect this way, you can use this table to check out your own English and see just what it does for each morphosyntactic category and property.

Table 2.5

Syntactic category	Morphosyntactic categories	Morphosyntactic properties	Grammatical words	Regular inflections
Noun	Number	1. Singular 2. Plural	1. Singular form 2. Plural form	None -s
Verb	Tense	1. Past 2. Present	1. Past tense form 2. Non-3rd person singular present form	-ed no inflection
	Number	1. Singular 2. Plural	3. 3rd person singular present form	-s
	Person	1. First person 2. Second person 3. Third person	4. Progressive participle 5. Perfect participle	-ing -ed/-en
Adjective/ Adverb	Comparison	1. Positive 2. Comparative 3. Superlative	1. Positive form 2. Comparative form 3. Superlative form	no inflection -er -est
Preposition	none	none	none	none

Identify the grammatical category of the italicized words in the following passage:　　**EXERCISE 2.4**

The *witches hopped in* their *red* Mini and *drove gently to* the convocation for an *evening* of fine *wines*, *entertaining* conversation and new spells.

· ·

2.2　WORD FORMATION

We assumed in the previous section that the lexemes we looked at were simple in not being made up themselves of other lexemes (although they were in many cases inflected). In this section we will look at complex lexemes which have other lexemes as component parts.

compound

There are two main ways in which English lexemes may have other lexemes as constituents. Two lexemes may be put together to make a compound lexeme. For example, the lexeme BOOKSHELF consists, very obviously, of the lexeme BOOK followed by the lexeme SHELF. A lexeme can also have as constituents a single lexeme plus an ending. These endings are generally termed affixes. The grammatical endings we looked at in the previous section are inflectional affixes. The ones which are constituents of complex lexemes are derivational affixes since they derive one lexeme from another. Look, for instance, at the word GENTLENESS. This lexeme, again obviously, consists of the lexeme GENTLE followed by the affix *-ness*. In the following two sections we will look first at compounding and then at derivation.

affix

derivational affix

derivation

When we looked at simple lexemes we saw that they had phonological, syntactic, and semantic properties. Compound lexemes too have all three sets of properties but, in their case, these properties are, in part, predictable in a way that they are not for simple lexemes. In general a compound lexeme has the sounds of its component lexemes in that order. This seems very obvious but, as we shall see in the case of derivation, this isn't always the case. For example, when the lexeme ELECTRIC has the derivational affix *-ity* added to it, it becomes *electricity*. The *k* sound has changed to an *s* sound. Compounding does not make changes to the sounds of the component lexemes.

Compound words in English usually have the main emphasis on the first word. For example, *income tax* has the main stress on the *in* of *income* and not on the *tax*. *Whitewash* has primary stress on *white* and *soulsearching* has primary stress on *soul*. There is debate as to whether this is always so. It certainly is generally the case.

As far as their syntactic properties go, compounds have a rather simple, regular set of properties.

First they are always binary in structure. In other words they always consist of two and only two constituent lexemes. This means that a compound which has three or more constituents must have them in pairs. For example, *washing-machine manufacturer* consists of *washingmachine* and *manufacturer,* while *washingmachine,* in turn, consists of *washing* and *machine*. A simple tree diagram of such a word would show its binary structure, as in Figure 2.1.

head

Compound words also usually have a head constituent. By a head constituent we mean one which determines the syntactic properties of the whole lexeme. For example, the compound lexeme LONGBOAT consists of an adjective, LONG, and a noun, BOAT. The compound lexeme LONGBOAT is a noun, and it is a noun because *boat* is a noun, that is, *boat* is the head constituent of *longboat*. One interesting piece of support for the existence of heads comes from compound nouns which have two nouns as constituents. In such a case, how can you tell which is the head? Well if one of them has an irregular plural, then only if it is the head does

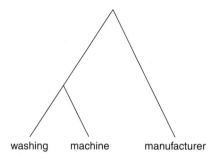

Figure 2.1

the whole compound have that form of the plural. For example, the plural form of *snowgoose* is *snowgeese,* that is, the form of the plural of the whole compound word is the form of its head constituent because the plural of *goose* is *geese.* The same goes for *snowman* and *snowmen, flowerchild* and *flowerchildren.* In English, of the two constituents of a compound, the right-hand one is normally its head.

There are exceptions to the generalization that compounds are syntactically headed. For example, *income* is a noun consisting of a preposition followed by a verb. Neither of these constituents determine that the compound is a noun since neither is itself a noun.

Compound words can belong to all the major syntactic categories we looked at in the previous section. Here are some examples of each:

Nouns: *signpost, sunlight, coatrack, bluebird, redwood, swearword, outhouse*

Verbs: *window shop, stargaze, outlive, undertake*

Adjectives: *icecold, hellbent, undersized*

Prepositions: *into, onto, upon*

Some of the constituent structures for compounds are productive in the sense that speakers can make up new ones on the same pattern readily. For example, a compound noun consisting of a noun plus noun, or adjective plus noun, is easy to make up. In the computer industry new compounds like this are being created almost daily. For example, many of the following are now familiar words to anyone with a computer: *pendrive, hard drive, mousemat, screensaver, screendump.*

Those constituent patterns where compounding is productive also allow compounds themselves to have compounds as constituents, as we saw when looking at the binary structure of compounds. For example, *floppy disk drive cleaner* has the compound noun *floppy disk* compounded with *drive* to create *floppy disk drive.* That compound noun in turn is compounded with *cleaner.* On the other hand, new compound prepositions, as we saw earlier, seem impossible to create. So it should not be possible to create new prepositions by compounding them.

As far as their meaning is concerned, compound words are often headed in another way. If we look at a compound like *dinnersuit,* then a dinner suit is a kind of suit, not a kind of dinner. *Undereating* is a variety of eating, and for something to be overgrown is for it to be grown in a special way. In other words, the lexeme which is the head of the compound from a syntactic point of view is also central to its meaning. The non-head modifies the meaning of the head, making it more specific in some way or other.

There are exceptions to semantic headedness. Redbacks, with which you will become familiar in Chapter 4, are a variety of Australian spider and not a variety of back.

lexical item

This allows us to make an important distinction. *Redback* is a lexical item, in other words, it is listed in the lexicon of many (if not most) Australian speakers of English. Lexical items have a tendency to become specialized and idiosyncratic. That is why they must be listed in the lexicon since their idiosyncrasy is something speakers have to learn and cannot deduce. If we make up a new compound word, for instance *radiodog,* with the stress on the word *radio,* then we know that it is a noun because its head, *dog,* is a noun and we infer that a radiodog is a kind of dog. Further than that, we do not know what this noun designates. But if it became a lexical item, we would have to know more, for instance that it was the dog that a particular radio station used in order to bark the hours of the day before the reading of the hourly news bulletin. (Heaven forbid.)

Here again we have an important distinction between lexemes, which are abstract words that may or may not be lexical items, and lexical items, which are actual words. We would want to say that *radiodog* is a possible word of English but not a lexical item of English (although it may just have become one in the previous discussion).

EXERCISE 2.5

Compounds are often frequent in modern technical areas where new vocabulary is being created. Find the compounds in the following passage:

A LaserWriter can print a document more quickly if the fonts used in the document are stored in the printer's memory or on a hard disk attached to the printer. Some LaserWriter printers come with built-in fonts, which are stored in the printer's read-only memory (ROM). You can transfer, or download, additional fonts to the printer's random access memory (RAM) or to a hard disk attached to the printer.

Apple Computer, Inc., *System 7 Reference Manual*

. . . .

2.2.2 DERIVATIONAL AFFIXATION

We have seen so far that although words in a dictionary are represented by sequences of letters and a grammatical category, they may have more structure than the dictionary usually provides. Some are compounds consisting of two lexemes. Still others have affixes as constituents. Look, for example, at a word like *loveliness.* Its form is a sequence of sounds, but it can also be divided into three sections. It is made up of *love* plus *li* plus *ness*. One of these is a lexeme. The other two are affixes.

Divide the following words into these same kinds of building blocks.

movement, lowly, nationhood

You will almost certainly have got the following divisions: move+ment, low+ly, nation+hood. These minimal building blocks of lexemes are called morphemes. **morpheme** Why are morphemes and not speech sounds the basic building blocks of complex lexemes?

A morpheme is usually realized (given form) as a speech sound or sequence of speech sounds just as a lexeme is, and it functions as part (or all) of a word. Morphemes also contribute to the meaning of a lexeme. For example, the word *girlhood* consists of two morphemes *girl* and *-hood*. The *girl* part means 'young female person' and the *-hood* bit means 'abstract property or state of being a ...'. So the word *girlhood* means 'the abstract property or state of being a girl'. A linguistic unit whose meaning is the sum of the meanings of its structural parts is described as 'compositional' and it has the abstract property of compositionality. **compositional**

Another property of morphemes which they share with lexemes is that the relationship between their form, that is, the sounds of which they are constructed, and their meaning is arbitrary. Any sequence of speech sounds that the language allows can be a morpheme. There is nothing in the sequence of sounds that go to make up the morpheme *-hood* that makes it particularly suitable to be a morpheme, or the morpheme *-hood* in particular. The great Swiss linguist Ferdinand de Saussure termed this property of words and morphemes 'the arbitrariness of the sign'.

So morphemes are the basic building blocks of lexemes because they are essentially made the same way, that is, as symbols. Morphemes are building blocks of words just as lexemes are building blocks of phrases. The inflections which we looked at in section 2.1 are clearly morphemes, as are the derivational affixes which we will look at now.

The creation of new lexemes by the process of derivation involves word formation rules. These rules specify what happens in the process of using one lexeme to derive another. A word formation rule operates on a base, that is, a lexeme **base** with all the properties lexemes have: form, syntactic category and meaning. It then specifies what happens to the base in the process of the derivation. The stem is the form of the base, that is, its phonological shape, and that is how we **stem** have been using the term.

Let us look at an example. Take the nouns ending in *-ness*. The base for such nouns is a set of adjectives, for example: *happy, sad, cheerful, gentle, soft, prickly*. The word-formation rule which derives the nouns *happiness, sadness, cheerfulness, gentleness, softness* and *prickliness* from their respective bases only takes adjectives as a base, as we can see because the following are not possible English words: **shipness, *slowliness, *putness*, since these have a noun, adverb and verb respectively as base and are therefore not well-formed. Secondly, the word-formation rule specifies that the meaning of the new word will be something like 'the state of being A', where A is the meaning of the base. So the meaning of *happiness* is something like 'the state of being happy'. Thirdly, the word-formation rule specifies the form of the new lexeme by indicating that the new lexeme has the suffix *-ness* attached to the right-hand end of the stem.

Things are not always so simple. Many word-formation rules specify their bases more narrowly than this. Look, for example, at the suffix *-ee* in words such as *addressee* and *payee*. The base for this word-formation rule is a set of verbs, and the meaning of the resulting lexeme is something like 'the one who is V-ed', the one who is addressed or paid. But this means that the verb which is the base for the word-formation rule and to which the *-ee* suffix attaches must be the kind of verb which has both someone to do the V-ing and someone to whom the V-ing is done. It would, for example, not be possible to attach *-ee* to a verb like *breathe* because when breathing takes place no one gets breathed, nor to a verb like *mow* since what gets mowed is not a person. On the other hand, not all verbs which look as though they should be eligible permit this, in that the process denoted by the verb cannot be something like that denoted by *kiss* or *thump*. We do not get *kissee* or *thumpee*.

The suffix *-able,* by way of comparison, does attach to *mow* and *sing,* but not to *sit*. The reason for this is that there are at least things like grass and songs which get mowed and sung but nothing gets sat. The word-formation rule for *-able* takes as its bases verbs which are not just actions but actions done to things or people. So people who might be loved are lovable; the things that could get mowed are mowable, and so on. Clearly things might also be kissable or thumpable.

The exact limitations on these particular word-formation rules are not perhaps as significant as the fact that they involve rather delicate facts to do with the meaning of the base, and these facts must be accessible to the rules of word formation.

In other cases, word formation rules specify that their base must belong to a sub-class of lexemes which came into the English language originally from another language. Look, for example, at the suffix *-ion* and the lexemes to which it attaches, like *decision, induction, conclusion* and *allusion*. The verb bases to which *-ion* is attached here are *decide, induce, conclude* and *allude*. All of them have Latin as their language of origin. Native English verbs like *break, run* and *breathe* cannot take *-ion,* as you can work out for yourself. Another suffix which attaches to such Latin bases is *-ity*. Thus *domesticity, reciprocity* and *anonymity* are well-formed English words since their bases are foreign imports, but **hardity, *greyity* and **loneity* are not, because their bases are lexemes which have been part of English vocabulary for a very long time and were not 'borrowed' from other languages.

Word-formation rules may also be sensitive to the phonological properties of bases. The prefix *de-* with the meaning 'take off' seems typically to apply to monosyllabic bases as in *delouse, dehorn, degrease*.

A word-formation rule may also be sensitive to what word-formation process (if any) took place to create its base. For example, the suffix *-ity* happily attaches to bases ending in *-able,* for example, *readable, readability*; *taxable, taxability.* But it is not happy to attach itself to lexemes ending in *-ful,* for example, *thoughtful, *thoughtfulity*; *restful, *restfulity.* On the other hand, *-hood* will not attach to any base which is anything but a single morpheme. For example, *sisterhood, parent-hood* and *priesthood* are well-formed but **blackbirdhood* is not.

All this suggests that the processes of derivation are potentially sensitive to all of the following properties of bases: their phonological form, their syntactic properties, their semantic properties, their derivational source and even their historical provenance.

Their effects, you might imagine, would also include the same range of possible properties. We have already seen that derivational processes have the basic phonological effect of adding an affix which determines the syntactic category of the new lexeme and its meaning. But these are not the end of the matter.

Word-formation rules which add derivational affixes may be divided into three groups. There are those which add stress-bearing affixes to their stems and those which cause the stress to shift, and those, like inflectional affixes, which have no influence on stress placement. We will look at this phenomenon from a phonological point of view in Chapter 6. The first group includes: *-ee, -ese* and *-esque.* All three suffixes take stress, for example:

pa'role – paro'lee, Su'dan – Sudan'ese, 'Roman – Roman'esque

Note that the ' mark coming before a syllable indicates that the following syllable is stressed.

The second group includes: *-eons, -y, -ial, -ion,* and *-ity.* The addition of one of these suffixes results in the stress shifting towards the suffix, for example:

'outrage – out'rageous, 'spectrograph – spec'trography

'adverb – ad'verbial, 'renovate – reno'vation, e'lectric – elec'tricity

The third group does not have any influence on the placement of stress. This group includes: *-able, -age, -en, -ful, -ing, -like, -ment,* and *-wise.*

Word-formation processes may also have phonological effects other than that affecting stress placement.

Look at the following bases and derived words. What sound changes do you notice?

commit	commission
submit	submission
admit	admission
revert	reversion
dominate	domination

morpho-phonemic

Clearly the addition of the noun-forming suffix *-ion* has had more phonological effects on the base than you might expect from just the addition of *-ion,* and don't let the spelling of the last example fool you. In each case the final sound of the base has undergone a change. This change is morpho-phonemic: that is, it is a phonemic change caused by a morphological process. There are many such processes and they lead us to the concept of allomorphy. Just as a speech sound in a language may have a variety of different realizations in different contexts, so a morpheme may have different phonemic realizations in different contexts. The plural in English, for example, has a variety of forms. Each of these: /s/, /z/, and /ɪz/, is an allomorph of the plural morpheme.

Allomorphs may be stem allomorphs or affixal allomorphs depending on what has the variant forms. In the case of the stem to which the *-ion* affix attaches we are dealing with stem allomorphs whereas the plural forms are affixal allomorphs.

EXERCISE 2.6

Separate the affixes from the following words and divide them into inflectional and derivational sub-classes:

singularities, neglectful, soils, deliberation, sacrifices, artificially.

. . . .

2.2.3 CONVERSION

conversion

There is a third word-formation process which is rather difficult to deal with because nothing happens to the lexeme's form in the process. Look at the following pairs: [N DRINK], e.g. *Give me a drink,* [V DRINK], e.g. *She drank the water;* [N JOKE], e.g. *That's a good joke,* [V JOKE], e.g. *They joked about the Minister of Finance;* [N AXE], e.g. *I have an axe for chopping firewood,* [V AXE], e.g. *The Prime Minister decided to axe the Minister of Finance.* The noun *drink* and the verb *drink* have exactly the same form but differ in their syntactic category and consequentially also in their meaning. Because they differ in both their syntactic category and their meaning these pairs contain different lexemes. The process which connects them is often termed conversion. Conversion is different from derivational affixation. There we can see the way in which the new lexeme has been derived from the base lexeme by the addition of an affix. The process has a directionality to it. But, in the above pairs, since there is no change to the form it is hard to say which of the pair is more basic. In some cases the meaning helps. Drinking is semantically more verb-like, while an axe is more noun-like. But in many cases it is not at all obvious. How do you know which is which in a particular context? Generally an inflection test will confirm which category it is. In *They axed his job* there is a past tense inflection on *axe.* So here *axe* must be a verb.

One problematic case of conversion is that of the participles. These can be verbs but they can also be adjectives as in *a growing child* and *drawn blinds.* Since these are not gradable adjectives the inflection test using *-er* or *-est* will not help. The progressive participle can also be a noun as in *Walking is good exercise.* Here *walking* is a noun but, since it is not countable, the plural inflection test doesn't work. For an explanation as to why these are adjectives and nouns we have to wait until Chapter 7.

Conversion is very common in English. Take most nouns and they can be converted to verbs. *Supermarket* could easily become a verb, for example, *We are going to be supermarketting until 11 o'clock.* Conversion also happens with adjectives, as the following examples show: [A YELLOW], e.g. *a yellow tulip,* [V YELLOW], e.g. *The paper yellowed gradually;* [A DARK], e.g. *a dark corner,* [N DARK], e.g. *in the dark.* Even compound verbs can be converted. The verb *to put someone down* can be converted into the noun *putdown.*

2.3 KINDS OF MORPHEMES

Now that we have seen how inflections and derivational affixes function, we can look at morphemes in a more general way so as to gain an understanding of some of their general properties.

2.3.1 BOUND AND FREE MORPHEMES

Some morphemes which are parts of complex lexemes are lexemes in their own right. In the lexemes *movement, lowly* and *national* the morphemes *move, low* and *nation* have this property. They are called free morphemes. Those, like *-ment,* that cannot stand on their own as lexemes, are termed bound morphemes.

free morpheme
bound morpheme

Divide the following morphemes into free and bound sets:

ation, nation, pre, post, angle, ible, infra, out.

EXERCISE 2.7

· ·

2.3.2 STEMS AND AFFIXES

A second classification of morphemes involves looking at the morphemes that are tacked on at the beginning or end of a word. It is a positional classification. Usually the stem is a free morpheme, as in the case of *lovely* where *love* is the stem of the word and a free morpheme. However, this is not always the case. For example, in the word *possible* the *-ible* seems to be attached to the stem *poss,* which is itself bound. There are other cases, like the word *cranberry* where *cran* occurs nowhere but in this word and seems, therefore, to be a bound stem. The bound morphemes which are attached to a set of stems are collectively known as affixes, as you will recall.

Separate the affixes from the stems in the following words:

trains, succeeded, lighter, predetermined, retroactive, confusions, instructional.

• •

prefix
suffix

Affixes in English have two locations where they can be attached to stems. The obvious places are before and after the stem. In a word like *recreate,* the stem is *create* and the affix attached at its left-hand end is *re-*. Affixes which attach at the left-hand end of a stem are termed prefixes. Affixes such as *-ation,* which are attached at the right-hand end of stems, are termed suffixes. It is one of the interesting properties of affixes that a given affix is either a prefix or a suffix. It cannot be both. We can think of this property as being rather like a hook that the affix is provided with which is at one end only. A prefix comes equipped with hook, hooking onto a stem at the affix's right-hand end and a suffix hooks onto a stem at the affix's left-hand end. Free stems, by contrast, have no hooks. We can see that this is the case by the fact that many stems will take both prefixes and suffixes.

What about bound stems? Since they must be attached to either an affix or another stem to form a word, they too must come equipped with a hook. Look, for example, at the *cran* in *cranberry.* It clearly hooks onto a stem to its right.

2.3.3   MORE ON INFLECTIONAL MORPHEMES

We have seen that there is an important distinction between derivation and inflection. In the case of derivation, an affix is involved in creating a new lexeme, whereas in the case of inflection the affix is the realization of a set of morphosyntactic properties.

Inflections tend to appear regularly on almost all the words of a particular grammatical class, as we saw in the previous section. You will recall that English countable nouns take the morphosyntactic property *plural,* and this is often realized in the form of a plural suffix. All English verbs can take a past tense and this morphosyntactic property is often realized in the form of a past tense suffix.

All inflections in English are suffixes and if a word has an inflection attached to it then it will be the last morpheme in the word, since English only allows a single inflectional suffix to appear on any word. Inflections never attach to bound stems.

suppletive form

In some cases, as we saw in the introduction to this chapter, verbs and nouns do not have regular forms of particular morphosyntactic categories, but have what are termed suppletive forms, that is, completely unpredictable ones. We saw suppletion in the earlier discussion in which we decided that word forms and lexemes had to be distinguished. The example we used was the past tense form of the lexeme GO, namely, *went.* This form is suppletive.

What are the comparative and superlative forms of GOOD and BAD?

Answer:

They are *better* and *best,* and *worse* and *worst.* Their form is totally unpredictable on the basis of that of *good* and *bad.* Therefore, their formation cannot be rule-governed and so they are also suppletive forms.

On the other hand, sometimes words which really are different in their inflectional morphology are identical in form. As we saw in section 2.1, the perfect participle in English is often indistinguishable in form from the past tense form. For instance, *Joanna has towed the boat* and *Joanna towed the boat* have identically inflected forms of the verb TOW. In the first sentence, *tow* has the perfect participle form and in the second, it has the past tense form. We can tell this is so because, for other verbs, the two forms are different. For example, the verb BREAK in the following two sentences has different forms: *Joanna has broken the mower* and *Joanna broke the mower.* The situation where two different grammatical words have the same inflected form is termed syncretism. Someone who wants **syncretism** to speak English must learn these forms separately. Allomorphy and syncretism will therefore create difficulties for foreign-language learners of English.

Find five further English verbs which show syncretism between the past tense and past participle forms.

Remove all the inflectional affixes from the following passage:

The privileged man opened the packet, looked in, then, laying it down, went to the window. His rooms were the highest flat of a lofty building, and his glance could travel afar beyond the clear panes of glass, as though he were looking out of the lantern of a lighthouse.

Joseph Conrad, *Lord Jim*

Answer:

The privileged man open the packet, look in, then, lay it down, went to the window. His room were the high flat of a lofty building, and his glance could travel afar beyond the clear pane of glass, as though he were look out of the lantern of a lighthouse.

You can see from this exercise that two things have happened. First, the English sounds more telegraphic and quite ungrammatical. Also, the removal of some inflections, such as the plural, creates a different meaning and changes other things such as the fact that the word *were* is no longer the correct word to use if there is only one room. Other instances, such as the loss of the *-ing* in *were looking,* make the sentence ungrammatical since *-ing* is a necessary ending. You can see that inflectional affixes are an essential part of the language, even in a language which has as few of them as English does.

There are varieties of English where even the few inflections which English has are dispensed with. This happens in pidgin Englishes. In a pidgin language, usually used for trading and basic communication, there are no inflections. For example, in Bislama which is now one of the national languages of Vanuatu you might want to ask, 'Can you tell me of any good restaurants?' and say, 'Yu save talem mi eni gudfala restoron blong kakae long hem?' Notice that *restoron* has no plural.

Inflection stripping is not limited to pidgin languages. You might also have noticed that the inflectionless text sounds like some forms of 'foreigner talk'. When adults first begin to learn a foreign language they tend to leave out the inflections, particularly if they normally speak languages like the Chinese ones which have no inflections.

EXERCISE 2.9   More exercises on the structure of words:

(a)   Divide the following words into their constituent morphemes by placing a plus sign (+) between the morphemes, and indicate for each morpheme whether it is bound or free:

cleaning lady, anti-skidding device, mushroom, nationhood, deputize, derailments, predestination, internationalization.

(b)   Indicate for each of the following words, which have been divided up into morphemes, which are the affixes and, for each affix, what is its associated stem:

involve+ment, in+support+able, sub+profess+or+ial, inter+sub+ject+iv+ity.

(c)   A number of morphemes in the following passage are italicised. For each, say whether it is bound or free; if bound, whether it is an inflection or a derivational affix:

We are at once the most resilient, most resource*ful*, most rest*ive*, most receptive, most radical, most reaction*ary* people who ever liv*ed*. We have had time and the tide for every*thing* but those moments of thought necessary to reverse the priorities to cause us occasionally to look before leaping.

2.4 MORPHOLOGICAL PROPERTIES

2.4.1 EXISTING AND NON-EXISTING, POSSIBLE AND IMPOSSIBLE WORDS

If we look again at the distinction between inflectional and derivational affixes you will recall that adding an inflectional affix to a stem does not make a new lexeme. There is just the word with an affix added, whereas if we add a derivational affix to a stem then we have a new lexeme. That enables us to make two further distinctions which are important. There are words which we have stored in our brains as words, that is, words that we know. We have earlier called these 'lexical items'. All native English speakers are likely to know the words *tree* and *sister*. They are words which exist in a native speaker's lexicon, the internalized store of words in his or her brain. Then there are words which do not exist in anyone's brain, perhaps – for example, the following word: *insultability*. There is no reason why this should not be a lexeme of English. It just doesn't seem to *be* a lexical item of English. So it is a possible but non-existing word. A word like *fmukg* is also non-existing, but it is also impossible in English for reasons having to do with the sequencing of its sounds as we will see in Chapter 5.3.2.

Not all bases for word formation need to be existing words, that is, lexical items. For example, adjectives ending in the suffix *-ly* can provide the base for the word-formation rule which creates words ending in the suffix *-ness*, for example *friendliness*. So the number of lexemes in a language is infinite but the number of lexical items anyone actually has stored in their brain at one time is, of course, finite.

2.4.2 PRODUCTIVITY

Earlier we found that some affixes appear to attach to a limited set of bases.

How many lexemes can you find ending in *-hood*?

You will not have found more than two dozen. However, in theory it looks as though *-hood* is restricted to bases which are nouns and which are morphologically simple. So, again in theory, *-hood* should attach to base lexemes such as *soldier, friend, parson, nurse,* and many others. But you will be aware that *soldierhood, friendhood, parsonhood* and *nursehood* are not English words. So as well as the potential set of lexemes of which a derivational morpheme might be a constituent, the actual set of lexical items that it is a constituent of may be much smaller. By contrast, *-ness* attaches to adjectives and creates nouns. It is hard to find any adjective to which it cannot attach. It therefore appears that affixes may differ in their productivity.

Productivity can be looked at in a number of ways: *-hood* has a limited potential for creating new lexemes in that it will only attach to lexemes consisting of a single morpheme, and the lexeme must be a noun. However, the set of such lexemes is quite large. But *-hood* does not form new lexemes from most of the set. In other words its productivity, given its potential, is quite small; *-ness,* however, is very productive given its potential.

Another way to look at productivity is to see how freely people use the affix in making new lexemes. If speakers commonly use the affix in coining new words, then the affix is productive. Sometimes this is very much a matter of time and place. In New Zealand there were charity events on television which were dubbed *telethons*. To raise money, clubs and families would run cakeathons, jogathons, bathathons. and many more. So, for the duration of the fund-raising event, *-athon* became a productive suffix, thereafter disappearing.

Clearly productivity is a matter of degree. Some affixes may be highly productive, some middlingly so and some may be totally unproductive, that is, never used to create new lexemes. The prefix *a-* in such words as *astern, adrift* and *asleep* is now completely unproductive, whereas the prefix *non-* can be quite freely attached to adjectives.

APPLICATION

It is useful to be able to look at the morpheme structure of words because you can often get a good idea of a writer's style from looking at the structure of the words they use. When words of only one morpheme are used the style will appear to be very simple, whereas if words made up of a number of morphemes are used the style will appear to be more complex.

EXERCISE 2.10

Compare the extracts below by splitting words up into morphemes. Try and come to some conclusions about the authors' styles.

I was away for two days at the posts. When I got home it was too late and I did not see Miss Barkley until the next evening. She was not in the garden and I had to wait in the office of the hospital until she came down.

Ernest Hemingway, *A Farewell to Arms*

The author of these Essays is so sensible of their defects that he has repeatedly refused to let them appear in a form which might seem to indicate that he thought them worthy of a permanent place in English literature. Nor would he now give his consent to the republication of pieces so imperfect, if, by withholding his consent, he could make republication impossible.

Thomas Babington Macaulay, *Critical and Historical Essays*

I have allowed the Preface to the former edition of these Poems to stand almost without change, because I still believe it to be, in the main, true. I must not, however, be supposed insensible to the force of much that has been alleged against portions of it, or unaware that it contains many things incompletely stated. It leaves, too, untouched the question, how far, and in what manner the opinions there expressed respecting the choice of subjects apply to lyric poetry, that region of the poetical field which is chiefly cultivated at present. But neither have I time now to supply these deficiencies, nor is this the proper place for attempting it: on one or two points alone I wish to offer, in the briefest possible way, some explanation.

Matthew Arnold, Preface to *Second Edition of Poems*

2.4.3 DIAGRAMMING WORD STRUCTURE

Now that we have looked at both the functions of words and their internal structure we can put the work of the last two sections together to show the structure of words, and their function, in diagrams. If two lexemes are put together to form another lexeme then this is like a Chinese box arrangement with units existing within other units, as we saw in the case of *bookshelf*. We can represent this structure by the use of tree diagrams, as we saw in Chapter 1. A tree diagram for *blackboard* would look like the one shown in Figure 2.2. What it shows is that we have one unit consisting of two sub-units, and these sub-units come in a fixed order.

However, there is more to the structure of this word than just the fact that it consists of two units in a fixed order. We also know that each unit belongs to a grammatical category, such as noun or verb. We can add this information into the Chinese box structure and it will look like Figure 2.3. The equivalent tree diagram would look like Figure 2.4.

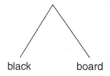

Figure 2.2

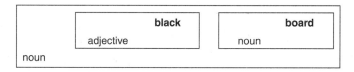

Figure 2.3

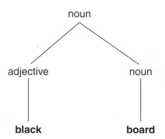

Figure 2.4

Both these representations are difficult to produce on a normal keyboard and so a third representation has been devised which essentially cuts the lines that join the ends of the boxes in the Chinese box representation and turns the ends into square brackets, so that the word *blackboard* can be represented as shown in Figure 2.5. This representation is called, rather obviously, labelled bracketed notation.

labelled bracketed notation

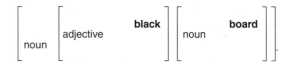

Figure 2.5

What about affixes? Since they are bound in a particular direction and are not themselves lexemes, their structure in the Chinese box representation looks like that in Figure 2.6. Notice that only the unit *slow* has a syntactic category and so there is no labelled box around *ly*.

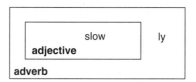

Figure 2.6

It follows that the tree diagram for this word will look like Figure 2.7.

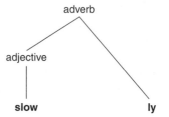

Figure 2.7

The labelled bracketed form will look like this:

[adverb [adjective **slow**] **ly**]

So far each example has consisted of only two parts. It seems that words always consist of two parts, that is, two parts at a time. *Nationalization* consists of *nationalize* plus *-ation* tacked onto it. *Nationalize*, in turn, consists of *national* plus *-ize* tacked on the end of it, and so forth. So the structure of this word in tree notation looks like Figure 2.8. Or in labelled bracketed notation it looks like this:

[Noun [Verb [Adjective [Noun **nation**] **al**] **ize**] **ation**]

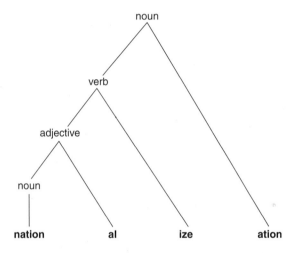

Figure 2.8

Now try to represent the following words both in tree diagrams and in labelled bracketed notation:

                                                      EXERCISE 2.11

bookworm

singer

mislay

tax collector

physical sciences library

unanalysable

inexcusable

internationalization

· ·

We have taken some time to introduce three different notations to represent the structure of words because each provides a different way of visualizing the same facts, namely, that words which have internal structure consist of units, which may or may not belong to syntactic categories and which come in a fixed order. In the case of words, such structures are relatively simple. When we look in Chapter 7 at the structure of sentences we will find that the structure of sentences can be represented in the same ways, but the syntactic categories are not just the by-now familiar lexical categories which we introduced in section 2.1. It is well worth taking time over drawing both tree and labelled bracketed diagrams of word structure. Doing so will help you become familiar with visualizing linguistic structure and representing it graphically.

Further exercises •

EXERCISE 2.12•

What is the grammatical category of the italicized words?

Two *old* Daimlers were parked in a line *by* the traffic lights. One *of* them *seemed* to have *lost* its *headlights*.

EXERCISE 2.13•

In each of the following words, separate the affixes from their respective stems. For each, decide whether it is a stem or an affix, bound or free, and if it is an affix, whether it is derivational or inflectional:

derivational, headstrong, unlikely, locator beacons.

Draw tree diagrams of the structure of each word.

EXERCISE 2.14••

Study the following passage and then answer the questions given below. *Take your examples from the passage*:

The crowd, in general more pleased with the bull even than with the peanut vendor, started to cheer. Newcomers gracefully jumped up on to fences, to appear standing there, marvellously balanced, on the top railings. Muscular hawkers lifted aloft, in one sinewy stretch of the forearm, heavy trays brimmed with multi-coloured fruits.

Malcolm Lowry, *Under the Volcano*

(a) Identify two compound words, name the grammatical category of each compound, and the grammatical categories of the elements that compose it.
(Example: *blackbird* is a noun, made up of adjective + noun.)

(b) Identify the class-changing derivational suffixes, name the grammatical category of the stem to which the suffix is attached and the grammatical category of the derived word.

(c) Divide the following words into their component morphemes:

newcomers, marvellously

(d)   What kind of word-formation process links the noun *hawker* and the verb
       hawk.

(e)   Identify an inflectional suffix other than the plural and explain its function or
       functions.

Study the following passage and then answer the questions given below. *Take*   **EXERCISE 2.15**••
your examples from the passage.

> The dog swam ahead, fatuously important; the foals, nodding solemnly, swayed
> along behind up to their necks; sunlight sparkled on the calm water, which fur-
> ther downstream where the river narrowed broke into furious little waves, swirl-
> ing and eddying close inshore against black rocks, giving an effect of wildness,
> almost of rapids; low over their heads an ecstatic lightning of strange birds
> manoeuvred, looping-the-loop and immelmanning at unbelievable speed,
> aerobatic as new-born dragonflies. The opposite shore was thickly wooded.
>
> Malcolm Lowry, *Under the Volcano*

(a)   Identify three compound words. For each one, name the grammatical cat-
       egory of the compound, and the grammatical category of the elements that
       compose it.
       (Example: *watertight* is an adjective, made up of noun + adjective.)

(b)   Divide the following words into their component morphemes, labelling each
       morpheme F (free), I (inflectional), or D (derivational):

       unbelievable, dragonflies

(c)   What is the function of the suffix -*ly* in the words *fatuously*, *solemnly* and
       thickly?

(d)   Identify two other words containing (different) derivational suffixes, name
       the grammatical category of the stem to which the suffix is attached, and the
       grammatical category of the derived word.

(e)   Describe the function of the suffix -*s* in *foals* and *waves*, and that of the suffix
       -*ed* in *swayed* and *sparkled*.

(f)   Comment on the past tense forms *swam* and *broke*.

(g)   The *Collins English Dictionary* contains the following entry:

       Immelmann turn or *Immelmann*... *n.* an aircraft manoeuvre used to gain
       height while reversing the direction of flight. It consists of a halfloop fol-
       lowed by a half roll. [C20: named after Max Immelmann (1890–1916),
       German aviator.]

Comment on the word-formation processes which have led, first, to the inclusion
of the above expressions in the *Dictionary*, and secondly, to the author's use of the
progressive participle form *immelmanning* in line 7.

Look carefully at the choice of vocabulary in the following passages. What differences in the styles can you discern and what do the differences in vocabulary choice suggest about the narrators of the two stories?

Mrs Clegg was quite a decent sort, but she had a glass eye that was cracked right down the middle, and it was funny the way she sort of looked out at you through the crack. Her old man was out of a job and that was why she was running the joint, though seeing she only had three rooms to let she said she wasn't making a fortune.

When she'd fixed my bed up she took me down to the kitchen to give me the teapot, and her old man was reading the paper, and their little girl was saying pretty boy to a budgie that was answering her back. Though sometimes it would ring a little bell instead. Mr Clegg told me he'd been a cook on a boat but now he couldn't get a keel. It was hard, he said, because he liked being at sea, though I thought by the look of him it must have been only a coastal or even a scow he'd worked on. He was pretty red too, though he said he hadn't been until he'd had experience of being on relief.

Frank Sargeson, 'That Summer'

It is perhaps an indication of the unusual features of my nature that for some days following the party, far from finding myself melted into a state of rapturous languor, I should find instead my mental capacities taxed by harder thinking than I had experienced during all that year. If I continued my association with Betty and the Gower-Johnsons, I foresaw that it would be elaborated to such a degree that my entire future might well be involved; and apart from minor advantages, such as benefiting from Betty's financial generosity, I saw my problem, if it was reduced to its bare, ineluctable elements, was nothing more or less than the same old problem which had first presented itself to me when I had finished with being a primary school boy: that is to say, the day-to-day activities of the environment I inhabited appeared not to be connected with what I conceived to be my major interests.

Frank Sargeson, *Memoirs of a Peon*

Word Meanings and Vocabularies

3.1 THE MEANING OF WORDS

What does a word mean? What are meanings and how does a word mean more or less the same thing to anyone who knows it? We can start again by looking in the traditional place people look for meanings, a dictionary. As well as telling us the spelling of a word and its syntactic category, dictionaries try to tell us the word's meaning or meanings. Let us look again at an example:

imposter, *n*. One who assumes a false character or personality; swindler.

Oxford Dictionary of Current English

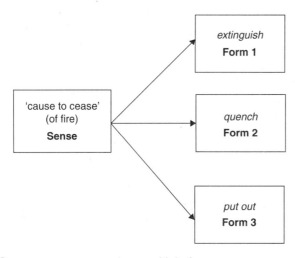

Figure 3.1 Synonymy: one meaning; multiple forms

This dictionary entry tells us that a word that is spelled *imposter* has a meaning given by other words. These words are not the meaning but have the same meaning as the word being defined. So here is a first important fact about word meanings. We can recognize sameness of meaning when we come across it just as we can recognize the sameness of two affixes which are allomorphs of the same morpheme. When expressions share the same meaning they are 'synonymous'. Where one word or expression has the same meaning as another, the two are called synonyms.

synonym

Which of the following words or expressions appear to have the same or very similar meanings; list them in pairs of letters:

(a) effluent	(h) the day after today
(b) knock over	(i) endure
(c) sympathize	(j) build up
(d) boycott	(k) put up with
(e) outflow	(l) tomorrow
(f) construct	(m) take a calculated guess at
(g) show sympathy	(n) estimate

Your answers should be:

(a), (e); (c), (g); (i), (k); (h), (l); (m), (n); (f), (j).

3.1.1 SAMENESS AND DIFFERENCE OF SENSE

The fact that this exercise proved to be so easy shows that we know the meanings of these words, and we, as speakers of English, share this knowledge.

If two words are synonymous then this allows us to make certain inferences. For example, if *car* and *automobile* are synonyms, then it follows from the fact that I am driving an automobile then I am driving a car, and conversely that if I am driving a car then I am driving an automobile, that is, if one is true then the other will be true and vice versa. The relationship where if one sentence is true, then the other is true, is termed entailment.

entailment

EXERCISE 3.1   *Synonymy and entailment*

In the following examples, what the first sentence expresses entails what the second expresses. Does the second sentence also entail the first? If it does, is this due to the synonymy of words or phrases in each sentence or not?

(a)   Evelyn won the race. The race was won by Evelyn.

(b)   Greg has hit the ball too hard. Greg has struck the ball too hard.

(c)   My socks are both scarlet. My socks are both red.

(d)   I bought some ripe tomatoes. I purchased some ripe tomatoes.

(e)   My dog is bigger than your dog. Your dog is smaller than my dog.

(f)   Her dad likes me a lot. Her father likes me a lot.

(g)   This pencil belongs to Roger. Roger owns this pencil.

(h)   Ken almost shot his foot. Ken nearly shot his foot.

(i)   My neighbour owns a pistol. My neighbour owns a firearm.

• •

In the above dictionary entry for *imposter,* the word has only one meaning, but this is not always the case. Words often have different but related meanings. When this happens one can often see quite clearly how the meanings relate to one another. For example, the lexeme SIGHT has the general meaning of 'the capacity to see', as in *Jerry slowly regained his sight,* but also the more special-ized meaning of a particular 'view', *The Grand Canyon is a magnificent sight.* The two meanings are obviously related. When this is the case the lexeme is said to be 'polysemous', and the property of having multiple meanings of this kind is called polysemy.   **polysemy**

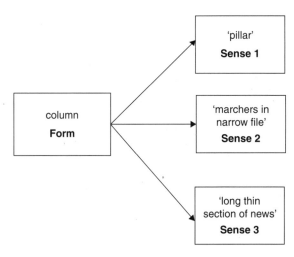

Figure 3.2 Polysemy: one form; multiple related meanings

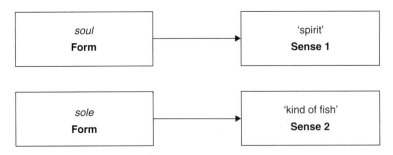

Figure 3.3 Homonymy: accidentally similar in form; unrelated meanings

homonym

Sometimes two quite different words accidentally have the same form. For example, *sight* and *site* are both nouns and both have identical phonological form. But native speakers know that these are two different lexemes and not one lexeme with two senses. Cases like that are called homonyms. Homonymy exists in both writing and speech. When two words are spelled identically, for example *lead* as in what you take your dog for a walk on, and *lead,* the heavy metal, the result is homography, and when they are spoken identically, for example *soul* and *sole,* it is homophony.

It needs to be noted that it is not always clear whether one is dealing with polysemy or homonymy in a particular instance. A chair that people sit on and the position of being a professor in a university, that is, holding a chair, probably are not seen by most speakers as being related in meaning.

EXERCISE 3.2   *Polysemy and homonymy*

Are the senses of the italicized words related, that is, is there one word with polysemous senses, or are these homonyms?

(a)   The ship was *listing* badly.
      We are *listing* the requirements for the course.

(b)   He gave her a diamond *ring*.
      His glass left a *ring* on the table.

(c)   They came to a *fork* in the road.
      He placed the *fork* beside the knife on the plate.

(d)   The dog tried to *lap* the water.
      The cat sat in my *lap*.

(e)   The dog had no *bark*.
      Don't remove the *bark* from the tree.

(f)   It is *hard* to play the violin.
      Ebony is a *hard*wood.

. . . .

Puns are a form of word play which relies on a word being polysemous or homonymous. For example, Hamlet, in the play of the same name, calls Rosenkrantz and Guildenstern *recorders*, because they have been sent to record what he says and does. But he then accuses them of treating him like the musical instrument, the recorder. The source of the pun is the homonymy of the two words *recorder*. **pun**

Think of five jokes that rely on puns and then look up in a dictionary the words on which they are based, for an explanation of how the joke works. **EXERCISE 3.3**

· ·

3.1.2 OPPOSITENESS OF SENSE

While some words have senses which are the same as one another, other sets of words have senses which are 'opposite' to one another. The senses of words can be opposite in a number of quite distinct ways. Some of these words with opposite senses are called antonyms. Some of them are gradable, a category we have already met in Chapter 2.1. Others are not gradable. Gradable antonyms are typically opposites near the ends of a scale, such as *hot* and *cold*. Their scale is the temperature scale. Antonyms of this kind have many interesting properties. Being gradable they can be modified by words like *very*, for example *very cold*, and can take comparative and superlative forms, as we saw in Chapter 2.1, for example *hotter, hottest*. Gradability has to do with the fact that the position of the antonym on its scale is not an absolute but a relative one. Consequently an antonym's sense cannot be right at the end of the scale. If we can modify it then there are temperatures which are hotter than hot and colder than cold. It is also a consequence that there are positions in between. This can be seen clearly in the case of *hot* and *cold* by the fact that there is another antonym pair, *cool* and *warm*, which take up intermediate positions between *hot* and *cold*. It is an inherent feature of the meanings of gradable antonyms that this should be so. **antonym**

When we look at the temperature scale on which *cold, cool, warm* and *hot* indicate ranges of temperatures, we find that the scale is not precise. Each range has fuzzy edges so that we can't be sure where *hot* finishes and *warm* takes over. The range also depends on what is being talked about. A hot day has a different temperature range, when measured in degrees, from a hot drink. A cold star is hotter than either with a surface temperature of somewhere about 2000 degrees centigrade. (Not something to put in a cup.)

A further property of gradable antonyms is that often one of the pair has two senses: one being its position on the scale and the other representing the whole scale. For example, if we ask how old someone is, we don't intend that to signify that the person is old. We can ask it of a week-old baby. This neutral sense is often termed the unmarked sense of the antonym. We can tell that only one of the pair has this unmarked sense because we can't ask how young someone is without that implying that they are young. **unmarked**

complementary senses

Not all antonyms are gradable, as we saw in Chapter 2.1. For example, the pair *alive* and *dead* have senses which are not a matter of degree. Expressions like *half dead* can be used literally only if they mean that half of whatever it is, say a tree, is completely dead and the other half is alive. These are mutually exclusive opposites or complementary senses. Complementaries may have only two words in the set, like *boy* and *girl*, or they may be multiple, like *solid, liquid* and *gas,* when they denote the only three states of matter in the set. Notice again that complementaries are only gradable in a metaphorical sense. When we say that someone is very much a boy we are referring to some of the additional properties of boys and not the primary one of being a boy.

converse senses

Words with converse senses, such as *buy* and *sell,* or *husband* and *wife,* look as though they are opposite in sense but strictly speaking they are not, since they denote the same action or relationship but from a different perspective. A person who is buying something from someone is having the someone sell something to them. If there is a married relationship then on one side of it there is a wife and on the other side there is a husband.

These three kinds of sense relationship: gradable antonymy, complementarity, and converseness all have repercussions for entailments. Antonyms can be involved in entailments in that if something has as a property one which is denoted by one of a pair of gradable antonymous senses, then it does not have the property at the other end of the scale. For instance, if someone is old then they are not young. However, the entailment doesn't work the other way round with negatives. If someone is not young, it does not follow that they are old.

With complementaries the comparison is between equivalents. If someone is not married then they are single and if they are not single then they are married. This is a direct consequence of the fact that complementary senses are mutually exclusive.

Converses also have interesting entailment consequences. If A buys X from B, then it follows that B has sold X to A. But not all senses that look like converses work this way. If someone sends something to someone else then the latter doesn't necessarily receive it. That depends on the dependability of the postal service, as well as the senses of the words *send* and *receive.* So there are no entailments.

Words with opposite senses enable us to discover some important facts about word meanings. The first is that word meanings can be broken down into smaller components. Look at *boy* and *girl.* Although their meanings are different, they still have a lot in common. Boys and girls are both young humans. They differ in only one aspect of their meaning, namely that girls are young female humans and boys are young male humans. So the meanings of these words consist of sub-components of meaning and the difference is in only one of these components. They have the other components in common.

3.1.3 SENSE COMPONENTS

componential analysis

Finding the component parts of the meanings of words is usually termed componential analysis. To discover what the components of a meaning of a word are, we can make use of a second fact we have also discovered with the aid of antonyms, and that is that antonyms belong to groups of words denoting related things. *Boy* and *girl* both denote children, *hot* and *cold* both denote temperatures. The word *child* and the word *temperature* are sometimes called the superordinates (or hypernyms) when we talk about their relation to the words 'under' them. These words which are included under a superordinate are termed hyponyms. You can check that a word is a superordinate of some other by putting them in sentences like this:

**superordinate
hypernyms
hyponym**

'Hot' is a temperature.

'Cold' is a temperature.

but not

'Temperature' is a kind of cold.

A 'girl' is a kind of child.

but not

A 'child' is a kind of girl.

Hyponymy

EXERCISE 3.4

Arrange the words in each group so that every word is a hyponym of the word immediately before it:

(a) mouse, rodent, mammal

(b) house, building, bungalow, structure

(c) run, jog, move

(d) pistol, weapon, firearm, revolver

(e) person, uncle, relative

(f) dog, beast, beagle, hound

(g) pilfer, steal, take

Hyponymy

EXERCISE 3.5

Arrange the following sets of words in a tree diagram to show which words are hyponyms of which. (Note that these tree diagrams do not show linear order, just hierarchical order.)

(a) Bic, biro, fountain pen, pen

(b) station wagon, car, convertible, vehicle, bus, van

(c) shrub, tree, plant, poppy, rhododendron, flower, marigold

(d)   steal, borrow, embezzle, get, burgle, buy

(e)   sing, speak, croon, chat, vocalize, yodel

(f)   denim, worsted, cotton, muslin, fabric, tweed, wool

(g)   amble, run, sprint, locomote, stroll, jog, walk

• •

When senses are hyponymous, that can give rise to entailments. For example, it follows from the fact that something is a chair that it is an item of furniture. But it does not follow that, if something is an item of furniture, then it will be a chair. As we have seen, not all entailments come about because of hyponymy but, when they do, it should be possible to determine the superordinate sense and the hyponymous sense which are responsible for the entailment by the fact that they are not reversible.

EXERCISE 3.6   *Hyponymy and entailment*

Does the first sentence entail the second? If it does, is this due to hyponymy or not?

(a)   All dogs have fleas. My dog has fleas.

(b)   Bob killed Charles. Charles is not alive.

(c)   The bus is late. The bus is very late.

(d)   Alan has planted marigolds. Alan has planted flowers.

(e)   Tom took a pig. Tom stole a pig.

(f)   Goldie ate the porridge. Someone ate the porridge.

(g)   I saw a human being. I saw a person.

(h)   Betty has not planted tulips. Betty has not planted flowers.

(i)   I am wearing black boots. I am wearing black footwear.

(j)   A tall pygmy came in. A tall person came in.

(k)   I ran home last night. I went home last night.

(l)   Bob killed Charles. Bob murdered Charles.

(m)   My socks are bright red. My socks are red.

(n)   My socks are almost dry. My socks are dry.

• •

co-hyponym   When we look at all the co-hyponyms, senses which are all hyponyms of the same superordinate sense, we can often sort out some of their meaning components. For example, look at the other words denoting temperatures: *freezing,* *frigid, cold, cool, tepid, lukewarm, warm, hot, boiling.* Each of these means what it does because of what the others mean. Warm is a temperature between hot and cool, wherever they are. Cold is colder than cool, and so on. Groups of words that cover one territory are often described as covering a 'semantic domain' or semantic field. Some of these fields are rather simple, such as the scale we have just looked at, and some are very complex, such as the terms we use for members of our family or for vehicles.

semantic field

Semantic fields and components

EXERCISE 3.7

Examine the following words. Sort out which sense components differentiate the senses of the various words:

   rope, twine, cable, hawser, wire, string, thread, cord.

• •

Semantic fields and components

EXERCISE 3.8

Find all the words that English makes available for us to use for members of a family, and see if you can work out how they relate to each other.

• •

Semantic domains and fields are an interesting source of information about the way a linguistic community thinks about a particular area. Current Western culture's love affair with the internal combustion engine has given rise to a large number of hyponyms of the sense 'vehicle'. Not only that, many of these hyponyms, such as 'car', have hyponyms in turn, such as 'sedan', 'coupe', and so forth. Other societies have similarly complex fields to deal with, say, an item of staple diet such as taro. This is the case in the Raga language spoken on the island of Pentecost in Vanuatu where the semantic field for 'taro' is as complex as ours for 'motor vehicles'.

   If we return now to the dictionary, it will be clear that it often tries to give the meaning of a word in terms of its semantic components. When we read in the dictionary that *mother* means 'female parent', we have two of the major components of the word given in the form of the words which have that component as their sense. These components are relevant to some field – in this case, the field of kinship words.

   In many cases, however, the semantic components of a word are relevant not just to the meaning of the individual word in its semantic field but also to the way the word functions with other words in sentences. This is true of the ways in which, for instance, adjectives fit semantically with nouns, and the way verbs fit semantically with their noun phrase participants. Let us take, for example, a noun like *woman*. We know that one of the semantic components of this word is that of humanness, and that humans are animate, or alive. So we can talk about *old women* and *young women* since these adjectives can be used of things that are alive. We can talk of *little men* and *big men* because we can use these adjectives with concrete objects. But we could not talk literally of *young* and *old comfort*, or *big* and *little sincerity*. When we speak literally, the meanings of words restrict the other words with which they will semantically fit. Such restrictions are termed selectional restrictions. People cannot eat gasses. You can sew only things that are sewable. Only female mammals can be pregnant. Only humans can pray. Events can only last periods of time and not locations, for example *The party lasted three days* is in accord with the selection restrictions which the verb *last* imposes while *The party lasted three houses* is not, even if the party was held at three houses.

Clearly many of these restrictions come about because of the way we conceive of the world, but that is not invariably so. For example, the verb *honour* seems to need the thing which is honoured to be a person or a human quality. We might say that the Nobel Prize committee honoured Nelson Mandela or that they honoured his courage. But it seems a bit odd to say that an architectural committee honoured a building. Here the selectional restriction seems to be rather more language-internal since there is nothing seriously incoherent about the idea of honouring a building.

Some breaches of selectional restrictions are minor, in that they don't do very serious violence to our view of the way things are. Others are egregious. For example, in a phrase like *the wind breathes in*, we can see our way through to how one might animate the wind so that it breathes. It is also a conventional way to treat the wind. However, if we say *the large boulder contemplated suicide*, then we are in more difficulty in that the selectional features of contemplating suicide are difficult to ascribe to boulders.

To summarize: synonyms cover the same bit of semantic territory, antonyms differ in meaning from each other by having one of their semantic components opposite to the other. Superordinates define semantic fields great or small, and within each field semantic components sort out the meaning of one word's semantic territory from that of the others in the field. We can also see these semantic components at work in the selectional restrictions that words have when they are put into sentences. What may look like, and in fact be, a perfectly grammatical sentence, may make little literal sense if the right semantic components are not meshed together.

Selectional restrictions are a factor in some sentences containing contradictions. Look at the following two sentences:

(a)   My male aunt bought a piano.

(b)   Babies are adults.

It is very easy to pick what causes the contradictions. In (a) the contradiction is in the words *male aunt*. Why is this? It is because one of the semantic components of the sense of the word *aunt* is the component 'female'. That clashes with the meaning of the adjective *male*. Similarly, it is part of the meaning of the word *baby* that babies are not adults.

Just as selecting incompatible semantic features can create contradictions, so selecting other ones can create semantic redundancy (tautology), as in the following two sentences:

(a)   Degas painted naked nudes.

(b)   I bought a male bull at the market

It is a semantic component of the meaning of *nude* that it is a figure which is naked, as it is a semantic feature of the word *bull* that bulls are male. Thus significant semantic components of *nude* and *male* are redundant.

3.1.4 TROPES

This brings us directly to metaphor and other figures of speech (often called tropes). We are used to looking in poetry for metaphors but metaphor is more common outside of poetry in normal language use than we might think. A simple way to look at metaphor is to see it as a breaking down of the literal selectional restrictions that the semantic components of words have in a sentence. When we talk about, for instance, a window onto the future, we have to ignore some of the semantic components of the word *window* – for example, that it is a concrete object – and just take the fact that windows are things that allow us to look from an enclosed space outwards. The metaphor could also be seen the other way about, where the future is seen as something concrete that can be seen out of a window. The metaphor lies in the suppression of some of each word's semantic features. The figure of speech called personification is a special case. Here, words that have the semantic component 'not human' have this suppressed so that these words are allowed to function in sentences as though they were human. *Freedom was at the helm of the ship of state*. Helmsmen are normally human. *Freedom*, the word, is allowed to perform an action normally reserved for words that have the semantic component 'human'. *The ship of state* too is a metaphor. In this metaphor the state is being seen as a ship with a captain and crew (presumably the government and its leader), and citizens, who might end up as metaphorical passengers. So the fact that states are not physical entities is being suppressed in the metaphor.

metaphor
trope

personification

Sometimes the underlying basis for a metaphor is carried on for more than one instance, as is the ship metaphor above. Ships have helms and helmsmen to steer them. You will find such extended metaphors commonly used in political speeches. Here is an example from a poem by Shakespeare, where you have to think a bit to figure out the source of the metaphors. The poem begins,

**extended
metaphors**

> When to the sessions of sweet silent thought
> I summon up remembrance of things past.

'Sessions' are times when legal cases are tried, and witnesses are 'summoned up' to such sessions. So both these are metaphors drawn from legal proceedings.

The nature of metaphors is that they are literally false, and therefore either baldly state a literal falsehood, or allow for the metaphor to be paraphrased by a literal falsehood. For example, if we describe someone as empty-headed, then this is literally untrue. The person does have things inside their head: a brain,

simile

blood vessels, bones, and so on. If we say that the car is a beast, then this is also literally false.

Similes avoid the falsehood by saying not that something is something that it is not, but rather that it is like something else, leaving the speaker to determine wherein the likeness lies. For example, we might say that a person acts as though there is nothing in their head, or that the car is like a beast. Using *as* or *like* in this way creates a simile.

There are other tropes which create literal falsehoods, for example, by using either something with which a thing is associated for the thing itself, or by using a part of something in the place of all of it. When people interested in motor racing talk about Le Mans, they are using the place, at which a yearly 24-hour endurance race is held, for the event itself. Such a figure of naming by association is called a metonymy. If you are asked to lend a hand, then it is not literally a hand which is being looked for but the whole person who is attached to the hand. Such a part – whole figure of speech is called a synecdoche. Perhaps the most famous such case is the opening of Mark Anthony's speech in Shakespeare's play *Julius Caesar* when he says,

metonymy

synecdoche

> Friends, Romans, countrymen, lend me your ears.

Both these figures of speech tell us that word meanings are not just sets of semantic components. The denotations of words have real-world associations. The American Grand Prix might be raced at the Indianapolis Motor Speedway, which is often called 'the brick yard'. So if we ask 'How did David Coulthard do at the brick yard?' we might be asking how he performed in the US Grand Prix Formula 1 motor race. We also know that there are whole things that have parts. When we use words to denote things like that, their parts come along as associates. So if we say 'Was Coulthard at the wheel?' we are thinking of him driving the whole car, not just clutching the steering wheel (which is now detachable in Formula 1 cars).

Look at the vocabulary associated with a particular sport and see what metaphors, similes, metonymies and synecdoches you can find.

The vocabulary of sport is often full of tropes, for example, military metaphors. The word *captain* was originally a military rank whose use was extended to sports teams. You will be able to find many more metaphors to do with sport. The metaphors tend to draw on an interesting and limited set of domains.

EXERCISE 3.9   *The lexical semantics of political rhetoric*

Look at this paragraph from the famous 'I have a dream' speech by Martin Luther King and see how he has used semantic fields and metaphors:

Fivescore years ago, a great American, in whose symbolic shadow we stand today, signed the Emancipation Proclamation. This momentous decree came as a great beacon light of hope to millions of Negro slaves who had been seared in the flames of withering injustice. It came as a joyous daybreak to end the long night of their captivity.

• •

3.1.5 WORD MEANINGS IN CONTEXT

So far you may have got the impression that word meanings are entirely stable collections of semantic components which only change in the case of metaphor. This is a half-truth. The meaning of a word given by its semantic components is more like a set of potential meanings. You were given some preliminary warning of this when we looked at the temperature field earlier in the chapter. A hot day and a hot iron are both hot but for a day to be hot is not the same as for an iron to be hot. It was said at the time that *hot* is a relative term, and it is relative not just to the other words on the temperature scale; what the whole scale denotes or what any meaning on it denotes depends on the context in which it is being used. Although terms on this scale retain the same relative positions, the scale changes its value for different types of things.

Furthermore, if all we had at our disposal to convey messages to one another were the meanings of individual words, we would be restricted, in what we could say, to as many messages as we had words in our vocabulary. But that isn't the case because we put words into sentences and combine the meanings of words into complex messages using the syntax of the language we happen to be speaking.

In their interaction with one another in grammatical sequences, the meanings of words undergo a number of changes. For instance, while a word may be polysemous on its own, when placed in grammatical sequences some of its senses can be excluded. For example, the adjective *single* has a sense meaning 'only one'. It also has a sense of 'unmarried'. If we put *single* with the noun *book* then the possibility that *single* means unmarried is excluded by the semantic features of the sense of *book*.

There is something, therefore, which allows us to combine the meanings of words into the meanings of phrases, and this process is rule-governed.

Let us begin by looking at the meaning of a very simple phrase, *big car*, and let us suppose we know the senses *big* and *car*. *Car* has semantic components which might include the following: vehicle, internal-combustion powered, for passengers, having wheels, driving on roads. *Big* has the sense of having physical dimensions larger than the norm. But, like temperatures, what constitutes *big* for a car is different from what constitutes *big* for an ant. It seems that to explain what such a simple phrase means we have to dive from the English language into the real world of cars and their relative sizes, and back into language again.

To explain why this is necessary we need to make a distinction between the sense of a word and its denotation. What we have looked at so far as meaning – that is, basically, semantic components – gives words a denotation. The sense of **sense denotation** the word *car* allows it to denote the set of all possible cars, actual or imaginary. It does not specify the exact boundaries of the set. Look, for example, at the word *fruit* and the word *berry*. We know that apples, oranges, pears and bananas are fruit and that raspberries, strawberries and gooseberries are berries, but what of tomatoes? We may think of tomatoes as vegetables but can see them as either fruit or berries without it bothering us. (Think of those delicious cherry tomatoes.)

Words in human languages usually do not denote well-defined sets of things, actions and properties but sets, whose boundaries are fuzzy. We may think this is very sloppy, but it actually allows words to denote things which do not seem clearly one thing or another. If we always had to be sure what it was we were talking about most of us would have to stop talking altogether.

Try holding a brief conversation with someone in which you have to define exactly what you mean for every noun you utter.

That should have been virtually impossible. Even if you felt you were doing quite a good job, your conversation will have taken much longer than normal and probably you gave up very quickly.

Let us now return to the phrase *big car*. It is clear that the senses of *big* and *car* are amalgamated somehow and thus that the denotation of the phrase *big car* is a subset of that denoted by *car*. So, just as we saw earlier that some of the senses of words may be excluded when those senses are put alongside others in grammatical sequences, so other senses combine with those of neighbouring words to enable complex messages to be constructed from their component parts. Here we are again looking at compositionality.

So far we have talked about words that have a fairly clear denotation, namely, of concrete objects. It is sometimes said that other words, like abstract nouns and nouns that denote internal states such as *pain*, are meaningless, that they are vague or useless. Strictly speaking, none of these statements is correct. Words like *courage* are harder to define than concrete nouns, because they denote social or cultural properties. Showing courage, roughly speaking, entails putting oneself at risk for some cause. Most people in English-speaking society would agree about that, so we know what the sense of the word is. What we might disagree about is whether a certain action by someone was courageous. But that is no different really from the problem of whether a bean bag can properly be referred to as a chair. The same goes for *pain*. I know what pain feels like and I assume other people do too even though an actor can simulate pain when he has not got it.

The use of words such as these can lead to communication breakdowns. On one side there are those who say that such and such an action is courageous, and on the other side are the other generation saying that such an action is not courageous but stupid. This is a disagreement about people's values that is connected with language where sense makes denotation possible.

Similar areas of disagreement and breakdown come about because of what words denote in different speech communities. In the 1960s a big car in the United

States was much bigger than a big car in Europe. So when someone from Europe asked to rent a small car in America and got what they thought was a big car, miscommunication about exactly what that involved resulted in a bemused client.

Let us return now to the way in which the senses of words combine. Recall that the set of entities denoted by *big car* was a subset of the entities denoted by *car,* just as the set of actions denoted by *run swiftly* is a subset of the actions denoted by *run.*

In some instances words come to be strongly associated with each other. When this happens their senses combine in a more idiosyncratic way than in the above examples.

What actual colour are the following?

white coffee, white wine, white sugar,

black coffee, red wine, brown sugar;

and how raw are raw meat and raw sugar?

Of the first three items only white sugar is actually white. White coffee is a muddy kind of colour and white wine has a yellowish colour. Black coffee is dark brown, red wine is more red than anything else but not scarlet, and brown sugar really is brown. Raw meat denotes uncooked meat, not unprocessed meat, whereas raw sugar is rather less refined than some more refined sugars such as white and brown sugar. How does this come about? Coffee comes either with or without milk and these two states are really what *white coffee* and *black coffee* denote, just as white and red wine are two generic kinds of wine. Imagine trying to sell light green wine (although some wines are light green)? The same situation often occurs with verbs and prepositions. We talk of living in North America or the Caribbean. But surely *in* does not make as much sense as *on*? We walk up the street when the street is not vertical.

To cover this sort of situation the term 'restricted collocation' has been invented. **restricted** Restricted collocations are linear associations of one word with another that give **collocation** a rather special sense and often denotation to one or both words a meaning that the words have by virtue of being together. Some restricted collocations are quite habitual. *Black tea, white wine, dry wine* show how much we take the facts that the tea is not really black nor the wine either white or dry for granted.

3.1.6 REFERENCE

What do the following phrases refer to:

the Taj Mahal, Alexander Graham Bell, Rover?

referring expression

Each of these phrases is a referring expression, that is, it has the potential to refer to someone or something or a group of people or things. But what does a referring expression actually refer to? It is tempting to think that the answer is simple. *The Taj Mahal* refers to a mausoleum in India. *Alexander Graham Bell* refers to the inventor of the telephone, and *Rover* refers to my dog. But the latter example shows that this cannot be the case. *Rover* is not only the name of a particular dog, it is the name of many dogs. There are also, no doubt, a number of people called Alexander Graham Bell, and there are a number of places called the Taj Mahal, as you can verify by looking up the Indian restaurants in many large cities.

We can instead think of there being referring expressions. Referring expressions can be used to refer but they only refer when a speaker is attempting to get a hearer (or hearers) to pick out an entity or set of entities on a particular occasion. For example, if I ask you whether you intend to go to the Taj Mahal, what *the Taj Mahal* refers to depends on whether I have just asked you to fetch a take-away Tandoori, or know you are going to India. This suggests that what a referring expression refers to is a matter of what the speaker intends the hearer to pick out, and the context in which the expression is used. We can conclude, therefore, that words and phrases do not refer of themselves.

3.1.7   WORD ASSOCIATIONS AND CONNOTATIONS

There are other aspects of meaning that are like referring in that they require us to look beyond the language and into the non-linguistic context where words are used. Such aspects of meaning are often termed 'pragmatic', and their study 'pragmatics'. By way of illustration, we will look at an example of pragmatics related to the sense of words. It is often said that there are no true synonyms because, although two words may denote the same range of things, they have different **associations** or **connotations**. Typically associations and connotations have to do with the positive and negative feelings people have towards things, properties, actions and the like. For example, if we feel badly disposed towards someone we might use words with negative connotations. An unreliable acquaintance will be called a rat because rats are animals which are not generally well thought of. We might term words with strong negative connotations 'snarl words' (or boo words) and words with positive connotations 'purr words' (or hurray words). In advertising it is typical to use purr words to accentuate the positive qualities of the product which is being advertised. You can hardly imagine a perfume advertisement which has the following slogan successfully selling the product even though the perfume may contain musk and attar of roses:

associations connotations

The stench of armpits and shrivelled petals.

Since connotations are based on social attitudes, they can reveal social attitudes.

What words can you find which are animal metaphors and used to denote women? What connotations do these words have? What does this tell you about social attitudes towards women?

Repeat the exercise for words used to denote men.

The majority of animal metaphors for women in English, such as *bitch*, have negative connotations, whereas many of the animal metaphors for men have positive connotations. Look, for example, at the word *dog*. Used of a woman in North America it refers to a woman who is not considered good-looking, and therefore it has negative connotations. However, referring to a man, as in *you old dog*, it has positive connotations. There are exceptions. The word *foxy* has positive connotations when used of women and the word *rat* negative ones when used of men.

One area where connotations and social attitudes can be clearly seen is in the case of euphemism. When people must talk about something unpleasant or embarrassing, some of the words dealing with this area come to have negative connotations. Many of the classical English 'four-letter words' are like this. Words like *piss* were once just simple one-syllable words to describe a perfectly normal activity. However, when English society became squeamish about certain bodily functions, the word *piss* came to have negative connotations and was replaced in polite speech by a variety of euphemisms such as the clinical word *urinate,* the   **euphemism** baby word *pee,* or the phrase *going to the toilet*. The word *sweat* had a similar fate. The polite synonymous word *perspire* came to rescue speakers who did not wish to be associated with the negative connotations of *sweat*. As you might imagine, euphemisms have a way of taking on the same opprobrium as their less polite synonyms. English has gone through quite a few words to designate the room in the house where the toilet is, including *toilet, bathroom, powder room, WC, loo*. Terms used for handicapped people have gone through the same process, giving us *cretin, idiot, mentally retarded, educationally subnormal, learning disabled* and currently *special needs*.

When the senses of words have very negative connotations they sometimes become taboo, that is, their use is socially forbidden.   **taboo**

Think of as many euphemisms as you can for the death of people. How many of these words are taboo?

You will find that because they are social, taboos are context-determined. One would not expect a priest at a funeral to say that the person being buried had snuffed it, while this might be acceptable in another context.

People swear in order to express their negative emotions and so they use words with strong negative connotations, often taboo words. In English these words often deal with religion, sex or excretion since these are major topic areas in which words have developed strong negative connotations (and, consequently, euphemisms). To swear, one utters one of the words with powerful connotations to express one's negative feelings about something such as hitting one's thumb with a hammer. The stronger the negative feelings, the closer to a taboo word speakers tend to get. So it does not do to use a euphemism instead. Swearing at something by saying 'Oh, excrement!' is funny just because *excrement* is a clinical term and therefore a way to escape saying the word *shit*, which is taboo in many situations, but therefore suitable as a swearword.

Again, swearing is a contextual matter and so part of pragmatics.

3.2 VOCABULARIES

So far we have looked at words as individual units but they can also be looked at in sets.

Do you know how many words there are in the English language?

How many words do you think you know?

It is impossible to know exactly how many words there are in the English language. New words are being added to the language all the time, while others are being lost. For example, the word *dryhten* used to be part of the English vocabulary. It meant 'lord'. Not even the most recent and comprehensive dictionary will list all the words in the language. The average educated adult speaker of English may know as many as 60,000 or more words. That is a lot of words. This is even more of a feat when we consider that, for each word, we know how to pronounce it, what it means, what part of speech it is, and what other words may appear with it.

vocabulary   Any well-defined group of words, such as all the words of the language, can be called a vocabulary. A language has a total vocabulary of all the words that there are in the language. No person knows all these words. Individual people have their own total vocabulary consisting of all the words they know.

Take a small pocket dictionary, and taking five pages at random, see how many words on each page you know. You can calculate roughly what proportion of the words in the dictionary you know by taking the proportion of words you know in these five pages and multiplying that proportion by the total number of pages in the whole dictionary and an approximation of how many words there are on each page.

You should also take into account that most dictionaries contain only a small sample of the total number of words in English. Of course these words are usually the more common ones, so that the chances are you will know an even smaller proportion of the total vocabulary of English.

The total vocabulary of an individual person can be subdivided into active vocabulary and passive vocabulary. Many of the words we know, we do not use ourselves, but we recognize them when other people use them. Think of weather forecasters and the technical vocabulary they use to talk about the weather. For them words like *precipitation* and *isobar* are active vocabulary, but they are passive vocabulary for the rest of us. We may know what they are talking about when they talk about precipitation but ordinary folks talk about rain. As people pass through the education system the size of their total vocabulary increases. Usually this happens when words first pass into people's passive vocabulary and then move from there into their active vocabulary. In this book, the words in bold in the margins are in many cases moving from being not part of your vocabulary at all, to being part of your passive vocabulary. But when you sit a test on the material, these words must become part of your active vocabulary when you actually use them and write about them.

active vocabulary
passive vocabulary

3.2.1   ADDING TO VOCABULARIES

The total vocabulary of a language is never static. Nor is that of a speaker. Words pass into and out of both. We have already seen how new lexemes can be made from pre-existing ones in a language through word formation processes: compounding, derivation and conversion.

Another common way of adding to vocabulary is through a process that can be called lexical borrowing (usually just termed borrowing). Lexical borrowing involves a word being copied from the vocabulary of one language into that of another. Many of the words of current English came originally from other languages and were borrowed into English. For example, the word *wienerschnitzel* does not look like a native English word and isn't. It came originally from German and arrived quite recently.

lexical borrowing

Borrowing takes place when two speech communities are in contact. If we look at the speech communities with which English speakers have been in contact then, most of these contacts have left a record of themselves in the form of borrowed words. In the early Middle Ages, Vikings raided and then settled northern England. Words from the Norse dialects which the Vikings spoke and which were borrowed into English include: *egg, husband* and *window*. Later in the Middle Ages, the Normans invaded and settled in England. Norman French was spoken by William the Conqueror and those who came with him from Normandy in 1066. Borrowed vocabulary which dates from this period includes the words *warden* and *castle*. If one traces the colonial period of settlement, when, unlike the previous situation where foreign speakers settled in England, English speakers settled in places like North America and India, then we find that most of these language contacts lead to some degree of borrowing. *Tomahawk* came from North America and *curry* from India.

More recently English has become a language spoken by settler populations all over the world including countries with many languages other than English.

Borrowings can come from any of these languages. For example, in the Republic of South Africa there are many indigenous languages including Zulu, Xhosa, Sesotho, Ndebele and Khoikhoi. All of these have provided loans for contemporary South African English including the following:

Zulu:	*bonsella* 'a small gift'
Xhosa:	*dagha* 'plaster'
Sesotho:	*morogo* 'wild spinach'
Ndebele:	*fundi* 'expert'
Khoikhoi:	*kierie* 'a wooden club'

Other immigrant populations speak languages which also provide loans for English:

Afrikaans:	*stoep* 'front porch, verandah'
Malay:	*sjambok* 'a heavy whip'
Hindustani:	*roti* a type of Indian bread
Yiddish:	*schlenter* 'a fake diamond'

You can see from this small set of examples that borrowed vocabulary can reflect cultural influences within a society and language and cultural contact. A regional dialect vocabulary based on borrowing may also result.

One of the consequences of borrowing words is that occasionally some of their internal structure remains marginally in evidence in the English form of the word, particularly when a number of words with the same structure are copied. This has happened with both Latin and French borrowings in English. Look, for example, at the following words: *incline, recline, decline.* They look as though they are formed with a prefix added to a bound stem. They were. But not in English. That is why we feel a bit uneasy about placing a morpheme boundary here while a speaker of Latin would have been in no doubt. A borrowing like *blitzkrieg*, which clearly still shows evidence of its German origins, is a compound in German. Is it still a compound in English where a speaker may not know that its two constituents are both words? Well, neither constituent is an English word and so the internal structure is not available to us unless someone tells us about the German origins of the word.

EXERCISE 3.10

Finding source languages

From which languages did the following words come and when did they transfer into English?

yacht, curry, transfer, pyjama

You could now try to find some interesting source languages for words of your own choice in a good dictionary and see if your friends can guess where the words come from. In many cases you will be able to trace why the words came to be borrowed from the languages they did, which makes for its own interesting stories.

APPLICATION

Considered stylistically, native words, words which were not borrowed, often belong to basic central vocabulary whereas borrowed words belong to more peripheral areas. As a result a piece of writing largely made up of native vocabulary often has a very simple style.

Look, for example, at the following two texts. Find out which are the native and which the borrowed words and then see what impact the word choice (or diction) has had on the style of the writing.

(a)
Conversation

Said my daughter, It rained
cats and dragons, and the wind –
you know – lay down
in our house, licking
its wounds and panting
and wagging its tail;
it had eyes as large
as mine, you know.

Asked her mother, What
happened next?

Said Sina, Oh nothing.
It just died.

Albert Wendt

(b)   ...discrimination against women violates the principles of equality of rights and respect for human dignity, is an obstacle to the participation of women, on equal terms with men, in the political, social, economic and cultural life of their countries, hampers the growth of the prosperity of society and the family and makes more difficult the full development of the potentialities of women in the service of their countries and of humanity ...

from the *United Nations Convention on the Elimination of All Forms of Discrimination against Women*

Lexical borrowing is usually a two-way traffic, but the majority of the traffic is from the vocabulary of people who are seen as being more powerful or more advanced in a particular area. So, for example, words having to do with computing are currently transferring from English into many of the world's other languages. Words to do with cooking and wine have transferred to English from French. For example, in the Middle Ages, the French word for sheep, *mouton*, became the English word for sheep meat, *mutton*. In more recent times words like *casserole, sauté* and *soufflé* have been borrowed from French. When one wants to go out to a particular kind of fast-food chain in Japan, which we call *McDonald's*, one asks one's friends to *Makudonaru*. Lexical borrowing in the early days of colonization in New Zealand saw many Maori words transfer into New Zealand English and many English words transfer into Maori. Early colonists saw Maori as being knowledgeable about the land and its flora and fauna and borrowed Maori words for these, for example the word *kiwi* for a native flightless bird. The colonists also brought with them the Christian religion, and many early borrowings from English into Maori were of biblical origin.

One area where cultural contact has given rise to a number of interesting borrowings is in the Antarctic. English in the Antarctic has adapted to its new environment by taking in vocabulary from other languages where these languages have more to do with snow and ice: loans from Norwegian, for example *blaahval*; Icelandic, for example *jokulhlaup*; Russian, for example *polynya*; Eskimo, for example *kamik*.

Vocabularies can also be added to by tools that each language has for making new words. We have already looked at the major tools in the case of compounding, derivation and conversion. However, there are some interesting minor tools for creating new words. They are not rule-governed in the way that derivation and compounding are, but are the result of people being lexically creative.

blend   New words are occasionally made by putting the first part of one word together with the second part of another as a blend. The word *smog* is a blend of *smoke* and *fog*. A cross between a tiger and a lion is called a *liger*. *Avionics* is aviation electronics. A blend from the Antarctic is *snotsicle*, being a bend of *snot* and *icicle*. Given Antarctic temperatures one can see how this might be a useful new word. Again you can make up such blends yourself, although it takes some ingenuity to make them stick. For example, you might want to call blithering idiots *blithiots*.

acronym   A relatively new way of creating new words is through the use of acronyms. An acronym is a word made up from the first letters or syllables of a phrase. For example, one United Nations agency is the United Nations Educational, Scientific and Cultural Organization. This has given rise to the acronym *Unesco*. Acronyms are of two kinds. Some sets of initial letters actually make up possible words, such as *Unesco*. Others do not, for example the United States Central Intelligence Agency is usually called the CIA. It is pronounced with each of its letters being pronounced separately rather than being pronounced 'keeya' or 'seeya'. Only acronyms which are pronounced as words really constitute new words. Other acronyms are just sets of initials which are stored in the memory.

Sometimes acronyms incorporate a syllable as well as just the first letters of words. Two examples from the US navy are the ranks of 'cincpac' and 'cinclant': Commander in Chief Pacific Forces and Commander in Chief Atlantic Forces. The Gestapo were the **Ge**heime **Staa**ts**Po**lizei. The Benelux countries are **Be**lgium, the **Ne**therlands and **Lux**emburg.

Like all lexical items, acronyms do not carry their history about with them. So if you want to know what that history is, you normally have to look it up.

Find the sources of the following acronyms:

EXERCISE 3.11

    radar, laser, IATA, NATO, quango, AIDS, NASA, RAM

• •

Acronym formation has become very productive in some areas of society, particularly in high-tech development. For example, the United States defence agencies such as the navy have created thousands of acronyms, to the point where they employ specialists whose task it is to write dictionaries of all the acronyms they currently use, ICBM, 'intercontinental ballistic missile', being one example. You can imagine how important it might be in areas where military hardware is concerned, not to get your acronyms mixed up.

Very occasionally words are created from scratch. Someone puts some sounds together and gives them a grammatical function and new meaning. The brand names *Kodak* and *Exxon* are reputed to have come into existence that way. This might be termed 'root creation'.

root creation

Very occasionally also, something gets named after the sound it makes. For example, the English bird the peewit, and the New Zealand native owl, the morepork, are reputed to make birdcalls something like their names. In the movie of the same name there is an early car called 'Chitty Chitty Bang Bang'. (No prizes for guessing how it got its name.) These can be termed 'echo words'. However, both these last, rather obvious ways of creating new words are nowhere near as productive as compounding, derivation and, in modern English-speaking society, acronym creation.

echo word

3.2.2 COINING NEW WORDS

When a new word is first created one talks of it being coined. This is an apt metaphor because after the coining of a word, one of two things can happen to it. It may be used once, for the purpose for which it was coined by whoever coined it. Most such words, termed nonce words, are used just the once and then are not used again. However, if the coinage gains currency, that is, other people use it as a medium of linguistic exchange, then it has become lexicalized, that is, it has been copied into the lexicons of a number of speakers who all know it and perhaps use it. What causes lexicalization has nothing to do with the language but a great deal to do with social factors. A word is lexicalized when it meets a lexical need, usually because there isn't already a word to fill the particular conceptual niche it comes to occupy. For example, in computer technology, new items of technology are invented frequently. They have to be called something. Usually

coined
coining

nonce word

lexicalization

someone comes up with a word by accident. The word catches on and then gains currency. Someone must have coined the term *harddrive*. It has certainly gained currency. Coiners of words are normally unsung heroes and heroines. Occasionally the coiner is known. For example, the scientist who gave the sub-atomic particles called quarks their name is Murray Gell-Mann. (But he actually borrowed it from the Irish writer James Joyce, for whom it certainly didn't name a class of sub-atomic particles.)

3.2.3 CHANGE THROUGH TIME

After a word has been coined and then lexicalized it normally undergoes some-times subtle, but often wide-ranging changes. Most common are changes in meaning. While a morphologically complex word is often compositional when it is coined, it is coined for specific purposes and those purposes end up affecting it in the lexicon. For example, a blackboard is, in many cases, a black board. But there is more to it than that. It is actually a board of any kind which is made so that one can write on it with chalk. As a result, blackboards can be green without this being a logical contradiction. Virtually every compound noun which is lexicalized has some such idiosyncrasy built into its lexical entry as the result of its lexicalization.

drift   The meanings of complex words also change over time. Meanings drift. The word *revolver*, for example, might mean 'something which revolves', but is now normally used to refer to a kind of pistol with a revolving firing chamber. The word *communism* originally had to do with living in communes, but has now only a non-compositional meaning to do with a political ideology.

Word meanings also drift in different directions in different places. A paddock in England is a small enclosed area near a house or agricultural building in which horses are turned out to grass. In Australia and New Zealand it is any fenced rural enclosure. They can be anywhere and any size.

widening   There are some general directions in which word meanings change over time. They may widen so that their denotation covers more than it did. For example, the word *barn* used to denote a storage place for barley but its denotation generalized to cover any kind of farm-based storage shed. Similarly the word *mill* used to denote a place where grain was ground. Now it denotes a much larger set of places where things are made, for example a woollen mill. *Paddock* has also therefore widened its denotation, but only in Australia and New Zealand.

narrowing   The opposite effect is narrowing, where the denotation of a word shrinks. The word *starve* used to denote dying in general but now denotes dying of hunger. (It is probably also currently expanding again to denote the state of being very hungry.) The word *disease* used to be compositional in its semantics, that is, it meant not being at ease. It has now narrowed the source of the lack of ease, specifically, to some kind of medical source. In Ghana the word *donation* has narrowed so that it denotes a financial gift provided to pay for funerals.

pejoration   The connotations of words can also change. They can worsen (which is termed
amelioration   pejoration) or they can get better (which is termed amelioration). *Lewd* started out denoting those who were lay people as opposed to clergy. Since the clergy were educated and the lay people, by and large, were not, it then narrowed to denote

those who were ignorant, and from there narrowed to mean obscene, clearly with worse connotations. *Knight*, by contrast, at one time denoted a male servant, and then a special kind of servant of the sovereign who had been knighted. Along with the new denotation came better connotations. The Neo-Melanesian word *bagarap* means 'broken' without negative connotations whereas the original verb, *bugger up*, does have negative connotations.

One of the mechanisms for changing meaning is the persistent use of a word in a non-literal sense using figures of speech like metaphor, which we looked at earlier. Look, for example, at these phrases: *a tall story, a blind alley, a strong smell*. In each case the adjective is used metaphorically rather than literally. When all hands are called on deck on a ship, *hand* now just means 'member of the crew', an additional sense for the word *hand* created by synecdoche. In time, such usages can become institutionalized as a further sense of the word. For example, the word *grasp* has a metaphorical sense of 'understand'. (You cannot literally grasp an idea.)

While meanings may drift, all aspects of a word's representation can change over time. For example, its phonological form can change. One notable change is clipping. If a word's form seems rather long and cumbersome it is sometimes shortened. When motorized public vehicles first came to be used, a Latin name was used for them. They were called 'omnibuses', which meant, in Latin, 'for everyone'. But it was a long word and so has been clipped to *bus*, so that now almost no one remembers the old form. However, that depends on which form of English you speak. In Zimbabwe they are still called *omnibuses*. *Influenza* has also been clipped in many dialects of English, and numerous other words are routinely clipped when they are used in casual speech. In New York City the Metropolitan Opera is usually called the Met. Usually the clipped form exists alongside the unclipped form as in the case of the Australian clipping *beaut*, which is a common clipped form of *beautiful*, and *fab*, a clipping of *fabulous*, in most teen slang. The clipped form is usually more informal.

clipping

Can you think of any vocabulary items which you might clip in informal speech?

The internal structure of a word can drift to the point where it is no longer recognizable. The word *window* was once a compound noun and its first constituent word is still the same one, *wind*. The second constituent was, a thousand or so years ago, the word *eye*. So a window was a wind *eye*. Before the advent of glass, one can see how this would be so. However, the word has now drifted to the point where its internal structure has dissolved and it is just a single morpheme.

A word's syntactic functions can also change. The word *freight* was able to be used as an adjective once, as in *a truck freight with apples*. That possibility is now gone.

Another way in which the syntactic representation may change is if a proper noun becomes a common noun. For example, one of the pioneers of automotive engineering was a European engineer named Diesel. His name has now become a common noun denoting a type of engine with which he was associated. This kind of change is sometimes termed 'proper noun conversion'.

proper noun conversion

The best source for studying the individual history of words is the *Oxford English Dictionary*, which contains the history of a great number of English words. This dictionary is an essential aid when reading texts from earlier periods of English because one can never be sure what words meant in the past or even whether a particular spelling represents the same word that it does now. It is now on-line and so you can enter a word and its recorded history appears in the form of quotations illustrating that history. More of this in section 3.2.9.

EXERCISE 3.12   *Drift and reading early texts in English*

The following poem by John Donne was written in about 1600 in England. Using the *Oxford English Dictionary*, find the contemporary meanings of the underlined words and see what they add to your understanding of the poem:

Aire and Angels

Twice or thrice had I loved thee,
Before I knew thy face or name;
So in a voice, so in a shapelesse flame,
Angells affect us oft, and worship'd be.
    Still when, to where thou wert, I came
Some lovely glorious nothing I did see,
    But since, my soule, whose child love is,
Takes limmes of flesh, and else could nothing doe,
    More <u>subtile</u> than the parent is,
Love must not be, <u>but</u> take a body too,
    And therefore what thou <u>wert</u>, and who
        I did Love aske, and now
That it assume thy body, I <u>allow,</u>
And fixe it selfe in thy lip, eye, and brow.

Whilst thus to <u>ballast</u> love, I thought,
And so more steddily to have gone,
With wares which would sinke admiration,
I saw, I had love's <u>pinnace</u> <u>overfraught,</u>
    Ev'ry thy haire for love to worke upon
Is much too much, some fitter must be sought;
    For, nor in nothing, nor in things
Extreme, and scattring bright, can love <u>inhere;</u>
    Then as an <u>Angell,</u> face, and wings
Of afire, not pure as it, yet pure doth weare,
    So thy love may be my loves <u>spheare;</u>
        Just such disparitie
As is <u>twixt</u> Aire and Angells puritie,
T'wixt womens love, and mens will ever bee.

John Donne

. . . .

3.2.4   REDUCED USAGE, ARCHAISM AND LOSS

The ultimate drift is for a word to drift right out of the language. In a pre-literate society this happens when no one can remember the word. At that point it has disappeared. In a written language things are not as clear cut. So long as a word is written down somewhere, it is at least accessible even if it is not part of anyone's passive vocabulary except that of the editor of the *Oxford English Dictionary*. We can therefore talk of various degrees of archaism. Look at the following passage on nineteenth-century horse-drawn carriages:

archaism

> Of the various types of carriages now in vogue, the Victoria, in its many varieties of form, is the most popular, accompanied, as of necessity by the Double Victoria, Sociable, Brougham, Landaulet and Landau.
>
> From the entry for *Carriage,* in the
> 10th edition of the *Encyclopedia Britannica*

None of these types of carriage will be familiar to most English speakers. For anyone except an antiquarian or specialist, these words are now archaisms. They were in quite common use but have now dropped out of common use.

Medieval armour similarly consisted of many different pieces with a term for each. In a short passage describing the arming of Sir Gawain in the medieval poem *Sir Gawayne and the Green Knight*, a prose translation provides the following italicized terms:

> He stayed there all that day, and dressed the next morning, asked early for his armour, and it was all brought. First a red carpet was laid on the floor and heaped with much gleaming gilded clothing. The sturdy man stepped onto the carpet and picked up the steel equipment dressed in a doublet of expensive Turkistan cloth and skilfully cut cape, fur lined and fastened at the neck. Then they put the *sabbatouns* on his powerful feet, bound his legs in steel with lovely *greaves* and cleanly polished *polaynes* which were fastened round his knees with golden knots. Then came the goodly *cuisses* which skilfully encased his thick thighs and were tied on with thongs. Then the *hauberk* of bright steel rings resting on bright fabric was wrapped about the warrior and well burnished *braces* placed on both his arms along with bright, goodly *cowters* and gloves of plate armour.

We can guess what most of these terms mean. Gawayne is being dressed from foot to head, with steel shoes (sabbatouns) and greaves on his lower legs, polaynes at the knees, and cuisses on the upper leg, a chainmail corslet over the torso, braces on the lower and upper arm, and cowters at the elbow. All these terms have become archaisms and are now known only to those with a specialist interest in armour.

Word loss is particularly common in slang, the everyday colloquial in-talk vocabulary used particularly by teenagers. Words go into and out of use with great rapidity in teen vocabularies. Some years ago there were groups of young people in Great Britain called 'teddyboys'. There were also 'mods' and 'rockers'. With the teddyboys having grown up, the word *teddyboy* has begun a journey out of the active vocabulary of most speakers of British English, as have *mods* and *rockers*, although no doubt in the passive vocabulary of nostalgia they live on. In one hundred years these words are likely to be known only to social historians. In other words, they will have become specialist vocabulary items like those of medieval armour and Victorian horse-drawn carriages. In a thousand years they will probably have gone the way of *dryhten*.

3.2.5 WORD HISTORIES

etymology

The historical development of a word is its etymology. Some words have an etymology which is entirely native. This means the words have been in the language for as far back as one can tell. Some have a history that is lost in pre-literate times. Others were coined through the processes of word formation we have looked at. Still other words are non-native having been borrowed at some point during the history of the language and since then have evolved within it.

folk etymology

Coming to the wrong conclusion about the origins and particularly the meaning of words is termed folk etymology. It is very entertaining for others when people make such mistakes. Folk etymologies also make good puns and jokes; for example, the definition of the word *briefcase* given in a cartoon strip was 'a trial where the jury goes out to form a lynching party'. Another splendid folk etymology is the word *wealth fair*, constructed by a North American student on a folk etymology of the word *welfare*. Welfare is something which gives people some wealth and it makes things more fair. However, in modern English *welfare* is not a compound word and the student who made up the etymology clearly thought that it was.

EXERCISE 3.13

Create your own folk etymologies

Find five compound words and say what they mean. Then make up two other meanings that they could have, for example *treetrunk* means 'the trunk of a tree'. It could mean 'a trunk of an elephant shaped like a tree' or 'a wooden suitcase'. Then try and construct a joke using one of the folk etymologies you have made.

• •

3.2.6 DIALECT VOCABULARIES

So far we have been looking at total vocabularies, both those of individuals and of languages. But there are also partial vocabularies of various kinds. Like the sounds of a language, the words of a language can often belong to particular dialects. For example, the word *croft* is used in parts of Scotland for the houses

of tenants on an estate. So this is a regional dialect word. In the southern prov- **regional dialect**
inces of Otago and Southland in New Zealand, locals may call a holiday cottage **word**
a *crib,* while northerners call it a *bach.* Speakers of English elsewhere might call
such places *holiday homes.* In every new English, such as those of Singapore
and Hong Kong, there are words borrowed from local languages, like Malay and
Cantonese. Most of these words are used only by people who live in the area.
Makan is Malay for 'food' or 'eating' but it can be heard in Singapore if people are
speaking English. It is thus a regional dialect word.

APPLICATION

When authors convey the regional dialect speech of their characters they
can do so by using dialect words or words which have dialect senses, that
is, meanings which the words have only in a particular regional dialect. If an
author chooses a word which is spoken only in the area in which his story
is set, then what the character says may be opaque to the reader, whereas
if the words are common in other dialects then the regional flavour of the
speaker may not be clear. Look at the following two passages of Scots and
North Country English dialect respectively and see what kind of balance has
been struck:

> 'Bide a wee – bide a wee; you southrons are aye in sic a hurry, and this
> is something concerns yoursell, an ye wad tak patience to hear't – Yill? –
> deil a drap o' yill did Pate offer me; but Mattie gae us baith a drap o'
> skimmed milk, and ane o' her thick ait jannocks, that was as wat and raw
> as a divot. – O, for the bonnie girdle-cakes o' the North! – and sae we sat
> doun and took out our clavers.'
>
> Sir Walter Scott, *Rob Roy*

> Just as I was going back up the yard to get my tea at home, hoping the
> others had come back from the pictures so's I wouldn't have anything
> to keep on being black about, a copper passed me and headed for the
> bloke's door. He was striding quickly with his head bent forward, and I
> knew that somebody had narked. They must have seen him buy the rope
> and then tipped-off the cop. Or happen the old hen at the yard-end had
> finally caught on.
>
> Alan Sillitoe, 'On Saturday Afternoon'

In the passage from *Rob Roy* the regional dialect vocabulary is almost impen- **dialect vocabulary**
etrable without the aid of a dialect dictionary. Words such as *jannocks* and *clav-*
ers cannot be understood by people from outside the dialect area. The Sillitoe
extract, on the other hand, allows us to guess what the dialect words might mean.

We can guess that the *yard* must be something like a street. *Being black* presumably means being in a bad humour. *Narked* must mean something like 'informed'. A *hen* must be a woman. You find many more works of fiction which make similar interesting contrasts, particularly in the literatures of countries where the English spoken is richly influenced in its vocabulary by words borrowed from indigenous languages. Such literatures are to be found, for example, in Africa and the West Indies. It has become more common for regional dialect vocabulary to appear in literature written in New Englishes as the local market for such literature has expanded. For those who are interested in Harry Potter, however, it is nice to know that the word *dumbledore* is an unborrowed English dialect word used, for example, in the Isle of Wight meaning 'bumblebee'.

If regional dialect vocabulary items are spoken in geographically distinct areas then it should be possible to survey an area to find out where particular words are spoken. Such a regional dialect survey is, as you can imagine, a delicate operation. There is no point in surveying the local doctor who comes from another region. But, with all their difficulties, regional dialect surveys of a number of areas in the English-speaking world have been conducted. There are notable dialect surveys of England and the United States, for example: Orton and Halliday's *Survey of English Dialects* (Harald Orton and Wilfred J. Halliday, *Survey of English Dialects*, vols I and II, Leeds, 1962–3); and Kurath's *A Word Geography of the Eastern United States* (Hans Kurath, *A Word Geography of the Eastern United States*, Ann Arbor, MI, 1949). As a result of doing such surveys, maps can be drawn which contain isoglosses, lines which mark the approximate boundaries for the use of a particular linguistic feature of a dialect, such as the use of a particular dialect word.

isogloss

Figure 3.4 is a dialect map marking the division in the United States between the areas where people call a kind of fresh cheese either *Dutch cheese, pot cheese* or *smear case*.

social dialect vocabulary

Authors who wish to represent the social status of speakers will often include social dialect words. Social dialect vocabularies are determined on the basis of the social class or status of the speaker. For example, what you call the *toilet* tends to be part of your social dialect; some people might call it *the loo*. For London, there is even *The Good Loo Guide* providing information about public toilets. There is a set of words for the last course of a meal: *pudding, dessert, afters*. There is a set of words for the most important room in a house. It can be called the *sitting room,* the *parlour,* the *living* room, the *lounge*. What you call it is often a matter of social dialect. In Chapter 1 we saw that such a set of words is a linguistic variable.

It has been found that linguistic clues such as social dialect vocabulary are often powerful indicators of a speaker's social status and therefore of how they will be regarded by others. Many linguists see the responses which the speech of lower socio-economic speakers evoke in middle-class people as being the result of prejudice. By analysing the actual linguistic form that gives rise to these responses linguists have been able to explain that, contrary to the prejudice, there is nothing in the speech forms themselves that is inferior. That only leaves the prejudices of the hearer, about which, as a linguist, it is hard to do much.

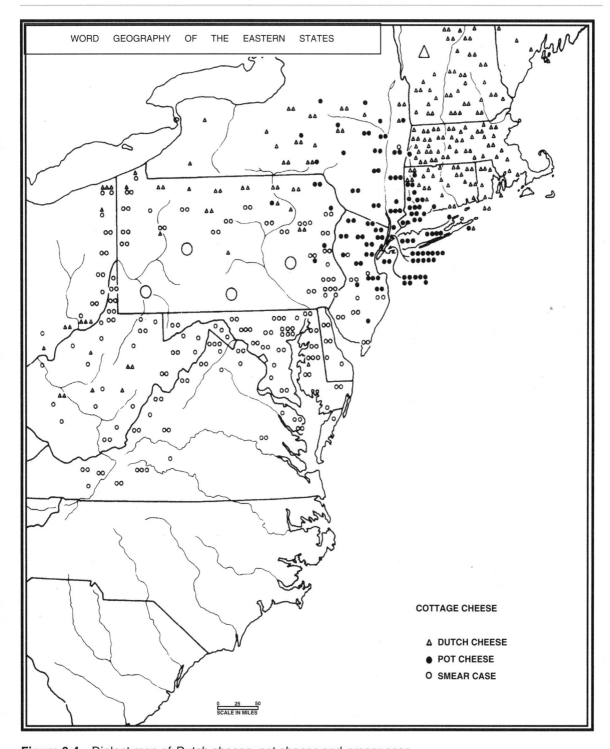

Figure 3.4 Dialect map of *Dutch cheese, pot cheese* and *smear case*

Which words in the following passage tell you about the speakers' probable social status, and what is that status likely to be?

> 'Mrs Barrows has worked hard, Martin, very hard. It grieves me to report that she has suffered a severe breakdown. It has taken the form of a persecution complex accompanied by distressing hallucinations.'
>
> 'I am very sorry, sir,' said Mr Martin.
>
> 'Mrs Barrows is under the delusion,' continued Mr Fitweiler, 'that you visited her last evening and behaved yourself in an – uh – unseemly manner.'
>
> James Thurber, 'The Catbird Seat'

Clearly Mr Martin is a subordinate because he addresses Mr Fitweiler as *Sir*. Mr Fitweiler is in a socially superior position and probably polite upper middle class, to judge by vocabulary such as: *grieves, report, distressing, delusion* and *unseemly*.

ethnic dialect vocabulary

Ethnic dialect vocabulary consists of words used by people who belong to particular ethnic groups and is characteristic of these groups. These are usually words which have been borrowed from the language or languages that members of the ethnic group spoke when they emigrated or before they became a colonized people. For example, there are quite a number of Yiddish borrowings in the English spoken by people of Jewish origin in New York City. The word *lox*, which denotes thinly sliced kosher smoked salmon, often eaten with cream cheese on bagels, is a borrowing from Yiddish and originally an ethnic dialect word. The words *chutzpah, mensch, schlemiel*, are also of Yiddish origin. In African American Vernacular English there are words of African origin such as *goober*, 'peanut', and *juju*, 'amulet'. In New Zealand English there are words which were previously ethnic dialect words for Maori speakers of English such as *whakapapa*, 'genealogy', and *kaumatua*, 'tribal elder'. Samoan speakers call white people *palagi* when they are speaking English.

Such ethnic dialect words and expressions can be and often are in turn borrowed into the more general vocabulary where they can then become part of a regional dialect. Pragmatic particles like *lah* and *ah* used at the end of Singaporean English sentences to indicate, for example, agreement or doubt, are borrowed from southern Chinese dialects but are now used by Singaporeans in general, including people who are ethnically Malay or Indian. So these words have moved from being ethnic dialect words to being regional dialect words.

3.2.7 SPECIALIST VOCABULARIES

A speaker has a regional, social and ethnic dialect vocabulary because of where he or she comes from, either regionally or socially or ethnically. But every speaker is also in command of a number of specialist vocabularies that relate to particular interests and occupations. Doctors, when they are speaking as doctors to other doctors or to their patients, use some vocabulary items that are peculiar to their occupation, words such as *tonsilectomy* and *hypertension*. So do surfies and drug addicts. Rock music has its own vocabulary which is different from that of jazz music.

specialist vocabulary

Here is a piece of scientific writing. Notice how difficult it is to understand because of its specialist technical vocabulary:

> Assuming conversions of gluons into sea quark-antiquark pairs, any gluon contribution is implicitly taken into account in the sea quark distribution.
>
> Gensch and Kriegel, 'Discussions of Vector Meson Production in Kp Interactions in Terms of a Simple Quark Fusion Model'

How big are specialist vocabularies? They can be very big indeed. There are hundreds of thousands of names for chemical compounds as you can tell by looking up web-based dictionaries of chemical compounds.. The maintenance manuals for the European airbus airliner are reputed to weigh more than the airbus itself. Imagine how many specialist vocabulary items there will be in such manuals. And imagine the task of translating them into other languages.

APPLICATION

Below is a piece of dialogue containing a number of specialist vocabulary items. Which words seem to have developed specialist senses? Can you guess what they might mean?

> 'Ah well, Toby's come up in the world since your day, Mr Smiley,' Tarr explained. 'They tell me even his pavement artists ride around in Cadillacs. Steal the scalphunters' bread out of their mouths too, if they get the chance, right, Mr Guillam?'
> 'They've become the general footpads for London Station,' Guillam said shortly. 'Part of lateralism.'
>
> John le Carré, *Tinker, Tailor, Soldier, Spy*

Pavement artists, scalphunters, footpads and *lateralism* all seem to be specialist terms. Since John le Carré's novels are usually about spying, the first three must be occupations, and lateralism some kind of policy concerned with spying. Without reading the rest of the novel, it is difficult to get much further.

Find an area in which you have a specialist vocabulary, for example in a hobby or sports area, and note down ten words from it that you think at least some of your

EXERCISE 3.14

friends will not know. Try to write good definitions of the meaning of these words and try to discover their etymologies to see how they have come to have the meaning and structure that they do. Frequently, you will not be able to find specialist words or specialist meanings in a dictionary. For example: the word *tube*, used in the vocabulary of surfing, is a metaphor because waves that are tubes are similar to literal tubes. The iTunes player categorizes pop music into many different categories. How many of these terms would your grandparents recognize: blues, country and western, heavy metal, grunge?

. . . .

3.2.8 FORMALITY AND VOCABULARY

Many vocabulary items can only be appropriately used in certain environments. For example, slang or colloquial vocabulary is out of place at a formal church service or on being presented to royalty. Conversely, formal vocabulary is out of place in a school playground unless it is used for humorous or ironic effect.

hypercorrect

Many speakers are uncomfortable with very formal situations, do not quite know which words to choose and therefore remain tongue-tied. However, this is a matter of how familiar one is with the situation. Ambassadors are not tongue-tied at embassy parties because they have been to many such parties and thus know what to say. Students entering tertiary education are, by contrast, often not sure how formal their writing must be. In such a situation people often hypercorrect, that is, they use what they consider more prestigious linguistic forms than are the norm for the situation. However, once one is familiar with a situation, the language, including vocabulary choice, usually looks after itself.

APPLICATION

Here is Joe Gargery, the blacksmith in Charles Dickens's novel *Great Expectations*, hypercorrecting when he is in London visiting his nephew and step-son Pip, now a gentleman:

'Us two being now alone, Sir,' resumed Joe, 'and me having the intentions and abilities to stay not many minutes more, I will now conclude – leastways begin – to mention that which have led to my having the present honour. For if it was not,' said Joe, with his old air of lucid exposition, 'that my only wish were to be useful to you, I should not have had the honour of breaking wittles in the company and abode of gentlemen.'

Joe and Pip are together in private, which is not a context in which two relatives need to be formal with one another. However, Joe feels so out of his social depth that he is more formal in his choice of vocabulary than is required. So he uses words which are morphologically more complex than one would normally expect a blacksmith to use in any context, for example *intentions, abilities*. Also he uses formulae in an interesting way. *Having the present honour* is formal, whereas *breaking wittles* is not. In other words the hypercorrection is not consistent.

This brings us to the question of what constitutes the right form to use in any situation. We can say that one might be a native speaker of a language but still not have native-like competence in it in every situation. To gain that, one must become a native speaker in each situation in turn. That takes time. So hypercorrecting is only hypercorrecting by reference to some norm of native-like performance in a particular situation or range of situations.

3.2.9 DICTIONARIES

Whole vocabularies, as we have seen, exist in languages, and in people's heads. In a society where there was no writing, dictionaries would not exist but then neither would they be needed. Speakers would learn all the words they needed from others' use of them. However, writing makes it possible to look up in dictionaries words which one might not come across in the normal course of events. Indeed, the first dictionaries of English were published with this in mind. As the speakers of English became more socially stratified and as literacy became more common among middle-class people, there were words in writing that were not in people's own vocabularies. Clearly they needed a dictionary, and that market niche was filled first by rather simple lists of 'hard' words but later and most notably by Samuel Johnson's dictionary, in which he attempted to list all of the words in the eighteenth-century English of his time.

Currently many kinds of dictionaries exist for particular purposes. There are bilingual dictionaries, dictionaries of idioms, technical dictionaries, large dictionaries and small dictionaries. To understand what all these different dictionaries can do for those who consult them we need to understand two things: the way dictionaries come into existence and how they compare with the internalized vocabularies of actual speakers, with which we have dealt earlier.

Dictionaries are books compiled by lexicographers and published by publishers. Since they are published by publishers, they are, for the most part, written for particular markets and in the hope that they will make a profit. (Even Samuel Johnson, in one of his more cynical moods, said, 'No man but a blockhead ever wrote, except for money.') This means that dictionaries are always a compromise. In a reasonably sized, and therefore reasonably priced, dictionary of English it isn't possible to list all the words a reader might conceivably want to look up. So lexicographers make a choice of the words which they think more people will want to look up, and leave out the more marginal and arcane words, which are less likely to be useful. This choice can now be made easier by searching large computer-based corpora of text looking for each word, its context, and how frequently it appears in the corpora.

In order to make things easier and therefore cheaper, publishers who publish dictionaries will often publish various versions of the same dictionary materials by selecting entries and what is said about each entry. Small pocket dictionaries will be cheap and will contain a smaller number of entries than desk dictionaries.

Dictionaries for tourists going away for their annual holidays to Crete will be bilingual and include Greek vocabulary to do with meals, postage, finding your way around, booking hotels, finding a health professional, but not specialist terms for parts of jet engines. They will also be cheap since you might part company with a small sum in an airport bookshop before you go but you will be price sensitive given that you are only going for two weeks.

Knowing all this, it is clear that dictionaries cannot be authoritative in all respects. They attempt, as best they can, to list as many words as possible within the bounds of the particular dictionary format. They attempt to give as many senses of the words as they can. They provide a few examples and hints of how the words might be used but they cannot be authoritative in the sense that they provide unimpeachable information on all the aspects of all the words of the language that the totality of its native speakers might want to know. That is why, when playing Scrabble, one must nominate a dictionary as an authority even though it cannot be an authority. There is no other option.

So how can you tell a good dictionary from a bad one? That depends on the purpose you have for referring to a dictionary. Most native speakers use dictionaries to check the spellings of words. Dictionaries don't normally get spelling wrong. People also look in dictionaries for unfamiliar words. Here, the bigger the dictionary the more likely it is to contain an unfamiliar word. But not necessarily. A very large number of technical words will not appear in a standard dictionary. For them you must turn to a technical dictionary in the subject area.

If a word is unfamiliar then one usually looks it up for its meaning. Here one is again at the mercy of the lexicographer who wrote the entry. There is an art to writing good glosses for the meaning of words and for getting all the ones that a reader might need. For example, in section 3.1 we saw that the word *imposter* is glossed as 'swindler'. This is clearly not a full synonym and thus can lead a reader astray. Many words have multiple meanings and so a reader wants as many of the meanings represented as is possible within the limits set by the dictionary. Again, if you do not find what seems like the right meaning, it may well be a shortcoming of the dictionary.

Figures 3.5 and 3.6 give two sample entries for the same word to illustrate some of the things we have been saying.

The first entry for the word *freight* is from the *Concise Oxford English Dictionary*. It begins with the spelling of the word and this is followed by its pronunciation

freight /freɪt/ *n. & v.* ● *n.* **1** the transport of goods in containers or by water or air or *US* by land. **2** goods transported; cargo. **3** a charge for transportation of goods. **4** the hire of a ship, aircraft, etc., for transporting goods. **5** a load or burden. ● *v.tr.* **1** transport (goods) as freight. **2** load with freight. **3** hire or let out (a ship) for the carriage of goods and passengers. [Middle Dutch, Middle Low German *vrecht*, variant of *vracht*: cf. FRAUGHT]

Figure 3.5 Entry for *freight* in the *Concise Oxford English Dictionary*

Freight (frāt), *sb.* Also 5 freyte, freyght, 6–7 fraight, 6 frate. [prob. a. MDu. or MLG. *vrecht*, var. of *vracht*: see FRAUGHT *sb.* The word has passed from Du. or LG. into some of the Rom. langs.; F. *fret* hire of a ship (from 13th c.), Sp. *flete*, Pg. *frete*]

1. Hire of a vessel for the transport of goods; the service of transporting goods (originally, by water; now extended, esp. in *U.S.*, to land-transit); the sum of money paid for this. In early use also: Passage-money.

1463 *Mann. & Househ. Exp.* 194 My mastyr toke hym ffor his ffreyte to Caleys..vj. li. 1483 CAXTON *Gold. Leg.* 283/2 Whome they receyued in to theyr Shippe gladly and sayd they wold brynge hym thyder without ony freyght or huyr. 1538 STARKEY *England* II. i. 172 Specyally yf to that were joynyd a nother ordynance..wych ys, concernyng the frate of marchandyse. 1580 HOLLYBAND *Treas. Fr. Tong, Naulage,* the fraight or fare payed for passage ouer the water. *a* 1687 PETTY *Pol. Arith* (1690) 19 Those who have the command of the Sea Trade may Work at easier Freight with more profit. 1712 E. COOKE *Voy. S. Sea* 353 Having agreed to pay no Freight there. 1764 BURN *Poor Laws* 180 Let a small deduction be made from the freights of ships, and from seamens wages. 1765 T. HUTCHINSON *Hist. Mass.* I. ii. 257 They purchased a ship-load of masts, the freight whereof cost them sixteen hundred pounds. 1854 HAWTHORNE *Eng. Note-bks.* (1883) II. 123 The captains talk together about..how freights are in America. 1861 GOSCHEN *For. Exch.* 18 The charge for freight acts with the same force as a charge for a commodity actually produced and exported. 1868 ROGERS *Pol. Econ.* ix. 1876) 83 The passage from the East to Europe has been so shortened, that a freight from thence to England is reduced to one-fourth.

† b. *To take freight:* to take passage for oneself and goods. *Obs.*

1719 DE FOE *Crusoe* II. xvi, We all took freight with him.

2. The cargo or lading (of a ship); a ship-load. In *U.S.* by extension: Anything carried by sea or land (a general term for 'goods' in transit). *Fast freight* (*U.S.*): see FAST *a.* 11.

1502 ARNOLDE *Chron.* (1811) 229 We..charge you precisely that the forsayd [merchants] wyth their shyp's freight .. ye suffer and let go passe. 1540 *Act 32 Hen. VIII,* c. 14 Beyng mynded..to take any freight or ladynge..into any of the saide shyppes. 1694 *Acc. Sev. Late Voy.* II. (1711) 3 When they have their full Fraught of Whales, they put up their great Flag. 1789 BRAND *Hist. Newcastle* II. 255 [A vessel] trading to Newcastle upon Tyne with corn, and returning with a freight of sea coals. 1832 HT. MARTINEAU *Ireland* 131 Do you know that Vessel? You cannot be aware what freight it bears? 1856 KANE *Arct. Expl.* II. xix. 196 They contrived to exclude both clothes and food in favor of a full freight of these treasures.

b. *transf.* A load, burden.

1618 CHAPMAN *Hesiod* I. 574 At thy purse's height, And when it fights low, give thy use his freight. 1697 DRYDEN *Virg. Georg.* II. 599 With the ruddy Freight the bending Branches groan. 1805 WORDSW. *Prelude* v. 84, I..looked self-questioned what the new comer carried.. Could mean. 1878 HUXLEY *Physiogr.* 73 These warm moist winds..deposit their freight of moisture in showers of rain.

c. *fig.*

a 1631 DONNE in *Select.* (1840) 43 Keep up that holy cheerfulness, which Christ makes the ballast of a Christian, and his freight too. 1755 YOUNG *Centaur* v. Wks. 1757 IV. 223 Every moment shall return, and lay its whole freight..before the Throne. 1812 J. WILSON *Isle of Palms* I. 127 An earthly freight she bears Of joys and sorrows. 1872 HOLLAND *Marb. Proph.* 97 A man who lisped On ready words his freight of gratitude.

† 3. A journey of a laden vessel. *Obs.*

1716 CHURCH *Philip's War* (1865) I. 157 He made use of Canoo's: But by that time they had made two fraights.. the Wind sprung up.

4. *U.S.* Short for *freight-train*: a goods-train. *By freight*: by the usual means of transportation, as opposed to *by express*.

1881 *Chicago Times* 18 June, A freight of thirty loaded cars..collided with the other train.

5. *attrib.* and *Comb.* (esp. *U.S.* in reference to the carriage of goods by railway), as *freight car* (= goods truck or van), *carriage, engine, -man, route, shed, steamer, traffic, train* (= goods train); also *freight-handler, -handling.* Also † *freight-money*, payment for conveyance of freight.

1856 OLMSTED *Slave States* 55 There were, in the train, two first-class passenger cars, and two *freight cars. 1884 *Pall Mall G.* 25 Sept. 5/2 They will put up their rates on the *freight carriage eastward. 1882 *Ibid.* 12 July 8/2 A riot has occurred [at Jersey city] between the *freight-handlers on strike and the Italian labourers. 1887 *Bureau Statist. Labour* (N. Y.) 327 There was also a great interruption of *freight traffic. 1855 *Gen. Term Rep..* should be sent forward by a carrier, or *freightman. 1755 MAGENS *Insurances* II. 189 All Insurances on expected Gain..future *Freight-Monies, Seamens Wages and Mens Lives are universally forbid. 1881 *Chicago Times* 12 Mar., This has been the cheapest *freight route to New York. *Ibid.* 17 June, Between the gas-works and the *freight-shed of the..railway. 1891 *Pall Mall G.* 3 Dec. 6/2 The St. John's Board of Trade..thinks that the interest of the country would be better served by grants to *freight steamers. 1885 *Ibid.* 10 Sept. 6/1 Goods traffic —called in America *'freight' traffic. 1872 *Japanese in America* 199 *Freight-trains frequently number..one hundred cars.

Freight (frāt), *v.* Forms: 6–7 fraight, (6 freith), 7– freight. *Pa. t.* and *pa. pple.* 6 freyghted, frayted, 6–7 fraighted, 7– freighted. [f. prec. *sb.*; cf. FRAUGHT *v.*]

1. *trans.* To furnish or load (a vessel) with a cargo; to hire or let out (a vessel) for the carriage of goods and passengers. Also with *out* and *to* or *for* (a place).

1485 in Arnolde *Chron.* (1811) 229 For too..lade and freith and cary awaye. 1555 EDEN *Decades* 296 Donco, where the marchauntes..fraight theyr shyppes. 1651 HOBBES *Leviath.* II. xxii. 119 With the Merchandise they buy at home, can fraight a Ship, to export it. 1671 CLARENDON *Dialog.* Tracts (1727) 293 They who freighted them out. 1702 C. MATHER *Magn. Chr.* I. vi. (1852) 84 They build one ship more, which they fraighted for England. 1800 WELLESLEY in Owen *Desp.* 707 The British merchants..not having obtained the expected permission to freight their ships to the port of London. 1831 SIR J. SINCLAIR *Corr.* II 223 An opportunity of making immense sums of money, by freighting their ships to the powers at war. 1878 SIMPSON *Sch. Shaks.* I. 120 He proposed to freight as many English vessels as possible by Flemings, Frenchmen, Spaniards, and Italians.

b. *transf.* To load, store. Also *fig.* of a burden: To bear upon as a load.

1839 LYTTON *Devereux* I. vii, Fortune freights not your channel with her hoarded stores. 1838 SPARKS *Biog.* IX. *Eaton* xi. 301 The caravan had been freighted by the Ba-shaw only to this place. 1892 TALMAGE in *N. Y. Weekly Witness* 13 Jan. 7/5 All the sins of the past and of the present freighting him.

c. *U.S. intr. To freight up:* to take in a cargo. *fig.*

1889 'MARK TWAIN' *Yank. at Crt. K. Arth.* (Tauchn.) I. 128 How to freight up against probable fasts before starting.

2. To carry or transport (goods) as freight.

1540 *Act 32 Hen. VIII,* c. 14 Euery brode wollen cloth freyghted to Daunske. 1697 DAMPIER *Voy.* I. xv. 412 Every man freights his Goods in his own room; and probably lodges there, if he be on board himself. 1881 HENTY *Cornet of Horse* xvi. (1888) 160 Van Duyk would have freighted a shipful of presents to Rupert's friends.

Hence **Freighting** *vbl. sb.*

1672 *Essex Papers* (Camden) I. 7, I Incourage all I possibly can buildinge of Ships of our owne (for Fraigtinge of Forringhners distresse us). 1867 SMYTH *Sailor's Word-bk., Freighting,* a letting out of vessels on freight or hire. 1884 L. HAMILTON *Mexican Hand-bk.* 67 The water flowing down from the various ravines..fills the arroyo and renders freighting in wagons difficult. *attrib.* 1769 BURKE *Late St. Nat.* Wks. 1842 I. 83 The freighting business revived. The ships were fewer, but much larger. 1856 OLMSTED *Slave States* 396 The roads seemed to be doing a heavy freighting business with cotton. 1850 N. H. BISHOP 4 *Months in Sneak-Box* 15 There appears to be no fixed freighting tariff established for boats.

Figure 3.6 Part of the entry for *freight* from the *Oxford English Dictionary*

in brackets, in the characters of the International Phonetic Alphabet, which you will learn to use in Chapter 4. Other dictionaries may use systems devised by the dictionary editors. To understand what they mean you must look up the section on the pronunciation guides at the beginning of the dictionary. Next are the word's two syntactic categories, in italics and abbreviated. Again, if you are not sure what these abbreviations mean you must look them up at the front of the dictionary. In the case of *freight*, it has two categories: noun and verb. Then come the senses of the word, each numbered and related to the syntactic category of the word. Only the main senses are given, each introduced by a number, the first set being the meanings the word has when it is a noun, and the second set being the senses the word has when it is a transitive verb. The last piece of the entry, given in square brackets, is its etymology. Often the abbreviations must be looked up if you don't know what MDu happens to be. In this case the etymology section indicates that the word *freight* was borrowed from the Middle Dutch word *vrecht*, which was a variant spelling of the word *vracht*, and it is related to the English word *fraught*, which comes from the same historical source.

This entry is an edited-down version of the entry in the *Oxford English Dictionary*, often called the Big Oxford. The Big Oxford started to be compiled in the mid-nineteenth century and took four editors to finish. The most remarkable of these was James Murray who started life as the son of a tailor in a small Scottish town. Murray was a man of insatiable curiosity and with an iron will. The dictionary was modelled on that of the brothers Grimm in Germany who not only collected fairy tales but also words. It was based on the idea that entries should show the development of a word over the whole of its recorded history. That history would come from quotations containing the word in its various uses. The quotations were written on slips of paper by volunteers, sent to Murray and then sorted, including by Murray's children who were paid by the slip; less when they were younger and more as they got older.

Part of the entry for *freight* from the Big Oxford is shown in Figure 3.6.

You can see from the size of this one entry that the Big Oxford is going to be a big dictionary. It is, in fact, 20 volumes in its second edition.

You may ask what place a huge dictionary like this has in the study of English. In the·first place it can be used just for its own sake, to look up the historical development of a word. But it is also an essential tool when reading English written in earlier periods when some English words did not mean what they do now. When you do that and are not sure about the meaning of a word, when it sounds as though it can't mean what it does now, or perhaps the word is so archaic that you don't know it at all, then by searching for the word in the CD ROM or on-line versions of the OED and checking the dates of the illustrative quotations so as to find a quotation near the period in which the book was written, you can understand what the writer at the time actually meant. Many Shakespeare editors do some of this work for you in the notes to editions of Shakespeare's plays. But in many other cases the Big Oxford must be accessed by you, the reader. Doing that with the paper version of the dictionary is a long business. Doing it with a CD ROM version or on line is easy.

Dictionaries, by convention, arrange their entries according to alphabetical order of the written version of the word. Clearly that is a useful way to look words up. However, there are other ways that have their uses. A rhyming dictionary often lists words in reverse alphabetical order, and that way all the words which rhyme with each other are listed together.

rhyming dictionary

Words can also be listed according to their meaning. Essentially this is what a thesaurus does. If you want a word with the same meaning as a given word, you look it up in the thesaurus. Again, computer technology is able to help here. In many modern computers a thesaurus is available as a piece of software, and thus if you are writing and would like to use a different word, but one which has the same meaning as the one you have just thought of, you can get a range of options from the thesaurus.

thesaurus

Further exercises •

Are the italicized words synonyms?

EXERCISE 3.15•

(a)   I want to *buy/purchase* some tomatoes.

(b)   My *mother/mum* doesn't like you.

(c)   These tomatoes are *red/ripe*.

(d)   I nearly fell into the *river/stream*.

(e)   Your tie is too *broad/wide*.

(f)   I *almost/nearly* fell in.

(g)   Denis has bought a *house/home*.

(h)   He's not a bad *bloke/fellow*.

(i)   That car needs a new *muffler/silencer*.

(j)   My *arm/elbow* still hurts.

(k)   Our host was *drunk/intoxicated*.

(l)   His father is even *slimmer/skinnier*.

(m)   This model is *expensive/valuable*.

Put the following set of words into pairs with opposite senses. Then work out whether the words are an antonym pair, a complementary pair, or a converse pair:

EXERCISE 3.16•

(a)   high   (f)   whisper

(b)   cold   (g)   aunt

(c)   tender   (h)   shout

(d)   uncle   (i)   hot

(e)   accept   (j)   low

EXERCISE 3.17 Examine the following list of words and then answer the questions given below, taking your examples from the list. (*Note*: some words can be used more than once.)

deep, villain, buy, animal, illegal, by, profound, legal, deer, shallow, sell.

(a) Identify a pair of gradable antonyms.

(b) Comment on the polysemy of the pair of gradable antonyms.

(c) Identify a pair of converses.

(d) Identify a pair of complementaries (ungradable opposites).

(e) Identify a pair of words related by hyponymy.

(f) Identify which is the hyponym and which the superordinate.

(g) Identify a pair of partial synonyms.

(h) Explain briefly why the two words are not perfectly synonymous.

(i) Identify a pair of homophones.

EXERCISE 3.18 How have synonyms and antonyms been put to use in this poem:

love is more thicker than forget
more thinner than recall
more seldom than a wave is wet
more frequent than to fail

it is most mad and moonly
and less it shall unbe
than all the sea which only
is deeper than the sea

love is less always than to
win less never than alive
less bigger than the least begin
less littler than forgive

it is most sane and sunly
and more it cannot die
than all the sky which only
is higher than the sky

e. e. cummings

Glossary •

Acronym   Word made up from the first sounds or syllables of words in a phrase.

Active vocabulary   The words that a speaker uses in speaking or writing.

Adjective   Head word of an adjective phrase. *See* Chapter 7. Some adjectives inflect for the morphosyntactic category of comparison.

Adverb   Head word of an adverb phrase. *See* Chapter 7.

Affix   General name for prefixes and suffixes.

Agreement   takes place when the choice of an inflectional morpheme on one word is triggered by the morphosyntactic properties of another word.

Allomorphy   The various forms of the same morpheme.

Amelioration   The historical change which improves a word's connotations.

Antonym   A word that has the opposite sense to another where the opposite-ness comes about from the senses' being at the ends of a scale, for example, *young* and *old.*

Archaism   The historical process whereby a word comes no longer to be in use, or a word which is no longer in use.

Associations   The associations of words come about because of the attitudes people have to the word and its sense.

Auxiliary verb   Verb which modifies a lexical verb in a verb phrase. Auxiliary verbs appear to the left of, or before, lexical verbs. *See* Chapter 7.

Base   The lexeme (or set of lexemes) which a word formation rule takes and turns into a constituent (or constituents) of the new lexeme(s) created by the rule.

Blend   A word whose phonological form is formed from the first half of the phonological form of one word and the second half of another, for example *smog* is a blend of *smoke* and *fog.*

Bound morpheme   A morpheme that cannot function as an independent word, that is, a morpheme which must attach to a stem to form a word.

Clipping   Shortening the phonological representation of a word.

Closed class   Classes of words where no new members of the class can be created by regular word-formation rules.

Co-hyponym   Two or more words whose senses are hyponyms of the same superordinate, *chair* and *table* are co-hyponyms of *furniture.*

Coining   Making up a new word.

Common noun   A noun that will go with *the.*

Comparative   A morphosyntactic property of an adjective or adverb. Its form may be the inflectional suffix -*er* or alternatively the word *more* used immediately before the adjective or adverb. The comparative form is usually used in the context where the referents of two noun phrases are being compared in respect of some property, as in *the Atlantic Ocean is smaller than the Pacific Ocean.*

Comparison   A morphosyntactic category of adjectives and adverbs having three morphosyntactic properties: **positive,** the unmarked form of the word, **comparative** and **superlative**.

Complementary senses   Words have complementary senses if they belong to a semantic field with only their senses in it.

Componential analysis   Finding the sense components of the meanings of words.

Compositional   If the meaning of a linguistic unit which is itself made up of constituents is made up in a predictable way out of the meanings of its constituent parts then it is semantically compositional.

Compound   A word made up from two other words.

Conjunction   Word that links two grammatical structures. *See* Chapter 7.

Connotation   The connotations of words are conventional social associations that words have developed. They tend to be negative or positive depending on people's attitudes to what the words denote.

Converse senses   Two words have converse senses if they are essentially synonyms but the 'actors' or relationship which they denote are differently allocated by the two senses. For example: *buy* and *sell*, *husband* and *wife*.

Conversion   The word-formation process whereby a lexeme having one syntactic category acquires a further syntactic category, thus creating a new lexeme.

Count noun   Noun that takes plural inflection and can occur with the determiner *a*.

Denotation   The set of things, actions, properties etc. that a word's sense gives it the potential to refer to.

Derivation   The formation of lexemes by means of adding a derivational affix.

Derivational affix   *See* **Derivation**.

Derivational morpheme   An affix which is part of the word-building system. Derivational affixes take as input one lexeme and through the addition of the affix create a new lexeme.

Determiner   One of: *a, the, this, that, these, those. See* Chapter 7.

Dialect vocabulary   Vocabulary that is (recognizably) used by a subgroup of speakers of the language.

Distribution A grammatical constituent's characteristic place(s) in sequence with other grammatical constituents.

Drift The changes which take place in the representation of a word in the lexicon after it has been lexicalized.

Echo words Words made up by attempting to imitate the sound of the thing the word denotes.

Entailment When what one sentence means follows logically from what another sentence means, the meaning of the second sentence entails the meaning of the first.

Ethnic dialect vocabulary Words that are distinctive of the speech of members of an ethnic subgroup of society.

Etymology The origin and history of words.

Euphemism A word or expression which tries to evade drawing attention to the socially uncomfortable nature of what it denotes.

Extended metaphors These are the result of taking a set of metaphors from the same semantic domain. For example, boxing can be the domain from which one might draw more than one metaphor in a description of a political debate by saying that a speaker was *really punching hard* and that a particular argument was *a knockout blow*.

Folk etymology A plausible but incorrect guess about the origin of a word.

First person A **morphosyntactic property** pertaining to the speaker (*I* and *we*).

Free morpheme A morpheme that can function as a word.

Gradable adjective An adjective that will take comparison.

Grammatical category The syntactic function of a word, for example, noun.

Grammatical word The form a lexeme takes when it includes one of its possible morphosyntactic properties, for example, the plural form of a noun, such as *women*.

Head The head of a lexeme is that constituent which determines the syntactic properties of the whole lexeme.

Homonym A word that has the same form as another but is otherwise unrelated to it.

Hypercorrect To use linguistic forms which are more formal than is considered appropriate by the speakers who are familiar with the situation.

Hypernym Synonym for **superordinate**.

Hyponym A word whose sense is a more particular instance of that of its superordinate, for example, *chair* is a hyponym of *furniture*.

Infinitive   Form of a verb having no inflection.

Inflection   An affix that is part of the grammatical system of a language.

Isogloss   Line on a map representing the boundary between geographic areas where two alternative regional dialect features are used.

Labelled bracketed notation   A way of showing hierarchical organization by surrounding each unit in a structure with two brackets and enclosing within them a label to show to which category the unit inside the brackets belongs.

Lexeme   A word as an abstract entity, distinct from the inflected forms which it may assume in different syntactic contexts, for example, *write, writes, wrote, writing, written* are forms of the lexeme WRITE.

Lexical borrowing   The adoption of a word from the vocabulary of one language by that of another.

Lexical item   An entry in the lexicon of a speaker or language.

Lexical verb   Head of a verb phrase. *See* Chapter 7. Verbs inflect for the morphosyntactic category of tense.

Lexicalization   The process whereby a coinage becomes an established lexical item.

Lexicon   Used in three senses:

1. the dictionary which a speaker of a language has in his or her head;
2. the set of lexemes of a language, and the processes which relate them;
3. the set of lexical items of a language.

Metaphor   Use of a word while breaking some of its selectional restrictions.

Metonymy   A trope where something associated with a thing is used for the thing itself, for example, calling someone who stays at home a *house-mouse.*

Morpheme   An element of word structure.

Morphology   Word form or the study of word form.

Morphophonemic   Having to do with the phonemic form of morphemes.

Morphosyntactic category   Grammatical category which has to do with both morphology and syntax, such as tense, case, number. *See also* **Morphosyntactic property**.

Morphosyntactic property   One of the grammatically relevant properties within a morphosyntactic category. For example, in English, the category *Number* in nouns contains the properties *Singular* and *Plural,* and the category *Tense* contains the properties *Present* and *Past.*

Narrowing   The historical process whereby the denotation of a word covers less than it did.

Non-count noun Noun that does not take plural inflection and cannot occur with the determiner *a*.

Non-gradable adjective An adjective that will not take comparison.

Nonce word A word coined and used once but not lexicalized.

Noun Head word of a noun phrase. *See* Chapter 7.

Number The morphosyntactic category indicating how many.

Open class Classes of words that can be added to by the word-formation processes of a language.

Orthography Writing systems and the study of writing systems.

Part of speech A traditional name for **grammatical category.**

Participle Verb form with some adjectival properties. In English, most participles end in *-ing, -en,* or *-ed*.

Passive vocabulary The words a speaker knows but does not use in speech or writing.

Pejoration The historical process whereby a word comes to have worse connotations than it previously had.

Perfect participle A form of the verb regularly ending in the inflection *-en* or *-ed* (provided the *-ed* is not the past tense), or irregularly formed by such means as a change in the vowel, for example *sung,* traditionally termed the past participle.

Person A **morphosyntactic category** affecting agreement between verbs and subjects as well as agreement between **pronouns** and their **antecedents**.

Personification A particular kind of **metaphor** where something that is not human is given human attributes.

Phonological form The way the sound of a word is represented in the **lexicon**.

Plural The **morphosyntactic property** indicating more than one.

Polysemy The property of having different but semantically related senses.

Positive A **morphosyntactic property** of adjectives or adverbs. Its form is the standard form, i.e., without inflection.

Prefix An **affix** that attaches to the left of the stem of a word.

Preposition Head of a prepositional phrase, for example *in. See* Chapter 7.

Productivity The extent to which a word-formation process, such as affixation, is able to apply to lexemes of the appropriate kind to create new words.

Progressive participle A form of verb regularly ending in the inflection *-ing,* traditionally termed the present participle.

Proper noun   A noun that will not go with the determiner *the*. The name of a person, or thing, e.g. *Sally* or *Brighton*.

Proper noun conversion   A change in a proper noun's syntactic representation whereby it becomes a common noun, for example *Bowler,* the man, to *bowler,* the hat.

Pun   The use of a word that has two senses, for humorous effect.

Reference   Words, through their denotation, can be used by speakers to refer to things, actions, properties, relationships etc., that is, to pick them out for the hearer from other things, actions etc. This activity is called reference.

Referring expression   A word or phrase which can be used to refer.

Regional dialect word   Word characteristically used by speakers from a particular geographic region.

Restricted collocation   This occurs where two words are conventionally associated with each other in a more restricted way than the grammar of the language might suggest. Some words develop idiosyncratic meanings as a result of such associations. For example, we talk about *white coffee,* not *light brown coffee*.

Rhyming dictionary   A dictionary which lists words by their reverse spelling or the sound of their last syllable.

Root creation   Words being made up from scratch by putting together a new phonological, syntactic and semantic representation.

Second person   A **morphosyntactic property** pertaining to the person spoken to (*you*).

Selectional restrictions   Restrictions created by the way senses fit with each other in phrases and sentences.

Semantic field   An area of meaning covered by words with related senses.

Semantic redundancy   Semantic redundancy occurs when the sense of, say, an adjective has a semantic component (or components) which is already present in the sense of, say, a noun of which it is a modifier.

Semantic representation   The representation of a word's meaning.

Sense   The meaning of a word excluding its connotations or associations. Meanings of words as seen from within the language.

Simile   A comparison in which one thing is said to be *like* or *as* another, for example, 'Britten motorcycles ride like the wind'.

Singular   The **morphosyntactic property** indicating one only.

Social dialect vocabulary   Words characteristically used by members of a particular social class.

Specialist vocabulary   Technical vocabulary of a group of specialists.

Standard form   Form of the adjective not inflected for either the comparative or the superlative.

Stem   The form of a word to which affixes are attached.

Suffix   An **affix** that attaches to the right of its stem.

Superlative   A **morphosyntactic property** of adjectives or adverbs. Its form is usually an inflection *-est,* or alternatively the word *most,* placed immediately before the adjective or adverb.

Superordinate   A word has a superordinate sense to another word (or words) if its sense is that of the whole set where the sense of the other word(s) denotes sub-categories of the set, for example *furniture* has the superordinate sense where *table, chair, stool,* etc. have hyponymous senses.

Suppletive form   An unpredictable and unrelated form of a word for a particular morphosyntactic realization, for example *better* as the comparative form of *good.*

Syncretism   This occurs when a morphosyntactic contrast systematically shows no difference in form even though elsewhere the **morphosyntactic properties** concerned are distinguished inflectionally. For example, both the perfect and past tense forms of regular verbs in English are the same, e.g. *John called the office* and *John has called the office.*

Synecdoche   A **trope** where part of something is used for the whole of it, for example, the villain in the James Bond movie *Goldfinger* was not a finger but a person.

Synonym   A word or expression that has the same sense as another.

Syntactic category   A word's part-of-speech label representing where a word will fit in a sentence. Synonymous with **grammatical category** and **part of speech.**

Taboo   A taboo word is one whose use is socially prohibited (at least in some contexts).

Tautology   Synonym for **semantic redundancy.**

Thesaurus   A dictionary which lists together words which have the same meaning.

Third person   A **morphosyntactic property** pertaining to the person or thing spoken about (*he, she, it, they*).

Trope   Non-literal uses of words or expressions. Examples are: **simile, metaphor, synecdoche** and **metonymy.** Also called 'figure of speech'.

Unmarked   In the case of pairs of antonymous senses and the lexical items which bear those senses, one of the pair of lexical items often has, as well as one of the antonymous senses, a neutral sense which subsumes both antonymous senses. This is the unmarked sense. It is the **lexical item** we use in questions such as 'How tall is she?', where we do not have any idea whether the person is tall or short.

Vocabulary   A set of words that have something other than their linguistic form, **grammatical category**, or meaning in common, particularly a property relating to their use.

Widen   The historical process whereby a word's denotation comes to encompass more than it did.

Further reading •

Abrams, M. H., *A Glossary of Literary Terms,* 9th edn (New York: Harcourt Brace, 2008).

Aitchison, J., *Words in the Mind: An Introduction to the Mental Lexicon,* 3rd edn (Oxford: Blackwell, 2002).

Bauer, L., *Introducing Linguistic Morphology,* 2nd edn (Edinburgh: Edinburgh University Press, 2003).

Blakemore, D., *Understanding Utterances: An Introduction to Pragmatics* (Oxford: Blackwell, 1992).

Chierchia, G., and McConnell-Ginet, S., *Meaning and Grammar: An Introduction* to *Semantics,* 2nd edn (Cambridge, MA: MIT Press, 2000).

Green, G., *Pragmatics and Natural Language Understanding*, 2nd edn (New York: Erlbaum, 1996).

Green, J., *Chasing the Sun: Dictionary-Makers and the Dictionaries They Made* (London: Pimlico, 1997).

Hince, B., *The Antarctic Dictionary: A Complete Guide to Antarctic English* (Coilingwood: CSIRO Publishing, 2000).

Hughes, G., *Swearing: A Social History of Foul Language, Oaths and Profanity in English*, 2nd edn (Oxford: Blackwell, 1998).

Hurford, J. R., Heasley, B. and Smith, M. B., *Semantics: A Coursebook*, 2nd edn (Cambridge: Cambridge University Press, 2007).

Katamba, F. and Stonham, J., *Morphology,* 2nd edn (Basingstoke: Palgrave Macmillan, 2006).

Kearns, K., *Semantics* (Basingstoke: Macmillan, 2000).

Marchand, H., *The Categories and Types of Present-Day English Word-Formation,* 2nd edn (Munich: C. H. Beck'sche Verlagsbuchhandlung, 1969).

Matthews, P. H., *Morphology,* 2nd edn (Cambridge: Cambridge University Press, 1991).

Murray, K. M. E., *Caught in the Web of Words: James Murray and the Oxford English Dictionary* (New Haven, NJ: Yale University Press, 1995).

Neaman, J. S. and Silver, C. G., *A Dictionary of Euphemisms* (London: Unwin Paperbacks, 1983).

Palmer, F. R., *Semantics*, 2nd edn (Cambridge: Cambridge University Press, 1981).

Partridge, E., *A Dictionary of Slang and Unconventional English: Colloquialisms and Catch-phrases, Solecisms and Catachreses, Nicknames, Vulgarisms, and such Americanisms as have been Naturalized* (London, Routledge & Kegan Paul, 1970).

Spencer, A., *Morphological Theory* (Oxford: Blackwell, 1991).

Szymanek, B., *Introduction to Morphological Analysis* (Warsaw: Panstwowe Wydawnictwo
    Naukowe, 1989).

Thomas, O., *Metaphor and Related Subjects* (New York: Random House, 1969).

Electronic resources •

http://www.palgrave.com/language/kuiperandallan/
This site provides electronic resources related to Part I of this book.

http://dictionary.oed.com/entrance.dtl
This is the web site for the OED.

http://www.writeexpress.com/online.html
One of a number of on-line rhyming dictionaries which help you find rhymes for words you
    enter into the dictionary.

http://wordnet.princeton.edu/
A rich resource on words particularly their semantics.

part two

Sounds

Part Two deals with the sounds of the English language.

- We will look at the way speech sounds are produced and the way these sounds are organized in English into distinctively different segments of sound, and suprasegmental sound patterns.
- To deal with articulatory phonetics we will look at the organs of speech and speech production processes, and provide an introduction to the broad phonetic transcription of English and to the International Phonetic Alphabet.
- We will introduce the basic concepts of segmental phonology. These include phonemes, allophones, distinctive features, contrastive, complementary, parallel and defective distribution, and phonotactics and allophonic rules.
- We will also introduce some of the more common allophones and allophonic processes in a number of varieties of English.
- Then we will look at the syllable and at how syllables are structured, at stress patterning, rhythm, tone and intonation.
- We will show that phonological concepts play a significant role in the terminology used to describe sound patterns in poetry.

SKILLS

By the end of this part of the book you should be able to:

- identify the organs of speech, describe speech production and describe any individual speech sound;
- produce and read transcriptions of English in IPA;
- identify phonemes and their allophones, write allophonic rules and identify the more common allophonic processes in English and English dialects;

- distinguish syllables of English and their structure and the major stress and intonation patterns of English; and
- recognize different rhyme schemes and meter in poetry.

Speech Sounds

We take our capacity to communicate through speech for granted. Each day we may utter tens of thousands of words without stopping to consider what we are doing or how we do it. Although communication through speech is our most common form of communication and we think of it as uttering words, the study of the production of speech as sound is the farthest removed of all the branches of linguistics from our intuitions about language. We have intuitions about the grammatical structure of sentences, and the meaning and structure of words, but we have few intuitions about how we produce speech sounds. For example, few speakers have any precise notion of what is physically involved in the production of the word *eye* (which consists of a single speech sound), or the production of the two sounds that constitute the word *me*. Furthermore, they would probably find it difficult if not impossible to describe how these sounds are produced.

This lack of intuition where the production of speech sounds is concerned is all the more surprising when we consider that we often make social judgements about people on the basis of their speech. We may be able to locate them geographically and socially from their pronunciation of a single sentence. Think how easily you can identify someone on the phone from just a few sounds. Yet we often have no idea, in precise phonetic terms, why the speech of one speaker differs from that of another. Furthermore, although some speakers are able to mimic successfully the speech of others, they may have no precise idea of how they achieve this.

The study of the production, perception, and analysis of speech sounds is called 'phonetics'. Phonetics is not a new or recent subject but is centuries old. The Sanskrit grammarian Panini, who lived in India in *c.*500 BC, included material on the subject in his grammar of Sanskrit. In George Bernard Shaw's play *Pygmalion*, and the musical *My Fair Lady*, one of the main characters, Professor Henry Higgins, is a phonetician. He records in detail, using a special set of symbols, what a speaker says so that he can reproduce it exactly.

In this chapter we are going to look at the production of speech sounds (phonetics). But first we shall look at the relationship between sound and spelling, because letters on a page are usually considered to represent the speech sounds of a language (which, in some ways, they do).

4.1   SOUNDS AND SPELLING

The spelling system of English aims to represent in writing the sounds used by speakers of English when they speak their language. It should be fairly easy to achieve this aim. All we need to do is identify the sounds of English, and then assign a unique symbol to each sound. However, what seems straightforward in theory turns out to be more complex in practice.

Consider the following words. Say them out loud and write down how many sounds you make for each one.

(a)	fill	(b)	feel	(c)	tree	(d)	bitter
(e)	thesis	(f)	sing	(g)	drunk	(h)	single
(i)	many	(j)	Mary	(k)	jungle	(l)	meander
(m)	theory	(n)	beer	(o)	furious	(p)	tune
(q)	chew	(r)	tew	(s)	cheer	(t)	phone

Your answers may be something like this:

(a)	3	(b)	3	(c)	3	(d)	4 or 5
(e)	5	(f)	3	(g)	5	(h)	5 or 6
(i)	4	(j)	4	(k)	5	(l)	6 or 7
(m)	4 or 5	(n)	3	(o)	7	(p)	3 or 4
(q)	2	(r)	3 or 4	(s)	3	(t)	3

It would appear that the number of spelling symbols or letters in a word does not necessarily correspond to the number of sounds. Consequently, we cannot tell how many sounds there are in a particular word just by looking at its spelling.

(a)   How many different ways can you find to spell the sound represented by the *ee* of *keep?*

(b)   How many different pronunciations can you find for the spelling ... *ough?*

Answer:

(a)   *e* as in *me*; *ey* as in *key*; *e ... e* as in *scene*; *ee* as in *keep*; *ea* as in *reap*; *ie* as in *belief*; *ie ... e* as in *believe*; *ei* as in *receipt*; *ei ... e* as in *receive*; *i ... e* as in *machine*; *oe* as in *amoeba*; *uay* as in *quay*.

(b)   *though, cough, through, bough, thought, rough, thorough.*

Clearly there is more than one way of spelling a single sound, and a particular spelling may represent more than a single sound. This takes us farther away from our seemingly achievable goal of one sound, one spelling symbol.

To make matters worse, the spelling of a word may contain 'silent' letters. These letters have no sound associated with them (although they may have been pronounced at some earlier time in the history of English). Furthermore, the pronunciation of a word may include a sound that is not represented in the spelling.

(a)   What silent letter can you find in the words *sword, knight, mortgage, doubt, align, would, psychology, honest, who?*

(b)   What 'extra' sound can you find in the pronunciation of the words *use, cute,* and *one?*

(c)   What mismatch do you find between the pronunciation and the spelling in the words *answer* and *salmon?*

Answer:

(a)   s*w*ord, *k*night, mor*t*gage, dou*b*t, a*l*ign, wou*l*d, *p*sychology, *h*onest, *w*ho.

(b)   A *y* sound before the *u* in *use* and *cute,* a *w* sound at the beginning of *one.*

(c)   There is no *w* sound associated with the *w* in *answer,* and no *l* sound in *salmon.*

The following exercise is a listening one. The aim is to listen to words for sounds that are the same.

Can you find examples of the same sound as that italicized in the initial word, in the sentence that follows it?
(*For example*: fea*t*   The old *t*ree in the garden)

(a)   *f*oot   Taking off his gloves, he coughed.

(b)   *b*ook   The bomb went off.

(c)	*scene*	You must clean the window.
(d)	*chin*	To which gin did you switch?
(e)	*your*	Pure acid is bad for the digestion.
(f)	*zoo*	This is a bad business.
(g)	*luck*	I have had enough trouble today.
(h)	*bath*	There's a draught out there.
(i)	*watch*	Which question was that?
(j)	*say*	I saw the fish take the bait.

Having completed this exercise, what can you tell about the relationship between spelling and sound?

Answer:

(a) Taking *off* his gloves, he cou*gh*ed.

(b) The *b*omb went off.

(c) You must cl*ea*n the windows.

(d) To whi*ch* gin did you swi*tch*?

(e) P*u*re acid is bad for the diges*ti*on.　　[*second one only for some pronunciations*]

(f) This i*s* a bad business.

(g) I have had en*ou*gh tr*ou*ble today.

(h) There's a dr*au*ght out there.

(i) Which question *w*as that?　　[*first one only for some pronunciations*]

(j) I saw the fish t*a*ke the b*ai*t.

Some things are again obvious from this exercise:

1. The same written letter does not always represent the same sound.

2. The same sound is not always represented by the same letter.

3. Some letters are not pronounced at all.

4. We pronounce sounds in some places where there is no letter.

Find examples of each case in the above exercise.

. . . .

Many people find spelling difficult. It takes years of practice to be a good speller, and one reason for this is that English spelling does not always directly reflect the sounds people make when they say a word.

From all the above exercises, it is clear that:

1. We interpret words as sequences of sound segments rather than as continuous streams of sound. This is important because we tend to think of words as written rather than spoken.

2. The number of letters in the written version of a word, and the number of sound segments in the spoken version, are not necessarily the same.

3. Sometimes the same word can be pronounced with different sequences of sound segments. For example, *single* can be pronounced with or without a second vowel, *single* or *singil*.

So the English spelling system, which is based on Roman orthography, does not enter into a one-to-one relationship with the sounds of our language. This problem is not unique to English. It occurs, for example, with French, and Scots and Irish Gaelic. However, there are other languages, for example Dutch, German, Italian and Maori, where the relationship between the sounds of the spoken language and the letters of the written language, which represent those sounds, is much more regular than that of English. Even in these languages it is not perfect. That being the case, in the Netherlands and Flanders spelling reform takes place from time to time to regularize the spelling of Dutch.

Given the problems associated with the English spelling system discussed above, it is clear that it is not an ideal means for recording the sounds of English. Furthermore, many languages possess sounds for which there is no symbol in the English spelling system. For example, one of the click sounds found in the Zulu language Xhosa is represented by the English spelling symbol !.

4.1.1   THE INTERNATIONAL PHONETIC ALPHABET

To allow the sounds of English, and any other language, to be written down, a phonetic alphabet was developed, the International Phonetic Alphabet (or IPA). In this alphabet the relationship between symbol and sound is one-to-one. Although we shall be discussing this alphabet in relation to English, it should be kept in mind that the IPA is universal, and that it contains symbols for all the sounds in all known languages. Figure 4.1 is the IPA chart for consonants.

You will see that the table has two dimensions each providing a 'cell' in which there are, at most, two symbols. The horizontal dimension has to do with where in the mouth the sound is produced and the vertical one with how it is produced. Within each cell, the first symbol is for the voiceless one of the pair. The other is voiced. In section 4.2 we will be looking closely at these three factors: voicing, and how and where the sound is produced.

The symbols required for English form a subset of the IPA since not all the possible sounds used in all the world's languages are used in English. In this book

CONSONANTS (PULMONIC)   © 1996 IPA

	Bilabial	Labiodental	Dental	Alveolar	Post alveolar	Retroflex	Palatal	Velar	Uvular	Pharyngeal	Glottal
Plosive	p b			t d		ʈ ɖ	c ɟ	k ɡ	q ɢ		ʔ
Nasal	m	ɱ		n		ɳ	ɲ	ŋ	ɴ		
Trill	ʙ			r					ʀ		
Tap or Flap				ɾ		ɽ					
Fricative	ɸ β	f v	θ ð	s z	ʃ ʒ	ʂ ʐ	ç ʝ	x ɣ	χ ʁ	ħ ʕ	h ɦ
Lateral fricative				ɬ ɮ							
Approximant		ʋ		ɹ		ɻ	j	ɰ			
Lateral approximant				l		ɭ	ʎ	ʟ			

Where symbols appear in pairs, the one to the right represents a voiced consonant. Shaded areas denote articulations judged impossible.

Figure 4.1 The International Phonetic Alphabet – consonants (pulmonic)

broad transcription

narrow transcription

we shall be interested only in the symbols that represent the sounds of English. The IPA 'letters' we will use are also not as detailed as they can be. We will use them for 'broad' transcription leaving out the fine detail. In Chapter 5 we will look at some of the fine detail when we examine how the pronunciation of speech sounds can vary in different situations. Transcriptions which provide this extra detail are termed 'narrow' transcriptions. They use symbols called 'diacritics' to provide the extra detail.

The symbols in the left-hand column of Table 4.1 represent the consonant sounds of English. We may define each symbol in two ways. First, each is assigned a three-term label, which provides a phonetic definition of how the sound represented by a symbol is articulated. These labels are given in the centre column and the terms are explained in section 4.2. Secondly, each phonetic symbol may be associated with a spelling symbol or symbols. Each phonetic symbol represents the sound associated with the underlined spelling symbols in the right-hand column.

Figure 4.2 shows the IPA symbols for vowels. The vowels are arranged on a quadrilateral the significance of which will be explained in section 4.2.3. Of the vowels available, only the ones in Table 4.2 are used in English. The symbols in the left-hand column of this table represent the vowel sounds associated with the underlined spelling symbols in the words that form the centre column. A transcribed version of each word is given in the right-hand column.

By now it should also not surprise you to learn that the sounds of English are not always the same everywhere in the world. The sounds presented here will do for a number of varieties of standard spoken English. We will find out later when we look again at dialects that some of these sounds are not used in some dialects of English, still others are pronounced differently in different places.

Table 4.1   Consonantal sounds of English and their descriptive labels

Stops

[p]	voiceless labial stop	put	capable	cup
[b]	voiced labial stop	but	abandon	cub
[t]	voiceless alveolar stop	tab	butter	put
[d]	voiced alveolar stop	done	edit	pad
[k]	voiceless velar stop	cat	succulent	break
[g]	voiced velar stop	get	begging	drug

Nasals

[m]	voiced labial nasal	mint	examine	drum
[n]	voiced alveolar nasal	nut	money	can
[ŋ]	voiced velar nasal	finger	drink	sing

Fricatives

[f]	voiceless labio-dental fricative	fly	coffee	calf
[v]	voiced labio-dental fricative	verb	having	cave
[θ]	voiceless dental fricative	thin	nothing	moth
[ð]	voiced dental fricative	the	wither	bathe
[s]	voiceless alveolar fricative	sing	blessing	cats
[z]	voiced alveolar fricative	zinc	breeze	rose
[ʃ] or [š]	voiceless post-alveolar fricative	ship	brushing	crush
[ʒ] or [ž]	voiced post-alveolar fricative	rouge	measure	seizure
[h]	voiceless glottal fricative	hope	ahead	

Affricates

[tʃ] or [č]	voiceless post-alveolar affricate	chalk	catching	clutch
[dʒ] or [ǰ]	voiced post-alveolar affricate	jump	digest	rage

Approximants

[w]	voiced labio-velar approximant	watch	away
[l]	voiced alveolar lateral approximant	lie	pulling pull
[r]	voiced alveolar approximant	roast	pouring
[j]	voiced palatal approximant	yacht	cube

To begin our gradual introduction to the dialect sounds of English, you should note that the vowel sounds in Figure 4.2 are based on standard Southern British English, which is a non-rhotic dialect variety of English as is rural southern United States English. In non-rhotic dialect varieties *r* is pronounced only when it is followed by a vowel sound. Speakers of rhotic varieties (for example Irish, General

Table 4.2 The vowel sounds of English

Monophthongs

[iː]	bead	[biːd]
[ɪ] or [i]	bid	[bɪd]
[e] or [ɛ]	bed	[bed]
[æ]	bad	[bæd]
[ɑː]	bard	[bɑːd]
[ɒ]	hot	[hɒt]
[ɔː]	bought	[bɔːt]
[ʊ]	book	[bʊk]
[uː]	booed	[buːd]
[ɜː]	burn	[bɜːn]
[ʌ]	bud	[bʌd]
[ə]	about	[əbaut]

Diphthongs

[ei]	bay	[bei]
[ai]	buy	[bai]
[ɔi]	boy	[bɔi]
[ou]	boat	[bout]
[au]	bough	[bau]
[iə]	beer	[biə]
[eə]	bear	[beə]
[uə]	tour	[tuə]

American or Scottish English) always pronounce *r* no matter what follows. This difference leads to differences in some of the vowel sounds as you can see in Table 4.3.

EXERCISE 4.1

Using the above tables convert the following piece of phonetic script into regular English spelling. Notice that in the phonetic script no use is made of either capital letters or punctuation. You will need to add these to the orthographic representation yourself.

[bʌt ðə riːl hɒrə ʌmʌŋst spaidəz wəz mɔː laiklı tə biː eŋkauntəd ın ðə lævətrı ıtself ðıs wəz ðə red bæk ðə red bæk ız meinlı blæk wıθ ə skɑːlət straip weə ıts spain wʊd bi ıf ıt wɜː ə vɜːtıbreit]

Clive James, *Unreliable Memoirs*

VOWELS

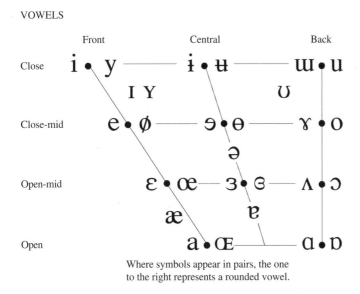

Where symbols appear in pairs, the one
to the right represents a rounded vowel.

Figure 4.2   The International Phonetic Alphabet – vowels

Table 4.3   Differences between a rhotic and non-rhotic variety of English

		Non-rhotic	*Rhotic (Scottish English)*
[ɪə]	beer	[bɪə]	[biːr]
[eə]	bear	[beə]	[beːr]
[uə]	tour	[tuə]	[tuːr]
[ɔː]	four	[fɔː]	[foːr]
[ɜː]	burn	[bɜːn]	[bʌrn]

Using the above tables, transcribe the following text into phonetic script. Remember **EXERCISE 4.2**
that you do not use either capital letters or punctuation in your transcribed
version.

One of the most interesting things about the six-headed Omni-Quarrgs of the
planet Cygo-Swarreldong in the star system of Grudni-Vogar-Actinax, in the
constellation of 'Go-and-upset-another-scrabble-board-Les-I-need-a-new-
name', is that they have only one word to stand for all 400 million nouns,
adjectives, prepositions, verbs and adverbs.

From *The Faber Book of Parodies*,
ed. Andrew Marshall and David Renwick

We can see from the above tables that the phonetic alphabet establishes a one-to-one correspondence between symbol and sound. Each sound is represented by one and only one symbol, while each symbol represents one and only one sound. Given any sound, we can represent it with a single symbol, and given a single symbol, we know which sound it represents. This differs from regular English spelling (or orthography), where one symbol may represent a number of different sounds. As an illustration, first consider the orthographic letter *a*, which represents three different sounds. For example, *a* represents the vowel in the words: *ban, barn,* and *bane.* We transcribe these sounds as [æ], [ɑː] and [eɪ] respectively. Secondly, consider the sound [f], which may be represented in English orthography by *f* as in *fine, ph* as in *physics,* or *gh* as in *laugh.*

Furthermore, the symbols retain their value irrespective of which language is being described. For example, the symbol [t] (which represents the final sound in *put*) represents the same sound in all languages.

The above tables introduce various terms, for example, stop, fricative, labial, velar and monophthong, which are used by phoneticians to describe sounds. To understand these terms we need to consider how sounds are produced.

4.2 ARTICULATORY PHONETICS

Articulatory phonetics is the name given to the study of how we produce speech sounds. To understand how we produce speech sounds, it is necessary to identify the organs involved in the articulation of these sounds.

4.2.1 ORGANS OF SPEECH

In identifying the organs of speech, we shall start at the lips and work our way down to the lungs.

1. Upper and lower lips

    labial

    These are used in the production of labial sounds, and certain vowels. When at rest, the lips usually remain in the closed position, forming an air-tight seal.

2. Upper and lower teeth

3. The roof of the mouth
    If you run the tip of your tongue backwards from your upper front teeth you should feel:

    alveolar ridge

    (a) The alveolar ridge: a hump directly behind the teeth.

    hard palate

    (b) The hard palate: running your tongue tip back from the alveolar ridge you should feel a bony structure, which may rise up quite steeply before it levels out. This is the hard palate.

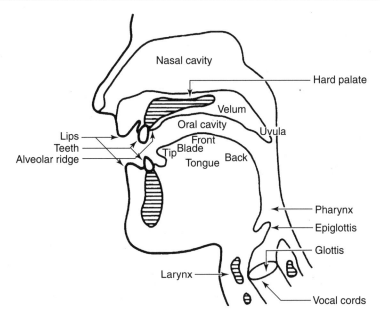

Figure 4.3

(c)   The soft palate or velum, and uvula: as you continue to run your tongue   **soft palate, velum,**
      tip back along the hard palate you should detect a change from the bony   **uvula**
      hard palate to the soft velum, which ends in the uvula. The velum is a
      muscle, which can be raised against the back wall of the pharynx to
      create an air-tight seal between the oral and nasal cavities. When the
      velum is closed, air from the lungs is directed out through the oral cavity.
      During normal breathing the velum is in the lowered position and, with
      the lips forming a seal, air is forced through the nasal cavity. The uvula is
      the short dangling central end of the velum which you can see hanging
      down at the back of the mouth when you look at the back of your throat
      in a mirror.

4. The tongue
    This is a complex muscle, whose flexibility allows it to be moved into a
    number of different positions and shapes. Although there are no obvious divi-
    sions on the surface of the tongue itself, for the description of sounds it may
    be divided into a number of sections:

    (a)   tip or point;

    (b)   blade – this lies below the alveolar ridge;

    (c)   front – this is the middle section which lies below the hard palate;

    (d)   back – this section lies opposite the velum and the uvula;

pharynx

(e)   root – a relatively vertical section which faces backwards towards the back wall of the pharynx.

The tongue is larger than the portion we can see when we look in the mirror. When it is not being used, it does not lie on the floor of the mouth but is held mid-way between the roof and floor of the mouth, approximately in the position it would be if we were to make the vowel sound at the end of *sofa*.

5.   The upper and lower jaws
These bones contain the teeth. The lower jaw is attached to the skull at a point just in front of the bottom of the ears. If you place your first fingers in this position and move your jaw up and down you will feel the hinge. Only the lower jaw will move. The upper jaw is part of the skull.

larynx

6.   The larynx and the vocal cords
The larynx is positioned at the top of the trachea (windpipe). It is a box-like construction consisting of cartilage. The protuberance known as the Adam's apple is the top of the larynx. The vocal cords are located inside the larynx just below the level of the Adam's apple. If you place your thumb and first finger on your larynx and make the sound at the beginning of *mouse* you should feel the vocal cords vibrating.

We refer to the space bounded by the lips and the vocal cords as the vocal tract. It is usual to divide the vocal tract into two cavities:

(a)   the pharynx – this begins behind the velum and ends at the larynx, and

(b)   the oral cavity (mouth) – this runs from the velum to the lips.

The pharynx and the oral cavity are two of the three resonating cavities of the head and neck. The third of these cavities is the nasal cavity, which is divided from the oral cavity by the hard palate. As we noted above, it may be either cut off from or connected to the vocal tract by the action of the velum.

4.2.2   SPEECH PRODUCTION

The production of speech involves three distinct processes. Although each process is independent of the other two, they may interact with each other. It is the interaction of these processes that allows for the great range of possible speech sounds. The three speech production processes are:

initiation
phonation
articulation

(a) initiation, (b) phonation, and (c) articulation.

4.2.2.1   Initiation
The production of any speech sound requires the creation of an airstream in the vocal tract. We create an airstream during breathing when we expand the chest cavity using muscles of the diaphragm at the bottom of the chest cavity and the

intercostal muscles which run between the ribs. The greater volume of the chest cavity created in this way causes air to rush into the lungs providing a fresh oxygen supply for the body. When the intercostal muscles and the diaphragm relax, the volume of the chest cavity decreases causing air to be pushed out of the lungs.

To produce English sounds, the airstream for speech is initiated by the lungs in this way. When the chest contracts air is pushed out of the lungs, creating an out-flowing airstream. We call this airstream 'pulmonic egressive' – pulmonic because it is initiated by the lungs, and egressive because it is out-flowing. The advantages of this airstream can be easily illustrated. Take a deep breath and as you breathe out count aloud. Note how high you managed to count before you ran out of breath. Now breathe out and as you breathe in try counting aloud again. Note how high you manage to count before it becomes impossible to count any further. You should find that you cannot count as high when you breathe in as you can when you breathe out. Speaking while breathing in requires considerably more effort than when breathing out. Imagine the difficulties that would arise if we used only an ingressive airstream.

Although all languages use a pulmonic egressive airstream, there are some languages that use alternative initiation types besides the pulmonic egressive one. Xhosa, a language spoken in South Africa, uses air which is sucked in to produce some of its sounds called 'clicks'. One click sound is similar to the 'tutting' sound we make when telling off someone. The click sounds do not require air to flow either in or out of the lungs, but air does flow into the oral cavity. Consequently, you can make clicks for as long as you like since, while you are making them in your mouth, you can breathe through your nose. But a pulmonic egressive airstream, since it comes from the lungs, requires you to breathe in every now and again. Try making a click slowly and see how you create the suction which allows the air to flow in past the tongue and teeth making the clicking, sucking sound.

4.2.2.2 Phonation

The pulmonic egressive airstream, as it passes through the larynx, may be modified by the vocal cords, through the introduction of voice. Without voice, speech **voice** would be reduced to a barely audible whisper. When the vocal cords are brought together, air passing out from the lungs causes them to vibrate, and voice is produced. Sounds produced with the vocal cords vibrating are called voiced. If the vocal cords are pulled back, they cannot vibrate. Sounds produced without the vocal cords vibrating are called voiceless. When we breathe, the vocal cords are pulled back allowing the air to pass freely in and out of the lungs.

To identify voiced and voiceless sounds, place your thumb and first finger on either side at the top of your larynx. Now make the sound at the beginning of the word *zoo*. You should feel the vocal cords vibrating. Keep your fingers in position but this time make the sound at the beginning of the word *sue*. This time you should not feel your vocal cords vibrating. The first example is a voiced sound, and the second is a voiceless one. Another way to test for a sound's voicing is if you can hold a note while producing it. Only when the vocal cords vibrate can you create a note, that is, sing. You can go up the scale singing *z* sounds but not *s* sounds.

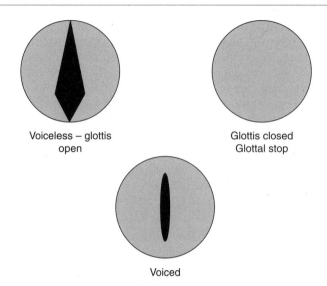

Voiceless – glottis open

Glottis closed Glottal stop

Voiced

Figure 4.4

In Table 4.4 below is a list of words. Say each one out loud, and decide if the sound associated with the underlined letter (or letters) is voiced or voiceless.

Table 4.4

	Voiced	*Voiceless*		*Voiced*	*Voiceless*
bacon			cheese		
salami			cream		
rice			shrimp		
orange			flour		
walnut			grape		

4.2.2.3 Articulation

articulators

active articulator
passive articulator

As the airstream passes through the vocal tract, it may be modified by the movement of the articulators, that is, by the lips and the tongue obstructing its passage through the vocal tract to varying degrees. This process is called articulation. The obstruction of the airstream may occur at any point in the vocal tract, and is the result of an active articulator (one which can move) moving towards a passive articulator (which cannot move). The active articulators are the lips and the tongue, and the passive articulators are locations on the roof of the mouth, for example the alveolar ridge, hard palate, etc.

We usually subdivide the articulatory process into two sections: place (where in the vocal tract obstruction of the air flow occurs) and manner (the degree to which the flow of air is obstructed). The second term of the three-term phonetic labels introduced in Table 4.1 (section 4.11) refers to a place of articulation, and the third to a manner of articulation. In the following sections we shall define and discuss these terms.

4.2.2.3.1 *Place of articulation*   The number of places of articulation may vary from one language to another. The following are those which are required for English and were introduced in section 4.1.1:

1. Labial: these are sounds formed by the articulation of the upper and lower **labial**
    lips, for example [p] as in *pit*.

2. Labio-dental: labio-dental sounds are produced by the lower lip and the
    upper incisors, for example [f] as in *fat*.

3. Dental: make the sound at the beginning of *thick* and prolong it. You   **dental**
    should find that the tip of your tongue makes contact with your incisors. It
    may either make contact with the back of your incisors or protrude slightly
    between them. The symbol for this sound is [θ].

4. Alveolar: to produce an alveolar sound the blade (or tip and blade) of the   **alveolar**
    tongue touches or comes close to the alveolar ridge. The sounds associ-
    ated with the underlined segments in the following words are all alveolar:
    tip [t], *dip* [d], *sip* [s], *zip* [z], and *nip* [n].

5. Post-alveolar (sometimes called alveopalatal or palato-alveolar): these
    sounds are produced by the blade of the tongue articulating with the junc-
    tion of the alveolar ridge and the hard palate. In English the sound at the
    beginning of *church* [tʃ] is post-alveolar.

6. In Indian English the bottom surface of the tongue rather than the top
    touches the alveolar ridge, that is, the tongue is turned downside up. This
    is termed a retroflex *t* and is symbolized as [ʈ]. (Remember, phonetics has   **retroflex**
    to have a symbol for all speech sounds and here is another one.)

7. Palatal: make the sound at the beginning of *yacht* and prolong it. This is   **palatal**
    a palatal sound produced by the front of the tongue articulating with the
    hard palate. (Remember the front of the tongue is the middle section and
    not the tip or blade.)

8. Velar: velar sounds are the result of the back of the tongue articulating with   **velar**
    the soft palate or velum: [k] in *cat*, [g] in *golf*, and [ŋ] in *hang* are all velar.

The places of articulation described above are those necessary for the description of English. Although these places are sufficient for some other lan-guages as well as for English, there are many languages whose speakers use speech sounds which require additional places of articulation. For some French speech sounds the back of the tongue articulates with the uvula. The Dravidian languages of southern India have a series of retroflex consonants for which the tongue is curled backwards so that the underside may make contact with the alveolar ridge.

4.2.2.3.2 *Manner of articulation*   Just as the vocal tract may be obstructed at any point, it is also possible to vary the degree of obstruction, giving a range of 'manners of articulation'. To describe the consonant sounds of English we require the following manners of articulation:

nasal, oral

Nasal vs. oral

As we saw in section 4.2.1 above, the nasal cavity is one of the three cavities of the head and neck involved in speech production. The flow of air from the lungs into the nasal cavity is controlled by the velum, which may be either raised or lowered. If it is lowered then air is free to flow out through the nasal cavity. We call segments produced with air flowing through the nasal cavity 'nasals'. The addition of voice will result in nasal resonance. Any segment produced with the velum raised, closing off the nasal cavity, is oral. You can test for whether a sound is nasal or not by holding your nose to close your nostrils. If a sound is a nasal stop, then the sound cannot exit from your nose once the nostrils are closed since the oral tract is also closed.

If you make the sound at the beginning of *mad* you should find that although your lips form an air-tight seal, air flows out through the nasal cavity. Now make the sound at the beginning of *bad*. You should find that no air flows out at all. Not only do the lips form an air-tight seal, as with the *m* of *mad*, but the velum is raised, sealing off the nasal cavity as well.

The position of the velum may be varied independently of the other speech production processes. Consequently, it is possible to nasalize any segment type, or to have voiceless nasals. For example, French has a set of nasalized vowels, and Hopi (a North American native language) has a set of voiceless nasals.

There are three nasal segments in English – labial [m], alveolar [n] and the velar [ŋ]. All other sounds are oral, that is, the velum is raised and the airstream from the lungs is forced to flow out through the oral cavity.

stop

Stops

To make a stop, the articulators form an air-tight seal somewhere in the vocal tract, and the air flow in the vocal tract is completely obstructed. [p b t d k g] are all stops. Such oral stops are also termed 'plosives'.

The nasals [m n] and [ŋ] are also stops. Although air from the lungs is free to flow out through the nasal cavity, each of these sounds involves a complete obstruction at some point in the oral cavity. Consequently, we also classify nasals as stops.

We can identify three stages in the production of a plosive consonant. The first is the closing stage, where the active articulator approaches the passive one. In the hold stage, the active articulator forms the air-tight seal. As air continues to come out of the lungs, the air pressure behind the seal increases. The release stage occurs when the active articulator is pulled rapidly away from the passive one. This is accompanied by a small explosion as the air behind the seal is released. Occasionally plosives may lack the closing or release stages, but they must always have a hold stage.

fricative

Fricatives

In the production of a fricative, the active articulator comes close enough to the passive one to restrict the flow of air but not to stop it completely. As the air is

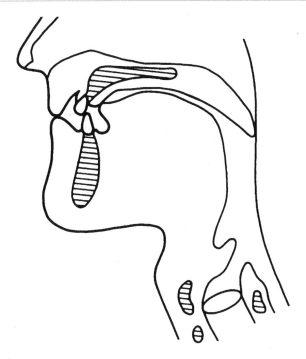

Figure 4.5(a) Position of the articulators for a bilabial oral stop
Note that the lips are shut and the velum is shutting off the nasal passage.

squeezed through the narrow gap between the articulators, it becomes turbulent and an audible hiss is produced: [f v s z] are all fricatives.

Approximants   **approximant**

With approximants the vocal tract is narrowed by the movement of the active articulator towards the passive one. However, unlike fricatives the gap is not narrow enough to produce turbulence. Consequently no audible hiss is produced. The sound at the beginning of *yacht*, [j], is an approximant as is [r].

We can divide the set of approximants into two classes: liquids [l r], and semi-   **liquid** vowels or glides [j w]. The glides are phonetically like vowels. If you make the   **glide** sound at the beginning of *yield,* that is [j], and prolong it, you should find quite quickly that you are actually making [iː], the vowel sound in *bead*. The articulation of [j] is almost identical to that of [iː], but is extremely short. The articulation of [w] is close to that of [uː]. As with [j], if you prolong the initial sound of *wood,* you will find that, just as a prolonged [j] quickly developed into [iː], a prolonged [w] will develop into [uː]; [j] is an extremely short [iː], and [w] is an extremely short [uː].

Despite being phonetically vowels, the glides behave like consonants, and we   **consonant** shall still classify them as such. We can easily illustrate the consonantal behaviour   **consonantal** of the glides. In English the indefinite article occurs as *a* before a noun beginning with a consonant, for example, *a mouse, a frog,* and *an* before a noun beginning with a vowel, for example, *an aardvark, an emu*. Before nouns beginning with either [j] or [w], we find the pre-consonantal form *a,* for example, *a yacht, a wombat.*

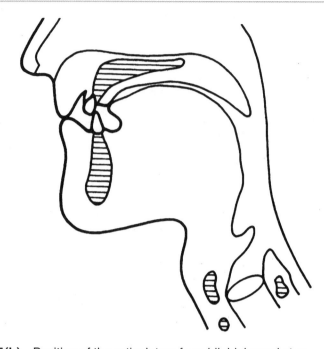

Figure 4.5(b) Position of the articulators for a bilabial nasal stop

Note that the lips are shut but the velum is away from the back wall of the pharynx opening the nasal passage.

Affricates

affricate

Like stops, affricates involve a complete obstruction of the air flow at some point in the vocal tract. However, unlike stops, the obstruction is released gradually. The gradual movement of the active articulator away from the passive one allows the air, which has built up behind the obstruction, to squeeze through the gap, creating turbulence. As with fricatives, the turbulence creates audible friction manifested in a 'hissy' kind of sound. [tʃ], as in the initial sound in *church,* and [dʒ], as in the initial sound in *judge,* are both affricates.

trills, taps, flaps

Trills, taps and flaps

These three manners are less common than those discussed above but do occur in some dialects of English as we shall see later.

For trills the active articulator is held in such a position that the airstream flowing over it causes it to vibrate rapidly against the passive one. The vocal tract is alternately open and closed. In some dialects of Scottish English, the sound at the beginning of *rabbit* is a voiced alveolar trill. French speakers often articulate the same phoneme when they speak English as a uvular trill.

In the articulation of taps and flaps, the active articulator makes a single fast contact with the passive one. In many US dialects of English the alveolar stops are articulated as taps when they occur between two vowels, for example the *t* in *phonetic* or *butter* would be a voiced alveolar tap, [ɾ].

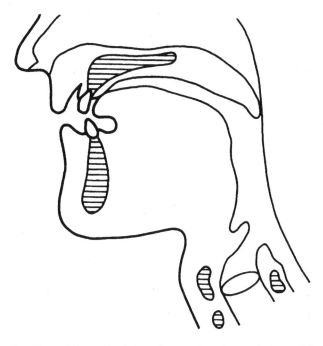

Figure 4.6   Position of the articulators for an alveolar oral stop – [t] or [d]

Note that the blade of the tongue is completely blocking the air flow at the alveolar ridge and the velum is shutting off the nasal passage.

Central vs. lateral   **central, lateral**

This distinction describes the route the airstream takes as it passes out through the oral cavity. In the production of all consonantal segments, except stops, the passage of the pulmonic airstream through the oral cavity may be either central or lateral:

Central.   Make [ʃ] but instead of breathing out, breathe in. The centre of your tongue should feel cold as the air passes over it. [ʃ] is a central sound. For these sounds, the side rims of the tongue form an air-tight seal with the upper molars and gums. This forces the airstream out over the centre of the tongue.

Lateral.   Make [l] and, as above, breath in. This time the sides of your tongue should feel cold as the air passes over them. For lateral segments, a closure is formed somewhere in the centre of the vocal tract. Air passes round this obstruction and out over the sides of the tongue. In English only [l], for example _like_, is lateral. All other segments are central.

From the list of English words below, put the underlined segments into classes   **EXERCISE 4.4**
according to manner of articulation:

   ca̱bin, s̱hips̱, ṯhanks̱, y̱achṯ, g̱aṯher, ḏrop

• •

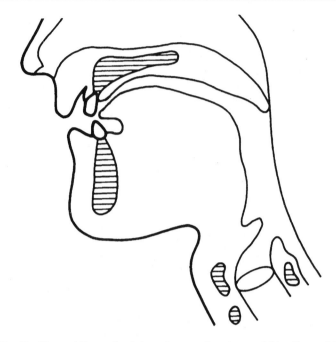

Figure 4.7 Position of the articulators for an alveolar oral fricative – [s] or [z]
Note that the velum is shutting off the nasal passage while a very small gap between the
alveolar ridge and the blade of the tongue exists.

We can use the speech production processes to provide a descriptive framework
for consonants. As we saw in section 4.1.1, it is possible to identify most English consonant segments by a three-term label.

1. The first term will always be either 'voiced' or 'voiceless'.

2. The second term will always refer to the place of articulation, for example
    'labial', 'alveolar' or 'velar'.

3. The third term always refers to the manner of articulation, for example 'stop',
    'fricative', 'affricate', 'approximant', or 'nasal'.

Consider, as an example, [k]:

- In the production of this segment the vocal cords do not vibrate. Therefore,
  [k] is 'voiceless'.

- To produce [k] the back of the tongue articulates with the velum. The place of
  articulation is 'velar'.

- The airstream is completely blocked. Segments produced in this manner are
  'stops'.

[k] is a 'voiceless velar stop'.

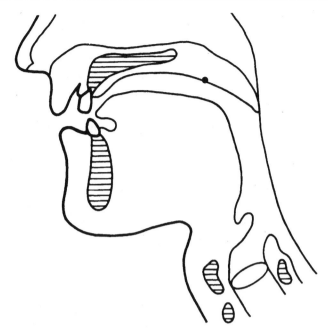

Figure 4.8 Position of the articulators for an alveolar approximant – [r]

Note that the articulators are in almost the same position as for [s] and [z] but the blade of the tongue and the alveolar ridge are a little further apart.

[l] requires an extra label. It is usually described as a 'voiced alveolar lateral approximant'. The term 'lateral' is required to distinguish [l] from [r], which is a 'voiced alveolar approximant'. Note that as all segments in English, apart from [l], are central, we do not include central in our description of consonants.

Provide three-term labels for the following segments: **EXERCISE 4.5**

[p]

[g]

[z]

[j]

· ·

In this exercise do not be misled by the orthography.   **EXERCISE 4.6**

(a)   Identify all the words in the following that contain an alveolar fricative
       between two vowel sounds:

         craze, case, rose, busy, doze, electricity, ace, raising, pleasing

(b)   Identify all the words in the following that begin with an approximant:

link, talk, quick, unit, sew, judge, youth, write, onion

(c)   Identify all the words in the following that end with a voiceless fricative:

dogs, laugh, boxes, rags, cuts, through, tough, bath

(d)   Identify all the words in the following that end with a vowel sound:

fly, put, stop, flow, lime, bit, name, through, rose, type

· ·

4.2.3 VOWELS

vowel

The description of consonants is based on a combination of the following: voicing, that is all consonants are either voiced or voiceless, the place of obstruction, for example dental, alveolar or palatal, and the degree of obstruction of the air flow, for example stop, fricative or approximant. Since it is the combination of voice, place and manner that defines the quality of each consonant, by using these three qualities we are able (as we saw above in section 4.2.2) to provide descriptive labels for all English consonants. Unlike consonants, the quality of a vowel is not the product of a combination of voice, and place and manner of articulation, but is determined by the shape of the vocal tract.

We can alter the shape of the vocal tract by varying the position of the tongue and the lips: the height of the tongue, which part of the tongue is raised or lowered, and the shape of the lips. With the addition of voice we create a range of different vowel sounds.

In describing vowels we refer to the position of the tongue and lips, and not to the place or degree of obstruction. Tongue position may be specified in two ways: vertically (how high or low is the tongue) and horizontally (which section of the tongue is raised or lowered). The lips are either rounded or unrounded. It is these three parameters (vertical and horizontal tongue position, and lip rounding) that are used to describe the articulation of vowels.

4.2.3.1 Tongue position
In section 4.2.1 we said that, when at rest, the tongue does not lie on the floor of the mouth but is held mid-way between the roof and the floor of the mouth, approximately in the position for the final vowel sound in *sofa*. If we take the rest position as the starting point, we may plot tongue position in the articulation of vowels in terms of movement from this point.

To establish the rest position of the tongue, produce the final vowel in *sofa*, [ə]. Try to maintain this articulation and then make the vowel in *bead*, [iː]. Alternate between these two vowels until you feel confident about your perception of the movement of your tongue. Do you detect any movement and if so in which direction?

In producing [iː], you should detect a forward and upward movement of the front of your tongue from the rest position towards the hard palate. You may check this by making [iː] and then, while articulating this vowel, move your tongue up until it touches the roof of your mouth and forms a stop. The front of your tongue will most likely be in contact with your hard palate. Now try alternating [ə] with [æ], as in *bad*. As you articulate [æ], you should detect a downward movement of both the front of your tongue and your lower jaw (away from the rest position and hard palate).

Relative to [ə], the tongue moves forwards and up for [iː]. Consequently we refer to [iː] as a close or high vowel. For [æ] there is lowering of the tongue and jaw relative to [ə], and therefore we refer to [æ] as a low or open vowel. **high** **low**

If you alternate [ə] with the vowel in *bed*, [e], your tongue will move forwards but will probably only move up or down very slightly if at all. Given this lack of vertical movement, we refer to this vowel as a mid vowel. This gives us a three-place scale for tongue movement in the vertical axis: high, mid and low. Try articulating these three vowels in sequence. You should become aware of the progressive lowering of the tongue and opening of the mouth as your lower jaw moves down. **mid vowel**

For some languages we may require a four-place scale, for example if we have [iː], [e], [ɛ] and [æ]. It is easy to accommodate this series into our three-place division by dividing the mid-point in two, giving high-mid, [e], and low-mid, [ɛ]. These four places are also called *open, half open, half close* and *close*. **high-mid** **low-mid**

In the articulation of [iː], [e] and [æ] it was the front of the tongue that moved, either up (towards the hard palate) or down (away from the hard palate). Vowels that involve the movement of the front of the tongue in the region below the hard palate we shall label as front vowels. This now gives us a two-term label for each of these vowels: [iː] is a 'high front vowel', [e] is a 'mid front vowel', and [æ] is a 'low front vowel'. The first term defines the position of the tongue in the vertical axis while the second identifies which horizontal section of the tongue is involved. **front vowel**

If [iː], [e] and [æ] are all front vowels, then what horizontal section is involved in the articulation of the vowels in *bard*, [ɑː], *bought*, [ɔː], and *booed*, [uː]? In attempting this exercise, contrast each of the vowels given above with [ə] as in the previous exercise. In doing this it may be useful to begin with [uː] and then [ɑː].

With [ɑː], [ɔː], and [uː] you should notice that it is the back of your tongue that moves from the rest position. In the articulation of [uː], the back of the tongue moves up and back from the rest position towards the soft palate or velum. You may check this by articulating [uː] and then moving the tongue slightly up until it makes contact with the soft palate. At this point you should have made a velar stop, either [k] or [g] depending on whether or not you retain the voicing of the vowel: [uː] is a 'high back' vowel. For [ɑː] your tongue (and perhaps your lower jaw) will **back** move down: [ɑː] is a 'low back' vowel. In articulating [ɔː] your tongue may move only slightly up or down (if at all) but will move back: [ɔː] is a 'mid back' vowel.

It is not just the front and the back of the tongue that are involved in the articulation of vowels, the centre is also used. In English, [ə], [ʌ] and [ɜː] are all central vowels. The middle of the tongue is involved in the articulation of these vowels.

4.2.3.2 Lip position

The position of the lips, as well as the tongue, contributes to vowel quality. Alternate the vowels [iː] and [uː]. You should notice that, apart from sounding like a klaxon, you change the position of your lips as you move from one to the other. For [iː] the lips are unrounded, whereas for [uː] they are rounded. Lip position may be varied independently of the tongue position. Make the [iː] vowel again, round your lips but do not move your tongue. When you round your lips you should produce a close (high) front rounded vowel. This vowel is identified by the symbol [y] and occurs in French *bureau*. While making a close front rounded vowel, move your tongue from the close position to the open position. How open does the vowel become before it ceases to be round? You should be able to produce high, high-mid, and low-mid front rounded vowels. It is rather difficult to produce a low rounded vowel. The symbols [ø] and [œ] are used to represent the high-mid and low-mid front rounded vowels, respectively. Such vowels occur in many languages, for example French, German, Swedish and Danish. (If you alternate between the rounded and unrounded sounds in the high-mid or low-mid area you sound more like a Swedish klaxon.) Just as it is possible to find front rounded and unrounded vowels in languages, central rounded and back unrounded vowels also occur in languages. For example, Mandarin, Japanese, and Fe?Fe? (an African language) all have a high back unrounded vowel, [ɯ].

4.2.3.3 Monophthong and diphthong

monophthong

If the sound of a vowel remains relatively unchanged during its production, then we call it a monophthong (one sound): [e] and [ɑː] are monophthongs.

diphthong

If the sound of a vowel continually changes within a single syllable then we call it a diphthong (2 sounds). The change in sound quality may be achieved by a movement of the tongue and/or lips. The vowels in *toy, tie* and *town* ([ɔi], [ɑi], and [ɑu] respectively) are all diphthongs. A diphthong thus moves from a starting position to a finishing position. Accordingly they are often classified as opening, in which case the mouth opens during their production, or closing in which case the mouth moves to a closer position, or centring in which case the final element on the diphthong is a central vowel.

opening diphthong
closing diphthong
centring diphthong

vowel quadrilateral

It is possible to represent graphically the position of the tongue in the articulation of vowels using a vowel quadrilateral. The quadrilateral represents the shape of the inside of the mouth in cross-section. The vertical axis represents the vertical position of the tongue on the high–low scale, while the horizontal is used to identify which section of the tongue is involved in the vertical movement. Using these two axes, we may position vowels on the chart in relation to the position of the tongue in their articulation.

While monophthongs may be indicated by a single point (or area) on the chart, diphthongs require a starting point, direction of movement, and a finishing point.

The IPA, as you saw in Figure 4.2, has a set of vowels which it uses as reference points: four front vowel positions and four back vowel positions, each with a rounded and unrounded version. They are at the four corners of the vowel quadrilateral and at two equally distanced points from the extremities at the mid-high and mid-low positions. These are called the cardinal vowels. They are not the **cardinal vowels** vowels of any particular language but can be used to locate vowels in general. If you know what they sound like, then you can compare other vowel sounds with them to get an idea of their position.

4.2.3.4 Long and short vowels

Vowels in English, and other languages, may be either long or short. This is referred to as 'length' or 'quantity'. (The difference between the vowel sounds is referred to as 'quality'.) All vowels are either long or short; [ɪ e æ ʌ ə ɒ ʊ] are all short in English. The remaining monophthongs and all diphthongs are long.

To conclude this section on speech production, we can compare the whole process, and the anatomy that makes it possible, to the bagpipes. Bagpipes

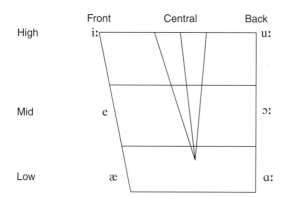

Figure 4.9

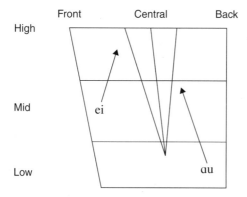

Figure 4.10

consist of a bag, which is full of air, connected to pipes. Similarly, the lungs are a pair of bags connected to tubes. The pipes of the bagpipes have a double reed inside at their base. When the bag is compressed, the air is forced out and passes between the reeds causing them to vibrate just like the vocal folds are caused to vibrate when the lungs are compressed. The sound created by the vibration in both cases then travels along the rest of the tube and we hear a single note droned by the pipe. This is much the same as the nasal cavity, whose air volume cannot be changed. If the sound created at the vocal folds produces a single note that passes out through the nose, we will hear a single note being droned. One of the pipes on the bagpipes, called the chanter, has holes in it so that the volume of air may be more radically altered. As the player covers or uncovers the holes, the note changes appreciably. This is like the oral cavity, which can have the volume of air within it changed by the degree to which the jaw is open, and by the placement of the tongue and the position of the lips. As a result it can produce different harmonics of the note created at the vocal folds.

In essence, then, the vocal mechanism looks rather like the diagram in Figure 4.11.

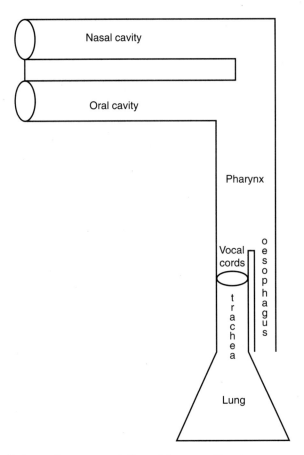

Figure 4.11   Schematic representation of the vocal tract

The differences between the vocal tract and the bagpipes are also of course important. The note created by the vocal folds can change in a way that the double reed's note in a bagpipe cannot. The vocal tract has a valve in the form of the velum, which allows the airway to the nasal passage to be cut off. Bagpipes have no tongue within the chanter and no moveable lips at its extremity. Notwithstanding all these differences, you can see from the diagram in Figure 4.11 that the oral tract is essentially a bent tube through which exhaled air passes. As it passes out it may be modified in a variety of ways, many of which create speech sounds.

Further exercises. •

For each of the following phonetic labels provide the correct symbol and a word that begins with that sound.
(*For example*: voiced labial stop [b] *b*in)

EXERCISE 4.7•

(a)   voiced palatal approximant

(b)   high back vowel

(c)   voiceless post-alveolar fricative

(d)   voiced alveolar nasal

(e)   voiced labio-dental fricative

(f)   high front vowel

(g)   voiced velar stop

(h)   voiceless dental fricative

(i)   low front vowel

(j)   voiced alveolar lateral approximant

Convert the following passages of phonetic script into regular English orthography. Notice that in the phonetic script no use is made of either capital letters or punctuation. You will need to add these to the orthographic representation yourself.

EXERCISE 4.8•

[ɪf ə red bæk bɪt juː ɒn ðə bəhɑind juː wɜː left wɪθ ðə prɒbləm əv weə tə put ðə tʊənəkei ənd nɒt lɒŋ tə θɪŋk əbɑut ɪt nɔː kʊd juː ɑːsk eniːwʌn tə sʌk ɑut ðə pɔizən ʌnles juː njuː ðəm verɪ wel ɪndiːd]

Clive James, *Unreliable Memoirs*

[hiː mʌst həv hɜːd hɑu bɔːrɪŋ ðei wɜː sɪns hiː nevə əpiəd bʌt ɪt wɒz nɒt fə wɒnt əv hævɪŋ hɪz neim ɪnvoukt ðə houl fækəltɪ sælɪveitɪd ɒn mæs ət ðə miə menʃən əv hɪm]

Clive James, *Unreliable Memoirs*

EXERCISE 4.9 In each of the words in Table 4.5 there is an error in the transcription of the consonant sounds, resulting in a non-existent pronunciation of that word. Circle the error and write the correct version in the space provided.

Table 4.5

(a)	strength	[strengθ]	[	]
(b)	crime	[crɑim]	[	]
(c)	wishing	[wɪshɪŋ]	[	]
(d)	wives	[wɑivs]	[	]
(e)	these	[θiːz]	[	]
(f)	hijacking	[hɑijækɪŋ]	[	]
(g)	yellow	[jellou]	[	]
(h)	thesis	[ðiːsɪs]	[	]
(i)	extra	[extrə]	[	]
(j)	chop	[chɒp]	[	]

EXERCISE 4.10 In each of the words in Table 4.6 there is an error in the transcription of the vowel sounds, resulting in a non-existent pronunciation. Circle the error and write the correct version in the space provided in the table.

Table 4.6

(a)	eat	[eːt]	[	]
(b)	like	[liːk]	[	]
(c)	shout	[ʃout]	[	]
(d)	open	[ɔːpən]	[	]
(e)	bait	[bɑit]	[	]
(f)	equal	[ekwəl]	[	]
(g)	aura	[ɑurə]	[	]
(h)	bottle	[bɔːtəl]	[	]
(i)	seize	[seiz]	[	]
(j)	tough	[tɔːf]	[	]

The articulation of consonants involves the movement of an active articulator (the lips and tongue) towards a passive one (the teeth and points along the roof of the mouth). The passive articulator identifies the place of articulation. For example, if the passive articulator is the alveolar ridge, the place of articulation is alveolar. Given any two of the active articulator, passive articulator or the place of articulation, we can easily identify the third. For example, if the active articulator is the blade of the tongue, and the place of articulation is the alveolar ridge, then the passive articulator must be the alveolar ridge. Now fill in the blanks in Table 4.7.

EXERCISE 4.11 •

Table 4.7

Active articulator	Passive articulator	Place of articulation
Lower lip	Upper incisors	
	Soft palate	Velar
Front of tongue		Palatal
Tip of tongue		Dental

Provide the symbol that corresponds to each of the phonetic descriptions in Table 4.8, and provide a word that begins with that sound.
(*Example*: voiced velar stop   [g]   *gone*)

EXERCISE 4.12 •

Table 4.8

Phonetic description		Phonetic symbol	Example
(a)	voiceless labio-dental fricative		
(b)	voiced palatal approximant		
(c)	voiced post-alveolar affricate		
(d)	voiced dental fricative		
(e)	voiced alveolar lateral		
(f)	voiced velar nasal		
(g)	voiceless dental fricative		
(h)	voiced alveolar approximant		

EXERCISE 4.13 •   For each of the following symbols provide the correct phonetic label and a word that begins with that sound.
(*For example*: [s]   voiceless alveolar fricative   *stop*)

(a)   [d]

(b)   [m]

(c)   [uː]

(d)   [f]

(e)   [dʒ]

(f)   [æ]

(g)   [w]

(h)   [k]

(i)   [r]

(j)   [e]

EXERCISE 4.14 ••   Study the following piece of transcription carefully and then answer the questions below:

[ðə fɜːst vjuː əv ɑustreiljə wɒz ðə koust niə pɜːθ riːfs whait biːtʃəz ʃælow wɔːtə laik ðə juːs əv emrəldz huːndridz əv swimiŋ puːls ðə kʌlər əv pɔːl njuːmənz aiz ətestəd tʊ æfluːəns]

Clive James, *Flying Visits*

(a)   There are three errors in the transcription of vowels, and four errors in the transcription of consonants. Identify and list each of these errors, and provide a correct transcription of the words in which they occur. (*For example*: [qwɪk] – [q] should be [k] giving [kwɪk].)

(b)   Pick out one word that begins and ends with a voiceless stop, one that contains a diphthong between two alveolar approximants, and one that contains a cluster of three consonants.

EXERCISE 4.15 ••   Consider the passage below and answer the questions that follow:

[æt ðə swiːdɪʃ bɔːdə sʌm tuː ɑuəz frɒm ɒzlou ðə bʌs stɒpt æt ə kʌstəmz post in ðə wʊdz ænd whail ðə draivə went intə ðə hʌt tə sɔːt out ðə peipəwɜːk moust əv ðə pæsɪndʒəz incluːdɪŋ miː nd ðə tuː aid fɔːkaːst klætəd daun ðə steps nd stʊd stæmpɪŋ ɑuə fiːt in ðə kould snou nd smoukɪŋ sɪgəretts bai ðə fistfʊl]

Bill Bryson, *Neither Here nor There*

(a)   There are three words with consonant errors in the passage and two words with vowel errors. Find these words and provide a corrected transcription. Note: the vowel errors are not possible in any dialect of English.

(b)   Find two words containing a cluster of two stop consonants at the same place of articulation.

(c)   Find a word containing a fricative approximant cluster between two vowel sounds.

Convert the following passages into phonetic script: **EXERCISE 4.16••**

I caught this morning morning's minion, kingdom of daylight's dauphin,
    dapple-dawn-drawn Falcon, in his riding
Of the rolling level underneath him steady air, and striding High there,
    how he rung upon the rein of a wimpling wing

                                    Gerard Manley Hopkins, *The Windhover*

...so I made my way out, saying goodbye to Todd and Alison and Sue and all the other wonderful new friends, I'd made, and stole a cab. No, not literally. It's an old-established New York custom: when you see a luggage-laden traveller hailing a cab, you obstruct his passage while he's trying to haul his gear and jump into the cab ahead of him, laughing heartily as you do so.

                                    Stephen Brook, *New York Days, New York Nights*

There was trouble over the oranges. The customs officers started asking questions and making difficulties. Perhaps the right man wasn't on duty or hadn't been paid enough. It seemed a lot of fuss over a crate of fruit. Were the oranges stuffed with drugs, or diamonds, or explosives? Fantastic explanations proposed themselves more readily than answers.

                                    Simon Loftus, *A Pike in the Basement*

chapter 5

The Phonology of English

INTRODUCTION – SOUNDS: SAME vs DIFFERENT

In section 4.2, we established a framework for the description of sounds. This framework is based on articulatory phonetics. Although we concentrated on the sounds of English, with some additions to the framework it is possible to describe the sounds of any language that can be produced in the vocal tract. It is also possible to describe any sound in detail.

Consider the following words:

   1. s*t*em   2. *t*ip

Pronounce the first word with your hand held just in front of your mouth, and then pronounce the second word. Do you perceive any difference in your pronunciation of *t* between the two words?

aspirated

You should feel a burst of air as you make the *t* in the second word, but not in the first. The second *t* is usually described as aspirated, while the first is a voiceless alveolar stop. We do not introduce a completely new symbol to represent the second *t* sound but add a diacritic, an additional mark, to the original symbol. These diacritics have no sound value in themselves but give us more detail concerning the pronunciation of the symbol to which they are added. The diacritic that signals aspiration is a raised *h*, which occurs to the right of aspirated consonant. For *t* this gives [tʰ].

As you would expect, the IPA has a set of diacritics to show all such possible additional details in the articulation of speech sounds. If we include diacritics in our transcriptions, we are, as we said in the previous chapter, engaged in narrow phonetic transcription. The IPA diacritics are given in Figure 5.1.

146

DIACRITICS   Diatricis may be placed above a symbol with a descender, e.g. ŋ̊

̥	Voiceless	n̥ d̥	̈	Breathy voiced	b̤ a̤	̪	Dental	t̪ d̪
̬	Voiced	s̬ t̬	̰	Creaky voiced	b̰ a̰	̺	Apical	t̺ d̺
ʰ	Aspirated	tʰ dʰ	̼	Linguolabial	t̼ d̼	̻	Laminal	t̻ d̻
̹	More rounded	ɔ̹	ʷ	Labialized	tʷ dʷ	̃	Nasalized	ẽ
̜	Less rounded	ɔ̜	ʲ	Palatalized	tʲ dʲ	ⁿ	Nasal release	dⁿ
̟	Advanced	u̟	ˠ	Velarized	tˠ dˠ	ˡ	Lateral release	dˡ
̠	Retracted	e̠	ˤ	Pharyngealized	tˤ dˤ	̚	No audible release	d̚
̈	Centralized	ë	̴	Velarized or Pharyngealized	ɫ			
̽	Mid-centralized	e̽	̝	Raised	e̝	(ɹ̝ = voiced alveolar fricative)		
̩	Syllabic	n̩	̞	Lowered	e̞	(β̞ = voiced bilabial approximant)		
̯	Non-syllabic	e̯	̘	Advanced Tongue Root	e̘			
˞	Rhoticity	ɚ a˞	̙	Retracted Tongue Root	e̙			

Figure 5.1   The International Phonetic Alphabet – diacritics

Now pronounce:

   3. no*t* yet   4. a*t*las   5. no*t* now   6. eigh*t*h   7. ha*t*pin,

paying attention to the position of your tongue in the articulation of *t*. Compare the position of your tongue in each case with its position for the *t* in *stem*. In *eighth*, try closing your teeth together as you make the *t*.

You should find that your articulation of *t* varies for each word. For *not yet*, your tongue is probably further back towards the hard palate. In this example [t] is described as 'palatalized'. The diacritic for palatalization is a raised *j* placed to the right of the symbol for the palatalized sound. This gives [tʲ]. If you say these words quickly enough you will probably pronounce the sequence of [t] [j] as [tʃ].

homorganic

lateral release

In *atlas* we have a sequence of two alveolar consonants, a voiceless stop and a lateral approximant. (We refer to sequences of consonants with the same place of articulation as homorganic sequences.) In releasing the stop you do not move the entire blade of the tongue but only the sides. The centre remains in contact with the alveolar ridge. We call this 'lateral release' and transcribe the *t* in this instance with a superscript l, [tˡ].

We have another homorganic sequence in *not now*, a voiceless stop and a nasal. As with the *t* in *atlas*, you do not release the *t* by moving the tongue from the alveolar ridge. In fact the tongue does not move at all. In this case the stop is released through the nasal cavity. The velum is in the raised position for the oral stop but is lowered for the homorganic nasal. The compressed air trapped in the oral cavity can then escape through the nasal cavity. We call this 'nasal release' and transcribe this *t* with a superscript n, [tⁿ].

nasal release

dentalized

If you try to close your teeth for the *t* in *eighth*, you may find your tongue in the way. In this case we have a dentalized version. For many speakers, their tongue protrudes between their incisors when they articulate dental or dentalized sounds. Speakers who do not put their tongue between their incisors for this sound will probably articulate this *t* by placing the tip of their tongue on the back of their incisors. Dentalization is indicated by a diacritic, which resembles a small incisor, placed below the appropriate symbol, [t̪].

In the final example, your tongue may move towards the alveolar ridge, and it may even make contact, but it is more than likely that you do not release the stop. If you consider your pronunciation carefully, you will probably find that you make and release the labial stop at the beginning of *pin*, but you do not release the stop at the end of *hat*. In this example [t] is described as 'unreleased', and transcribed as [t̚], where ˺ is the diacritic for an unreleased stop.

unreleased

This exercise demonstrates that there are, at least, seven ways of pronouncing *t* in English. It is possible, with an expanded phonetic framework, to describe these sounds in some detail. If there are seven types of *t* in English, then what use do speakers of the language make of these sounds? The answer is none. Until you were asked to consider carefully your pronunciation of the above words, you were probably unaware of these differences but simply thought of them all as *t*. Although they are all phonetically quite different you 'heard' them all as *t*. For speakers of English, whether a *t* is aspirated, dentalized, palatalized or unreleased is unimportant. None of these phonetic properties seems to be involved in recognizing *t*. Speakers of English are unaware of these differences. In fact, they consider all seven to be 'the same'. This point may be simply illustrated. Aspirate the *t* in *stem*. Does the substitution of the unaspirated *t* by the aspirated version give a different word? No. Substitution of one *t* sound for another does not produce a different word. It simply results in a somewhat unusual pronunciation of that word. You can test this further by replacing all the *t* sounds by the dentalized version. In each case the result will be the same. The meaning of the word will not change but your pronunciation will be slightly odd (and in some cases difficult).

Again, consider *tip*. Using the table of consonant sounds of English introduced in Chapter 4.1.1, try replacing the initial sound (a voiceless alveolar stop) by another single consonant sound from the list, for example [d] (a voiced alveolar stop). Each time where replacement results in a different word, record the consonant involved and its three- (or four-) term label.

You should have found that at least: [p] voiceless labial stop, [d] voiced alveolar stop, [n] voiced alveolar nasal, [s] voiceless alveolar fricative, [z] voiced alveolar fricative, [l] voiced alveolar lateral approximant, and [w] voiced labio-velar approximant may be substituted for [t] and make another word. Whereas the phonetically different *t* sounds in the earlier exercise could be considered as the 'same' sound, speakers of English clearly consider each of the sounds in the above exercise to be different. These sounds are used to distinguish one English word from another.

Phonetic properties such as aspiration and palatalization are not distinctive in English. Their use does not distinguish one word from another. However, properties such as voiced, voiceless, labial, alveolar, stop, fricative, approximant and nasal *are* distinctive. They are used to distinguish one word from another. A change in one or more of these phonetic properties in a single sound may result in what a speaker considers to be a different sound, or, if that sound is part of a word, then such a change may result in a different word.

In English, phonetic properties such as aspiration and palatalization are automatic, that is, they are not within the speaker's control. Native speakers of English have to try hard not to aspirate the *t* sound in words like *ten* or *top*. However, phonetic properties like voiced and voiceless; labial, dental and velar; and stop, fricative and approximant are within the control of the speaker. It is these properties that speakers of English use to distinguish one sound from another, and one word from another.

It would appear that we can identify two different sets of phonetic properties in English. First, there are those that distinguish one sound from another, and therefore one word from another. These properties are information-bearing. If we change the initial voiceless stop of *tip* to a voiced one, we know that a different word has been uttered. Secondly, there is the set of properties that provide a more detailed description of the pronunciation of a sound, but do not distinguish one sound (or word) from another. The members of this second set are not information-bearing. In distinguishing the initial sound of *tip* from that of *dip*, a property such as aspiration is unnecessary or redundant. The presence versus absence of aspiration is not necessary to distinguish [t] from [d], whereas voiceless versus voiced is.

The first set of (information bearing) properties we shall describe as distinctive, and the second as non-distinctive. This division of phonetic properties may be extended to the segments themselves. We have a set of distinctive segments

phoneme

allophone

that are defined solely by distinctive phonetic properties, those that speakers of the language use to distinguish one word from another. We shall call the members of this set 'phonemes', and indicate their status by placing them inside slanting brackets, for example /t/ and /d/. Sounds whose description includes one or more non-distinctive properties, and does not distinguish one word from another, we shall call 'allophones' (variant forms of a phoneme) and place them inside square brackets, for example [tʰ] and [t˥] in English. The identification and study of these distinctive sounds, and their relation to the non-distinctive sounds, is, as we indicated in Chapter 1, called phonology.

The set of properties that are distinctive is not constant throughout the world's languages. Consequently, the set of distinctive sound segments may differ from language to language. Although, for example, aspiration is non-distinctive in English, it is distinctive in languages such as Korean and Thai. Speakers of these languages will hear the difference between, for example, [tʰ] and [t]. These two languages have phonemic voiceless aspirated stops /pʰ tʰ kʰ/, whereas in English such segments are allophones of the voiceless stops. A speaker of English does not 'hear' the difference between the aspirated and unaspirated voiceless stops, but a speaker of Korean or Thai listening to English will hear the difference. Furthermore, whereas the distinction between voiced and voiceless stops is distinctive in English, there are languages such as Maori and Tongan where it is not. In these languages sounds such as [b d g] are not phonemes, but are allophones of /p t k/ respectively. Speakers of Tongan do not 'hear' the difference between /p/ and /b/ in English. For them these two sounds are the 'same'.

5.1   IDENTIFICATION OF PHONEMES

We may test whether the difference between two sounds is phonologically important by substituting one sound for another in a word. If this substitution produces a different word then we have identified a phoneme. For example, earlier we replaced the [t] in *tip* with [d]. This gave us *dip*, which is different from *tip*. We can conclude that [t] and [d] are allophones of different phonemes and, as such, we place them in slanted brackets rather than square ones to identify them as phonemes, that is /t/ and /d/, rather than [t] and [d].

minimal pair test
minimal pair

This method of testing for the phonological importance of a sound is called the minimal pair test. The two words, for example *tip* and *dip*, which differ in one and only one sound are called a minimal pair. Any two words that differ in one and only one sound are a minimal pair, for example *cheap* and *jeep* – [tʃiːp] vs [dʒiːp]; *wing* and *sing* – [wɪŋ] vs [sɪŋ]; and *fill* and *kill* – [fɪl] vs [kɪl]. Pairs of words that differ in more than a single sound are not minimal pairs, for example *kill* and *thrill* – [kɪl] vs [θrɪl]; and *wing* and *fling* – [wɪŋ] vs [flɪŋ] are not minimal pairs. To establish the phonemic status of a sound, it is only necessary to identify one minimal pair. Always remember that we are considering sounds and not spelling symbols. *Hand* and *hang* differ in a single spelling symbol but in two sounds – [hænd] vs [hæŋ], and therefore are not a minimal pair.

> Consider the word *pin*, /pɪn/. Substitute the other consonant sounds from Table 4.1 for /p/. Which ones, when substituted for /p/, give another English word?

You should have found that /b t d k f θ s ʃ tʃ dʒ w l/ (*bin, tin, din, kin, fin, thin, sin, shin, chin, gin, win* and *Lynn*) can all be substituted for /p/ to give another English word.

In the above exercise, we established a phonetic frame – [__ɪn], and then substituted various sounds in the initial position of this frame. Each time the placing of a sound in this frame resulted in a different word, we identified a phoneme of English. All the sounds that can be substituted for /p/ to make another English word are phonemes of English.

This method of identification of phonemes (the minimal pair test) is based on the notion of 'minimal contrast'. Two or more sounds in a language contrast if they can appear in the same position in the same frame. All the sounds you identified above appear in the same position in the same frame, that is, before [ɪn]. These sounds are said to be in contrastive distribution. The minimal pair test relies on the notion of contrastive distribution.

contrastive distribution

What do we mean by distribution? Remember the train analogy from Chapter 1. We suggested that every unit in the train has a special position vis-à-vis the other units in the train. This position is its distribution, that is, its place in the sequence. Contrastive distribution is, therefore, a place in a sequence where two sounds contrast one with the other. In a train, if we put a freight car in the location where we had a passenger car, they would be in contrastive distribution. We perceive them to be different in this location.

Although we have applied the minimal pair test only to the consonant phonemes of English, it is possible to use this method to identify the vowel phonemes of English. For example, taking /pɪn/ as our frame, we can try substituting various vowel sounds for /ɪ/, and as for the consonants, each time we get a new word we have identified a vowel phoneme of English, for example *pen, pan, pain, pun* and *pine*, /pen pæn peɪn pʌn paɪn/. We can also substitute other consonant sounds for /n/, for example *pip, pit, pill, pith, pitch, pick, pig* and *ping*, /pɪp pɪt pɪl pɪθ pɪtʃ pɪk pɪg pɪŋ/.

• •

How many minimal pairs can you find for (a) *pill*, (b) *hot* and (c) *high*?

EXERCISE 5.1

• •

5.1.1 COMPLEMENTARY DISTRIBUTION

In the introduction to this chapter we identified a number of different *t* sounds. All of these *t* sounds appear in different (or mutually exclusive) environments, for instance, the laterally released allophone occurs only before a lateral, the dental allophone only before a dental, and the palatalized allophone only before a palatal sound. We never find the palatalized allophone before a dental sound or the laterally released allophone before a palatal. For example, we never find [eitʲθ]. Sounds in a language that never occur in the same environment can never contrast or have the potential to contrast. Therefore, they cannot be in contrastive distribution. We say that sounds that only ever occur in different (or mutually exclusive) environments are in complementary distribution.

complementary distribution

The situation is rather like werewolves. The story goes that there are some people who turn into werewolves at night by the light of the full moon. So by day there is someone you know as John Smith who on certain nights grows fur and howls. But how do you know that the John Smith you meet by day is the werewolf you hear howling some nights? You can never put them one beside the other and see that they are two different people, that is, you can never put them into a situation where they are in contrastive distribution. There is a good reason for that, they are one and the same person. So it is with phonemes. But by itself, that is not sufficient. Let us suppose that Fred Jones also turns into a werewolf at night. How can you tell the two werewolves apart? Well, both might grow fur and howl, but one is very short and the other tall. That does not change. So it is with sounds which are in complementary distribution. They must have a lot in common to be different versions of the same phoneme. When John becomes a werewolf, he remains tall as a werewolf; when Fred becomes a werewolf he remains short.

phonetic similarity

Sounds that are in complementary distribution may be allophones of a single phoneme. But for allophones to be assigned to a particular phoneme, not only must they be in complementary distribution, they must also have a phonetic similarity. If we consider again the many different *t* sounds, not only are they in complementary distribution, but they also have distinctive phonetic properties in common. They are all alveolar stops. Thus we would have no objections to assigning these sounds to the phoneme /t/. They are allophones of the phoneme /t/.

Phonetic similarity is not a precise notion. There are no rules or cut-off points that help us to decide to which phoneme a particular allophone should be assigned. However, it is usually easy to arrive at such decisions.

5.1.2 DEFECTIVE DISTRIBUTION

Consider the sounds [h] and [ŋ] in English. What is the distribution of these sounds?

These two sounds are in complementary distribution: [h] never occurs in word-final position, or before another consonant. In fact, it appears only in syllable-initial position; [ŋ] never occurs in word-initial position, but does occur in word- and syllable-final position. Given that these two sounds are in complementary distribution, we could claim that they are allophones of the same phoneme. But notice that they have almost nothing phonetically in common: [h] is a voiceless glottal fricative while [ŋ] is a voiced velar stop. So the suggestion that they are allophones of the same phoneme must be rejected on grounds of lack of phonetic similarity. Furthermore, native speakers of English would never consider [h] and [ŋ] to be allophones of the same phoneme. Native speakers do not hear them as being variant forms of the same sound. Unlike the allophones of /t/, which native speakers perceive as the 'same', no native speaker perceives [h] and [ŋ] as the same. They are clearly different.

The fact that /h/ and /ŋ/ fail to appear in contrastive distribution, but appear in complementary distribution, is an extreme example of defective distribution. This term is used to describe any phoneme that appears in some environments but not in others.

defective distribution

5.1.3 PARALLEL DISTRIBUTION

The minimal pair test is a simple and effective means for identifying the phonemes of a language, and only a single minimal pair is required for the phonemic status of a sound to be established through contrastive distribution. However, it may not always be possible to find a minimal pair.

When we cannot find minimal pairs and we are certain that the sounds in question are not allophones of a single phoneme, we need to consider the distribution of the sounds in question. What this involves is looking at the range of positions in a word in which the specific sounds may appear. For example, we might consider word-initial or word-final position, or which consonants and vowels the sounds under consideration may precede or follow. If the distribution of two sounds overlaps, then they are in parallel distribution. Sounds that are in parallel distribution have the potential to contrast with each other and, therefore, are phonemes. They cannot be allophones, because allophones, as we discussed above, appear in mutually exclusive positions. To establish parallel distribution, we have to find only a single environment in which both sounds appear.

parallel distribution

As an illustrative example, let us consider the distribution in English of /θ/ and /ʒ/. In word-final position, we find that the same vowels may precede /θ/ and /ʒ/ as we can see in Table 5.1.

We now have four environments in which both sounds appear, that is, after /iː ei ɑː or /uː/. Given the above examples, we can establish parallel distribution: /θ/ and /ʒ/ have the potential to contrast, and therefore must be assigned phonemic status.

Table 5.1

Final /θ/	Final /ʒ/	Vowel
teeth	liege	iː
faith	beige	ei
bath	camouflage	ɑː
booth	rouge	uː

Parallel and contrastive distribution are related. All sounds in contrastive distribution are also in parallel distribution. Minimal pairs, for example *slip* vs *snip*, [slɪp] vs [snɪp], contrast in a single sound. These sounds, which contrast, must appear in the same environment, [s__ɪp]. Therefore, they are also in parallel distribution. However, the reverse is not necessarily true. Sounds in parallel distribution, as we have seen in the above exercise, do not always occur in contrastive distribution.

The notions of contrast and distribution are fundamental concepts in phonology. It is through these notions that we identify all the phonemes of a language (its phonemic system) and the allophones of those phonemes. For reference, these concepts are summarized below.

> **Contrastive distribution** involves two or more sounds that occur in identical environments and for which at least one minimal pair can be found. A minimal pair is a pair of words that differ in one, and only one, sound.
>
> **Parallel distribution** involves two or more sounds that occur in identical environments. It is not always possible to find minimal pairs for sounds in parallel distribution.
>
> **Complementary distribution** involves two or more sounds that never occur in identical environments and for which no minimal pairs will ever be found.

Without a sound understanding of parallel, contrastive and complementary distribution, we cannot proceed with our study of phonology. Before continuing you should attempt Exercises 5.2 to 5.5. These are devised to reinforce the notions of contrastive, parallel and complementary distribution. In attempting these exercises you will find it useful to set out a distribution table for the sounds whose distribution you have been asked to investigate. The use of such a table will make it easier for you to identify the distribution of the sounds in question.

Positions to consider in setting up your table might include: #__ (word-initial), __# (word-final) (where # represents a word boundary); V__ (after a vowel), __V (before a vowel), V__V (between two vowels) (where V is any vowel); C__ (after a consonant), __C (before a consonant), and C__C (between two consonants) (where C is any consonant).

You should choose only those positions in which the sounds in question occur in the data you have been asked to consider. For example, if the sounds in question do not appear in either word-final or word-initial positions, do not include these in your table. If the sounds under investigation are consonants, and there are no consonant clusters in the data, then do not include C__, C__C, or __C. Similarly, if you are considering vowels and there are no clusters of monophthongs, then do not include V__, V__V, or __V in your table.

We will now demonstrate how such a table works and how it helps find distributions of sounds in a worked example. In the case of our own language, we have good intuitive judgements about which sounds sound the same and which sounds sound different. But we do not have such judgements to go on in the case of languages which we do not know. We will now look at a language other than

English to see how the way we have looked at distribution as a way to find phonemes might help.

Consider the distribution of [x] and [ç] in the following data based on German:

[dɑx]	roof	[mɑnç]	many
[deçɐʁ]	roofs	[çemi]	chemistry
[buːx]	book	[taoxən]	dive
[byːçɐʁ]	books	[hoːx]	high
[lox]	hole	[miç]	me
[lœçɐʁ]	holes	[lɑxən]	laugh
[stɒʁç]	stork	[milç]	milk

Given the environments in which [x] and [ç] appear in the data, our distribution table for these data would be as shown in Table 5.2.

Table 5.2

	#__	__#	V__	__V	V__V	C__
x	–	✓	✓	✓	✓	–
ç	✓	✓	✓	✓	✓	✓

From this table it appears that [x] and [ç] are in partial parallel distribution,
and therefore could be separate phonemes. However, notice that only [ç] appears
in word-initial position, and although both appear in word-final position, only [ç]
may be preceded by a consonant. Whenever [x] occurs in word-final position, it
is always preceded by a vowel, and never a consonant. These observations suggest that we should take a closer look at the environments in which both [x] and
[ç] occur.

If [x] and [ç] are in complementary distribution, then they must occur in mutually exclusive environments. As we noted above, only [ç] occurs in word-initial
position and in word-final position preceded by a consonant. In these positions it
is in complementary distribution with [x]. Both appear before, after and between
vowels. Closer inspection of the vowels that occur next to [x] and [ç] may show
that these consonants are in complementary distribution. Before we proceed,
can we eliminate any of the three environments (__V, V__, and V__V) from
consideration?

Above we noted that although both sounds occur in word-final position, only [ç] is preceded by a consonant. This suggests that the difference in environment is what precedes the sound and not what follows. If both sounds occur word-finally then they are in parallel distribution, but if only one can be preceded by other consonants then they are in complementary distribution. Let us look at the vowels that precede [x] and [ç], as shown in Table 5.3.

Table 5.3

	ɑ	e	ɒ	oː	uː	yː	œ	i
x	✓	–	✓	✓	✓	–	–	–
ç	–	✓	–	–	–	✓	✓	✓

We can see that [x] and [ç] are in complementary distribution. [x] is always preceded by [ɑ ɒ oː uː], and [ç] is preceded by [e yː i œ]. The vowels that precede [x] are all back vowels, while those that precede [ç] are all front vowels. Based on these data, [x] and [ç] are allophones of a single phoneme. Are they phonetically similar? To check you will have to look at the IPA chart since these are not English sounds. The answer is that they are. They are both voiceless fricatives. [x] is produced on the soft palate and [ç] on the hard palate, as you can see from the IPA table.

This way of looking at the context is a fail-safe system. You get to see every possibility and to check it out. It doesn't provide a motivation for why a phoneme has the allophones it does in some environments and other allophones in other environments. When you become more familiar with the processes which realize phonemes as their allophones, as you will in section 5.3.4, you will often be able to short-circuit the process to which we have introduced you so far because you will see a pattern. The pattern is caused by regular phonetic processes where something in the phonetic environment triggers a particular realization of a phoneme. For example, the environment may cause a voiceless phoneme to become voiced. However, once you have made such an analysis, you still need to check that the two allophones which you think are in complementary distribution really are, that is, by checking that their environments are mutually exclusive.

Now try the following exercises and see if you can figure out the distributions using distribution tables.

EXERCISE 5.2   The following data are words in the pseudolanguage, Xena.

1.a [pal]	1.b [pral]	1.c [aba]	1.d [lap]	1.e [larp]
2.a [tal]	2.b [tral]	2.c [ada]	2.d [tat]	2.e [lart]
3.a [kal]	3.b [kral]	3.c [aga]	3.d [lak]	3.e [lark]

How many oral stop sounds does Xena have?

How is the distribution of oral stop sounds influenced by neighbouring sounds?

How many oral stop *phonemes* does Xena have? Explain how you arrived at your answer.

· ·

In the pseudo-language Hercules, nasal consonants appear only before other consonants. Look carefully at the place of articulation of the nasal and the following consonant and see if the places of articulation of the nasals might be in complementary distribution.

EXERCISE 5.3

1. [ŋgap]   3. [mbat]   5. [bint]

2. [ndot]   4. [liŋk]   6. [srump]

· ·

We said earlier that English vowels are either long or short. But, in context, this can change. Long vowels can be shorter than usual and short vowels longer. If you listen to the words *feet* and *feed*, the vowel in *feet* is shorter than the vowel in *feed*. Consider the following data. See if you can find what it is in the phonetic environment that makes short vowels longer and long vowels shorter. No dot after a vowel means that it is short, one dot means it is half-long and two dots (like a colon) means it is fully long.

EXERCISE 5.4

1. [fiˑt]   [fiːd]   4. [set]   [seˑd]

2. [luˑt]   [luːd]   5. [kʌp]   [kʌˑb]

3. [hɔˑk]   [hɔːn]   6. [kæp]   [kæˑb]

· ·

Consider the following data from British English:

EXERCISE 5.5

[liːp]	*leap*	[bliːp]	*bleep*	[fiːɫ]	*feel*	[heɫd]	*held*
[led]	*lead*	[gluːm]	*gloom*	[feɫ]	*fell*	[sɒɫt]	*salt*
[leik]	*lake*	[mɪljən]	*million*	[puːɫ]	*pool*	[ɒɫraːit]	*alright*
[læp]	*lap*	[ɔili]	*oily*	[ɔiɫ]	*oil*	[fɪɫm]	*film*
[luːm]	*loom*	[səlekt]	*select*	[pouɫ]	*pole*	[bɪɫz]	*bills*
[lɒk]	*lock*	[jelou]	*yellow*	[peiɫ]	*pale*	[ʌɫsə]	*ulcer*

In British English [l] (clear *l* – voiced alveolar lateral, as described in Chapter 4.2.2.3.2) and [ɫ] (dark *l* – voiced velarized alveolar lateral) are in complementary distribution. (A velarized consonant has the back of the tongue much closer to the velum than a non-velarized consonant.) What is the distribution of these two sounds?

● ●

5.1.4 FREE VARIATION

In the previous section we used the notions of parallel and contrastive distribution to identify phonemes.

Consider the following transcriptions:

   [iːðə]   [ɑiðə]   [niːðə]   [nɑiðə]   [ekənɒmɪks]   [iːkənɒmɪks]

How many different words are there?

free variation

Although there are six different transcriptions, there are only three words. We know that /iː/, /ɑi/, and /e/ are all phonemes in English (see Chapter 4.1.1), but in the above examples, substitution of, for example, [ɑi] for [iː] in [iːðə] does not result in a new word. In these examples, the phonemic contrast between these vowels would appear to have been suspended. We call this situation, where the contrastive nature of the phoneme is suspended in isolated words, free variation.

Although phonemic contrast is occasionally suspended in free variation, sociolinguists have found that free variants may be sociologically significant. The choice between variants is often conditioned by the social situation. For example, speakers using one form might be associated with a particular social group or geographical area, or may be of higher prestige. These aspects will influence the speaker's choice. Often this is a matter of degree. Speakers with higher social prestige may use one free variant more frequently than speakers with lower prestige so that people living in a wealthy suburb may more often say [iːkənɒmɪks] while people in the same town but in a poor neighbourhood might more often say [ekənɒmɪks]. Only a careful sociolinguistic study will establish the social rules that determine the occurrence of the variants.

This approach may be applied to cases of free variation both with phonemes and also with allophones. Speakers may have a choice of two (or more) allophones in a particular environment. For example, after a stressed vowel speakers may choose either [t] or [ʔ], a glottal stop, as allophones of /t/. The selection of one of these allophones may depend on such factors as the class, sex, age, and even religion of the speaker. In a study of Scottish English, Macaulay and Trevelyan (1977) found that members of the professional and managerial class are less likely to use [ʔ] than members of the semi-skilled and unskilled class. Labov (1972) found that shop assistants in department stores in New York City used a rhotic pronunciation (one with a /r/ after vowels) more frequently if they worked in a high-class department store than a lower class department store. That was because in New York City it is not a matter of being rhotic or not. Rhoticity is a matter of free variation but the choice is sensitive (amongst other things) to socio-economic status.

5.1.5   VARIATION AND DIALECTS

Free variation accounts for only a fraction of the variation in language. Most of the variation we encounter results from exposure to different geographic dialects. In Chapter 1 and the introduction to Chapter 4, we noted that we may locate speakers geographically and socially from their pronunciation of the language. We usually say that a speaker has a particular accent, which we may describe geographically, **accent** for example, from Birmingham, Glasgow, New York, Australia or South Africa, or more subjectively, for example posh, plummy, broad, rustic, northern or soft. For New Englishes, we may say that they speak Singlish (Singapore English), Nigerian English, Jamaica talk or subcontinental English.

Variation between different geographical and social dialects of English may be accounted for in four different ways:

Systemic differences
Dialects that differ systemically have different phonemic systems. For example, **systemic difference** Scottish English has a voiceless velar fricative, /x/, which other English dialects **phonemic system** lack. Whereas *lock* and *loch* are a minimal pair in Scottish English (/lɒk/ vs /lɒx/), in other dialects they are homophones, that is, they sound identical. As a further example, many dialects of English lack /ʍ/, the voiceless counterpart of the voiced labio-velar approximant /w/. In fact many books which deal with the phonetics of English no longer include /ʍ/ as a phoneme of English. The opposition between the two sounds is still reflected in English orthography. *Wh* represents /ʍ/ and *w* represents /w/. Some words whose distinctiveness rested solely in this opposition are now, for many speakers, homophones (they sound identical), for example *whine* and *wine, which* and *witch,* and *whether* and *weather.*

Speakers of Irish English and many other regional Englishes such as those in Germany, may not make a distinction between the alveolar stops /t/ and /d/ and their fricative equivalents /θ/ and /ð/, making *then* sound the same as *den.* Consequently in Irish English *then* and *den* are no longer a minimal pair. New Zealand English is currently losing the distinction between the /iə/ and /eə/ dipthongs, making *here* and *hair* no longer minimal pairs and consequently giving rise to homophone jokes such as a hair salon calling itself 'Why not hair?' If this change is completed, then New Zealand English will be systemically different from Standard British English.

Distributional differences

With distributional differences, the phonemic systems may be the same, but the distribution of certain phonemes may differ between the dialects in question. This is best illustrated by an example. All dialects of English possess a voiced alveolar central approximant, /r/. However, if we were to compare Ulster English with southern British English, we would find that the distribution of this phoneme differs in these two dialects. In southern British English /r/ is restricted to pre-vocalic position only, that is only before vowels. However, in Ulster English /r/ has a full distribution. It occurs before vowels, consonants, and pauses. We call dialects such as southern British English, which have only pre-vocalic /r/, 'non-rhotic', as you will recall. Those dialects in which /r/ has a full distribution are 'rhotic'. Scottish, Welsh, West Country, and General American are all rhotic. Most dialects of British English, and Australian and New Zealand English, are non-rhotic. Many speakers of English who model their accents on that of the United States will be rhotic. Pop songs are often rhotic regardless of where the singer is from. Even if the singer is not rhotic at home, they become rhotic in the kareoke bar.

Rhoticity in North America is particularly interesting. We have already mentioned that in New York City it is a matter of free variation. The more rhotic you are there, the higher up the social class system you are heard as being. In Boston it can be the other way around in some areas. The Boston 'Brahmin' families are sometimes less rhotic. But in the American South rhoticity is a regional dialect feature. Particularly in the rural South many people are completely non-rhotic. The result is that if you say *car* in New York without an /r/ at the end you are heard as being lower on the social scale, in Boston you may be heard as being higher up the social scale, whereas in rural Alabama you are heard as being a local rather than a Yankee from the north.

Rhoticity can have an effect on the vowel system of English dialects as you can see from Table 5.4, which shows some of the similarities and differences between the vowel systems of the Northern Hemisphere Englishes of British Received Pronunciation (RP; upper- and upper middle-class standard speech), Scottish English and General American, using a set of test words developed by the English phonetician John Wells.

/r/'s closely related cousin /l/ is also undergoing changes in many Englishes when it occurs after vowels. In some southern US dialects the words *golf* and *help* are pronounced with no [l] at all as [gʌf] and [hep]. In some New Zealand speech the /l/ is replaced by the second element in a diphthong with these words becoming [gɒʊf] and [heʊp].

Realizational difference

As with distributional differences, two dialects may possess the same number of phonemic oppositions but differ in the phonetic realization of all instances of particular phonemes. For example, both southern British English and New Zealand English possess an opposition between the vowels in *bit* and *bet*. However, in New Zealand English the vowel in *bit* is more central than its counterpart in southern British English, while the vowel in *bet* is realized slightly higher.

Table 5.4

		General RP	Standard ScotE	General AmE
1.	kit	/ɪ/	/ɪ/	/ɪ/
2.	dress	/ɛ/	/ɛ/	/ɛ/
3.	trap	/æ/	/a/	/æ/
4.	lot	/ɒ/	/ɒ/	/ɑ/
5.	strut	/ʌ/	/ʌ/	/ʌ/
6.	foot	/ʊ/	/u/	/ʊ/
7.	bath	/ɑː/	/a/	/æ/
8.	cloth	/ɒ/	/ɒ/	/ɔ/
9.	nurse	/ɜː/	/ʌ/	/ɜr/
10.	fleece	/iː/	/i/	/i/
11.	face	/ei/	/e/	/ei/
12.	palm	/ɑː/	/æ/	/ɑ/
13.	thought	/ɔː/	/ɒ/	/ɔ/
14.	goat	/ou/	/o/	/o/
15.	goose	/uː/	/u/	/u/
16.	price	/ai/	/ʌi/	/ai/
17.	choice	/ɔi/	/ɔi/	/ɔi/
18.	mouth	/au/	/au/	/au/
19.	near	/iə/	/ir/	/ir/
20.	square	/eə/	/er/	/er/
21.	start	/ɑː/	/ær/	/ɑr/
22.	north	/ɔː/	/ɒr/	/ɔr/
23.	force	/ɔː/	/or/	/or/
24.	cure	/ʊə/	/ur/	/ur/

These realizational differences apply to all occurrences of the vowel phonemes in question. **realizational difference**

The related property, namely, how close the variant of a vowel is, is also a social dialect feature in Australian English. The closer the variant, the lower down the social scale you are heard as being.

We can map such realizational differences for the whole of a phoneme system. In Table 5.5 we display the long vowel and diphthong vowel realizations of the main Southern Hemisphere Englishes compared with Received Pronunciation of Standard British English. NZE is New Zealand English, AusE is Australian English and SAfE is South African English. Realization differences are given in narrow transcription. You can see that liberal use of diacritics provided by the IPA enables quite subtle differences in accent to be documented. You might need to refer back to Figure 5.1 to understand them all.

Table 5.5

			RP	NZE	AusEng	SAfEng
7.	bath	/ɑː/	[ɑː]	[ɐ̞ː] [a̠ː]	[aː]	[ɒː]
9.	nurse	/ɜː/	[ɜː]	[œ̈] [ö]	[ɨː] [œ] [ø̞ː]	[øː]
10.	fleece	/iː/	[i̞i]	[i̞i] [əi]	[əi]	[iː]
11.	face	/ei/	[eɪ]	[æe] [ɐə]	[ɐɪ]	[ɐe]
12.	price	/ai/	[aɪ]	[ɑ + e] [ɒe]	[ɒɪ]	[ɑ.ə]
13.	thought	/ɔː/	[ɔː]	[o̞] [oə] [oɐ]	[oː]	[oː]
14.	goat	/ou/	[əu]	[ɐö] [ɐ̈ÿ]	[ɐʉ]	[ʌ.ə]
15.	goose	/uː/	[ʉu]	[ʉ] [əɨ]	[ʊʉ]	[ʉː]
16.	palm	/ɑː/	[ɑː]	[ɐ̞ː] [a̠ː]	[aː]	[ɒː]
17.	choice	/ɔi/	[ɔi]	[œ]	[oɪ]	[oe]
18.	mouth	/au/	[aʊ]	[ä̞ö] [ɛɨ]	[æʊ]	[æə]
19.	near	/iə/	[iə]	[i̞ɐ] [eɐ]	[ɪ̈ː]	[eː]
20.	square	/eə/	[ɛə]	[eɐ] [ɪ̈ɐ]	[e̞ː]	[eː]
21.	start	/ɑː/	[ɑː]	[ɐ̞ː] [a̠ː]	[aː]	[ɒː]
22.	north	/ɔː/	[ɔː]	[o̞] [oə] [oɐ]	[oː]	[oː]
23.	force	/ɔː/	[ɔː]	[o̞] [oə] [oɐ]	[oː]	[oː]
24.	cure	/ʊə/	[ʊə]	[ʉɐ] [oə] [oɐ]	[ɔ] [ʊə]	[uə] [ɔː] [oː]

Selectional difference

**selectional
difference**

With selectional differences, two dialects have the same set of phonemic contrasts but particular words select different phonemes in each dialect. Again this is best illustrated with an example. The vowels /iː/ and /ɪ/ occur in both British and New Zealand English. However, for example in *cloudy,* speakers of New Zealand English select /iː/, while most speakers of standard British English select /ɪ/.

5.2   PHONEMES AND ALLOPHONES REVISITED

From the discussion of phonemes so far, it would appear that a phoneme is the minimal unit of sound in a language that is capable of distinguishing one word from another. For example, if [t] in *tip* is replaced by [d] this gives *dip,* which is a different word from *tip.* The difference is signalled by the difference between [t] and [d]. Therefore /t/ and /d/ must be phonemes of English.

Allophones of a single phoneme are in complementary distribution (they never contrast), and are usually phonetically similar. Furthermore, allophones are the predictable realizations of phonemes, and the factors that condition the occurrence of allophones are usually found in the immediate environment of the word in which the allophone occurs. This means that, for a given phoneme, we can predict where each of its allophones will occur, and we can capture such predictable behaviour in a rule. In the *t* example above it is possible to write rules that will predict where each allophone will occur. For example /t/ will be realized as [t̪] when it occurs next to a dental consonant. Similarly, /t/ will be realized as [tʲ] when it occurs next to a palatal sound. Although it is possible to predict where the allophones of a phoneme will occur, it is generally impossible to predict where phonemes will occur. We cannot write a rule, for instance, to account for the distribution of /t/ in English.

In the above discussion we claimed that allophones were the predictable realizations of phonemes. If allophones are phonetically real, that is, sounds that are actually produced and carried on the airwaves, then what exactly do they realize? What is the status of the phoneme?

In our discussion of the phoneme in the first section of this chapter, we identified two types of properties: distinctive and non-distinctive. Speakers do not 'hear' the non-distinctive properties but do 'hear' the distinctive ones. For example, because aspiration is non-distinctive in English, a speaker of English will 'hear' [kʰ] in *catch* as a voiceless velar stop, and not as an aspirated voiceless velar stop (which is what the speaker produced). Speakers listen for the distinctive properties of a sound, those on which contrasts are based, and not for the non-distinctive properties. Implicit in this is the claim that the phoneme is, in some sense, psychologically real. We may claim that the phoneme is an abstract psychological unit rather than a sound as such.

Speakers of English never pronounce, for example, /k/ exactly the same each time it is said. You might have a cold or be tired and that has an effect on your pronunciation. Yet neither speaker nor hearer is ever in any doubt over what was said. To allow for such variations, we can claim that both speaker and hearer must have a mental pattern or template of the sound. Speakers attempt to match their production to this mental pattern, and hearers match incoming sounds to their mental patterns. These mental patterns may also be defined in terms of the distinctive properties of the language. Allophones of a phoneme will be matched against these patterns and assigned to the closest one. For example [kʰ], which is voiceless, velar, aspirated and a stop, will be matched against /k/, which is (ideally) voiceless, velar, and a stop. As aspiration is non-distinctive, the hearer disregards it. In one sense the hearer does not 'perceive' it.

Further evidence for the psychological approach may be drawn from the behaviour of speakers when they encounter sounds that are not part of their own language. Speakers, in pronouncing non-native words, will match sounds that do not occur in their own language with the closest ones that do. For example, speakers of English often replace French nasalized vowels by vowel-plus-nasal sequences, and realize the voiceless velar fricative of German as a voiceless velar stop. French, Dutch and German have no dental fricatives, and speakers of these languages will often substitute dental stops or alveolar fricatives for these sounds when speaking English. For example, a German speaker might, when speaking English, say [sɪn] or [tɪn] but mean [θɪn]. A Samoan speaker might say [pɪn] but mean [bɪn] because Samoan has no voiced stops.

If an individual phoneme is an abstract unit, then any phonemic representation of a word form must also be abstract. For example, the phonemic representation of *pin* is /pɪn/. This consists of three phonemes, /p/, /ɪ/, and /n/. If each of these is an abstract entity, then any unit that consists wholly of abstract entities must also be abstract. We often refer to phonemic representations of word forms as 'underlying representations'. Underlying representations are also often referred to as lexical representations, and are thought to be the form in which a speaker stores words in their mental lexicon.

underlying representation

This way of thinking about speech sounds may seem rather convoluted, but it is actually the way humans work with the rest of their experience. Let us suppose that you have before you a hairless Chihuahua named Polly and a hairless Cornish Rex named Manuel. They are both about the same size, they have four legs, a head and a tail. They are both brown. But the Chihuaha is a dog and the Cornish Rex is a cat, regardless of all the similarities they might have. The concept of a cat, of course, is not a particular cat nor is the concept of a dog a particular dog. Polly must have distinctive features that allow us to suppose that she is a dog regardless of all the things that she shares with Manuel, who has distinctive features making him a cat. Manuel can't bark.

5.3 PHONEMIC ANALYSIS

How then should we set about analysing the phonemic system of a language in general? There are three parts to a phonemic analysis of a language: the phonemic system, a statement of the phonotactics, and a set of allophonic rules, which link phonemes to their allophones. Let us look at all of these.

5.3.1 THE PHONEMIC SYSTEM

The phonemic system of a language is a list of all the consonant and vowel phonemes of the language and the distinctive features which make each phoneme different from the others. The phonologist will identify the phonemes of a language through a careful analysis of phonetic data. Phonemic status will be assigned only to those units that occur in contrastive or parallel distribution. Units in complementary distribution are allophones of phonemes and will, on the basis of distribution and phonetic similarity, be assigned to the appropriate phoneme.

Here only the consonant phonemes of Standard British English are given. There are twenty-four consonant phonemes in the phonemic system of Standard British English. These may be divided into:

obstruent

obstruent

seventeen obstruents (oral stops, fricatives and affricates)

/p t k b d g f v θ ð s z ʃ ʒ tʃ dʒ h/

sonorant

> seven sonorants, consisting of: **sonorant**
>
> | three nasals | /m n ŋ/ |
> | two glides or semi-vowels | /j w/ |
> | two liquids | /l r/ |

The consonant phonemes of standard North American English are the same.

5.3.2 PHONOTACTICS

Consider the following transcriptions.

[sprʌdʒ]   [strɔiʃt]   [θmɜːjŋ]   [fniːz]   [gruːltʃ]   [swɒŋk]

Which of the above words could be English and which could not?

Answer:

[sprʌdʒ], [gruːltʃ] and [swɒŋk] could all be words of English, whereas [strɔiʃt], [θmɜːjŋ] and [fniːz] could not.

Although you are unlikely to have encountered any of the above words before, you should have had few, if any, problems in separating those words that could be English from those that could not. This is possible because, as part of your knowledge of English, you recognize which sequences of segments are possible, and which sequences do not occur, that is, you know the phonotactics of English. Notice that these are not phonetic facts. You can easily pronounce these impossible words. It follows that these facts are phonological.

The phonotactics of a language are a list of restrictions on the distribution   **phonotactics**
of segments, possible sequencing of segments into clusters, and admissible syllable types. Although there are twenty-four consonant phonemes in English, and consonant clusters both before and after vowels are permitted, it is certainly not the case that consonants may combine at random up to the maximum permitted limit. Some clusters are simply too difficult to pronounce, and free combination would place quite a burden on the language learner.

What is the largest cluster of consonants that may occur at the beginning of an English word? How many different clusters of this size can you find?

Answer:

The largest initial consonant cluster in English contains three consonants. There are only ten such clusters in English. They are:

s + p + l, r, j

s + t + r, j

s + k + l, r, j, w

s + m + j

Each of these clusters begins with /s/, the second element is always a stop, and the third is one of the non-nasal sonorants. Apart from /smj/ which occurs only in *smew* (the name of a bird), the second consonant in all other clusters is always a voiceless stop. In general, initial CCC clusters in English are of the form /s/ + voiceless stop + approximant.

However, we have to add four exceptions to this rule. First, there is /smj/, which is not covered by our general statement. Secondly, there are three combinations of /s/ + /p t k/ + /l r j w/ that do not occur. There are no /spw/, /stl/ or /stw/ initial clusters in English. These three clusters are different from clusters such as /pdz/, /bfn/ or /gtb/, which are ruled out by the general phonotactic restrictions on CCC clusters discussed above. The three clusters that do not occur have to be specifically identified and ruled out. To distinguish between clusters that are ruled out by general phonotactic statements, and ones that have to be specifically identified and ruled out, we shall call the former 'illicit clusters' and the latter 'potential clusters'. Illicit clusters never occur, and never could occur in the language. They are not permitted by general phonotactic rules of the language in question. Potential clusters (and words) could but have not (yet) occurred. They are permitted by the general phonotactic rules of the language in question but are excluded by specific statements.

illicit cluster
potential cluster

Repeat the previous exercise but with initial CC clusters. List any generalizations concerning the nature of CC clusters, for example: nasal + fricative clusters are illicit. Identify any illicit clusters and potential clusters.

Answer:

Only the following initial CC clusters occur in English:

p + l, r, j   b + l, r, j

t + r, j, w   d + r, j, w

k + l, r, j, w   g + l, r, j, w

m + j	n + j
l + j	
f + l, r, j	v + j
θ + r, j, w	s + l, j, w, p, t, k, m, n, f
f + r	h + j

Stops, both oral and nasal, and fricatives are followed by approximants. (Only /k/ and /g/ may be followed by any of the four approximants. All other stops and fricatives may be followed by a subset of the approximants.) The only exception to this is /s/. It may be followed by one of the voiceless stops, /m/ or /n/, or /f/, as well as by three of the approximants. Except for clusters beginning with /s/, there is an opening of the oral cavity as we move from initial to final consonant in most initial CC clusters.

In our discussion, we have concentrated on initial consonant clusters. However, phonotactics, as defined above, define the admissible syllable types of a language. Therefore, the phonotactic rules of a language should include statements concerning syllable-final clusters, and which vowels may combine with which consonants or consonant clusters. For example, no word in English may begin with /ŋ/, or with any of the following: /ðʊ θɔi zʌ/ or /jɑi/. Furthermore, none of /j w h/ or /e æ ʌ ɒ/ may occur in syllable-final position in English. As with initial consonant clusters, there are limits on the possible combinations of consonants in word-final clusters: for example, there are no /gb vŋ nð mθʒ/ final clusters. There are also restrictions on the vowels with which those consonants and clusters may combine, for example, /mf/ occurs only after /ʌ/, while /ŋ/ may only occur after /ɪ æ ʌ ɒ/.

Through defining the set of permissible syllable types in a language, phonotactics determine the range of phonologically permissible words. Consequently, our notion of illicit and potential clusters, introduced above, may be extended to words. Illicit words never occur, and never could occur in the language. They are not permitted by general phonotactic rules of the language in question. Potential words could but have not (yet) occurred. They are permitted by the general phonotactic rules of the language in question but are excluded by specific statements. For example, neither /ɒliːmdʒ/ nor /kjɒhw/ are words of English. Nor could they ever be. Both violate the phonotactics of English. However, both /vjuːlz/ and /skwɔːmθ/ could be words of English. They both conform to the phonotactics of English. It just happens that neither of these potential combinations actually occurs in English. Recall from Chapter 3.2.1 that root creation of new words is possible. To do that you need to pick a permissible phoneme sequence and put a meaning and grammatical category to it. New window drapes called /vjuːlz/ for anyone?

5.3.3 ALLOPHONIC RULES

In our discussion of phonemes and allophones (section 5.2), we claimed that allophones are the predictable realizations of phonemes, and as such their

allophonic rule

occurrence can be expressed formally by a rule. These rules that link an abstract phoneme to its allophonic realizations are called allophonic rules.

The function of the rules may be illustrated by the following diagram:

INPUT		OUTPUT
Phonemic Form	→ Acted on by →	Phonetic Representation
(Abstract Unit)	Allophonic Rule(s)	(What speakers produce)

The form of allophonic rules may be best illustrated by an example:

				(Context)
/t/	→	[tʲ]	/	___ j
(Input)		(Output)		(Conditioning factor)

This rule tells us that the phoneme /t/ is realized by its palatalized allophone when it occurs before a palatal approximant. Like all allophonic rules, this rule may be divided into two halves, which are separated from each other by a slash, /. We shall refer to the first half, on the left side of the slash, as the process side. On the process side of the rule we find the input segment to the rule and its output, in this case /t/ and [tʲ]. The part of the rule to the right of the slash specifies the context in which the rule operates and gives the conditioning factor. In this example the allophone occurs before a palatal approximant, which is the conditioning factor.

The process side of any allophonic rule is basically:

$$/X/ \rightarrow [Y] /$$

that is, phoneme X is realized as allophone Y.

The context of a rule may be quite complex, and there are three basic possibilities. First, the conditioning factor may occur to the right of the input phoneme:

/ ___ A

This possibility is illustrated by the palatalization of /t/ discussed above.

Secondly the conditioning factor may precede the input:

/ A ___

As an example, consider the realization of /t/ in *bathtap*. In this sequence /t/ may be dentalized under the influence of the preceding dental. We can capture this in the following rule:

/t/ → [t̪] / θ ___

Thirdly, the input phoneme occurs between two conditioning factors:

/ A____B

In some varieties of English /t/ and /d/ are realized between vowels as an alveolar tap, [ɾ]. If we take /t/ as our input, then the rule for this process would be:

/t/ → [ɾ] / V____V   (where V = any vowel)

In each of the examples above, the process applies in a single context. If a process applies in two (or more) contexts, do we write two rules or can we still write a single rule?

Consider our dentalized and unreleased allophones of /t/; /t/ is dentalized when it is followed by a dental fricative, for example in *eighth*. However, /t/ is also dentalized if it is word-final and the next word begins with a dental fricative, for example in *not think*. Dentalization occurs both within a word and over word boundaries. This gives us two rules:

/t/ → [t̪] / ___ θ   /t/ → [t̪] / ____ #θ   (# = word boundary)

In both of these rules the process is the same; only the context is different. We can collapse these two rules into one by isolating the common material, in this case the process and part of the environment, and then by placing the non-overlapping part of the contexts inside curved brackets or parentheses:

/t/ → [t̪] / ___(#)θ

The material inside the brackets is optional. It may or may not be present. The rule states that /t/ is realized by its dentalized allophone when it is followed by a voiceless dental fricative, and when it is followed by a word boundary *and* a voiceless dental fricative.

Now consider the unreleased /t/. /t/ is unreleased when it is followed by another stop, for example /d/, but let us say that it is also unreleased in word-final position. This would give us two rules:

/t/ → [t˺] / ___d   /t/ → [t˺] / ____ #

In both of these rules the process is the same: only the context is different. We can collapse these two rules into one by isolating the common material, in this case the process, and then by placing the non-overlapping part of the contexts inside braces:

$$/t/ → [t˺] / \underline{\quad} \left\{ \begin{array}{c} d \\ \# \end{array} \right\}$$

The braces indicate a disjunction (you must chose one or the other), /t/ is unreleased before either /d/ or a word boundary. The braces tell us that the rule will apply only if one of the contexts inside the braces is met.

The environment half of every allophonic rule is an account of the distribution of a particular allophone. As the allophones of a phoneme are in complementary distribution, that is, no two allophones of a phoneme occur in the same environment, then for any phoneme, the environment half of each allophonic rule for a particular phoneme must be different. If this were not the case, we would have parallel distribution, the potential for contrast, and the sounds in question would be phonemic rather than allophonic.

EXERCISE 5.6   Return to your solutions to Exercises 5.2 to 5.5. For each pair of allophones you identified in the data in these exercises, select one member as the underlying or phonemic form, and write an allophonic rule to derive the other member of the pair.

. . . .

5.4   ALLOPHONIC PROCESSES

Having introduced the notion and formalism of allophonic rules, we can now look at allophonic processes in English. These processes constitute the ways in which the realization of a phoneme is the result of the environment in which it appears. They thus explain why allophones take the form they do.

5.4.1   ASPIRATION

In English, one allophone of the voiceless stops is aspirated. Although the environment in which aspirated stops occur is more complex than that of [tʲ], it is possible to write a rule which predicts where these allophones will occur. Concentrating on the voiceless alveolar stop /t/, consider the following words:

*t*en

s*t*em

The /t/ in *ten* is aspirated, whereas in *stem* it is not. You can test this for yourselves. Put your hand close to your mouth and utter both words. You should feel a small puff of air on your hand when you release the /t/ in *ten* but not in *stem*. Based on these two words, it would appear that for /t/ to be aspirated it must appear in initial position in a word. We might posit as our rule that /t/ is realized as [tʰ] if it occurs in initial position in a word. Formally, this would be stated as:

/t/ → [tʰ] / #____

However, now consider *attack*. This contains [tʰ] but not in initial position. This violates our initial hypothesis. How might we rescue our hypothesis? We could simply add the new environment to our rule. However, that would suggest that aspiration of initial and non-initial stops is unrelated. It is unlikely that the same process would be triggered by two unrelated environments. Any solution should attempt to capture whatever is common to both the non-word-initial aspirated stop and the word-initial ones since it is likely that the same environmental factors are responsible for the particular allophone being the way it is. What do the stops in *ten* and *attack* share? It could be the case that /t/ is aspirated only when followed by a front vowel. However, words like *top* and *atop* with aspirated stops show that this is not the case. If we were to divide *attack* into syllables, we would find that it contains two syllables, with the dividing line falling between the initial vowel and the first consonant. Now although [tʰ] in *attack* does not occur word-initially, it does occur syllable-initially. Given that *ten is* a single or monosyllabic word, we can now see that syllable-initial position is the common factor, and revise our initial rule. A voiceless stop is aspirated if it occurs in syllable-initial position. Formally this gives:

/t/ → [tʰ] / .___   (. indicates a syllable boundary)

Finally, consider *tautology*. This word contains two occurrences of /t/ in syllable-initial position. For some of you, both *t*s are aspirated. However, for others, only one *t*, the second, is aspirated. The situation where only one /t/ is aspirated violates our hypothesis. This time we must discover why one syllable-initial stop is aspirated but not the other. Transcribe *tautology* and divide it into syllables. Repeat the word paying attention to the effort you put into pronouncing each syllable. Do you put more effort into one syllable which is more prominent than the others? If so which one? You should find that you put more effort into the second syllable. This increase of effort which is reflected in increased prominence, is called 'stress'. It is the stop at the beginning of this stressed syllable which is aspirated. We can now conclude that a voiceless stop is aspirated when it occurs in the initial position of a stressed syllable. Formally, this is stated as:

/t/ → [tʰ] / .___V
              [+stress]

In the above exercise we were presented with some data. On the basis of this data we set up a hypothesis concerning the aspiration of voiceless stops in English. When this database was expanded we saw that our initial hypothesis was no longer valid, and revised it to take account of the additional data. A further expansion of the database led to revision of the second hypothesis and rule. The setting up of a hypothesis which can be tested against the data is a common approach to problem solving and analysis of language. We did not attempt to arrive at an overall solution in a single step but set out an initial hypothesis which was gradually revised and refined.

5.4.2 ASSIMILATION

In speech, the sounds of a language do not occur in isolation but in sequences of variable length. When placed in a sequence, sounds may be influenced by their

assimilation

neighbours. They may acquire some of their neighbours' characteristics, and in doing so become more like their neighbours. Assimilation is the name we give to the process where one segment becomes more like (or identical to) another segment, or two segments become more like each other.

Consider the words *happen* and *input*. If they were pronounced carefully and transcribed, we would probably get:

[hæpən]   *happen*   [ɪnpʊt]   *input*

However, in a more natural speech style we might find:

[hæpm]   *happen*   [ɪmpʊt]   *input*

In both examples, the alveolar nasal, /n/, becomes more like the bilabial stop, /p/, by becoming a bilabial nasal, [m]. Furthermore, in both examples, the bilabial stop triggers the assimilation, and the alveolar nasal is the segment which changes. All assimilation processes involve at least one segment which is changed, and one which is the source of the change. We shall refer to the segment which is changed as the 'target', and the segment which influences the target as the 'source'.

Although all assimilation processes involve a source and a target, what may vary is the position of the source in relation to the target. Where the source comes before the target the direction of influence is from left to right, or forwards through the word. This is called 'progressive assimilation' because the influence progresses forwards through the word. This direction of assimilation is also referred to as 'perseverative assimilation', it preserves some aspect of a segment, beyond the segment from which it originates. Our first example, *happen*, is an example of progressive assimilation, which may be expressed by the following rule:

progressive (or perseverative) assimilation

/n/ → [m] / p$^{(source)}$ ____ $^{(target)}$

/n/ is realized as [m] when it is preceded by /p/.

regressive (or anticipatory) assimilation

'Regressive assimilation' is where the source comes after or to the right of the target, and the direction of influence is from right to left, or backwards through the word. This type of assimilation may also be called 'anticipatory assimilation' because a segment is altered in a way which anticipates a phonetic property of a segment which comes later in the word. *Input* is an example of regressive assimilation. The rule for this regressive assimilation is:

/n/ → [m] / ____$^{(source)}$p$^{(target)}$

/n/ is realized as [m] ·when it is followed by /p/.

5.4.2.1 Assimilation types

In discussing assimilation, not only do we identify the direction of the assimilation, but it is also useful to establish a list of assimilation types. The most common types of assimilation are: place, voice, nasalization, and lip attitude.

place, voice, nasalization, lip attitude

5.4.2.2 Place

The above examples involve assimilation of place. In both examples an alveolar nasal assimilated to a bilabial stop. The dentalized, palatalized, and retroflex allophones of /t/ we discussed above are all examples of assimilation of place.

In the discussion of *input,* although the alveolar nasal is realized as a labial nasal, this is not reflected in the spelling.

5.4.2.3 Voice

A second assimilation type involves phonation, or voice. In assimilations of voice, a sound becomes more like its neighbours by 'agreeing' in voice. Voiceless sounds become voiced, and voiced ones may become voiceless. We call the first type voicing, and the second type devoicing. As with assimilations of place, assimilations of voice may be either progressive or regressive.

voicing devoicing

Transcribe the following words. Do not be misled by the spelling system but pay particular attention to what you say.

town's, book's, people's, Pat's

You should have transcribed these words as:

[tɑunz bʊks piːpəlz pæts]

In the transcribed versions, the possessive marker *'s* has two versions, [s] and [z]. If we take the voiceless version as the phonemic form, /n/ and /l/ as the source, and /s/ as the target, then we have progressive assimilation of voice.

Now consider the following words:

small, slap, slush, trap, class, crush

If we were to transcribe these words phonemically we would probably transcribe them as:

/smɔːl slæp slʌʃ træp klɑːs krʌʃ/

However, if we were to listen carefully to a recording of these items we would find that the second consonant is either voiceless or only partially voiced. The voiced sound has assimilated to the initial voiceless one by becoming either fully or partially voiceless. Using the diacritic [̥] to indicate that a sound which is normally voiced has been devoiced, we may represent this in a phonetic version of our transcription, giving:

[sm̥ɔːl sl̥æp sl̥ʌʃ tr̥æp kl̥ɑːs kr̥ʌʃ]

These are examples of progressive assimilation, with the initial consonant being the source and the following sonorants being the target. We can also find examples of regressive devoicing. If we were to transcribe the following sequence phonemically and then phonetically:

have to

we would have:

/hæv tə/ and [hæf tə]

Again we have an example of devoicing. In this case we have regressive assimilation, with /t/ the source and /v/ the target.

5.4.2.4 Nasalization

velic closure

In the discussion of articulation, we pointed out that the velum or soft palate could be either raised or lowered. When it is raised, velic closure occurs and air flows from the lungs out through the oral cavity. However, when the velum is lowered the nasal cavity is open to the flow of air from the lungs. Air can now flow out through the nasal cavity, giving nasal sounds. In English the velum is usually lowered for only the three nasal stops, /m n ŋ]. However, the position of the velum is not dependent on the other processes and may be lowered during the production of other segments. 'Nasalization' occurs when the velum is lowered during the production of a segment which is not normally nasal. The most common occurrence of nasalization in English is regressive nasalization of vowels in vowel-nasal sequences. For example:

/kɒŋgres/ *congress* → [kʰɒ̃ŋgres]

In this example, the nasal is the source and the vowel is the target. The property of nasalization is transferred from the source leftwards to the target giving regressive nasalization. This may be represented by the following rule, where V represents any vowel, N any nasal, with the diacritic [˜] to indicate nasalization:

V → Ṽ / ___N

Whereas such nasalized vowels in English are allophones of oral vowels, French has a set of phonemic nasalized vowels. After vowel nasalization occurred in French, the nasal was deleted phonemically, although not in the spelling, giving sets of minimal pairs:

/pɛ̃/   *pain*   'bread'   /pɛ/   *paix*   'peace'

5.4.2.5   Lip attitude

'Lip attitude' refers to the position of the lips during the articulation of a sound. During the articulation of back rounded vowels, the lips are, of course, rounded. This lip rounding may spread to adjacent consonants manifested by labialization represented by the diacritic [ʷ]. (Look in the mirror to check this. Say *keel* and then *cool* and notice the lip rounding on the latter word.) This gives:

/kʊl/   *cool* → [kʷʰʊl]   /loub/   *lobe* → [lʷoub]

5.4.2.6   Fusion

Fusion is a type of assimilation where two segments assimilate to each other. **fusion**
The outcome of this assimilation is a third distinct segment which combines properties of the two assimilating segments. For example, in careful speech, *caught you* and *would you* would be realized as: [kʰɔːt juː] and [wʊd juː]; but in normal conversation they are more likely to be realized as: [kʰɔːtʃə] and [wʊdʒə]. In both examples the alveolar stop and following palatal approximant fuse to give the voiceless and voiced post-alveolar affricates [tʃ] and [dʒ]. The voice, place, and manner of articulation of the two input segments are combined to form a third segment. The voiced quality of the fused segment is decided by the voice quality of the first consonant. The place of articulation is mid-way between alveolar and palatal, and the manner of articulation of both input segments is reflected in the fused segment, which is both a stop and a continuant.

As well as these assimilatory processes, there are a number of other processes which affect segments in context.

5.4.3   ELISION

Consider the following list of words. Read each word aloud and then transcribe what you say, remembering to concentrate on what you say and not what you read.

handsome, windmill, handkerchief, mostly, kindness, attempts

In your transcription you may have omitted some of the consonants which you might have expected to be present. For example, you may have omitted the /d/ in *handsome, windmill, handkerchief* and *kindness,* the /t/ in *mostly,* and the second one in *attempts.* We call the deletion of a segment normally present in the stream of speech 'elision'. Elision is more common in less formal and more casual   **elision** speech styles. In careful speech most of the consonants which were elided in the above examples would be present.

The most frequently elided consonants in English are /t/ and /d/. For example:

West Cliff	/west klɪf/ →	[wes klɪf]
thousand points	/θɑuznd pɔints/ →	[θɑuzn pɔints]

The elision of a segment may allow a subsequent assimilation to occur. For example:

handbag	/hændbæg/ →	hænbæg →	[hæmbæg]

As well as consonants, vowels may also be elided. This is most obvious in the various contractions found in English, for example *I am* → *I'm, she is* → *she's*, and *do not* → *don't*. Vowel elision also occurs in other words, for example: *bottle* /bɒtəl/ → [bɒtl̩], *police* /pɒliːs/ → [pliːs], and *geography* /dʒiːɒgræfɪ/ → [dʒɒgrəfɪ]. The small diacritic line in [bɒtl̩] indicates that the [l] is a syllabic consonant, a one-consonant syllable. We shall have more to say about such consonants in Chapter 6.1.3.

These are some of the more obvious examples of elision. If you were to transcribe phonetically a passage of informal conversation you would find a far greater range of both consonant and vowel elision than the few examples discussed above.

Elision of segments is not confined to contemporary English but also occurred in the past. In many cases the elision of both consonants and vowels has taken place but the orthography has not been adjusted to take account of the 'new' pronunciation, and still retains symbols (silent letters) which reflect the earlier pronunciation. For example: *Wright, knee, gnaw, thistle, fasten, walk,* and *lamb* all contain symbols for consonants which are no longer pronounced even in careful speech. *Gloucester, Salisbury, evening, written,* and *time* all contain vowel symbols to which no sound value is now assigned. Sometimes these spellings reveal something of the etymology of a word. The *-cester* in *Gloucester* was Latin *castra* two thousand years ago showing that this was then a Roman town.

Elisions, some of them having become permanent, are the source of many of the 'silent letters' we noted in Chapter 4.1.

5.4.4 INSERTION

epenthesis

In the previous section, we saw that segments which are present in careful speech may be elided in more casual speech styles. It is also possible for segments not normally present in careful speech styles to be inserted. The term for such insertions is 'epenthesis'. Both consonant and vowel epenthesis occurs in English. In some dialects of English schwa [ə] is inserted between two consonants. For example: [fɪləm] *film,* [æθəliːt] *athlete,* [ɑːrəm] *arm,* and [gɪrəl] *girl*. Consonant epenthesis is most frequent, in English, between nasal-fricative and nasal-stop sequences such as: /ns/ and /mt/, giving [mɪnts] *mince/mints* and [drempt] *dreamt*. These insertions arise from timing errors. The velum closes before the oral consonant is formed, and this results in an epenthetic oral stop, with the same place of articulation as the nasal.

When words are borrowed, as we saw in Chapter 3, their phonological form adapts to that of the language into which they come. So, if the receiver language has restrictions on consonant clusters, then epenthetic vowels are introduced. This is clear when English words with an initial consonant cluster are borrowed into languages which do not allow such clusters. This includes all the Polynesian languages. So a word like *tree* might become [tɪriː].

5.5 ALLOPHONES

Having discussed some of the more common allophonic processes in English, let us look at some of the more common allophones of consonants. In the following discussion, it will become apparent that the various processes tend to affect classes of segments rather than individual segments. This is not to deny that some processes may only affect one or two members of a class, for example, only the alveolar stops, /t/ and /d/, are dentalized before the dental fricatives. Consequently, we shall structure our discussion around groups and processes rather than individual segments.

5.5.1 ORAL STOPS /p t k b d g/

There are a number of processes which affect the class of oral stops as a whole. All oral stops occur with nasal release when followed by a nasal. If the stop-nasal sequence is homorganic (both have the same place of articulation) then the complete closure in the oral cavity is not released and the air escapes through the nasal cavity when the velum is lowered. For example:

[tɒp^{n}moust]

If the stop-nasal sequence is not homorganic, then the oral stop is not normally released until the articulation of the following nasal is complete. For example:

[bɪg^{n}mɑus]

Although there is a difference between the homorganic and non-homorganic sequences, the term 'nasal release' applies to both.

With homorganic stop-lateral sequences we get lateral release. The stop is released by the lowering of the sides of the tongue for the following lateral, for example, *bottle, throttle, atlas, at last* and *coddle*. No other articulatory movement is involved. If the stop-lateral sequence is not homorganic, then it is usual for tongue tip contact to occur before the stop is released. Although an additional articulation is involved, the air escapes over the sides of the tongue. The non-homorganic stop-lateral cases are examples of lateral escape, for example,   **lateral escape**
please, black, quick lime and *big lake* all involve lateral escape.

We discovered in the first section of this chapter that /t/ was unreleased when followed by another stop. This applies to all stops, not just when they are followed by another stop but also when they occur in final position. With the voiced stops there may be some devoicing if the following stop is voiceless. Taking /p/ and /b/, these allophones are illustrated below:

[p˺] [rɪp˺]   [b˺] [rɪb˺keidʒ]

5.5.1.1   Voiceless stops   /p t k/

Aspiration is the one process which affects only the voiceless stops. Voiceless stops are aspirated, as we discovered in section 5.4.1, in initial position of a stressed syllable and immediately preceding the vowel. In our discussion, we looked only at /t/, but the same process under the same conditions applies to the other voiceless stops as well, for example, the /p/ in *post* and the /k/ in *keep* will both be aspirated.

5.5.1.2   Voiced stops   /b d g/

Devoicing is the main process which affects voiced but not voiceless stops. Voiced stops are partially devoiced when followed by a voiceless consonant, and in utterance-initial and utterance-final positions, that is, when either preceded or followed by silence. As we noted above, when a voiced stop occurs in final position, or is followed by a word beginning with a voiceless consonant, then it will be unreleased, as well as partially devoiced. Taking /d/ as an example, we have:

deep [d̥iːp],   *trod* [trɒd̥˺],   *board claims* [bɔːd̥˺kleimz]

5.5.2   VOICED FRICATIVES /v ð z ʒ/

These tend to devoice in utterance-initial or final position, or when followed by a voiceless consonant:

view [v̥juː],   *cave* [keiv̥],   *we've found* [wiːv̥ faund]

5.5.3   SONORANTS /m n ŋ r l j w/

As with voiced stops and fricatives, devoicing is the main process which affects sonorants. All sonorants devoice within a word if preceded by a voiceless consonant:

smile [sm̥ail]   *snow* [sn̥ou]   *cringe* [kr̥indʒ]

play [pl̥ei]   *refuse* [rəfjuːz]   *quick* [kw̥ɪk]

If /r/ is preceded by either /t/ or /d/, then it tends to be realized as a fricative rather than as an approximant. In the former combination devoicing also occurs.

When /j/ and /w/ follow a voiceless consonant, then they are realized as voiceless fricatives; /j/ is realized as a voiceless palatal fricative, and /w/ as a voiceless labio-velar fricative, [w]. In Chapter 4.2.2.3.2. we said that the glides, /j/ and /w/, were phonetically like vowels, but behaved like consonants. These allophones are clearly consonantal, that is, they are voiceless and fricative, and illustrate further the dual nature of the glides.

Apart from a voiceless allophone, /l/ has two other major allophones. The first is articulated with the blade of the tongue and the alveolar ridge. We call this allophone 'clear l'. It occurs before vowels:

leap [li:p]   *silly* [sɪlɪ]

This allophone also occurs if /l/ is in word-final position and the next word begins with a vowel:

fill in [fɪl ɪn]

The other is a velarized alveolar lateral, and occurs after a vowel or before a consonant:

fall [fɔːɫ]   *help* [heɫp]

We call this allophone 'dark l'.

5.5.4 VOWELS

In Chapter 4.2.3.4 we stated that vowels in English may be either long or short: /ɪ e æ ʌ ɒ ʊ/ are all short, while the remaining monophthongs and all diphthongs are long. However, the precise length of any vowel depends on its environment. Vowels followed by a voiceless consonant are shorter than those followed by a voiced consonant or in word-final position. In the following examples the vowels in the words in the first column are shorter than those in the second or third columns:

beat	bead	bee
bit	bid	
base	beige	bay
bet	bed	

Taking /iː/ as an illustrative example we might transcribe the words in the first line as follows:

[biˑt biːd biː]

5.6 DERIVATIONS

**surface
   representation
derived form**

derivation

From our discussion of some of the common allophonic processes and allo-phones of English, it should be apparent that although allophonic rules apply to individual phonemes, these phonemes do not occur in isolation but in the context of a phonological or underlying representation. Consequently, while allophonic rules do link phonemes to allophones, they also relate underlying representations to surface ones. For most phonologists surface representations (consisting of allophones) are derived from underlying ones (consisting of pho-nemes) thus giving a derived form, through the application of allophonic rules. We usually refer to the process of deriving (or determining) the pronunciation of an underlying representation as a derivation.

As an illustrative example of a derivation, let us consider *congress* and *ten past (eight)*:

	Underlying Representation
	/kɒngres/
Aspiration	kʰɒngres
Nasalization	kʰɒ̃ngres
Vowel Lengthening	kʰɒ̃·ngres
Nasal assimilation	kʰɒ̃·ŋgres
Surface Representation	[kʰɒ̃·ŋgres]

	Underlying Representation
	/ten pɑːst/
Aspiration	tʰen pɑːst
Assimilation	tʰempɑːst
Nasalization	tʰẽmpɑːst
Vowel Lengthening	tʰẽ·mpɑːst
Surface Representation	[tʰẽ·mpɑːst]

In the first example /k/ is aspirated and the following vowel is nasalized and lengthened. In the second example /t/ is aspirated, /n/ assimilates to /p/, and /e/ is nasalized and lengthened.

5.7 FEATURES

So far in our discussion of phonology we have established two different but related units, phonemes and allophones. Although both units may be described in articulatory terms, for example, the phoneme /t/ may be defined by a three-term label (voiceless, alveolar, stop), many phonologists have considered phonemes to be indivisible. They were the smallest units with which many phonologists worked. However, other phonologists proposed that phonemes were simply cover symbols, and could be decomposed into smaller units, which they called distinctive features. For these phonologists the fundamental or primitive unit of phonology was no longer the phoneme but the distinctive feature. They did not adopt this position without sound arguments.

distinctive feature

5.7.1   THE NECESSITY OF FEATURES

In section 5.4.1 we analysed the distribution of [tʰ], found that its distribution was predictable, and wrote a rule which derived it from /t/. Let us now consider the remaining English voiceless stops /p/ and /k/.

Consider the following two sets of data:

(a)   occur   (b)   preposterous

      concussion   pull

      acquire   spanner

      caught   oppose

For both sets, identify all occurrences of /k/ and /p/. Which occurrences are realized by the aspirated allophones [kʰ] and [pʰ]? Can you write the rules which predict the occurrence of these allophones?

Although the input and output of the two rules required here differ from that in the discussion of aspiration in section 5.4.1, the process of aspiration and the conditioning environment in which the rule operates are identical:

/t/ → [tʰ] / .____V
           [+stress]

/p/ → [pʰ] / .____V
           [+stress]

/k/ → [kʰ] / .____V
           [+stress]

Although these three rules may capture accurately what happens, they fail to capture a general point of English phonology: all voiceless stops are aspirated when they are the only consonant before a stressed vowel. Phonological rules tend to apply to classes of related phonemes, rather than to classes of unrelated ones. The members of these classes are related by virtue of sharing one or more aspects of their description. In the above example the members of the class share two features, they are voiceless and they are stops. So it must be the case that there is only one rule for aspiration here and not three. The way we have done rules up to now cannot express this.

One solution to this problem lies in our discussion of phonetics. Although we use symbols such as /p/, /z/, and /n/, these symbols may simply be an abbreviation for a set of phonetic properties. In Chapter 4.2.2.3.2 we assigned each consonantal phoneme of English a three- or four-term label of phonetic features – for example, /t/ is a voiceless alveolar stop. It may be possible to use these features rather than symbols to identify segments. This would certainly allow us to reduce the above three rules to one:

$$[\text{voiceless stop}] \rightarrow [\text{aspirated}] \ / \ .\underline{\quad}V$$
$$[+\text{stress}]$$

Already we can see that there is a sound argument for abandoning the notion that phonemes are indivisible, and seeing them as simply cover labels for sets of features.

Although such a system appears to provide a solution for the above example, it is somewhat simplistic, and soon runs into problems. In English the regular expression of the plural morpheme is *s*. This morpheme is realized in three different ways by speakers of English – /s/, /z/, and /əz/. Each realization is an 'allomorph'. Given any noun, a speaker of English will always choose the correct allomorph of the plural morpheme. Therefore, it should be possible to write a rule which will correctly predict the realization of the plural morpheme for any noun.

Draw up three columns – one for each allomorph of the plural – and then put each of the following nouns into one of the three columns according to which version it takes:

dog, cat, church, judge, book, zoo, base, bee, pod, tap, game, tone, brush, bruise, day, cuff, cub, move, month, lathe, pang

You will probably have got a set of answers like this:

/s/	tap, cat, book, cuff, month
/z/	cub, pod, dog, move, lathe, game, tone, pang, day, zoo, bee
/əz/	base, bruise, brush, church, judge

Can you identify the factor which determines which version occurs with which noun? You should pay particular attention to the final sound in each noun.

The final sound in the nouns which occur before /s/ is always voiceless. It is either a stop or a labio-dental or dental fricative. The nouns which occur with /z/ always end in a voiced sound, a vowel, voiced stop, nasal stop, or a voiced labio-dental or dental fricative. Those nouns which occur with /əz/ always end in a fricative, which may be either voiced or voiceless and is either alveolar or post-alveolar, or one of the two affricates. The choice is conditioned by the phonological properties of the final segment of the noun. This conditioning is a type of assimilation and is referred to as 'phonological conditioning'.

phonological conditioning

Each of the three classes is quite complex and cannot be easily identified. The first class, for example, consists of all voiceless stops and some voiceless fricatives. It is impossible, given the phonetic features introduced in Chapters 4.1.1 and 4.2.2.3.2, to provide a more concise description of this group of sounds. If we wish to capture these three classes, then we require a more comprehensive system of features which allows such classes of sounds to be determined as a bundle of distinctive features and just the right distinctive features. In this book we are not going to attempt this. It is the subject of most more advanced treatments of segmental phonology. Determining the set of distinctive features of a language and of languages in general is a fascinating process and leads to some interesting conclusions, not the least of which is that the number of distinctive features required to make up just the right classes to explain phonological processes in all the world's languages is quite a small set of the order of a dozen or so. While the number of phonemes in a language may range from in the twenties to over one hundred, all the phonemes of all the world's languages may just be different arrangements of a much smaller inventory of distinctive features. All of the phonological rules of all the world's languages appear also to be able to be expressed in terms of these features.

features

Further exercises •

We use the minimal pair test to identify the phonemes or distinctive sounds of a language. Find at least one minimal pair in English for each of the following sets of sounds:

EXERCISE 5.7°

(a)	[s] and [t]	(b)	[l] and [n]	(c)	[f] and [v]
(d)	[d] and [ʃ]	(e)	[s] and [ʒ]	(f)	[k] and [ŋ]
(g)	[z] and [tʃ]	(h)	[p] and [dʒ]	(i)	[m] and [l]
(j)	[iː] and [e]	(k)	[ou] and [ɑː]	(l)	[ɪ] and [ɒ]
(m)	[ei] and [ʌ]	(n)	[ɑu] and [ɔː]	(o)	[e] and [ɒ]
(p)	[ɑː] and [ɪ]	(q)	[ei] and [ɑu]	(r)	[iː] and [ou]

EXERCISE 5.8^{••}

Below are some data from the African language Swahili. Look at the distribution of the sounds [ɔ], an open 'o', and [o], a closed 'o'. The aim of the exercise is to find out if these two sounds are really alternative pronunciations of the same sound.

[ŋgɔma]	[watoto]
[bɔma]	[ndoto]
[ŋɔmbe]	[mboga]
[ɔna]	[ʃoka]
[ɔŋgeza]	[modʒa]

Check the distributions of the two sounds to see if they are complementary.

EXERCISE 5.9^{••}

Consider the following pairs of words:

possible	impossible	probable	improbable
opportune	inopportune	decisive	indecisive
edible	inedible	tangible	intangible
literate	illiterate	legal	illegal
reversible	irreversible	responsible	irresponsible

What is the difference in meaning between the members of each pair?

List the prefixes which are added to the first member of each pair to derive the second.

If each prefix has the same meaning then it is likely that they are allomorphs of a single morpheme.

Are the allomorphs phonologically conditioned? If so, select one allomorph as the underlying representation of this morpheme.

EXERCISE 5.10^{•••}

Consider the data below, which are based on Italian, and then answer the questions that follow:

[minɑ]	*mina*	'mine'	[nido]	*nido*	'nest'
[muffːɑ]	*muffa*	'mould'	[notʃe]	*noce*	'nut tree'
[limɑ]	*lima*	'file'	[kɑne]	*cane*	'dog'
[limone]	*limone*	'lemon'	[denaro]	*denaro*	'money'

[lombo]	*lombo*	'loin'		[andare]	*andare*	'go'
[pompa]	*pompa*	'pump'		[tondo]	*tondo*	'round'
[liŋgwa]	*lingua*	'tongue'		[tʃiŋkwe]	*cinque*	'five'
[fuŋgo]	*fungo*	'mushroom'		[baŋko]	*banco*	'bench'

How many different nasal sounds are there in the above data?

Are all the nasal sounds phonemic? You will need to set up a distribution table.

If one of the nasals is not phonemic, but an allophone of one of the other nasals, then write rules to derive the allophones.

Consider the following data from Scottish English: EXERCISE 5.11 •••

1.	iː	[liːv]	leave	[briːð]	breathe	[hiː]	he
		[hiːr]	hear	[briːz]	breeze		
	i	[lif]	leaf	[hiθ]	heath	[lis]	lease
		[hil]	heal	[bist]	beast	[sim]	seem
2.	eː	[breːv]	brave	[beːð]	bathe	[meː]	may
		[beːr]	bear	[heːz]	haze		
	e	[feθ]	faith	[len]	lane	[mes]	mace
		[mel]	mail	[met]	mate	[med]	maid
3.	uː	[muːv]	move	[smuːð]	smooth	[θruː]	threw
		[puːr]	poor	[snuːz]	snooze		
	ʊ	[rʊf]	roof	[rʊθ]	Ruth	[lʊs]	loose
		[mʊn]	moon	[tʊl]	tool	[hʊd]	hood
4.	oː	[groːv]	grove	[loːð]	loath	[loː]	low
		[doːr]	door	[doːz]	doze		
	o	[of]	oaf	[boθ]	both	[klos]	close
		[mol]	mole	[mod]	mode	[not]	note

In the above data, is the vowel length phonemic or allophonic? If it is allophonic, then taking the short vowels as underlying, attempt to provide the rule which lengthens the vowels. (*Hint*: Take V → V: as the input to the rule and provide the environment in which the rule applies.)

Now consider the following data:

[hid]	heed	[hiːd]	he'd
[pled]	plaid	[pleːd]	played
[brud]	brood	[bruːd]	brewed
[rod]	road	[roːd]	rowed

What problems, if any, do these data raise for our rule above? Can we account for them without abandoning our rule?

EXERCISE 5.12•••   The following data are based on Italian:

[kapo]	[gamba]	[tʃena]	[dʒiardino]
[kura]	[gufo]	[tʃirka]	[dʒentile]
[kolle]	[governo]	[tʃelebre]	[dʒenero]
[koɲato]	[grande]	[kutʃina]	[kudʒino]
[krude]	[gloria]	[kontʃepire]	[intellidʒente]
[biskotto]	[lago]	[innotʃente]	[voldʒeri]
[sikuro]	[organo]		
[lokale]	[negotsio]		
[perikolo]	[laguno]		

Consider [k] and [tʃ], and [g] and [dʒ] in the above data. The members of each pair are in complementary distribution with each other. Provide a statement of the distribution of each member of the pair confirming that they are in complementary distribution.

EXERCISE 5.13•••   Consider the following data based on Castilian Spanish:

[tiβio]	*tibio*	'lukewarm'	
[balsa]	*balsa*	'raft'	[la βalsa]

[luθiðo]   *lucido*   'lucid'

[demenθia]   *demencia*   'dementia'   [la ðemenθia]

[reɣaθo]   *regazo*   'backlog'

[gola]   *gola*   'throat'   [la ɣola]

The voiced oral stops and the voiced fricatives are in complementary distribution.

Provide a statement of the distribution of these sounds to support this claim.

Consider the following data based on Italian: **EXERCISE 5.14•••**

[skudo]	*scudo*	'shield'	[zbadato]	*sbadato*	'careless'
[sabato]	*sabato*	'Saturday'	[zlitta]	*slitta*	'sleigh'
[seta]	*seta*	'silk'	[zmalto]	*smalto*	'glaze'
[sfida]	*sfida*	'dare'	[zgorbio]	*sgorbio*	'daub'
[sindakato]	*sindacato*	'union'	[zvestire]	*suestire*	'undress'
[solo]	*solo*	'alone'	[vazo]	*vaso*	'vase'
[sperone]	*sperone*	'spur'	[ezame]	*esame*	'survey'
[stampo]	*stampo*	'stamp'	[uzo]	*use*	'use'
[sudore]	*sudore*	'sweat'	[vizo]	*viso*	'face'
[aspettare]	*aspettare*	'await'	[mizeria]	*miseria*	'misery'
[vista]	*vista*	'view'	[tezoro]	*tesoro*	'treasure'

[s] and [z] are in complementary distribution. Provide a distribution table for each sound.

Return to your solution to Exercises 5.12 to 5.14. For each pair of allophones you   **EXERCISE 5.15•••**
identified in the data in these exercises, select one member as the underlying
or phonemic form, and write an allophonic rule to derive the other member of
the pair.

Examine carefully the distribution of the phoneme /ŋ/ in English by looking at the   **EXERCISE 5.16•••**
following words: *long, length, longer, *ngep, *ngotop, *ngear*. What kind of distribution does the phoneme /ŋ/ have?

What kind of distribution do the other two nasal consonants /m/ and /n/ have?

Now look at the following words and the kind of assimilation that nasal consonants in English are subject to: *temporary, limp, tent, rend, longer, finger, *tenporary, *temd, *tengp*. What kind of assimilation are all the three nasals subject to?

Now look at the way in which the /ŋ/ phoneme appears in the following words: *long* vs *longer, strong* vs *stronger?* Where did the /g/ come from?

What kind of explanation might you want to provide on the basis of this data for the distribution of /ŋ/ by comparison with the other nasals?

Syllables and Suprasegmentals

In the previous chapter we concentrated on segmental phonology. We did not discuss any unit larger than the phoneme, or any aspect of phonology which may apply to more than a single segment. In this chapter we shall look at the syllable – a unit which may be larger than a single segment – and various suprasegmental aspects of phonology. Suprasegmentals are, as their name suggests, features of the sounds of a language which apply to units larger than a single segment. The IPA has special symbols to indicate these features.

6.1 SYLLABLES

Although the discussion of phonotactics above (see Chapter 5.3.2) introduced the term 'syllable', no attempt was made to define it. Most speakers of English, **syllable**

ˈ	Primary stress	
ˌ	Secondary stress	ˌfoʊnəˈtɪʃən
ː	Long	eː
ˑ	Half-long	eˑ
̆	Extra-short	ĕ
|	Minor (foot) group	
‖	Major (intonation) group	
.	Syllable break	ɹi.ækt
‿	Linking (absence of a break)	

Figure 6.1 Suprasegmentals

although probably unable to define the term 'syllable', have some intuitive notion of how many syllables a given word contains.

Transcribe each of the following words, divide them into syllables by inserting the syllable boundary marker (.) and list the number of syllables. For example:

divide   2 /də.vɑid/

phonetic, linguistics, member, wombat, data, ancestral, aardvark, communal, extra, monopoly, quickly, taboo

---

Your answers are probably something like this:

3	/fə.ne.tɪk/	3	/lɪŋ.gwɪs.tɪks/
2	/mem.bə/	2	/wɒm.bæt/
2	/dei.tə/	3	/æn.ses.trəl/
2	/ɑːd.vɑːk/	3	/kɒm.jə.nəl/
2	/ek.strə/	4	/mə.nɒ.pə.lɪ/
2	/kwɪ.klɪ/	2	/tə.buː/

While it is unlikely that we will have disagreed on the number of syllables each word contains, you may disagree, for some words, with our placement of the boundaries. For example, you may have /æn.se.strəl/, /kɒ.mjən.əl/, /kwɪk.lɪ/ or /eks.trə/. All of these alternatives are acceptable. For other words, for example *aardvark, wombat,* and *member,* the only possible syllabifications are those given above. Neither /me.mbə/ nor /memb.ə/ is acceptable. Any account of the syllable should explain why, for some words, there is only one possible syllabification but for others alternative syllabifications are possible.

6.1.1   SYLLABLE BOUNDARIES AND PHONOTACTICS

The number of syllables in any given word would appear, at least from the data considered above, to be related to the number of vowel sounds (monophthongs and diphthongs) the word contains. If a word contains two vowel sounds, for example *exclude,* then it contains two syllables. Clearly there is a principled means for arriving at the number of syllables in a word. There is also a principled means by which we can identify those words which have alternative syllabifications and what those alternatives are.

Consider the word *member,* which we transcribed as /membə/. *Member* may only be syllabified as /mem.bə/, and not as either /me.mbə/ or /memb.ə/. We may arrive at an understanding of why this is so if we consider the cluster /mb/. In our discussion of the phonotactics of English in Chapter 5.3.2, we identified the possible word-initial clusters of English. The list of possible word-initial CC clusters does not include /mb/. This is an illicit cluster, and no word or syllable may begin with this cluster. Consequently, *member* cannot be syllabified as /me.mbə/, as the second syllable would then begin with an illicit cluster. Although we did not identify or discuss the permissible word-final clusters, no English word may end with /mb/. It is both an illicit initial and an illicit final cluster. For /mb/ the only possibility is to place the syllable boundary between the two consonants.

We may use the phonotactics of the language as a principled basis for determining where syllable boundaries occur in bi- and polysyllabic words. Implicit in this approach is the claim that the phonotactic restrictions apply not to words but to syllables. If a cluster cannot occur at either the beginning or the end of a word, then it cannot either begin or end a syllable. Any consonants that occur between two vowels will be assigned to a vowel so as to produce permissible word-initial or final clusters. Although this is illustrated by *member*, consider, as a further example, *stalwart*. This word also contains two syllables, with the boundary occurring between /l/ and /w/. We know the boundary must occur between these two segments because there are no words which either begin or end with /lw/. Therefore, no syllable may either begin or end with this cluster.

These are unambiguous examples. It is clear where, given the phonotactics of English, the boundaries must occur. There are, however, a large number of cases for which it is not so clear where the syllable boundary should occur. As an illustrative example, consider *extra*. Transcribed phonemically, we have /ekstrə/. If we have one syllable per vowel, then this word contains two syllables. As /k/, /ks/, and /kst/ are all possible word-final clusters, the syllable boundary may be placed after any of these. The problem of where to place the boundary is complicated further when we take the second syllable into consideration. /r/, /tr/, and /str/ are all possible word-initial clusters, and therefore the boundary may be placed in any of these three positions. These positions coincide with the possible positions for the end of the preceding syllable:

/ek.strə/   /eks.trə/   /ekst.rə/

Some consonants may belong to more than one syllable. We refer to such consonants as ambisyllabic. In the above example, /s/ and /t/ are ambisyllabic **ambisyllabic** as they may belong to both the first and the second syllable. Individual speakers may differ on which of the three possible positions they choose, but all are possible.

6.1.2 SYLLABLE STRUCTURE

In our discussion of the syllable, we have assumed, so far, that a syllable consists of a vowel and initial and final consonant clusters. Of these three constituents only the vowel is obligatory. All syllables must contain a vocalic nucleus. The initial and final consonant clusters are optional. This means that the simplest syllable will be a vowel, for example *eye* or *a*. Such syllables are represented as V. The next simplest syllable types are consonant–vowel (CV) or vowel–consonant (VC), for example *me, he, go, on, at* and *an*.

We discussed the largest syllable-initial clusters in English in Chapter 5.3.2, above. These clusters contain three consonants, the first of which is always /s/, the second a voiceless stop /p t k/, and the third is an approximant /r l j w/. The largest syllable-final cluster in English contains four consonants, for example *sixths*, /ksθs/, and, as with the syllable-initial clusters, the range of possible combinations is limited.

6.1.3 NUCLEUS, RHYME, ONSET AND CODA

nucleus
onset
coda
rhyme

As we discussed above, all syllables must contain a vocalic element. This is called the nucleus. The optional initial consonant or consonants are called the onset, while the optional final consonant or consonants are called the coda. Together the nucleus and coda form the rhyme. We can now represent the structure of the syllable as a tree. Consider as an example *streets*, as shown in Figure 6.2. The onset and coda constituents are self-explanatory. They represent initial and final consonants or clusters. However, the inclusion of the rhyme requires some further explanation.

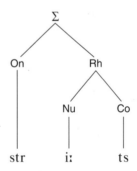

Figure 6.2

Σ is the Greek letter *sigma* and is used to represent the whole syllable.

The rhyme constituent consists of both the vocalic nucleus and the coda. There are a number of arguments for grouping these constituents together. First, in poetry the rhyme arises from the use of syllables whose nucleus and coda are identical but onsets differ. It is the nucleus and coda of the final word of one line which rhymes with the nucleus and coda of the final word of a later line, for example:

> The furl of fresh-leaved dogrose down
> His cheeks the forth-and-flaunting sun
> Had swarthed about with lion-brown
> Before the spring was done.

Gerard Manley Hopkins

Here the nucleus and coda of *down* rhymes with that of *brown*, and that of *sun* rhymes with that of *done*. The onset plays no role in these rhymes. The rhyme in poetry is carried by the rhyme constituent of the syllable. When the initial constituent of two or more syllables is identical, we refer to the resulting effect as alliteration, for example: **alliteration**

> Doom is dark and deeper than any sea-dingle

W. H. Auden

Secondly, we saw above that in the stream of speech some segments are elided (see Chapter 5.4.3). It is usually consonants which are elided, but vowels, especially short ones, may also be elided. Schwa, /ə/, is especially susceptible to elision. For example, in a word like *single,* the schwa of the final syllable may be elided:

single /sɪŋgəl/   →   [sɪŋgl]

When this vowel is elided, the final syllable no longer contains an obligatory nucleus. However, the syllable does not cease to exist, but a new nucleus is found. In this example, /l/ becomes the new nucleus. This is indicated in the transcription by placing a small vertical line, beneath the /l/, to indicate that it is now the nucleus:

[sɪŋgl̩]

You may recall that we used this symbol in Chapter 5.4.3.

We call consonants which may become the nucleus of a syllable 'syllabic **syllabic consonant** consonants'. In English, /l m n/ are the only consonants which may become the nucleus of a syllable. Not only is the number of syllabic consonants limited, but also these consonants must be part of the coda of the syllable. Consonants which become the nucleus of a syllable whose vocalic nucleus has been elided are never taken from the onset. This suggests that the relationship between the nucleus and coda differs from that between the onset and the nucleus. The nucleus and the coda are more directly related to each other. This more direct relationship is reflected in a structure of the syllable which groups these two constituents together as the rhyme.

Thirdly, the rhyme plays a role in stress placement in English. In all bi- and polysyllabic words, one syllable will always be more prominent than the others. We call this prominent syllable the 'stressed' syllable.

Identify the stressed syllable in each of the following words by placing a single quotation mark at its beginning:

monopoly, politics, wombat, become, dogma, algebra, phoneme, window, butcher, bromide, digital, promise

Speakers of English, even when presented with a word they have not previously seen or heard, are usually able to assign it the correct stress pattern. For example, the word *ambipedal*, which is a brand new coinage and means 'able to use both legs equally', has the main stress on the *ped* syllable. We can conclude from this that there must be a set of principles or rules which allows speakers to assign stress to the appropriate syllable of a word. Given that stress placement is quite complex, there will be (and are) exceptions to any such set of principles or rules.

Monosyllabic words pose no problems since there is only one syllable the speaker can stress. However, in more complex cases a number of factors influence the placement of stress. These factors include word-class membership, word structure, and the composition of the rhyme constituent.

Consider the following list of verbs and nouns. For each member of the list, provide a transcription, identify the stressed syllable by placing a single quotation mark before the stressed syllable, and draw syllable trees for each syllable.

ballot, exclude, attract, annoy, divide, abstract(v), enter, target, delight(n), money, abstract(n), canteen, incline, linguist, machine

Answer:

/'bælət ˌeksˈkluːd əˈtrækt əˈnɔi dəˈvaid əbˈstrʌkt 'entə 'taːgət dəˈlait 'mʌni 'æbstrækt kænˈtiːn inˈklain 'liŋgwist məˈʃiːn/

If we consider the verbs first, we can see that the stress may fall on either the first or the second syllable. In discussions of stress it is normal to refer to syllables by counting back from the end of the word. In a bisyllabic word the second syllable is the ultimate or final syllable and the first is the penultimate. The antepenultimate is the initial syllable of the three-syllable word. This is illustrated by considering, as an example, *rhododendron*, as shown in Figure 6.3.

To determine the rule for stress placement, we should consider the rhyme section of the stressed syllable and compare it with the rhyme of the unstressed syllable. Furthermore, stress placement rules usually apply to the final syllable first, so in your comparison compare the rhymes of stressed and unstressed final syllables.

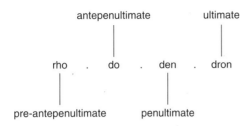

Figure 6.3

The rhyme constituent of those final syllables which are stressed contains either a diphthong, /də'vaid/, a long vowel, /eks'kluːd/, or a short vowel followed by a coda of two consonants, /əb'strækt/. The rhymes which contain either a long vowel or a diphthong may also contain a coda of one or more consonants, for example, /eks'kluːd/ and /də'vaid/. These consonants do not play a role in stress placement in these cases. However, if the rhyme contains a short vowel, it will only accept stress if it also contains a coda of two or more consonants. These rhymes are traditionally referred to as being 'heavy'.

Rhymes which consist of either a short vowel or a short vowel plus a single consonant are called 'light', for example, /'entə/. So if the rhyme constituent of the final syllable of a bisyllabic verb is heavy, it will accept stress. If it is not, it rejects stress which then falls on the penultimate syllable irrespective of its weight.

In our introductory discussion about stress placement, we noted that word-class membership, as well as the structure of the rhyme, plays a role in stress placement. If we now turn to the nouns, we see that they differ from verbs with respect to which rhyme types accept stress. Stress falls on a final syllable which contains either a long vowel or a diphthong. If the final syllable contains a short vowel and two or more consonants, then, unlike the verbs, it rejects stress. The notion of a heavy syllable is more restricted with nouns. This difference accounts for the different stress placement on noun–verb pairs such as *abstract, conduct, frequent,* and *protest.* In each pair, the verb is stressed on the final syllable, while the noun is stressed on the penultimate syllable.

One final point concerning the structure of the syllable concerns the distribution of sound types through the syllable. The nucleus is always either a vowel or a syllabic consonant, which in English is always a sonorant (either an approximant or a nasal). As we move out from the nucleus, we find that the sounds in consonant clusters become gradually less sonorant. In any cluster, approximants and nasals, if present, occur closer to the nucleus than obstruents. The less vowel-like a sound is, the further from the nucleus it occurs.

These sequencing tendencies can be seen as the result of speech being produced by the periodic opening and closing of the mouth. When the mouth is fully open you are likely to be producing a vowel. When your mouth is shut tight you are likely to be voiceless. So stops are more likely at the periphery of syllables and voiced sounds in the middle of them.

Turning now to speakers of English as a second or foreign language, they sometimes have a first language with different phonotactics and therefore different syllable structure from that of English. Some languages allow only a single optional consonant at the beginning of the syllable. When speakers of such languages speak English, they tend to put epenthetic vowels in to break up initial English consonant clusters giving more syllables as we saw in the previous chapter. For example, *spray* might become *peray*. They tend also to put vowels after final consonants to create the, for them, native-sounding syllables. So Japanese speakers of English will take a word like *cat* and put a vowel on the end of it. Then they get the right CVCV syllable structure. If there are enough such speakers in a speech community, then they develop their own variety of English with its own syllable structure.

Maori has a (C)V syllable structure. Could Maori have ambisyllabic consonants?

The answer has to be no because, if there was a consonant, it would have to belong to the beginning of a syllable.

6.1.4 RHYME SCHEMES

couplet

Most English poetry written before the Second World War made use of the fact that syllables had a rhyme constituent, by creating patterns with rhymes. These patterns involved the last rhyme of a line of a poem and the same rhyme at the end of a nearby line. We saw an example of this earlier. Different patterns of rhymes led to different rhyme schemes. When two lines rhyme, one below the other, this is called a 'couplet'. In the eighteenth century most English poetry was in couplets. The twentieth-century American poet Ogden Nash also used couplets. In his poems for the French composer Saint Sains's music *Carnival of the Animals* he wrote about cuckoos (which lay their eggs in the nests of other birds):

> Cuckoos lead Bohemian l**ives**.
> They fail as husbands and as w**ives**.
> That is why they cynically disp**arage**
> Everybody else's m**arriage**.

ballad

Traditional ballads have a rhyme syllable matching at the ends of their second and fourth lines. Samuel Taylor Coleridge's *The Rhyme of the Ancient Mariner* uses this style:

> It is an ancient Mariner,
> And he stoppeth one of thr**ee**.
> 'By thy long beard and glittering eye,
> Now wherefore stopp'st thou m**e**'?

Limericks consists of five lines, two couplets one after the other and the last line rhyming again with the first. You can make them up yourself. A web search will find hundreds which you may enjoy. **limerick**

Rhyme schemes are usually given by assigning a letter to each rhyme. So, for couplets, the rhyme is aa bb cc etc. while the scheme of a limerick goes: aabba.

One of the most complex forms is the sonnet, which has fourteen lines and two major rhyme schemes. The Petrarchan rhyme scheme goes: abbaabba cdecde, while the Shakespearean one goes: abab cdcd efef gg. **sonnet**

Poetry written without a rhyme scheme is called blank verse. Most post-Second World War poetry and most of Shakespeare's plays are written in blank verse. **blank verse**

6.2 SUPRASEGMENTAL FEATURES OF ENGLISH

In our discussions of English phonetics and phonology we have concentrated on the description of individual segments, consonants and vowels. We have also discussed a number of processes which affect these individual segments – for example, assimilation, elision, and aspiration. These individual segments may combine with each other to form larger units, such as syllables and words. There are a number of phonological features which extend or spread over more than a single segment. We call these features prosodies or suprasegmentals. Stress, pitch, and intonation are all suprasegmental features. **prosody** **suprasegmental** **stress** **pitch** **intonation**

6.2.1 PITCH

In Chapter 4.2.2.2 we discussed the contribution of the phonatory process to speech production. This process introduces voice into speech through the activity of the vocal cords. The rate at which the vocal cords may vibrate is not fixed but can be deliberately varied by the speaker.

Taking the syllable [juː], try saying this with your normal pitch, a low pitch, a high pitch, a rising and a falling pitch. This demonstrates that pitch is controlled by the speaker.

The faster the vocal cords vibrate, the higher the pitch of a sound, and the slower the rate of vibration, the lower the pitch will be. We can increase or decrease the rate at which our vocal cords vibrate in two ways. First, we can vary the pressure of the air coming out of the lungs. The greater the pressure, the higher the pitch, and vice versa. Secondly, any change in the tension of the vocal cords will result in a change of pitch. An increase in the tension of the vocal cords will raise the pitch of the voice.

All speakers have a pitch span, which ranges from the lowest note they can produce to the highest. In normal speech production, speakers do not make use of their entire pitch span, but only a middle portion. Movements out of this middle portion are often associated with particular emotional states or attitudes towards the topic of discussion. For example, if a speaker is happy, nervous, excited, or enthusiastic about the topic of discussion, then he or she will make more use of the upper portion of their pitch span. Use of the lower portion may occur when the speaker is sad, bored or unenthusiastic about the topic of discussion.

6.2.2 INTONATION

Consider the following sentence:

The doctor has been called.

Say it once as a statement, and a second time as if it were a question. Paying particular attention to the end of the sentence, do you notice any difference in the pitch of your voice between the two?

The pitch of your voice should have dropped on *called* when you uttered the sentence as a statement but risen when you uttered it as if it were a question. These variations in pitch contribute to our understanding of the utterance as a whole. Our response to the above sentence uttered with a falling pitch on the final word would differ from that to the same sentence uttered with a rise in pitch on the final word. These two pitch movements are not unique to this example but recur across the language. We call these recurrent changes in pitch movement 'intonation'. Intonation is another suprasegmental feature.

Intonation involves a limited number of recurrent pitch movements or patterns. Each pitch pattern may be used to convey the speaker's attitude to the topic of conversation, or to the hearer, or the speaker's personality, or to signal grammatical features such as whether the utterance is a question. We shall call

tone

these pitch patterns tones. We can identify, for English, three basic tones: (a) a fall from high to low, indicated by ˋ; (b) a rise from low to high, indicated by ˊ; and (c) a monotone, indicated by ˉ. The terms 'high' and 'low' are relative. There is no absolute value attached to these terms. What is important is that the finishing point is lower than the start, and not the value of either point.

Each of the tones introduced above may be associated with a typical meaning. A fall typically signals 'finality'. The speaker has concluded his or her contribution, or does not wish to say or hear any more on the topic being discussed. For example:

A   Did you see the documentary on sheep last night?

B   ˋNo (and I'm not interested).

A rise in the pitch is associated with 'questioning' or a desire to say or hear more. For example:

A   Did you see the documentary on sheep last night?

B   ´No (but I'm interested).

The monotone is relatively unnatural and is associated with routine. For example:

A   Have you ever been refused car insurance?

B   ¯No.

A   Have you ever been charged with a traffic violation, except parking?

B   ¯No.

There are two further tones, which are combinations of the rise and fall tones. These tones are the fall–rise, indicated by ˇ, and the rise–fall indicated by ˆ. The fall–rise signals 'limited agreement' or 'agreement with reservation'. For example:

A   Do you like my new shoes?

B   ˇYes.

Speaker A would expect B to continue and explain why he/she has reservations, and what they are. The rise–fall is associated with strong feelings of either approval or surprise. For example:

A   Do you like my new shoes?

B   ˆYes.

These tones do not change the meaning of the word with which they are associated, but change the meaning of the utterance as a whole. In the above examples, *no* retains the same lexical meaning no matter which tone the speaker uses. However, the tones modify the meaning of the utterance, as is illustrated by either the fall and rise examples, or the fall–rise and rise–fall examples.

The use of tone in English differs from that in languages such as Thai, Chinese, and Vietnamese. In these languages, unlike English, tone does change the meaning of a word. For example, in Thai the meaning of /naa/ changes with the tone: /naa/ plus a high tone means 'young maternal aunt or uncle', but when uttered with a mid tone it means 'rice paddy'. Tone in Thai is phonemic. To change the tone of a Thai word results in a different word, just as changing the initial /t/ of English /tɪp/ to /d/ results in a different word.

6.2.2.1 Tone groups and tonic syllables
Conversation does not consist of one-word utterances.

Draw two lines to represent the minimum and maximum pitch of your own voice, and then try to draw a line, as illustrated by the first example in Figure 6.4, to represent your intonation for the following sentences:

Figure 6.4
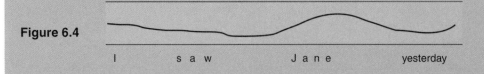

I   s a w   J a n e   yesterday

(a)   All the people are coming.

(b)   Are all the people coming?

(c)   I decided yesterday I didn't want to go.

Your answers might look like the drawings in Figure 6.5.

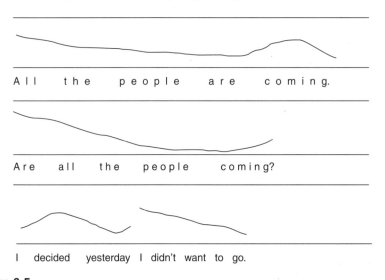

A l l   t h e   p e o p l e   a r e   c o m i n g.

A r e   a l l   t h e   p e o p l e   c o m i n g?

I   decided   yesterday   I   didn't   want   to   go.

Figure 6.5

We can see from these examples that major changes in pitch do not occur on all the syllables of an utterance. There is only a single tone in each of the first two examples. This tone falls on the first syllable of *coming*, which is the last stressed syllable of the utterance. In the third example there are two tones. The first falls on the final syllable of *yesterday*, while the second occurs on *go*. The distribution of tones in continuous speech has led to the establishment of a unit which is generally larger than a single syllable. We call this unit the 'tone group'.

tone group

Although tone groups are usually larger than a single syllable, both single syllable and multi-syllable tone groups are possible.

To clarify the notion 'tone group', let us consider some examples.

> Consider both the intonation contour assigned to the first example in the previous exercise, and those assigned to B's answers to A's questions. What do all of these tone groups have in common?

All of these tone groups contain one of the tones we identified above in section 6.2.2. Tone groups must contain a syllable on which a major change of pitch occurs. This syllable is called the 'tonic syllable' and is the only obligatory member of a tone group. The simplest tone group will consist only of a tonic syllable, while larger tone groups will contain a tonic syllable and a number of other syllables during the articulation of which no major change of pitch occurs. The pitch may change from one syllable to the next, but it remains constant throughout the production of these syllables. The obligatory tonic syllable is the only syllable in the tone group where the pitch changes during its production.

tonic syllable

The structure of the tone group proposed above parallels that which we proposed for the syllable. Both syllables and tone groups must contain an obligatory element. In the case of the syllable it is the vocalic nucleus, and for the tone group it is the tonic syllable. All other constituents (onset, and coda or non-tonic syllables) are optional.

In any tone group, we can identify the tonic syllable through its possession of the following properties. First, it carries the major pitch change, which will be one of the tones introduced above. Second, it will always be a stressed syllable, but it is more prominent than other stressed syllables. This additional prominence is called 'tonic stress'.

6.2.2.2 Tone groups and continuous speech

Any stretch of continuous conversation will consist of a number of tone groups. Although we have established a basic structure for tone groups, we have not discussed any criteria which would allow us to place boundaries between adjacent tone groups. We may use grammatical, semantic and phonetic criteria to delimit tone groups.

Tone group boundaries tend to occur at major grammatical boundaries, for example, those between phrases (about which we will have more to say in Chapter 7). This is illustrated by the examples in Figures 6.6 and 6.7 where the vertical stroke indicates a tone group boundary.

There are two tone groups in each of these examples. In the first example, the boundary falls between the two clauses, while in the second it falls between phrases, but not in the middle of them. The tone groups coincide with grammatical constituents, and also have meaning. If the boundary were to fall between *alligator* and *evil*, then the tone group would cut across a grammatical phrase,

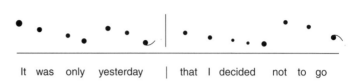

It   was   only   yesterday | that   I   decided   not   to   go

Figure 6.6

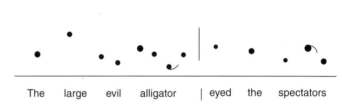

The   large   evil   alligator | eyed   the   spectators

Figure 6.7

and produce a tone group which was semantically anomalous. This tendency for tone group boundaries to coincide with major grammatical boundaries gives tone groups both grammatical and semantic coherence.

One possible phonetic marker of tone group boundaries is the pause. Furthermore, pauses may coincide with major phrase boundaries. The occurrence of a pause at a major phrase boundary suggests strongly that this is also the location of a tone group boundary. However, not all units that are bounded by pauses are tone groups. As tone groups must contain a tonic syllable, which is always stressed, then any unstressed syllable bounded by pauses cannot be a tone group.

Furthermore, it is also the case that an intonation contour which goes from one pause to the next is not necessarily a single tone group. Consider, for example, the third sentence in the exercise in section 6.2.2.1, above. Even if this sentence were uttered without any internal pauses, it would contain two tone groups. In most people's intonation there will be a break in the continuity of the intonation after *yesterday*. This break in continuity suggests that a boundary occurs at this point. Support for the placing of a tone group boundary in this position comes from the behaviour of the pitch of the voice. After the tonic syllable, which falls on the final syllable of *yesterday*, and is uttered with a falling tone, there is a slight step up in pitch to the next syllable, which is unstressed. This change of pitch between a stressed and an unstressed syllable usually indicates a tone group boundary.

Finally, the tonic syllable is often the stressed syllable of the final lexical word in a tone group. Having identified the tonic syllable, the tone group boundary may be placed after the tonic and any associated unstressed syllables. These associated syllables may be part of a syntactic constituent, or if the tonic does not fall on the final syllable of a word, then the boundary will occur after the remaining (unstressed) syllables.

Despite these guidelines, there are often cases where it is impossible to make a principled decision on the placement of tone group boundaries. This is especially the case in spontaneous conversation, where hesitation phenomena and other planning difficulties result in various anomalies. The problems posed by spontaneous conversation, and solutions to these problems, are discussed in Brown, Currie and Kenworthy (1980).

6.2.2.3 The functions of intonation

We can identify three functions for intonation: (i) attitudinal function, (ii) accentual function, and (iii) grammatical function. Let us look at each of these in more detail.

attitudinal function
accentual function
grammatical function

(i) attitudinal function

We may use intonation to indicate our attitude or emotions towards the topic being discussed. This involves not just intonation but also pitch placement, tempo, voice quality, and facial expressions. We have already encountered, above, a number of examples that illustrate this function of intonation. Our use of the fall to signal that we don't wish to say or hear any more on the topic being discussed, or the rise to signal that we are interested in the topic, are examples of attitudinal function. Both the fall–rise and rise–fall are also typically associated with a speaker's attitudes. (See section 6.2.2 above.)

(ii) accentual function

The tonic syllable is usually the stressed syllable of the final lexical word in the tone group. However, for contrastive purposes, it is possible to place the tonic syllable on any word. For this reason this function is sometimes called contrastive stress. This is illustrated by the following, where the italics indicate the tonic syllable:

(a)   He was wearing a blue *suit*.

(b)   (He wasn't wearing a *grey* suit.) He was wearing a *blue* suit.

In (a) the tonic syllable would normally fall on *suit*. However, if it were to fall on *blue*, this would imply a contrast, as illustrated by the (b) example. This contrastive use of intonation is accentual in that it draws attention to a word which would not otherwise have attention drawn to it. Similarly, prepositions are normally unstressed, and the placement of tonic stress on a preposition again implies a contrast, which is illustrated by the following:

(a)   Place the book on the *table*.

(b)   Place the book *on* the table. (Not under or next to it.)

For purposes of emphasis, the tonic may be placed on any syllable. For example:

(a) This is really *dull.*

(b) This is *really* dull.

(a) You mustn't run so *quickly.*

(b) You *mustn't* run so quickly.

The (a) examples are non-contrastive, while the (b) ones are contrastive.

The tonic syllable may be located earlier within a tone group if the later information in the tone group is taken as given. For example:

Here's the *book* you asked me to buy.

The request to buy the book is not new, that is, is taken as given. What is not taken as given is that it is a book which is involved and so the tonic is located earlier in the tone group.

(iii) grammatical function

In our discussion of tone group boundaries, we claimed that these boundaries normally coincide with the boundaries between major grammatical units. One consequence of this is that intonation may be used to disambiguate structures which, when written, are ambiguous. For example, in the sentence:

Those shareholders who bought quickly reaped the benefits.

there are two possible interpretations:

(a) Benefits were reaped by those shareholders who bought quickly.

(b) Benefits were reaped quickly by those shareholders who bought.

There are two possible ways of uttering this sentence. The first corresponds to the first interpretation, and the second to the second interpretation. These two possibilities are given below:

| Those shareholders who bought *quickly* | reaped the benefits |

| Those shareholders who *bought* | quickly reaped the benefits |

The first interpretation would have the tone group boundary between *quickly* and *reaped,* with the tonic falling on *quickly.* The second possibility has the boundary falling between *bought* and *quickly,* with the tonic falling on *bought.*

In poetry, when a line ends at the point at which there is a clear tone group boundary, the line is referred to as 'end stopped'. When there is no tone group boundary the line is referred to as 'run on'. Limericks usually have end stopped lines.

end stopped
run on

> There was an old lady of Ghent
> Who knew not if she came or she went.
> She'd lost most of her wits
> And would soon call it quits
> But for now she could still pay the rent.

6.3 STRESS

In our discussion of the syllable and intonation, we introduced the term 'stress' and discussed stress placement, but we did not provide a definition, nor did we discuss stress as a phenomenon. We said that stressed syllables tend to be more prominent but did not discuss what contributed to this prominence. Prominence of sounds is relative. There is no absolute measure of prominence. Sounds are only prominent in relation to another sound. Length, loudness, pitch and quality all contribute to a speaker's perception of a syllable as prominent.

Length   The length of a vowel contributes to prominence. Syllables containing long vowels and diphthongs tend to be more prominent than those which contain short vowels, even when they are unstressed.

Loudness   Hearers often perceive stressed syllables as louder than unstressed ones. This is a direct result of speech production factors such as greater muscular effort in forcing air between the vocal cords, which in turn vibrate more vigorously. This increased activity is ultimately perceived as an increase in loudness. Some linguists refer to loudness as 'intensity'.

Pitch   As we saw in section 6.2.1, this term is applied to the rate of vibration of the vocal cords. If the pitch changes on a syllable then that syllable will be perceived as prominent. This is often called 'pitch prominence'. It does not matter whether the pitch moves up or down; what counts is that it moves.

Quality   The quality of a sound also contributes to its prominence. In general, vowels are more prominent than consonants, but within each group there is a hierarchy. The more open a vowel is, the more prominent it is, thus /ɑi/ is more prominent than either /iː/ or /uː/. Approximants and nasals are more prominent than fricatives, which are more prominent than stops.

While all of these factors contribute to the prominence of syllables, some are more important than others in determining stress. It would seem logical that loudness is a major contributor to prominence, but this is not the case. As we discussed above, some sounds are more prominent, that is, they sound louder than others by virtue of their quality. While it is true that stressed syllables tend to be louder (or more intense) than unstressed ones, pitch movement is the most obvious cue to prominence for the hearer.

Of the remaining three factors, length contributes quite strongly to prominence. Quality also plays a role but to a lesser extent than either pitch movement or length. Although stressed syllables tend to be louder than unstressed ones, loudness by itself as a marker of prominence is the least effective of the four contributory factors. In general, a stressed syllable will tend to be marked by a change in pitch and, in comparison with unstressed ones, to be longer and louder. Stress is the result of the cumulation of two or more of these properties on a single syllable.

6.3.1   LEVELS OF STRESS

Some longer words have more than one stressed syllable. For example, the following words have two stressed syllables: 'mini'mize, 'circu'late, 'explan'ation, and 'deri'vation. Not only do these words have two stressed syllables, but when uttered in isolation, there would also appear to be a difference in the degree of stress. In the first two examples, the first stressed syllable appears to be more prominent than the second, while in the third example this position is reversed. We call the more prominent of the two stresses the primary stress and the lesser the secondary stress. For example, primary stress falls on the initial (or antepenultimate) syllable of *minimize,* while secondary stress falls on the final (or ultimate) syllable. We indicate primary stress with a raised mark and secondary stress, where it occurs, with a low mark before the stressed syllable. For example:

'mini,mize   'circu,late   ,expla'nation   ,deri'vation

Recall that when we discussed compound nouns in Chapter 2.2.1, we said that compound nouns had primary stress on the first word of the compound. So what would we expect to happen when a conversion takes place from a compound verb to a compound noun? We would expect the stress to shift to the first word. Here is an example of this happening. At a local drycleaning firm, sometimes stains cannot be removed and a little ticket is attached to the garment which says:

The stains on this garment have not been overlooked. We consider that any more work would result in loss of colour or damage to the fabric.

As you can imagine, referring to these as 'little white tickets for stains we can't get out' is a bit of a mouthful so these are called an 'overlook, which has different stress from the verb over'look.

6.3.2   STRESS IN CONNECTED SPEECH: RHYTHM

In isolation all English words have at least one stress. However, in connected speech certain words are commonly unstressed. For example, *the, a, be, have, he, she, it, and, but, in, to, on* and *at* are usually unstressed. Bi- and polysyllabic words will contain at least one unstressed syllable. Consequently, in connected speech there will be a large number of unstressed syllables, and a smaller number of stressed ones. Alternations between stressed and unstressed syllables provide connected speech with its rhythm.   **rhythm**

Read the following sentences aloud and tap with a finger on each stressed syllable:

(a)   What did you hope to discover by this test?

(b)   What's the problem with all these people?

(c)   What's the difference between a free and a bound morph?

Mark the beginning of each stressed syllable and count the number of syllables between each stress; and note the regularity with which you tap each stressed syllable. Does the number of unstressed syllables between each stressed one vary or remain constant? Does the rate at which you tap the stressed syllables remain constant or does it vary?

Answers:

(a)   'What did you 'hope to dis'cover by that 'test?

(b)   'What's the 'problem with 'all these 'people?

(c)   'What's the 'difference between a 'free and a 'bound 'morph?

The number of unstressed syllables between each stressed one varies: 2, 2, 3 in the first; 1, 2, 1 in the second; and 1, 4, 2, 0 in the third. However, the rate at which you tap does not vary. There is a regular beat in each of the above sentences. Stressed syllables in English occur at regular time intervals. This leads us to say that English is stress timed, that is, the period of time between each stressed syl-   **stress timed** lable, irrespective of the number of intervening unstressed syllables, is roughly equal. Each stressed syllable and the unstressed ones which follow it are grouped together to form a metrical unit we call the foot. All utterances may be divided up   **foot** into feet. We can illustrate this using one of the above sentences as an example:

| What's the | difference between a | free and a | bound | morph?

If stressed syllables occur at approximately regular intervals, then each foot, irrespective of the number of syllables it contains, should be of approximately equal length. To ensure that, for example, a foot of five syllables is of the same duration as one of two syllables, various phonological processes operate on the unstressed syllables. For example, unstressed vowels may be reduced, usually to [ə], or [ɪ]. We can see vowel reduction most readily in cases where we have the same stem with different word endings added. With the addition of further syllables the stress shifts (usually towards the end of the word), and the syllable which was formerly stressed has its vowel reduced:

de'rive [dəraɪv], de'rivative [dərɪvɪtɪv], deri'vation [derɪveɪʃən]

You will notice that the stressed syllable has the full phonemic value, the one we would expect from the spelling. When the stress is removed, the vowel is weakened. Sometimes instead of reducing, vowels can disappear altogether. When this happens the syllable is left without a vowel, and then, as we noted in section 6.1.3, one of the syllabic consonants, if present, takes over the function of the syllable. For example:

bottom [bɒtm̩], thicken [θɪkn̩], fiddle [fɪdl̩]

In some cases no syllabic consonant is present, and elision of the vowel may leave us with a 'syllable' which violates the phonotactics of English. For example:

should [ʃd], there is [ðz]

Sometimes unstressed syllables may be completely elided:

'sentences [senːzɪz]

syllable timing

mora timing

Not all languages have stress-timed rhythm. Some allocate more or less the same time to each syllable and are termed 'syllable timed'. French is one such language. Still others allocate about the same time to each short vowel so that a syllable containing a long vowel is about twice the length of a syllable containing a short vowel. This is termed 'mora timing'. In many parts of the world where English is spoken as a second or foreign language, the timing of English is not stress timing but syllable or mora timing. In Singapore, the New English spoken as a native language has taken on the timing of Chinese to a considerable extent and this is heard as a kind of rapid-fire staccato delivery with each syllable having about the same time devoted to it.

What do you think would be the effect on vowel weakening of speaking English with syllable or mora timing?

One of the likely results is that vowel weakening would occur less. So French speakers of English as a second language tend to have fewer syllables which phonetically have /ə/ as their nucleus. It might be that if we look at speakers of English around the world, perhaps a majority do not speak with stress-timed rhythm.

Although we said above that stressed syllables tend to occur at regular intervals, this is only a tendency. Speakers may, and do, vary the rhythmical patterns of their speech. If a speaker were to use a single rhythmical pattern, he or she would sound monotonous, and hearers would soon lose interest in what was being said. To avoid sounding monotonous, speakers vary the rhythmical patterns they use. Such variations are most obvious in poetry. In the following extract, W. H. Auden controls the rhythmical pattern and creates a rhythm which echoes the sound of a train:

Night Mail

This is the night mail crossing the border,
Bringing the cheque and the postal order,

Letters for the rich, letters for the poor,
The shop at the corner, the girl next door.

Pulling up Beattock, a steady climb:
The gradient's against her, but she's on time.

Past cotton-grass and moorland boulder,
Shovelling white steam over her shoulder,

Snorting noisily, she passes
Silent miles of wind-bent grasses.

Finally, syllables which are stressed are more prominent not just in their loudness but also in the way the phonemes in the syllable are perceived. In poetry the sound patterns made on stressed syllables are more significant than those of unstressed ones. A line of poetry which contains alliterating consonants in the onset of stressed syllables will sound a lot more 'noisy' than one which has those consonants in the coda of lightly stressed syllables. Compare: *play pool with a big, bad cannonball* with: *observation is a simple necessity*. Both have stops alliterating but the first line has them at the beginning of stressed syllables while the second has them at the beginning and end of unstressed syllables.

6.3.3 RHYTHM AND METER IN POETRY

Just as there are patterns for rhyme in poetry within traditional verse forms, so there are patterns of rhythm. These patterns form a kind of metrical grid within which the poetry is written. Meter has two aspects: the number of feet to a line **meter** and the positioning of weak and strong beats in a foot, that is, stress placement to a foot. If there are only two feet to a line, that is, two stressed syllables, then the meter is termed dimeter; if there are three, trimeter; four, tetrameter; five, pentameter; and six, hexameter.

trochee, trochaic iamb, iambic

Feet come in four traditional forms. If there are only two syllables in the foot then the stressed syllable must come first or second. If first, then the foot is termed a trochee and the meter trochaic. If second, then the foot is an iamb and the meter iambic. The child's rhyme *eeny meeny miney mo* is trochaic. The line starts with a stressed syllable followed by an unstressed one and carries on that way until the last syllable, which is also stressed. Iambic rhythm is much more commonly used in English poetry, for example, in Thomas Gray's *Elegy Written in a Country Churchyard,* which begins:

> The curfew tolls the knell of parting day,
> The lowing herd winds slowly o'er the lea,
> The ploughman homeward plods his weary way,
> And leaves the world to darkness and to me.

dactyl, dactylic anapaest, anapaestic

If there are three syllables to a foot, then, as far as traditional meter goes, they have the stressed syllable either first or last. If first, the foot is a dactyl and the meter dactylic, if last, the foot is an anapaest and the meter anapaestic. If we look again at the limerick, it has a complex mixture of feet. Each line starts with an iamb, followed in the case of the first two lines by two anapaests. The next two lines have only one anapaest after the iamb and the last line returns to the pattern of the first two lines.

scansion

When you put the two aspects of the meter together and examine a traditional verse form for its meter you are performing an operation called 'scansion'. An eighteenth-century couplet and poems with sonnet form are normally written in iambic pentameter, as are most of the lines in Shakespeare's plays (although Shakespeare's yokels often speak in free verse). Ballads alternate an iambic tetrameter line with an iambic trimeter line.

free verse doggerel

Poems which do not adhere to a traditional metrical grid pattern or rhyme scheme are written in free verse. Poems which adhere slavishly to both and have end stopped lines are called doggerel. Good poetry usually has some tension between the actual rhythm of the lines and the metrical grid patterns within which the poem or play is written. If we look at lines of Shakespeare's plays, they are normally ten syllables long and normally have five stressed syllables to a line. The meter is iambic pentameter. But the stressed syllables seldom line up exactly where the meter would have had them occur. Look, for example, at the opening lines from Shakespeare's *Richard III*:

> Now is the winter of our discontent
> Made glorious summer by this sun of York.

If these lines followed iambic meter exactly then the stresses would run as follows:

> Now **is** the **win**ter **of** our **dis**con**tent**

> Made **glo**rious **summ**er **by** this **sun** of **York**.

But some of these syllables would not normally take a heavy stress. A more normal way to say the lines would be:

> **Now** is the **win**ter of our **dis**con**tent**
>
> **Made glo**rious **sum**mer by this **sun** of **York**.

There is therefore a tension between the meter and the rhythm. Shakespeare does not write doggerel but he does write in iambic pentameter.

Further exercises •

Transcribe into phonetic script, and then provide syllable trees, for the following monosyllabic words. Remember that the only obligatory elements in a syllable are the rhyme and the nucleus. Both the onset and the coda are optional. If you are doing syllable trees for words with more than one syllable then each syllable gets its own syllable tree.

EXERCISE 6.1•

groan, keep, dog, through, ooze, pain, thought, wipe, egg, lamb

Indicate the primary and secondary stresses in the following words by putting the appropriate stress marks in front of the relevant syllables.

EXERCISE 6.2•

(a) likely

(b) perfection

(c) interference

(d) solidify

(e) singlehandedly

Indicate the likely tone unit boundaries in the following sentences, put the tonic syllable in capital letters and indicate the way you would normally expect the tone to be. For example, the sentence

EXERCISE 6.3•

We had decided some time ago that we would walk.

would probably have the following intonation:

We had decided some time aˊGO | that we would ˋWALK.

(a) What was her name?

(b) You did what?

(c)   We had decided, some time ago, that we would walk.

(d)   By the time the team had reached the top, the light was fading and it was too late to descend.

(e)   Is there really more to him than meets the eye?

EXERCISE 6.4•••   Consider the rhythmical patterns of the following poem. How does the rhythmical pattern contribute to the images created by the words?

Inversnaid

This darksome burn, horseback brown,
His rollrock highroad roaring down,
In coop and in comb the fleece of his foam
Flutes and low to the lake falls home.

A windpuff-bonnet of fáwn-fróth
Turns and twindles over the broth
Of a pool so pitchblack, féll-frówning,
It rounds and rounds Despair to drowning.

Degged with dew, dappled with dew
Are the groins of the braes that the brook treads through,
Wiry heathpacks, flitches of fern,
And the beadbonny ash that sits over the burn.

What would the world be, once bereft
Of wet and of wilderness? Let them be left,
O let them be left, wildness and wet;
Long live the weeds and the wilderness yet.

Gerard Manley Hopkins

EXERCISE 6.5•••   Look at the following verse of poetry and see how stress has foregrounded some of the phonemes. Ask what effect this has had on the sound of the poem.

The Moods

Time drops in decay,
Like a candle burnt out,
And the mountains and woods
Have their day, have their day;
What one in the rout
Of the fire-born moods
Has fallen away?

W. B. Yeats

Glossary •

Accent   Accent refers to variation in pronunciation between speakers (or groups of speakers) of the same language. The variation may have either a social or a geographic base, and may be systemic, distributional, realizational, or selectional. *See also* **Dialect**.

Accentual function   The contrastive use of intonation.

Active articulator   The articulator that moves during the production of a speech sound. In English the tongue and the lips are the active articulators.

Affricate   Affricate is a manner of articulation. It involves a complete closure in the oral cavity followed by a slow release, which results in friction. For example, the initial and final sounds in *judge*, [dʒ], are affricates.

Alliteration   The repetition of a consonant phoneme, particularly in the onset of nearby stressed syllables.

Allophone   An allophone is the phonetic realization of a phoneme. The allophones of a phoneme are in complementary distribution, phonetically similar, and are predictable. Being predictable, allophones are rule-governed, that is, we can write a rule to account for the occurrence of each allophone.

Allophonic rule   Allophonic rules link the abstract phonemes to their phonetically real allophones (or underlying representations to surface ones).

Alveolar   This is a place of articulation. Alveolar sounds are produced by the tip/blade of the tongue articulating with the alveolar ridge, which lies behind the upper front teeth.

Ambisyllabic   We label a consonant or group of consonants which belong to more than one syllable ambisyllabic, for example in *extra* the /s/ and /t/ may belong to either the first or the second syllable – /ek.strə/, /eks.trə/, or /ekst.rə/.

Anapaest, anapaestic   A poetic foot with two weakly stressed syllables followed by a strongly stressed one. Rhythms with such feet are termed anapaestic.

Approximant   Approximant is a manner of articulation. During the production of an approximant, the active and passive articulators come close to one another but not quite close enough to produce audible friction; [j] is an example of an approximant.

Articulation   Articulation is one of the three speech production processes. It can be divided into 'place of articulation' (where an articulation occurs), and 'manner' (what type of articulation). *See also* **Initiation** *and* **Phonation**.

Articulator   A part of the oral cavity that is directly involved in making a speech sound.

Aspirated   Aspiration is a short puff of breath which occurs between the release of a stop and the onset of voicing. In English the voiceless stops are aspirated when they are the only onset consonant in a stressed syllable.

Assimilation   The process by which one segment becomes more like another, or two segments become more like each other.

Attitudinal function   The use of intonation by the speaker to indicate his or her emotional attitude to the topic of conversation.

Ballad   A traditional form of poetry (often sung) which has four-line verses. The lines rhyme abcb and alternate with iambic tetrameter and trimeter meter.

Blank verse   Poetry written without a rhyme scheme.

Broad transcription   Transcription that indicates only phonemic differences and ignores all allophonic variation. The symbols used represent only phonemic contasts. Broad (or phonemic) transcription is the most common and straight-forward means of representing the spoken forms of a language.

Cardinal vowels   A set of vowels that do not occur in any known language but are used as reference points, like the points of a compass. These reference points are: four front vowel positions and four back vowel positions each with a rounded and unrounded version. They are at the four corners of the vowel quadrilateral and at two equally distanced points from the extremities at the mid-high and mid-low positions. These cardinal vowels are used to locate vowels in general. If you know what the cardinal vowels sound like, then you can compare other vowel sounds with them to get an idea of their position.

Central   In the articulation of central sounds the tongue forms an airtight seal with the upper molars and gums. This forces the airstream over the centre of the tongue. In English all sounds except /l/ are central. The articulation of some vowel sounds may also be referred to as central. Central vowels are articulated with the middle section of the tongue. In English, /ʌ/, /ɜː/ and /ə/ are all central vowels.

Centring diphthong   A diphthong the second vowel of which is in the central area of the vowel quadrilateral

Closing diphthong   A diphthong the second vowel of which is more close (higher) than the first vowel

Coda   In syllable structure the rhyme constituent consists of an obligatory nucleus and an optional coda. The optional coda consists of any postvocalic consonants, for example, in *text*, /kst/ constitutes the coda.

Complementary distribution   Sounds which only ever occur in different (or mutually exclusive) environments are in complementary distribution. If the sounds in question are phonetically similar then it is more than likely that they are allophones of the same phoneme. For example, the palatalized allophone of /t/ only occurs before the palatal approximant, whereas the dentalized allophone only ever occurs next to a dental. These two sounds are in complementary distribution; we never find the palatalized allophone before a dental. Furthermore, they are phonetically similar. Therefore, they are allophones of the phoneme /t/.

Consonant   This is one of the major classes of sounds. Consonants occur at the margins of syllables (in the onset and coda) and not normally in the nucleus. They involve some obstruction (complete or partial) of the flow of air through the vocal tract, and therefore are usually defined in articulatory terms, that is, voiced/voiceless, place of articulation, and manner of articulation.

Contrastive distribution   Contrastive distribution involves two or more sounds which occur in identical environments and for which at least one minimal pair can be found, for example /p/ and /t/ occur in contrastive distribution in the words *pan* and *tan*, /pæn/ and /tæn/.

Couplet   A pair of successive lines of a poem where the final syllables rhyme.

Dactyl, dactylic   A poetic foot with a strongly stressed syllable followed by two weakly stressed syllables. Rhythms consisting of such feet are termed dactylic.

Defective distribution   This term is used to describe any phoneme which appears in some environments but not in others. For example, /h/ appears only in syllable-initial position, whereas /ŋ/ appears only in syllable-final position.

Dental   Dental is a place of articulation involving the tip of the tongue and the front incisors. In English, /θ/ and /ð/ are both dental, while in French, /t/ and /d/ are dental and not alveolar as they are in English.

Dentalized   We call the assimilation of a segment to the dental place of articulation dentalization. The sounds thus articulated are dentalized sounds.

Derivation   For most phonologists, surface representations (consisting of allophones) are derived from underlying ones (consisting of phonemes), through the application of allophonic rules. We usually refer to the process of deriving (or determining) the pronunciation of an underlying representation as a derivation.

Derived form   Any representation to which one or more allophonic rules have been applied.

Devoicing   Devoicing is an assimilatory process whereby a normally voiced segment is realized as voiceless. Devoicing may be either partial or full. In full devoicing, a segment which is normally voiced remains voiceless throughout its entire production. In a partial devoicing, the onset of voicing is delayed.

Diphthong   A vowel of continually changing quality within one syllable is a diphthong. The change in quality may be caused by a movement of the tongue and/ or lips. The vowels in *house, high* and *toy* are diphthongs.

Distinctive feature   Distinctive features are the fundamental units of phonology. They are smaller than phonemes, which are composed of sets of features. The features are usually binary (they have two values, + or −). We use the term 'distinctive' because the features are primarily intended to capture only the phonological (or distinctive) oppositions in any language, and not necessarily the phonetic realization of these oppositions.

Distributional difference   This is one of the four ways in which dialects may differ. The dialects in question have the same set of phonemes, but the distribution of certain phonemes may differ between the dialects in question, for example all dialects of English possess a voiced alveolar central approximant, /r/, but in southern British English /r/ is restricted to prevocalic position only, while in Ulster English it has a full distribution. It occurs before vowels, consonants, and pauses. *See also* **Realizational, Selectional** *and* **Systemic difference**.

Doggerel   Poetry where the rhythm slavishly follows the meter, and lines are generally end stopped.

Elision   Elision is the deletion of a segment normally present in the stream of speech.

End stopped line   A line of poetry with a tone group boundary at its end.

Epenthesis   Epenthesis is the insertion of segments not normally present in careful speech.

Features   *See* **Distinctive feature**.

Flap   *See* **Tap**.

Foot   The foot is a metrical unit consisting of a stressed syllable and all unstressed syllables up to, but not including the next stressed syllable. This term is used slightly differently in the analysis of poetic meter, where each foot has a fixed sequence of stressed and unstressed syllables.

Free variation   We refer to the suspension of phonemic contrast in isolated examples as free variation. For example, although /iː/ and /ɑi/ contrast in English (and are therefore phonemes), in [iːðə] vs [ɑiðə] the contrast is suspended. The substitution of /ɑi/ for /iː/ (or vice versa) does not in this case result in a different word.

Free verse   Poetry which is not metrical and does not follow a traditional rhyme scheme.

Fricative   Fricative is a manner of articulation. In the production of a fricative, the active articulator comes sufficiently close to the passive one to impede the flow of air but not to stop it completely. As the airstream is squeezed through the narrow gap between the articulators, it becomes turbulent and an audible hiss is produced; [f v s z] are all fricatives.

Front vowel   In the articulation of front vowels the tongue is not retracted in the oral cavity; [iː] is an example of a front vowel.

Fusion   Fusion is a process whereby two segments fuse together to form a third segment which shares features of the two input segments. For example, in English, /t/ and /j/ often fuse together to form [tʃ].

Glide   Glides are a subset of approximants. The glides are also called semivowels. Phonetically glides are very short vowels, but phonologically they behave like consonants.

Grammatical function   The use of intonation to indicate grammatical boundaries. It can therefore be used to disambiguate structures that when written can be ambiguous.

Hard palate   The hard palate is a bone that separates the oral cavity from the nasal cavity. It runs from the alveolar ridge to the beginning of the velum or soft palate. Sounds for which an active articulator moves towards or articulates with the hard palate are palatal.

High   A high vowel is produced with the tongue moved as far towards the palate as is possible without a blockage and therefore a consonant being produced.

High-mid   A high-mid vowel is one made with the tongue moved up from its mid rest position. High-mid is half way between the rest or mid position and the high position.

Homorganic   Sequences of consonants which share the same place of articulation are homorganic, for example, /n/ and /t/ in *dent*, /dent/.

Iamb, iambic   A poetic **foot** which has a weakly stressed syllable followed by a strongly stressed one. Rhythms with such feet are termed 'iambic'.

Illicit cluster   Illicit clusters are those consonant clusters which are ruled out by the general phonotactic rules of the language.

Initiation   Initiation is one of the three speech production processes. Initiation involves the creation of an airstream, which may then be modified by the articulatory and/or phonatory processes. *See also* **Articulation** *and* **Phonation**.

Intonation   Intonation is a suprasegmental feature. It involves a limited number of recurrent pitch movements or patterns. Each pitch pattern may be used to convey the speaker's attitude to the topic of conversation, or to the hearer, or the speaker's personality, or to signal grammatical features such as whether a sentence is a question.

Labial   Labial is a place of articulation. Any sound involving the lips in its articulation is labial. In English there are six labial sounds: two labial stops, /p b/; one labial nasal /m/; two labio-dental fricatives, /f v/; and a labio-velar approximant, /w/.

Larynx   The larynx is positioned at the top of the trachea (windpipe). It is a box-like construction consisting of cartilage. The protuberance known as the 'Adam's apple' is the top of the larynx. The vocal cords are located inside the larynx just below the level of the Adam's apple.

Lateral   If the tongue forms an air-tight seal at some point in the centre of the vocal tract, then escaping air will pass round this obstruction and out over the sides of the tongue. The manner of articulation involved is described as lateral. For example, the initial sound in *lateral* is a lateral.

Lateral escape   In non-homorganic stop-lateral clusters the airstream trapped by the stop escapes over the sides of the tongue.

Lateral release Lateral release occurs in homorganic stop-lateral sequences. The stop is released by the lowering of the sides of the tongue.

Limerick A poetic form which has only a single verse of five lines, which rhymes aabba. Each line begins with an iamb followed by anapaests. The first couplet is a trimeter, the second couplet a dimeter and the last line a trimeter again.

Lip attitude This refers to the position of the lips during the articulation of a sound. Typically, the lips may be either rounded as for the back rounded vowels or /w/, or spread for all other sounds.

Liquid Liquid consonants, in English /l/ and /r/, are a subset of approximants. Unlike glides, liquids are phonetically consonants and they behave phonologically like consonants.

Low Low sounds are those produced with the tongue lowered from the rest position.

Low-mid A low-mid vowel is one made with the tongue moved down from its mid rest position. Low-mid is half way between the rest or mid position and the low position.

Meter The grid pattern of weakly and strongly stressed syllables in traditional poetic forms. It has two aspects: the number of poetic feet per line and the arrangement of weak and strong stresses in each **foot**.

Mid vowel A mid vowel is articulated with the tongue departing little from its rest position. Mid vowels are articulated between the position of high vowels and low vowels; [e] is a mid vowel.

Minimal pair Two words which differ in one and only one sound are a minimal pair, for example, *pit* and *pot*, or *pip* and *pit*.

Minimal pair test The minimal pair test is a simple and effective means for identifying the phonemes of any language. The test uses the notion of minimal contrast through the minimal pairs to identify phonemes.

Monophthong A monophthong is a vowel the quality of which remains relatively unchanged throughout its production. For example /i/ and /æ/ are both monophthongs.

Mora timing When a language is mora timed, the unit of timing is approximately the length of a short vowel.

Narrow transcription A transcription that includes information on allophonic variation. Through the use of diacritics, this transcription type can provide detailed information on the articulation of sounds.

Nasal Nasal is a manner of articulation. The term is usually applied to sounds that involve a complete obstruction in the oral cavity, that is a stop, but for which the velum is in the lowered position. This allows air to escape through the nasal cavity. The position of the velum is independent of all other speech production processes. Consequently, although we find only voiced nasal stops in English, it is possible for nasals to be voiceless, and for any segment to be articulated with the velum in the lowered position. In this latter case we describe the sound as being nasalized. For example, the vowel sound in the French word *bon,* /bõ/, is nasalized. Nasalization is signalled through the placing of a tilde, ~, over the nasalized sound.

Nasal release   Oral stops may be released either by releasing the closure in the oral cavity or by lowering the velum. We refer to the second possibility as nasal release.

Nasalization   See **Nasal**.

Nucleus The nucleus is the obligatory constituent of a syllable. It must be either a vowel or one of the few consonants which may function as the nucleus in the absence of a vowel. In English, only /l m/ and /n/ may function as a syllable nucleus.

Obstruent   A member of the set of oral stops, fricatives and affricates.

Onset   This term refers to the optional initial consonant or consonants of a syllable. For example, in *string* /strɪŋ/, the onset is /str/.

Opening diphthong   A diphthong the second vowel of which is more open (lower) than the first vowel.

Oral   Oral is a manner of articulation. Oral sounds are produced with velic closure. That is, the velum is raised, making contact with the back wall of the pharynx. This seals off the nasal cavity and air from the lungs is forced out through the oral cavity. Sounds produced in this manner are oral.

Palatal   Palatal is a place of articulation. Palatal sounds involve the front of the tongue and the hard palate. The sound at the beginning of *yacht* is palatal. Assimilation of a segment towards the palate is palatalization.

Parallel distribution   Two or more sounds are in parallel distribution when they occur in identical environments.

Passive articulator   In the articulation of a speech sound an active articulator moves towards a passive one. Passive articulators do not move. In English the passive articulators are the teeth and positions on the roof of the mouth.

Pharynx   This is part of the vocal tract. It extends from behind the velum to the larynx.

Phonation   Phonation is one of the three speech production processes. Phonation involves the modification of the airstream from the lungs by the vocal cords. The main phonation types in English are voiced and voiceless. *See also* **Articulation** *and* **Initiation**.

Phoneme   A single sound segment which is contrastive in a language.

Phonemic system   A list of the phonemes of a language or dialect.

Phonetic similarity   For two or more sounds to be considered allophones of a single phoneme they must be not only in complementary distribution, but also phonetically similar to each other.

Phonological conditioning   If the distribution of allomorphs is determined by phonological factors then we say that the allomorphs are phonologically conditioned.

Phonotactics   Phonotactics are a list of restrictions on the distribution of segments, possible combinations of segments into clusters, and admissible syllable types.

Pitch   Pitch, a suprasegmental, is the property of a sound which allows a hearer to judge it as having a higher or lower 'note'. It is related to the frequency at which the vocal cords vibrate.

Place   In the articulation of consonants, place is where in the vocal tract obstruction of the airflow occurs. Labial, labio-dental, dental, alveolar, post-alveolar, palatal, velar and glottal are all places of articulation.

Potential cluster   Potential clusters are consonant clusters which are not ruled out by the general phonotactic restrictions of the language, and have to be specifically identified and ruled out. *See* **Illicit cluster**.

Progressive (or perseverative) assimilation   Assimilation where the sound which is subject to change comes after the source of the change.

Prosody   *See* **Suprasegmental**.

Realizational difference   This is one of the four ways in which dialects of a language may differ. Two dialects may possess the same number of phonemic oppositions but differ in the phonetic realization of particular phonemes. For example, both southern British English and New Zealand English possess an opposition between the vowels in *bit* and *bet*. However, in New Zealand English the vowel in *bit* is more central than its counterpart in southern British English, while the vowel in *bet* is realized slightly higher. *See also* **Distributional, Selectional** *and* **Systemic differences**.

Regressive (or anticipatory) assimilation   Assimilation where the sound which is subject to change comes before the source of the change.

Retroflex   A consonant produced with the active articulator (the tongue) turned downside up so that the lower surface of the tongue makes contact with the passive articulator.

Rhotic   A rhotic dialect of English has the phoneme /r/ fully distributed, that is, before vowels, consonants and pauses. Scottish English is fully rhotic whereas Australian English is not.

Rhyme   The rhyme is an obligatory constituent of a syllable. It consists of an obligatory nucleus and an optional coda. *See also* **Coda, Nucleus,** *and* **Syllabic consonant**.

Rhythm   Rhythm can be defined as the regular occurrence of an event. In language, rhythmical patterns arise from the alternation between stressed and unstressed syllables.

Run on line   A line of poetry which does not have a tone group boundary at its end.

Scansion   The process of working out for a poem, or verse drama, what its **meter** is.

Selectional difference   This is one of the four ways in which dialects of a language may differ. With selectional differences, two dialects have the same set of phonemic contrasts but particular words select different phonemes in each dialect. Again this is best illustrated with an example. The vowels /iː/ and /ɪ/ occur in both British and New Zealand English. However, for example in *cloudy*, speakers of standard British English select /ɪ/ as the final vowel, while New Zealand English speakers select /iː/. *See also* **Distributional, Realizational** *and* **Systemic difference**.

Soft palate   *See* **Velum**.

Sonnet   A complex poetic form with 14 lines in iambic pentameter with a rhyme scheme of typically abba abba cde cde (the Petrarchan form) or abab cdcd efef gg (the Shakespearean form).

Sonorant   A member of the set of nasals, glides (or semi-vowels) and liquids

Stop   Stop refers to a manner of articulation. For all stops an air-tight seal is formed at some point in the oral tract. This completely obstructs (or stops) the flow of air from the lungs. In English, [p b t d k g m n] and [ŋ] all involve an air-tight oral tract seal in their production, and therefore, are all stops.

Stress   In an utterance, some syllables appear more prominent in relation to their neighbours. We refer to this relative prominence as stress. Length, loudness, pitch and quality all contribute to a speaker's perception of a syllable as prominent or stressed.

Stress timed   A kind of rhythm, which standard English has, where the length of time between stressed syllables is roughly equal no matter how many unstressed syllables come between the stressed syllables.

Suprasegmental   Suprasegmentals are those aspects of speech production which involve more than a single segment. Stress, tone and intonation are all suprasegmental features. Another term for these features is 'prosody'.

Surface representation   The term 'surface representation' refers to a phonetic word form, of which the constituent parts are phonetically real allophones.

Syllabic consonant   A syllabic consonant is any consonant which is functioning as the obligatory nucleus of a syllable. In English only /l m/ and /n/ may function as the nucleus of a syllable.

Syllable   The syllable is a phonological unit which may be larger than a single segment. It contains an obligatory nucleus, and optional initial and final consonant clusters. The syllable types and consonant clusters (if any) permitted in a language are defined by the phonotactic rules of the language.

Syllable timing   When a language is syllable timed, each syllable occupies approximately the same time.

Systemic difference   This is one of the four ways in which dialects may differ. Dialects which differ systemically have different phonemic systems. For example, Scottish English has a voiceless velar fricative, /x/, which other dialects lack. Irish English lacks /θ/ and /ð/ which many other varieties of English have. *See also* **Distributional, Realizational** *and* **Selectional difference**.

Tap   Tap and flap are manners of articulation. In the articulation of taps and flaps, the active articulator makes a single fast contact with the passive one. In many US dialects of English the alveolar stops are articulated as taps when they occur between two vowels, for example the *t* in *phonetic* would be a voiced alveolar tap, [ɾ].

Tone   Tone is the term used to refer to pitch movements. In some languages tone is phonemic, that is, it is used to distinguish words. For example, in Thai the meaning of /naa/ changes with the tone: /naa/ plus a high tone means 'young maternal aunt or uncle', but when uttered with a mid tone it means 'rice paddy'. In English, tones are the major changes in pitch which occur on a tonic syllable. Each pitch pattern or tone is associated with a typical meaning.

Tone group   A tone group may consist of a single syllable or a number of syllables over which an intonation contour extends. All tone groups contain an obligatory tonic syllable.

Tonic syllable   The tonic syllable is the obligatory element in a tone group. The tonic syllable will be stressed, but more prominent than other stressed syllables in the tone group. We call this additional prominence 'tonic stress'. It also carries the major change of pitch, which will be one of the intonation tones found in the language.

Trill   Trill is a manner of articulation. For trills the active articulator is positioned so that the airstream flowing over it causes it to vibrate rapidly against the passive one. The vocal tract is alternately open and closed. In some dialects of Scottish English the sound at the beginning of *rabbit* is a voiced alveolar trill. French speakers speaking English often use a uvular trill.

Trochee, trochaic   A metrical **foot** with a strong followed by a weak syllable. A rhythm with such feet is trochaic.

Underlying representation   An underlying representation is the phonemic representation of a sound or word. It is an abstract representation and is also referred to as the lexical or dictionary form.

Unreleased   Stops are unreleased when the active articulator makes contact with the passive one but does not move away.

Uvula   The uvula is the pendulum-like end of the velum. It is a place of articulation and any sound involving the uvula as the passive articulator is uvular.

Velar   Velar is a place of articulation. Velar sounds involve the back of the tongue and the soft plate or velum. Assimilation of a segment towards the velum is velarization.

Velic closure   This term is used to define the position of the velum during the articulation of oral sounds.

Velum   The velum is a muscle that separates the nasal and oral cavities. It may be raised to form a seal with the pharynx, closing off the nasal cavity. This is called **velic closure**. Any sound involving the velum as a passive articulator is velar. In English the sounds at the beginning of *call* and *golf* and the sound at the end of *hang* are velar. We refer to the assimilation of a sound to the velum as velarization.

Voice   Voice refers to the buzzing sound created by the vibration of the vocal cords. Any sound for whose production the vocal cords vibrate is voiced, for example /b d g m n ŋ v ð z ʒ dʒ l r w j/. Sounds produced without the vocal cords vibrating are voiceless, for example /p t k f s ʃ tʃ/.

Voicing   This is an assimilation process whereby a normally voiceless sound is realized as voiced under the influence of a neighbouring voiced sound.

Vowel   Vowels function as the nucleus of a syllable. No audible friction occurs during the production of a vowel. They are usually defined through reference to the tongue position on vertical and horizontal axes, and lip position, rather than through the place and type of stricture.

Vowel quadrilateral   An abstract visual representation of the oral cavity used to represent the tongue position in the articulation of vowels. It is usually divided horizontally into front, central, and back, and vertically into high, high-mid, low-mid, and low. Vowels can be plotted on this chart. For example, /i/ typically involves the front of the tongue moving towards the hard palate, with maximal upward displacement from the rest position. This gives a high front vowel which is plotted on the chart in the top left corner.

Further reading •

Ashby, M. and Maidment, J. *Introducing Phonetic Science* (Cambridge: Cambridge University Press, 2005).

Brown, G., *Listening to Spoken English*, 2nd edn (London: Longman, 1990).

Brown, G., Currie, K. L. and Kenworthy, J., *Questions of Intonation* (London: Croom Helm, 1980).

Carr, P., *English Phonetics and Phonology: An Introduction* (Oxford: Blackwell, 1999).

Catford, J. C., *A Practical Introduction to Phonetics*, 2nd edn (Oxford: Oxford University Press, 2002).

Chambers, J. K. and Trudgill, P., *Dialectology* (Cambridge: Cambridge University Press, 1998).

Cruttenden, A., *Intonation*, 2nd edn (Cambridge: Cambridge University Press, 1997).

Crystal, D., *The English Tone of Voice* (London: Edward Arnold, 1975).

Francis, W. N., *Dialectology: An Introduction* (London: Longman, 1983).

Giegerich, H., *English Phonology: An Introduction* (Cambridge: Cambridge University Press, 1992).

Gimson, A. C., *An Introduction to the Pronunciation of English*, 4th edn (London: Edward Arnold, 1989).

Halliday, M. A. K., *A Course in Spoken English Intonation* (Oxford: Oxford University Press, 1970).

Hawkins, P., *Introducing Phonology* (London: Routledge, 1992).

Hayes, B. *Introductory Phonology* (Oxford: Wiley-Blackwell, 2008).

Kreidler, C. W., *The Pronunciation of English: A Coursebook in Phonology*, 2nd edn (Oxford: Blackwell, 2004).

Labov, W. *Sociolinguistic Patterns* (Oxford: Blackwell, 1972).

Ladefoged, P., *A Course in Phonetics*, 5th edn (London: Thompson Learning, 2006).

Lass, R., *Phonology: An Introduction to Basic Concepts* (Cambridge: Cambridge University Press, 1984).

Macaulay, R. K. S. and Trevelyan, G. D., *Language, Social Class and Education: A Glasgow Study* (Edinburgh: Edinburgh University Press, 1977).

McMahon, A. M.S., *An Introduction to English Phonology* (Edinburgh: Edinburgh University Press, 2002).

O'Connor, J. D., *Phonetics* (Harmondsworth: Pelican, 1973).

Odden, D., *Introducing Phonology* (Cambridge: Cambridge University Press, 2005).

Roach, P., *English Phonetics and Phonology: A Practical Course*, 3rd edn (Cambridge: Cambridge University Press, 2000).

Electronic resources

http://www.palgrave.com/language/kuiperandallan/
This site provides electronic resources directly related to Part II of this book.

http://www.arts.gla.ac.uk/IPA/ipa.html
Home page of the International Phonetic Association, home of the IPA.

http://www.sil.org/computing/catalog/show_software_catalog.asp?by=cat&name=Font
Home page of the Summer Institute of Linguistics from where you can download fonts for many different languages as well as for the IPA.

http://web.uvic.ca/hrd/ipa/main.htm
IPA symbols for use in web interfaces. The symbols are fetched from this web site by inserting a pointer in your web page.

http://www.linguistics.ucla.edu/faciliti/uclaplab.html
Lots of help with phonetics including a slow motion movie of the vocal cords vibrating.

http://www.yorku.ca/earmstro/ipa/
IPA chart where you can hear the sounds of the IPA.

part three

Sentences

In this part of the book we will look at the linguistic properties of sentences, that is, their phrase structure and major internal functions.

- We will see that for each major lexical category there is a phrase of which it is the head. These phrases in turn perform functions within clauses, and clauses and phrases are constituents of sentences.
- We will also look at how constituents may occupy different positions within the phrase structure of sentences and how this gives rise to the structural properties of questions, relative clauses, passive constructions and imperatives.

By the end of this part of the book you should be able to:

- recognize noun phrases, adjective and adverb phrases, prepositional phrases, and verb phrases;
- determine the internal structure of these phrases and draw tree diagrams of their structure;
- identify the constituents of complex phrases and sentences and how movements may have altered the underlying structure of sentences.

The Structure of Simple Sentences

INTRODUCTION

We have seen earlier that morphemes are the building blocks that go to make up words. But English is not just a collection of words. If words were all we knew, then what we would be able to say would be limited to exactly the vocabulary in our lexicons. Fortunately for us, words are put together to form sentences. The way in which words are put together to form sentences is called the syntax of the language. To recall that there is such a thing as syntax, recall the following exercise from Chapter 1.

Make a sentence out of each of the following sets of words:

   (a)   sleeps, a, baby, newborn

   (b)   in, house, live, green, the, a, people

   (c)   the, kicked, boy, ball, a

If it were the case that English had no syntax, that is, no rules for creating sentences, then these words could be put together in any order. However, you will have noticed that there are only a very few orders that create grammatical English sentences. All the other possible orders (including the order the words are given in the above exercise) do not create English sentences.

But what is it exactly that enables you to do this ordering? We saw in Chapter 1 that there is an infinite number of sentences in English and that we create new ones all the time. So out of the building blocks of lexical items we are able to construct an infinite number of sentences. How exactly do the rules of syntax come into this? First, as we have decided, there must be such rules because they are what enables us to structure sets of words into sentences. Secondly, there must be a finite set of such rules.

There are a number of reasons why this must be so. First, if English had an infinite set of syntactic rules, no one would ever be able to learn them all. Yet we do learn them and do so quite early in life. Secondly, if the set of rules was infinite then we would not be able to understand sentences spoken by someone who had learned a different set of English rules, just as we have difficulty in understanding people who use words which we do not know. In practice, this happens very infrequently and only with the small number of syntactic rules which differ from one dialect to another. For the rest, our difficulties in understanding other speakers of English are not the result of their knowing and using different syntactic rules. Thirdly, the set of syntactic rules must be finite because they fit inside our heads, and heads, for all their capacity, are nevertheless finite.

So we have a finite set of syntactic rules and a finite set of lexical items. But we can use these finite means for infinite ends, the creation of new, never-before-uttered sentences.

We will suppose that the syntax of English has phrase structure, that is, the sentences are made up of phrases and the phrases are made up of words. In looking at the phrase structure of English we will begin by looking at simple phrases and seeing how they consist of heads and modifiers. We will then look at the major functions within clauses.

7.1 SIMPLE PHRASES

7.1.1   THREE WAYS TO IDENTIFY PHRASES

In this section we will be looking at simple phrases. To do that we must first have some idea of what a phrase is. The sentence *Mary swims*, whose structure we discussed in Chapter 1, contains only two words. These must come in the order they do if the sentence is to follow the rules of English syntax. In the box diagram we drew for it in Chapter 1, there is no unit between 'word' and 'sentence'. However, if we look again at the sentences you put together earlier we can identify an intermediate unit.

None of the following strings of words follows the rules of English syntax for making a sentence. Change the order of each so that it is a grammatical sentence.

(a)   Has been eating the chocolate cake the old man.

(b)   The old man the chocolate cake has been eating.

(c)   Has been eating the old man the chocolate cake.

To make each of the above strings of words conform to the rules of English syntax you will have moved not single words, but fixed sequences of words, for example, *the old man*, or *the chocolate cake*. Sequences of words which move as whole units are intermediate between words and sentences. They are called 'phrases'.   **phrase**

There are three tests we can use to identify which sequences of words in a sentence are phrases: movement, meaning, and substitution. To produce grammatical sentences in the above exercise you moved fixed sequences, and not individual words. If a phrase can be moved then it moves as a whole unit. This movement may be further illustrated by the following examples:

(a)   *The old man* ate *the chocolate cake.*

(b)   What *the old man* ate was *the chocolate cake.*

(c)   It was *the chocolate cake* that *the old man* ate.

(d)   *The chocolate cake* was eaten by *the old man.*

If we consider the italicized sequences of words in the first sentence above, we can see that when they are moved to give us the other sentences they always move as a whole. We do not find sentences such as:

(a)   *It was man the chocolate cake which the old ate.

(b)   *The the cake was eaten by chocolate old man.

These two examples are ungrammatical because only part phrases have been moved, leaving other parts of the phrase behind. For example, the phrase *the old man* has been broken into two parts: *man* and *the old* in the first example, and *the* and *old man* in the second. It seems, therefore, that it is not possible to move anything but a whole phrase.

Phrases do not just form grammatical units; they also form units of meaning. The following sequences of words all have a coherent identifiable meaning:

(a)   the old man, the chocolate cake,

(b)   the large evil leathery alligator,

(c)   in a bad mood,

(d)   unbelievably boring,

(e)   quite large,

(f)   is reading a book.

Each one of these sequences is a phrase.

Consider the following sets of words:

(a)   the the old,

(b)   cake which the,

(c)   the leathery,

(d)   in the,

(e)   cake ate,

(f)   large evil.

Can you figure out the meaning of these sequences of words?

It is difficult (if not impossible in many cases) to identify a meaning for each of these sequences. They do not form phrases.

EXERCISE 7.1   In each of the following sentences, identify sequences of three or more words which are phrases:

(a)   An ancient monument fell down during the bombing.

(b)   Several young Latvian artists danced gracefully before the Empress.

· ·

Finally, any sequence that will substitute for another, that is, which can occupy the same location, is also a phrase.

Look at the following sentence:

Davina sold *chocolates* yesterday *at the corner store.*

Substitute another phrase for each of the italicized phrases.

You might have got any of the following and innumerable other sentences:

(a)   *My old friend Ahmed* sold *carpets* yesterday *in the market at Zurich.*

(b)   *The angry tenants* sold *all of the furniture of the apartment block* yesterday *out of spite.*

Each of the italicized phrases which is substituting for the original phrase above is itself also a phrase.

Each of these tests, as you can see, is a test of the integrity of phrases. The constituents of phrases belong together; that is why they move together, have a coherent meaning and can be substituted for as a unit.

7.1.2 HEADS AND MODIFIERS

In Chapter 2.1 we looked at five major lexical categories: noun, verb, adjective, adverb and preposition. We said that each is the head of a phrase. We now need   **head** to come to a better understanding of what makes the head of a phrase significant. The major grammatical property which gives heads their distinctive role in phrases is that they determine the major grammatical properties of the whole phrase just as the heads of words determined the major morphosyntactic properties of words. Recall that grammatical properties have to do, basically, with where in a sequence a phrase will fit. When we talk about the order in which syntactic constituents come, we are talking of their 'distribution' or 'distributional'   **distribution** properties'.

Look at the following arrangements of the phrases we used as examples earlier.

(a)   *The old man in a bad mood.

(b)   *In a bad mood is reading a book unbelievably boring.

(c)   *Is reading a book the large evil leathery alligator.

None of these arrangements of phrases make grammatical sentences of English although the phrases themselves are internally grammatical. The reason for these arrangements being ungrammatical must therefore be that the phrases are in an ungrammatical sequence, that is, they are ungrammatically distributed.

What is it that determines how a phrase may be distributed? As with morphologically complex words, every phrase has one constituent which is responsible for determining this and that constituent is its head.

Look at the phrase *in a train*. It can fit in a variety of 'slots' in a sentence. For example, it can fit into the following places in sentences:

(a)   Granville met his beloved in a train.

(b)   You always get an odd range of smells in a train.

(c)   The emergency cord in a train should not be touched without good reason.

The phrase *a train* cannot fit in these places:

(a)   *Granville met his beloved a train.

(b)   *You always get an odd range of smells a train.

(c)   *The emergency cord a train should not be touched without good reason.

This shows that it is the preposition, and not the following words, which is responsible for the fact that the phrase *in a train* will fit where it does, that is, that it has its particular distribution.

noun phrase

Where a phrase consists only of its head, it often has the same distributional properties as a phrase with the same head as well as other constituents. A noun phrase like *gorgeous looking Bentleys with walnut dashboards* can be located in the same places in sentences as its head noun, *Bentleys*. For example, they both fit in the slots in the following sentences:

_____ make Clive drool.

Clive loves _____

Some of the inflectional properties of the phrase are also determined by its head. For example, noun phrases have number, either singular for one or plural for more than one. This is shown by the fact that the head noun inflects for number, as we saw in Chapter 2.1. It happens that when a head noun is singular or plural the whole noun phrase of which it is the head is also singular or plural. You can see this is so when the noun phrase is replaced by a pronoun, because then the pronoun has the number of the head noun and not of any other noun in the phrase. Take the noun phrase *the witches' discovery of the secrets of life*. This noun phrase is singular because *discovery*, which is its head noun, is singular. But the phrase also contains two plural nouns, *witches* and *secrets*, and another singular noun, *life*. The number of these nouns has nothing to do with the number of the phrase as a whole. In German, where all nouns have gender, it is the gender of the head noun which determines the gender of the whole phrase.

The heads of phrase we will deal with in this book are also obligatory. A phrase must have a word in head position. This is significant for the meaning of the phrase because the phrase is about the head in some very general sense. A red coat is a particular kind of coat. Here *coat* is the head of the phrase *a red coat*. Swimming in a pool is basically about swimming rather than about the pool. Again, *swimming* is the head of the phrase *swimming in a pool*. It is also significant because it means that there can be one-word phrases. In such cases, only the head is present.

EXERCISE 7.2

Using the above properties of phrases, find the heads of the following phrases. Note that in some cases there are phrases within these phrases. You should find only the word which is the head of the whole phrase, and not the heads of any of the phrase's other constituents:

(a)   the great big elephant

(b)   several very old books

(c)   all the women in the moon

(d)   excellently presented material on Lady Havisham

(e)   rather thick in the head

(f)   most awfully pleasant

(g)   delighted by their arrival

(h)   sitting in the room

(i)   bored out of his skull

(j)   having delayed writing to you

(k)   syncopated rhythms of Africa

(l)   very lovely

(m) in trouble with the law

(n)   almost out of the woods

(o)   right above his neighbour's house

(p)   singularly unimpressed with Jeffrey

(q)   is eating a big dinner

· ·

Now, by way of revision, identify the grammatical category (part of speech) of the heads of the following phrases: **EXERCISE 7.3**

(a)   out of the stratosphere

(b)   given his intransigence

(c)   cycled to work

(d)   dreadfully slowly

(e)   quite inappropriately large

(f)   tawdry work by the amateur painters

(g)   right up in Scotland

(h)   so nearly correct

(i)   genuinely silly about his aunt's fortune

(j)   right beside a dirty factory

· ·

Having looked in general at heads, we are now going to set objectives for the following account of English syntax. In doing so we are going to simplify things by

modifier

supposing that there is only one kind of functional constituent of phrases other than the head, namely the modifier (although there are many structurally different kinds of modifier). In other words, once you have found the head we are generally going to say that all the other constituents are modifiers. In more advanced treatments of grammar you would find that this is not correct. Later we will also explore at least one way in which this is an oversimplification.

We are also going to suppose that the structure of phrases is rather flat, that is, that it has fewer intermediate levels of structure than an advanced treatment of grammar would suppose phrases to have. The reason for this is that our objective will be to help you identify where phrases begin and end, what the head of a phrase is, and thus what its modifiers are. More detailed treatment can wait.

7.1.3 NOUN PHRASE

Look at the following phrases:

(a)   the dog

(b)   a moderately short programme

(c)   some very old cars

(d)   six bags of wholemeal flour

(e)   very dirty marks on the walls

Each of these phrases has a noun as head: *dog, programme, cars, bags* and *marks* respectively. The other constituents are, by our definition, modifiers. Roughly speaking the modifiers tell us about the head while the head does not tell us about the modifiers.

But what are these other modifier constituents? To decide this question we have to look whether they are themselves phrases. There is clear evidence that some of the constituents of these phrases are themselves phrases. *Moderately short* is a phrase, since it has a head, *short*, which has its own modifier, *moderately. Moderately* tells us how short but not how programme. So it must be modifying *short. Short* is an adjective, so *moderately short* must be an adjective phrase.

Find the clear cases of other phrases in the above examples.

You will probably have figured out at least some of the following: *very old, of wholemeal flour, wholemeal flour, very dirty, on the walls, the walls.*

We can see an important grammatical process at work within these phrases, namely that a phrase can function within another phrase. This process is termed embedding; one phrase is said to be embedded within another.

embedding

We can represent embeddedness by containing one phrase within another in a Chinese box arrangement, as in Figure 7.1. Such an arrangement will be familiar from the previous chapters where we used it to represent the structure of morphologically complex words.

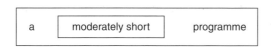

Figure 7.1

Tree diagrams can also be used as in Figures 7.2 and 7.3. (We have left out the labels of constituents we have not yet dealt with.)

The tree diagram in Figure 7.2 is a way of representing the fact that the phrase *the dog* consists of the word *the* and the noun *dog* and that the whole phrase is a noun phrase.

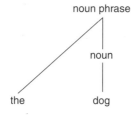

Figure 7.2

The tree diagram in Figure 7.3 represents the fact that the phrase *a moderately short programme* consists of the word *a* followed by the adjective phrase

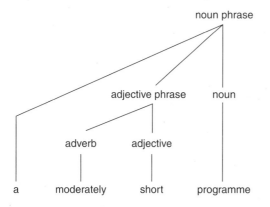

Figure 7.3

moderately short, which in turn consists of an adverb, *moderately*, and the head adjective, *short*. The final constituent of *a moderately short programme* is the head of the phrase, the noun *programme*, and since this is a noun, the whole phrase is a noun phrase.

Provide similar paraphrases for the two tree diagrams in Figures 7.4 and 7.5:

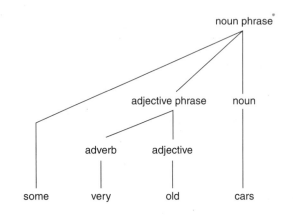

Figure 7.4

Note: Here we have just sketched the structure of the adjective phrase. Fuller structure is provided later when we deal with adjective phrases in section 7.1.4.

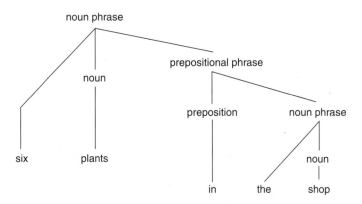

Figure 7.5

From the above examples, it would appear that two kinds of phrase can appear as modifiers within noun phrases: adjective phrases to the left of the head and prepositional phrases to the right.

We have so far not put a category label on every constituent in some of the noun phrases in the above examples. The first such category we need to deal with **determiners**   is exemplified by *a* and *the*. Words like these are generally called determiners.

English has a small closed class of determiners. (Recall that closed classes are closed because they cannot be added to.) Determiners come before adjectives in the noun phrase. You can tell that this is their distributional pattern by trying them out of position: *old the car, *very a long truck.

There are the two articles: *a* and *the*. *A* is often called the 'indefinite' article because the noun phrase it introduces is not one that the speaker and hearer have mentioned recently or that can be identified from the context. For example, if someone says, *I have a new car*, then we can take it that this is the first time the car has been mentioned, at least in the current conversation. *The* is termed the 'definite' article and is normally used when what its noun phrase denotes has been mentioned earlier or can be assumed from the context. For example, if someone says *I saw the teacher yesterday*, then we take it that there is only one teacher being referred to and both speaker and hearer(s) know which one. (These characterizations of the uses of articles are just to give an idea of their use. Their actual conditions of use are more complex.)

article
indefinite article

definite article

In some regional dialects of English articles are not used. For example in some dialects of Singaporean English, someone might say, *You got car key?*

The set of demonstratives: *this, that, these* and *those,* are a further sub-class of determiners. Their meaning is rather like that of antonyms. *This* and *these* are the singular and plural versions of a demonstrative which indicates that what the noun phrase refers to is to be regarded as in some way closer to the speaker than if *that* and *those* were used. The *this* set is usually termed 'proximal' and the *that* set 'distal'. So how close is close and is it just spatially close? When you say 'these friends of mine' as opposed to 'those friends of mine' what are you saying about closeness? Does it depend on the context? Notice too that there is a form of agreement here since, if the head of the noun phrase is plural, you must use the plural demonstrative. Notice also that this is a very small closed system. There are other languages which indicate such relationships by having inflectional morphemes to indicate proximal and distal noun phrases.

demonstrative

proximal
distal

agreement

Numerals like *six* and *sixth*, and quantifiers like *some* and *many*, appear between a determiner and adjective phrases within a noun phrase. *The six tall trees* but not **the tall six trees*. To make things easy we will just suppose that numerals are heads of adjective phrases.

Quantifiers, words like *many, most, some, all, few, several* and *both* are not so easy to assign to a syntactic category. Two of them, *all* and *both*, can come before the determiner slot, as in *all the cars* and *both the tandems*. Others seem to fit in the determiner slot, for example, *some*, as in *some red boats*, but not **the some red boats*. Still others come following the determiner, for example, *many* in *the many soldiers*. Because of this complexity we will leave quantifiers for more advanced treatments than this.

quantifier

Now look at the noun phrase *Joan's car*. The head noun of this phrase is *car*. But what of *Joan's?* It is clearly a modifier since it tells us more about the car. But it is a noun and therefore that noun must be the head of its own noun phrase. So we have two noun phrases, one a modifier of the head of the other. We can see the same thing with a more complex example. In the phrase *an old building's fences* the head noun of this phrase is *fences*. That is because the whole phrase is about these fences. If we look carefully at *an old building's,* then it consists of a noun phrase, *an old building,* with an *'s* added to it. This phrase has the identical distribution to that of determiners in that it comes in the same position in noun phrases, for example, *a park's six tall trees.* Notice that the indefinite article *a* in the above phrases is a modifier of *park* and not of *fences.* We can tell this is the case because *a* only agrees with head nouns which are singular. In *an old building's rather green fences* there is one building but a number of fences. What is happening here is that a noun phrase is itself a modifier of a head noun within a noun phrase. These noun phrases are termed 'possessive' noun phrases. They must take the possessive marker of apostrophe s if the noun phrase to which they are attached is singular, or s apostrophe where they are attached to a plural noun phrase. This possessive marker is distinct from the plural inflection, as you can see in the case of irregular plural inflection. For example, in the *oxen's yoke,* *oxen* is already plural but takes the possessive marker when it is functioning in the same slot as determiners.

possessive noun
phrase

A further fact to note about the possessive marker is that it is not an inflection since it does not attach to a word but comes at the end of the whole noun phrase. It is not attached to the head noun. In the phrase *the old mill by the stream's green fences,* the head noun of the whole phrase is *fences.* The possessive noun phrase is *the old mill by the stream.* Its head is *mill* and not *stream.* So the possessive marker attaches to the whole possessive noun phrase and not its head. (Of course if the head happens to be the last word in the phrase then it will look as if it is attached to the head.)

So how does one draw a tree diagram for such possessives? The easiest way is probably the one shown in Figure 7.6.

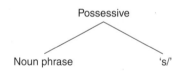

Figure 7.6

Pick out the heads and modifiers in the following noun phrases. (Pick out the head first and ignore phrases embedded in the example phrases.)

(a) the old grey mare down in the paddock

(b) my uncle with the fish and chip shop

(c) these three intelligent bus drivers I met yesterday

(d) an other person whom I don't know

(e) six goblins in green

APPLICATION

Compare the two small poems below for their use of modifiers in noun phrases.

Gipsy

I, the man with the red scarf,
Will give thee what I have, this last week's earnings.
Take them and buy thee a silver ring
And wed me, to ease my yearnings.

For the rest, when thou art wedded
I'll wet my brow for thee
With sweat, I'll enter a house for thy sake,
Thou shalt shut doors on me.

D. H. Lawrence

A White Blossom

A tiny moon as small and white as a single jasmine flower
Leans all alone above my window, on night's wintry bower,
Liquid as lime-tree blossoms, soft as brilliant water or rain
She shines, the first white love of my youth, passionless and in vain.

D. H. Lawrence

Discussion

The noun phrases in both poems tend to have modifiers to the left of the head, sometimes quite a few. The noun phrases in the first poem do not often have modifiers to the right whereas some of the noun phrases in the second poem have modifiers to the right of the head as well.

The first poem is more active than the second in that the speaker is making a proposal of marriage and making promises to the person he is addressing of what he will do for her after they are married. So there is relatively little modification of nouns since the emphasis is on the verbs. In the second poem the emphasis is on description of the blossom and so it is perhaps appropriate that there is rather more modification of nouns within noun phrases.

7.1.3.1 Pronouns

In dealing with words in Chapter 2 we did not discuss a further grammatical category that is relevant to noun phrases, namely, pronouns. Having looked at noun phrases we are now able to work out more exactly what pronouns are. Pronouns are traditionally thought of as standing for nouns. For example, in the sentence *Most teachers work very hard and they earn all the money they get*, we know that

pronoun

antecedent

they 'stands for' *most teachers,* or, to put it more technically, *most teachers* is the antecedent of the pronoun *they.* If we change this so that the sentence reads *All the older teachers at Bridgewood High work very hard and they earn all the money they get,* we can see that the pronoun *they* has the noun phrase *all the older teachers at Bridgewood High* as its antecedent. In these two examples, the pronouns do not have nouns but noun phrases as their antecedents. Sometimes it is true that a pronoun has only a single noun as antecedent but that is an accident. It comes about when the antecedent noun phrase happens to contain only one word, its head.

English pronouns take various forms according to the morphosyntactic categories of number and person, and according to the gender and grammatical role of the noun phrases which are their antecedents. Number, as we saw in Chapter 2, takes account of whether the antecedent is singular or plural. Person takes account of whether the antecedent is the speaker (the first person), the addressee (the second person), or is being spoken about (the third person). Gender takes account of whether the antecedent is male, female or neither. The grammatical functions of noun phrases for which pronouns vary in form will be dealt with in the next section.

Pronouns show a specific form for the possessive function. The fact that there are possessive pronouns such as *your, their,* and *her,* as in *her brother,* shows that possessive noun phrases really are noun phrases, because pronouns (which have noun phrases as antecedents) can substitute for them. For example, in the sentence *The old steam train travelled to its nearest destination, its* is in possessive form within the noun phrase *its nearest destination.* The antecedent of *its* is the noun phrase *the old steam train.* You can tell this is so because you can substitute the antecedent for the possessive pronoun as follows: *The old steam train travelled to the old steam train's nearest destination.*

We said earlier that these various forms of pronouns are in evidence if the antecedent is neither the speaker, that is, first person (*I, we*), nor the addressee, second person (*you*), that is, if it is third person. If such an antecedent is plural, then the pronoun will be either *they, their* or *them.*

See if you can work out which position the pronoun occupies for each of the three forms: *they, their* and *them.*

Their is clearly the possessive form, as you can tell from such noun phrases as *their old car* and *their many friends. They* is the form the pronoun characteristically takes when it comes in front of a verb, like *saw,* and *them* is the form the pronoun takes after *see,* for example, *they saw them.* We will look in greater detail at these roles which noun phrases play in section 7.2.

If the third person pronoun is singular then it is sensitive to the gender of the antecedent, and its forms are: *he, she, it,* or *his, hers, its,* and so forth. The various forms of personal pronouns are given in Table 7.1. The ways in which

Table 7.1 The pronoun categories

Person	Case	Gender	Number	
			Singular	Plural
First person	Subject		*I*	*we*
First person	Complement		*me*	*us*
First person	Possessive		*my/mine*	*our(s)*
Second Person	Subject		*you*	*you*
Second Person	Complement		*you*	*you*
Second Person	Possessive		*your(s)*	*your(s)*
Third Person	Subject	Feminine	*she*	*they*
Third Person	Subject	Masculine	*he*	*they*
Third Person	Subject	Neuter	*it*	*they*
Third Person	Complement	Feminine	*her*	*them*
Third Person	Complement	Masculine	*him*	*them*
Third Person	Complement	Neuter	*it*	*them*
Third Person	Possessive	Feminine	*her(s)*	*their(s)*
Third Person	Possessive	Masculine	*his*	*their(s)*
Third Person	Possessive	Neuter	*its*	*their(s)*

Note: The nature of complements will be discussed in section 7.2.3.

these vary are, recalling Chapter 2, dependent on morphosyntactic categories such as number as well as the gender of the antecedent and the grammatical function of the pronoun itself, which we will have more to say about later in this chapter.

Find the pronouns in the following passage and for each pronoun indicate its number, person, and gender. Remember that gender only appears in the third person singular.

EXERCISE 7.6

> Marie and her brother had worked together for a long time in the family business while it was developing. I had known them since school and you must have known them too. He was a short fellow while she was much taller.

· ·

Recall too that pronouns can be referring expressions when there is no explicit antecedent but what exactly they refer to is then a matter of context. We know that *she* must have a single female as its antecedent but exactly who that is depends.

7.1.4 ADJECTIVE PHRASE

Just as noun phrases have nouns as heads so adjective phrases have adjectives as heads.

Look, for example, at the following phrases:

(a)   quite old

(b)   moderately expensive

(c)   quite moderately long in the arms

The heads of these three phrases are *old, expensive,* and *long*. The other constituents are modifiers. The modifiers can be single-word degree adverbs like *very* and *quite*, which we will suppose to be the heads of adverb phrases. (Degree adverbs are adverbs which cannot themselves take modifiers.) They can be adverb phrases containing modifiers, as we saw earlier. They can also be prepositional phrases, as in the case of *quite moderately long in the arms,* where the head is *long* and *in the arms* modifies *long*.

Draw labelled tree diagrams of the three example phrases above.

Your answers should be as shown in Figures 7.7, 7.8 and 7.9.
Adjective phrases characteristically appear in two places, as illustrated by the following contrasting positions:

(a)   *the very old goat,   the goat was very old;*

(b)   *the rather dreadful holiday,   the holiday which was rather dreadful.*

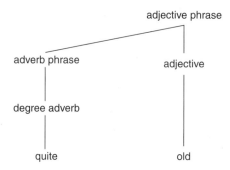

Figure 7.7

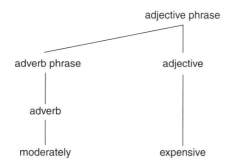

Figure 7.8

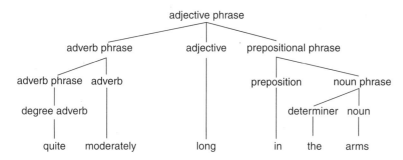

Figure 7.9

The first position is termed the 'attributive' position and adjectives which are located in this position are called 'attributive adjectives'. Here the adjective phrases come after determiners and before the head noun in noun phrases, for example, *the very old blanket* and *a moderately expensive shirt*. The other position is termed the 'predicate' position and the adjective phrases which are located in this position are called 'predicate adjectives'. It is the position an adjective phrase takes when it comes after verbs, for example, *John was very long in the arms*. (We briefly made mention of these two positions in Chapter 2.1.) In a number of varieties of English spoken as a foreign language, the BE before the predicate adjective is left out. So people say *John very long in the arms*. This happens because, for example in Chinese, there is no BE in this syntactic construction.

There are some interesting differences between the attributive and predicate positions for adjective phrases. First, attributive adjective phrases have a preferred sequence. For example, *a friendly former conductor* sounds better than *a former friendly conductor*, *a small blue car* is better than *a blue small car*. This ordering appears not to be grammatical, in that alternative orders are not totally prohibited. (There is some dispute not only about the facts of the matter but also concerning what to do about them and so we will say no more about it.) Adjective phrases in predicate position do not have this ordering property because it is not possible to put adjective phrases one next to the other in predicate position, for

attributive adjective

predicate
predicate adjective

example, *a car is small, blue*. Adjective phrases in predicate position can be co-ordinated, in which case they will not have a preferred order, for example, *the car is small and blue, the car is blue and small*. (We shall have more to say about coordination in Chapter 8.1.2.)

Secondly, attributive adjective phrases cannot have constituents after their heads, so that *the long in the arms young man* is ungrammatical, whereas in predicate position modifiers after the head are permitted, for example, *the young man is long in the arms* is grammatical.

EXERCISE 7.7

Identify the adjective phrases in the following passage and italicize their heads.

> In other ways he was a very hard man. He was big and rather clumsy-looking, with big heavy bones and long flat muscles, and he had a big, expressionless, broken-nosed face. Yet he moved with surprising ease and silence as well as having a gift for stillness.

> M. K. Joseph, *A Soldier's Tale*

· ·

APPLICATION

The choice between attributive and predicate adjectives can have an impact on descriptive writing. Look, for example, at the following description of an Icelandic warrior:

> ...he was <u>tall</u>, <u>strong</u>, and **skilled in arms**, <u>even-tempered</u> and <u>very shrewd</u>, **ruthless with his enemies** and **always reliable in matters of importance**.

> From *Njal's Saga*, translated by
> Magnus Magnusson and Hermann Palsson

Discussion

All of the underlined adjective phrases are in predicate position. The author had no choice but to choose predicate position for the adjective phrases in bold type because they contain constituents after the head adjective. Not only that, adjective phrases in predicate position can come in any order and so, by placing adjective phrases in predicate position, the writer of a description has a choice about the order in which the adjective phrases appear. The sequence here begins with the warrior's physical size, then moves on to his physical abilities, then mental attributes, and lastly his social attributes. You can see that this is a logical sequence if you want to introduce someone into a story for the first time. It is a sequence that is not available in attributive position since the sequencing of adjective phrases in attributive position is more fixed than in predicate position and also adjective phrases in attributive position cannot take modifiers after their heads.

7.1.4.1 Adverb phrase

Adverb phrases have a structure similar to that of adjective phrases. They have adverbs as their heads and the modifiers which they take on their left include degree adverbs as in the following examples: *very quickly, quite slowly*; or adverb phrases, for example, *quite moderately slowly*. Also, quite a number of words, such as *fast*, function as both adverbs and adjectives, as in *a fast boat* and *the boat sailed fast*. Given these similarities, it is often supposed that adjective and adverb phrases can be termed 'A phrases', or AP for short.

7.1.5 PREPOSITIONAL PHRASE

We can now revisit another of the word classes from Chapter 2.1, the preposition.

Look at the following verb phrases:

(a)   play *in the moonlight*

(b)   sat *by the gate*

(c)   has come home *within a couple of hours*

   on a motorbike

   through a tunnel

Each of the italicized phrases is a prepositional phrase. This is because the prep-   **prepositional**
osition is its head. Prepositional phrases can have just a head, as in the verb   **phrase**
phrase *take the book out*, where *out* is a prepositional phrase consisting only
of a preposition. Prepositions often have noun phrases immediately following
them within the phrase, as is the case in all the above examples. They can also
take adverb phrases to their left as modifiers, for example, *rather in trouble, very
directly in the way.*

In the above examples the prepositional phrases are clearly functioning as
modifiers in the verb phrase, telling us more about the action denoted by the
verb. Earlier, prepositional phrases also appeared as modifiers in noun phrases
(section 7.1.3) and adjective phrases (section 7.1.4). In a more general sense their
function is descriptive and you will notice a preponderance of them in descriptive writing.

Find the prepositional phrases in the following extract:

> At first it seemed there was no one about. Then he saw a single figure, a girl, far down the beach, close to where the surf was breaking, sitting under a beach umbrella. He went towards her. When he was close enough to see her clearly he sat down on the white sand.
>
>   He could not see her face. She sat with her back to the land, staring out to sea. The umbrella above her was dark blue, with white frills and tassels that swayed in the breeze. Her hair was long and blonde and it too was dragged at by the breeze from the sea. She was slender, her shoulders broad only in pro-portion to her long tapering back and narrow waist. She sat cross-legged, her knees appearing to Smith projecting on either side, like outriggers. She was pale-skinned, lightly tanned. She sat perfectly still. From where Smith watched the highest waves appeared to lift above her. He saw her framed in green. Then as the wave broke and shot forward up the sand he saw her against the white froth and the blue of the sky. Sometimes in the relative quiet between breakers he heard faintly the sound of music and guessed that somewhere among her things, scattered about the beach towel on which she sat, was a battery radio.
>
> C. K. Stead, *Smith's Dream*

Summary

To judge from the phrases we have looked at so far, it would seem that all phrases have heads, and modifiers either before the head or after it. The head of a phrase is the word that has the same category as the phrase as a whole. Nouns are the heads of noun phrases, adjectives are the heads of adjective phrases, and prepositions are the heads of prepositional phrases.

7.1.6 VERB PHRASE

verb phrase   Verb phrases, phrases with verbs as heads, have a complicated structure. That is why we have left them until last.

Look at the following verb phrases:

(a)   gave Jill a book,

(b)   has given Jill a book,

(c)   will be giving Jill a book.

We would all agree that in all three verb phrases an act of giving is central. In both *Fred has been putting money into the bank*, and *April could have been putting candles on the table*, an act of putting is central. But, in each example, as well as the head verb *give* and *put*, there are other verbs present: *have, be, will* and *could*. So we can draw a distinction between the head of the verb phrase, often called the 'lexical' verb, and verbs which precede it such as *will*, *have* and *is*, which are called 'auxiliary' verbs. They can be considered verbs because, for instance, they can change their form according to tense: *is* vs. *was*, *has* vs. *had*. Tense inflection, as we saw in Chapter 2.1, is a defining characteristic of verbs.

lexical verb
auxiliary verb

Auxiliary verbs are of three major kinds: modal auxiliary verbs: *can, could, shall, should, will, would, may, might* and *must*, which, if the verb phrase has one, always come first; the aspect auxiliaries, *have* and *be*, which, if they are present, come in that order and after any modal auxiliary verb; and the passive auxiliary, which is also *be* and which, if it is present, comes last. That means we should be able to find verb phrases such as *could have been being taken*. This is a complex verb phrase but it is certainly grammatically possible.

modal auxiliary
** verb**
aspect auxiliaries
passive auxiliary

There are other constituents which can precede lexical verbs.

Look again at some examples:

   (a)   does give Jill a book,

   (b)   did give Jill a book,

   (c)   doesn't give Jill a book,

   (d)   hasn't given Jill a book.

Under certain circumstances the auxiliary verb *do* appears before the lexical verb. It only appears when there is no other auxiliary verb and then only under two circumstances: if the verb phrase is emphasized strongly with a heavy stress on the *do*, or if there is a negative like *not* or *n't* in the verb phrase. The distribution of *do* is therefore very restricted. The negative *not* (or *n't*) is an optional constituent which, if it occurs, always comes just after the first auxiliary verb whatever that is. So, for example, we can get any of the following sequences:

(a)   hasn't given Jill the book,

(b)   isn't giving Jill the book,

(c)   will not give Jill the book.

Given the above restrictions, why are the following verb phrases ungrammatical?

(a) *does be giving Jill the book,

(b) *has beenn't giving Jill the book.

Answer:

They are ungrammatical because in (a) a form of *do* appears when there is another auxiliary present, and in (b) the negative is attached to the second auxiliary when it can only be attached to the first.

Now look at the following verb phrases:

(a)   has very suddenly given Jill the book

(b)   is almost certainly giving Jill the book,

(c)   could not very easily be giving Jill the book.

What constituents other than auxiliary verbs and negatives appear in front of the lexical verb?

These examples show that one further constituent can precede the lexical verb and that is an adverb phrase, specifically, in the above examples: *very suddenly, almost certainly* and *very easily*. Such adverb phrases tend to occupy the same position as the negative, that is, to come immediately after the first auxiliary verb if there is one, or, if there is also a negative, immediately following the negative. So much, for the meantime, for the distribution of auxiliary verbs.

So what do all these various auxiliary possibilities indicate? Modal auxiliaries deal with many different possible ways for seeing the action of the lexical verb. Recall from Chapter 2.1 that there is no future tense inflection in English. But that does not mean English speakers cannot refer to times in the future. Future time for the action is often expressed by the modal *will*. If Jill will give John a book, then the giving is to be in the future. Possible action is often indicated by *could*. For example, if Jill *could* give John a book, then she hasn't yet given it to him. It is just a possibility for the future. The perfective aspect auxiliary *have*, which we looked at in Chapter 2.1, indicates that the action is completed relative to a given point in time. For example, if we say, Jill *has given* John the book, then the action is over relative to now, when we are speaking.

perfective aspect

The progressive aspect auxiliary *be* indicates that the action is on-going at a **progressive aspect** particular point in time, so that if Jill *is giving* John a book, then it is happening now while we are talking.

A number of New Englishes and Englishes as a second language do not use aspect auxiliaries in quite the way we have described. For example it is common in India for the progressive to be used for current situations where speakers in the UK and USA would not use it. For example, an Indian speaker might say, 'Rajiv is having two cars' where an American speaker might say, 'Rajiv has two cars.' The progressive in Indian English is here not indicating an ongoing action but an ongoing state of affairs.

African American Vernacular English also shows interesting variation on the standard English patterns for the auxiliary verbs.

Look at the following dialogue between Huck Finn and Jim:

'Strawberries and such truck,' I says. 'Is that what you live on?'

'I couldn' git nuffn else,' he says.

'Why, how long you been on the island, Jim?'

'I come heah de night arter you's killed.

Mark Twain *Adventures of Huckleberry Finn*

What variant features of the phrasal syntax do you notice?

Answer:

In the second line, since the auxiliary part of the verb phrase contains a negative, it is non-standard for there to be a second negative in the form of *nothing*. Double negatives are common in many varieties of English. Here they do not add up to a positive but just make the negative more emphatic. In the third line the aspect auxiliary *have* would be present in standard English but it isn't here. This is also a common feature of the rural English of the American South. In the fourth line, the truncated form *you's* is for *you was*. This has a non-standard agreement between the subject and the verb. In standard English this would be *you were*.

The passive auxiliary *be* and its involvement with syntax is more complex. To understand the full import of that we must look at the grammatical units which follow the verb (which we do in section 7.2), and the way phrases may be moved (which we do in Chapter 8.2).

We saw earlier that, in total, it is possible for four auxiliaries to precede the lexical verb, for example, *The stone might have been being lifted by Brünhilde*. There are interesting relationships to do with inflections in such verb phrases between each auxiliary verb and the verb which follows it.

Let us look at some verb phrases which contain the perfective auxiliary *have*:

(a)   have eaten their breakfasts,

(b)   have taken the train to Blackpool,

(c)   have been opening many windows.

You will notice that the verb immediately following *have* takes the ending *-en*. This inflected form of the verb is the 'perfect participle', whose morphology we looked at in Chapter 2.1. The perfect auxiliary verb always selects the perfect participle form of the following verb, typically the affix *-en*, but also irregular forms such as *has sung*. The progressive auxiliary selects the progressive participle form of the following verb: *is eating, was walking, were riding*. The passive auxiliary selects the perfect participle form of the following verb: *was eaten, were tickled, have been cut*. A number of explanations have been offered for this selection process but for our purposes it is sufficient to point out that this is again a matter of distribution, that is, it has to do with where syntactic constituents come relative to others, and it is rule-governed. We will suppose that all auxiliaries are immediately dominated by a verb phrase in the tree diagrams as illustrated in Figure 7.10.

APPLICATION

Look carefully at tense inflection (past and present) and aspect (*have* and *be*) in the following narrative:

> The European Guest House stood two hundred feet above the water, on the crest of a rocky and wooded spur that jutted from the jungle. By the time Aziz arrived the water had paled to a film of mauve-grey, and the boat vanished entirely. A sentry slept in the Guest House porch, lamps burned in the cruciform of the deserted rooms. He went from one room to another, inquisitive, and malicious. Two letters lying on the piano rewarded him, and he pounced and read them promptly. He was not ashamed to do this. The sanctity of private correspondence has never been ratified in the East.
>
> E. M. Forster, *A Passage to India*

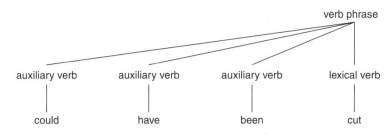

Figure 7.10

Discussion

Tenses and their relationship to modal and aspect auxiliary verbs as indicators of time relationships are a rich source of interest in narratives because there are so many ways of telling a story. If we look at the passage, we will see that it is, except for the last sentence, in the past tense. The first sentence has a plain past tense verb, *stood*. But after a second plain past tense verb, *arrived,* there is one verb phrase with perfective aspect, *had paled*. (This is perfective because of the presence of the perfective auxiliary *have*. But notice that *have* is itself inflected for past tense.) Since perfective aspects always require reference to a particular point in time, by which time the action of the verb was completed, in this case by which time the water had paled, the perfective arranges events around the arrival of Aziz. This pivotal event then leads on to the other events which happen after the arrival of Aziz and which are all again indicated by plain past tense forms of the verbs. The paragraph finishes with a present perfective passive verb with a negative after the first auxiliary, *has never been ratified*. This, a more complex form than all the preceding ones, does not deal with the actual events of the paragraph, but is a general comment on those events and so is not in the past tense.

Narratives can be examined in this way to see how the narrator uses tense and aspect to give focus to certain events and present other events as relating to these focal events.

Up until this point our examination of the verb phrase has looked only at what is on the head verb's left. We will return to look at what is to the verb's right in the verb phrase in the next section, since the constituents on the verb's right need to be looked at in the context of another unit, the clause.

Some hints for drawing tree diagrams of simple phrases

1. Find the head of the phrase. Remember that every noun, adjective, verb, adverb and preposition is the head of a phrase.

2. Find the modifiers which go with a head. Modifiers always tell you more about the head. For example, in the phrase *the red mill by the river, red* tells you more about the mill, and the fact that the mill is by the river tells you more about the mill. Even the determiner *the* tells you that there is a particular mill being mentioned. In the verb phrase *has swum the lake three times*, the head is *swum* and the *has* tells you that the swimming is completed; *the lake* is what was swum and *three times* is how often the lake was swum. So

all the modifiers add detail to the swimming. In the prepositional phrase *down the sink, the sink* indicates the location or direction of the *down*.

You should now be able to pick out what kinds of words and phrases function as modifiers. This exercise gives you some examples of three kinds of phrase. You should draw tree diagrams of all of them to get a feel for the structural properties of simple phrases. To make life easier you can use the following abbreviations, which we will use from now on:

N for noun

A for adjective and adverb

P for preposition

V for verb

DET for determiner

DEG for degree adverb

A also for numerals and quantifiers

PRON for pronoun

NP for noun phrase

POSS for possessive noun phrase

AP for adjective and adverb phrases

PP for prepositional phrase

VP for verb phrase

LexV for lexical verb

AuxV for auxiliary verb

Table 7.2 Noun phrases

	Modifiers	Head	Modifiers
(a)		Angus	
(b)	the	man	
(c)	the old	man	
(d)	a moderately old	man	
(e)	the seven very silly	people	
(f)	many	undertakers	
(g)	too many	undertakers	
(h)	the	cottage	in the woods
(i)	a very grim	beast	on the moors
(i)	the animals'	captivity	in dirty cages

Table 7.3 Prepositional phrases

	Modifiers	Head	Modifiers
(a)		in	
(b)		down	the hatch
(c)		across	the street
(d)		from	behind the house
(e)		down	into the mud
(f)	completely	down	the drain
(g)	right	after	the meeting

Table 7.4 Adjective phrases

	Modifiers	Head	Modifiers
(a)		silly	
(b)		fearful	of the consequences
(c)		yellow	with age
(d)	thoroughly	disreputable	
(e)	quite ecstatically	moved	by Englebert's music
(f)	so	boring	
(g)	too	involved	in Fred's affairs

· ·

Having now had some practice at drawing tree diagrams and seen how they represent syntactic structure, we are in a position to learn some basic terms to describe the relationships which units in a sentence have one to another. As we saw in Chapter 1, a tree diagram shows the units of which a sentence is constructed in two dimensions. The horizontal dimension represents the sequence of units in the order they come – that is, the precedence of syntactic units (that is, how one word precedes the next). When we speak, this precedence order is the order in which words come out of our mouths over time. In writing, the precedence order is given spatially from left to right on the page. The vertical dimension represents the way in which words are linked together into phrases – that is, the dominance of syntactic units.

precedence

dominance

Some basic relationships in tree diagrams can be seen in the tree diagram in Figure 7.11, which indicates the relationships in tree diagrams and the terminology used to refer to those relationships. Some of this terminology we have already used. Some will be new.

Examine the tree diagram in Figure 7.12 and then find the constituents and nodes listed below:

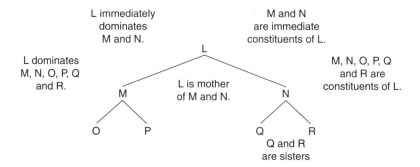

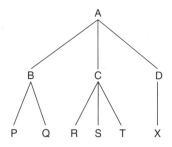

Figure 7.11

Figure 7.12

(a)   the sisters of D

(b)   the daughters of C

(c)   the immediate constituents of A

(d)   the constituents of A

(e)   the node which immediately dominates T

(f)   the daughters of A

· ·

Recall that what a tree diagram represents can also be represented by placing labelled brackets round each constituent. For example, the tree in the above exercise can be represented as follows:

$[_A [_B PQ] [_C RST] [_D X]]$

The A brackets surround the whole structure. The B brackets surround the constituents PQ, and so on. Labelled bracketed notation can be useful as a shorthand way of drawing trees, although it is also more difficult to 'read' than a tree representation of syntactic structure.

Convert (a) and (b) to tree diagrams, and (c) and (d) in Figures 7.13 and 7.14 to labelled bracketings.

(a) $[_A [_B CD]]$

(b) $[_A [_B [_C D] [_E FG]] H]$

(c) 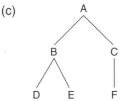   (d)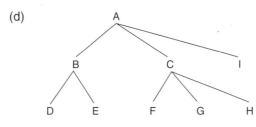

Figure 7.14

Figure 7.13

· ·

7.2   SIMPLE CLAUSES AND THEIR FUNCTIONAL CONSTITUENTS

7.2.1   SUBJECT

Having looked at the structure of simple phrases we can return now to the simple two-word sentence, *Mary swims*, which we looked at in Chapter 1, and look at it in more detail. Sentences clearly consist of phrases and we now need to look at how those phrases function in sentences. Recall that in Chapter 1 we made a distinction between the form of a unit which has to do with its internal structure while the function of a unit has to do with where the unit fits in a larger structure. We also decided then that the simplest complete sentence has two constituents and each constituent, at its simplest, is a single word.

Let us look at some further examples:

(a)   The dogs played in the park.

(b)   Some elephants were chewing the acacia trees.

(c)   The film crew left the location for lunch.

(d)   Sandra didn't like the neighbours.

(e)   The building looked unstable.

(f)   A journey up the Nile might take three months.

subject

In each case someone or something does something, or has a property. For example, in (a) the dogs are doing something, namely, playing in the park; in (e) the building has the property of looking unstable. The unit which does something or has a property is called the 'subject'. So the way to pick the subject is to ask who or what is doing things or who or what has the particular property mentioned. The answer to that question is given by the subject. On that basis the subjects of the above simple sentences are:

(a)   the dogs

(b)   some elephants

(c)   the film crew

(d)   Sandra

(e)   the building

(f)   a journey up the Nile

If the verb has to do with an activity then the subject is often the person or thing that is performing the action. In the sentence *Chopin composes many polkas*, the subject is *Chopin* since he is composing the polkas. Unfortunately this semantic relationship is not a hard-and-fast test. For example, in the sentence *Many polkas are composed by Chopin*, *Chopin* is not the subject but *many polkas* is (although Chopin is still doing the composing).

The 'who or what' approach needs to be used carefully. It tells us what the subject is only if we use both the auxiliary verbs and the lexical verb. For example, Chopin is (as we saw) the one doing the composing in both versions of the sentence. But if we ask 'who or what are composed by Chopin' then we get the answer 'many polkas' and not 'Chopin' in the second case.

A second relationship to check is one involving inflectional morphology. If the subject of an English sentence can be substituted for by the pronouns *he, she* or *it,* and the tense of the sentence is the present tense, then the inflection *-s* must appear on the first verb in the sentence. Look, for instance, at the example sentences above. If we substituted *Polish composers* for *Chopin* we would get *Polish composers compose many polkas*. Notice that the *-s* on the end of the verb *compose* has disappeared. This is because the subject is no longer replaceable by *he, she* or *it,* that is, it is plural and not singular in number. This relationship between the subject and the presence or absence of *-s* inflection is a reliable indicator of what is the subject of the sentence. Of course if the subject is plural there is no *-s* and if the sentence has past tense there will be no *-s,* but you can always change both to check out your hunch about the subject. Look at the following example sentence: *In the twilight six dragoons gathered the prisoners together.* The sentence has past tense indicated by the *-ed* ending on *gathered.* So it needs to be changed to present tense if we are to have any chance of using the *-s* test. That would change the sentence to *In the twilight six dragoons gather the prisoners together.* We can now look for an *-s*. There is none. That means *the twilight* cannot be the subject because it is singular, but the *six dragoons* could be substituted for by *they* and could be the subject, since it is plural. If we change them to singular then an *-s* should be required: *In the twilight one dragoon gathers the prisoners together.* And there it is. So six *dragoons* must be the subject of the sentence. Notice that we are again using a substitution test here, this time for checking syntactic properties of phrases.

7.2.2 PREDICATE

Let us turn now to the thing the subject is doing or the property it has; this is called the predicate. So the predicates of the above sentences are:

predicate

(a) played in the park

(b) were chewing the acacia tree

(c) left the location for lunch

(d) didn't like the neighbours

(e) looked unstable

(f) might take three months

Find the subjects of the following sentences:

EXERCISE 7.12

(a) Peter joins the Navy tomorrow.

(b) The greatest magician of all time performs here next week.

(c) On Saturday morning three monkeys escaped from the zoo.

(d) They hate performing.

(e) That Lionel saw the escape interests the police.

· ·

Predicates can themselves contain a number of important functional units. At this point we will be looking at those units to the right of the head of a VP (that is, to the right of the lexical verb), which we left out of the discussion when we looked at the VP. This is because VPs are the phrases that perform the predicate function.

7.2.3 OBJECTS

Look at the following three-word sentences:

(a)   Martha kissed Jim.

(b)   Elephants enjoy soccer.

(c)   Sopranos sing arias.

The first unit in these sentences is clearly the subject and therefore the rest is the predicate. (*Who or what kissed Jim? Martha.*) But within the predicate there are now two further units. We can see that these two units belong together. They can, for example, be in a different location as a single unit (recall the movement test for phrases):

(a)   What Martha did was *kiss Jim*.

(b)   What elephants do is *enjoy soccer*.

(c)   What sopranos do is *sing arias*.

And we can also say that:

(a)   The person Martha kissed was Jim.

(b)   What elephants enjoy is soccer.

(c)   What sopranos sing is arias.

object

The second two elements together are the predicate and, as such, a single functional unit, but you can see that the verb phrase which is functioning as the predicate has within it a separate phrase. This third element in these examples is called the 'object'. Object and verb are closely related because verbs frequently require particular kinds of objects to complete their meaning. Laughing does not require anything to be laughed, but patting, kissing or enjoying requires that there be something to be patted, kissed or enjoyed. The object of the verb is usually that something. So the reason that the verb and its object form a functional unit is not only that they may be moved as a single unit but also that they form a unit of meaning.

To find whether a verb has an object we can say *who?* or *what?* after the verb. The answer to that question is given by the object. *Martha kissed who?, Elephants enjoy what?, Sopranos sing what?* The answer in each case is the object of the verb.

Each of the following sentences either has, or does not have, an object. (Remember, complete sentences must have both a subject and a predicate.) Sort out those sentences that have an object from those that do not:

(a) John was eating.

(b) Henry drank a milkshake.

(c) Martha fainted.

(d) She needed a milkshake.

(e) Henry fed his dog.

(f) The dog fainted suddenly.

Your answers should be:

(a) no object.

(b) object

(c) no object

(d) object

(e) object

(f) no object

Sometimes a simple sentence will contain two objects.

Each of the following sentences has either no, one, or two objects. In each case, sort out how many objects there are:

(a) John gave his mother a present.

(b) Henry told me a story.

(c) Henry told a story.

(d) I took the dog.

(e) I asked my aunt a question.

(f) Geoffrey walked.

(g)   Geoffrey walked his dog.

(h)   She called.

(i)   She called the general.

Your answers should be: (a) 2, (b) 2, (c) 1, (d) 1, (e) 2, (f) 0, (g) 1, (h) 0, (i) 1.

7.2.3.1   Kinds of objects

Look at the verb *tell* and its possible objects. *Tell* can have either one, or two objects. If there is one object, that object is either what was told or who it was told to. *Samantha told a story, Samantha told Jim.* However, in each case we know that telling involves both these items. The thing that is told or given is called the **direct object** 'direct object' and the person or thing it is told or given to or for is called the 'indi- **indirect object** rect object'. Again it is because the meaning of some verbs requires it that some verbs have both direct and indirect objects. Giving requires someone to do the giving, something to be given and someone to whom it is given.

When a verb takes two objects, the objects can often come in two different grammatical orders. We can say *Mary gave Freda a boat* or *Mary gave a boat to Freda.*

For each of the objects in the following sentences, say whether it is the direct object or the indirect object:

(a)   Karl rode his bike.

(b)   Nathan gave Sarah her breakfast.

(c)   The postmaster sent a parcel to Henry.

(d)   Freda owed Marcia a dollar.

(e)   Eve saw the serpent.

(f)   Mary gave her aunt breakfast.

Answers:

(a)   His *bike* is the direct object.

(b)   *Sarah* is the indirect object while *her breakfast* is the direct object.

(c)   *A parcel* is the direct object and *to Henry* is the indirect object.

(d)   *Marcia* is the indirect object while *a dollar* is the direct object.

(e)   *The serpent* is the direct object.

(f)   *Her aunt* is the indirect object and *breakfast* is the direct object.

We found when we looked at the structure of words and that of simple phrases that it was possible to represent their structure by tree diagrams. The same is true of sentence structure. If the subject and predicate are two units in the structure of a sentence then they form a simple binary tree as in Figure 7.15, and, looking at both the form of the constituents and their function, a Chinese box arrangement as in Figure 7.16.

If the predicate, in turn, consists of a verb plus an object, then the tree looks like that in Figure 7.17. Notice that we have one new abbreviation, namely S standing for sentence, and that tree diagrams give only structural information.

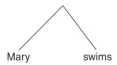

Figure 7.15

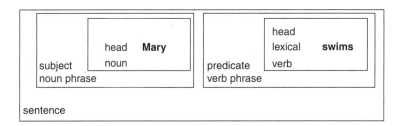

Figure 7.16

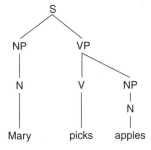

Figure 7.17

You will probably have realized that predicates are VPs and, up to now, that both subjects and objects can be NPs. This again illustrates the difference between form and function. The form of a phrase may be that of a noun phrase while its function might be that of subject or object depending on its relationship to other constituents in the sentence.

EXERCISE 7.13

Draw tree diagrams for the following sentences:

(a)   Dougal breeds rabbits.

(b)   Hans sent Arthur oranges.

(c)   Chieko told stories.

(d)   Alexander smiles.

(e)   Norah fed her dog his dinner.

· ·

complement

As we said above, objects are required to complete the meaning of some verbs. Because of this property they are often termed 'complements', since they complement the meaning of the verb. Both types of object are clear cases of a complement but they are not the only kinds of complements. There are, for example, some verbs which require an adverb phrase to complete their meaning, an instance being the verb *behave*. You can behave *very badly*, or *well* or *perfectly*. (If we use the verb *behave* without a complement then it is assumed that this means 'behave well'.) The verb *put* requires both a direct object and a location. You cannot just put the car. You have to put it somewhere.

This allows us to distinguish genuine indirect objects, where the lexical verb requires there to be an object, from cases which have the same structure but where the constituent in question is not an object. Compare, for example, *Joanna fastened the picture for her mother* and *Joanna bought the picture for her mother*. The latter can take the form *Joanna bought her mother a picture* but the former cannot take the form *Joanna fastened her mother the picture*. It seems that in buying someone something there is a closer relationship between the buying and the one for whom something is bought than there is between the act of fastening something and the one for whom one might do that.

7.2.4   INTENSIVE COMPLEMENTS

intensive
complement

Objects of both sorts are always different things from the subject. If Lisa welds axles, then Lisa and the axles are different things. If Lisa gives Henry an axle then Henry and the axle are different things. But if she says that Fred seems an idiot, then Fred and the idiot are one and the same person. So *an idiot* is not an object. We may call it an intensive complement. Intensive complements appear after only a few verbs; typically after any form of the verb *be* (such as *is, was, were*) when it is used as a lexical verb (but not when it is used as an auxiliary verb), or verbs such as *seem, appear* and *become*.

Look at the following examples:

(a)   The car appeared a wreck.

(b)   The jury seemed a disgruntled group.

(c)   A whole town became a disturbed community.

Do the subject and complement refer to the same entity or group?

Answer:

The complements clearly refer to the same thing or things as the subject and they are thus not objects but intensive complements.

   All the above examples have NPs acting as intensive complements but they are not the only type of phrase which can do so.

Look at the following examples:

(a)   The car appeared in a mess.

(b)   The jury seemed very nasty.

What phrase types are these complements and does the complement tell us more about the subject?

Answer:

In (a) the complement is a PP; in (b) an AP. But the complement still relates back to the subject just as it does if the structure is an NP. So these too are intensive complements. Adjective phrases in predicate position, which we looked at earlier, are therefore functioning as intensive complements.

   There are also intensive complements which come after objects, and therefore look like a second object but are not. If we compare the sentence *Janet sold her brother a bike* with the sentence *Janet called her brother an idiot*, you will see that in the first sentence, there are two phrases after the verb, each one referring to someone or something different, whereas in the second sentence, although there are also two noun phrases after the verb they refer to the same person. So the second complement in *Janet called her brother an idiot* is an intensive complement. It is telling you more about Janet's brother, just as the intensive complements which directly follow verbs tell you more about the subject. Complements of this sort come after a small class of verbs such as *call, name, elect* and *appoint*. One more thing which these intensive complements have in common with those which follow directly after verbs is that, as well as being NPs, they too can be APs and PPs, as the following cases show:

   (a)   George thought Frederick [$_{AP}$rather silly].

   (b)   Jemma found her dog [$_{PP}$in great spirits].

EXERCISE 7.14   The following examples all contain complements. For each, determine whether it is a direct object, an indirect object, or an intensive complement:

   (a)   Jean sold Freda a bicycle.

   (b)   Tom owned a new camera.

   (c)   Sylvia likes her breakfast hot.

   (d)   Jonty appeared very shy.

   (e)   The captain judged Harriet the most valuable player.

. . . .

7.2.5 ADVERBIALS

adverbial

We have now examined four main functional units in the sentence: the subject, and, within the predicate, the lexical verb and its possible complements. The last units that we still have to look at are the adverbials. Adverbials characteristically appear after the subject, verb and object/complement core of the sentence and indicate things like how, when, where and why the things that are described by the sentence are going on. As you might guess, adverb phrases can and do function as adverbials; for example, the adverb phrase *rather clumsily* in *Derek dried the dishes rather clumsily*. But adverb phrases are not the only phrase types which can function as adverbials.

Look, for example, at the following sentences:

   (a)   John helped his father *in many situations*.

   (b)   Sally wanted him home *at the film's conclusion*.

   (c)   The team played very badly *by their standards*.

The italicized units are all adverbials. What is their form?

Answer:

They are clearly prepositional phrases.

> In the three example sentences above, where else might the adverbials be able to appear in the given sentences?

Your answers might include the following possibilities:

(a)   In many situations John helped his father.

      John, in many situations, helped his father.

(b)   At the film's conclusion Sally walked Jim home.

(c)   By their standards the team played very badly.

We already saw when we looked at the verb phrase in the previous section that adverb phrases can come after the first auxiliary verb. This exercise shows that adverbials can appear in various other places in sentences and not just at the end after the subject, verb and any complements.

Adverbials are often sub-classified according to their content. If they deal with the time at which an event took place they are termed 'time' adverbials. If they deal with the location of the event(s), they are 'place' adverbials. If they deal with the way in which the events were performed or took place then they are 'manner' adverbials and if they deal with the reason for the events taking place then they are termed 'reason' adverbials: when, where, how and why respectively.

time adverbial
place adverbial
manner adverbial

reason adverbial

In each of the sentences below, find the subject and any objects, intensive complements and adverbials:

EXERCISE 7.15

(a)   Heather took the ferry across to Istanbul yesterday.

(b)   Isabelle trimmed the lamp lightly.

(c)   Bricks are best because they are heavy.

(d)   Cotton fabrics suit everyone this season.

(e)   This season everyone is sending expensive presents to their friends for Christmas.

· ·

We can now summarize some of what we have found by formulating a table (Table 7.5) which indicates what kinds of phrases perform the various functions in simple sentences.

Table 7.5 Summary of simple sentence functions and the phrases that can perform them

Function	*Structures*
subject:	noun phrase, e.g. *The boy* screamed.
predicate:	verb phrase, e.g. John *had been eating his lunch.*
complements:	
direct object	noun phrase, e.g. He rode *a large horse.*
indirect object	(a) noun phrase, e.g. I gave *Fred* a new bike.
	(b) prepositional phrase starting with *to* or *for.* (For such a prepositional phrase to be an indirect object it can be paraphrased with a simple noun phrase, *e.g. John gave a present to his mother* can be paraphrased as *John gave his mother a present.*)
intensive complements:	(a) noun phrase, e.g. She seemed *a nice person.*
	(b) adjective phrase, e.g. She appeared *very angry.*
	(c) prepositional phrase, e.g. She was *over the moon.*
adverbials:	(a) adverb phrase, e.g. She ran *very quickly.*
	(b) prepositional phrase, e.g. She walked *by the river.*

Further exercises •

EXERCISE 7.16• Draw tree diagrams of the following phrases:

(a)   the red tulip

(b)   is selling the silver

(c)   very deeply troubled

(d)   on the afternoon of the party

(e)   is cycling into town this afternoon

(f)   my auntie with the red hair

EXERCISE 7.17• Identify and label all the functional constituents: subjects, predicates, objects, intensive complements and adverbials, except heads and modifiers, in each of the following sentences:

(a)   We gave him a raise.

(b)   He donated his stamp collection to the gallery.

(c)   She put the wombat in the alligator's cage.

(d)   Xavier cried.

(e)   The key opened the door.

(f)   The alligator ate its prey.

Study the following passage, identify all the verbs and assign them to the categories 'lexical' or 'auxiliary'. For each lexical verb decide whether it denotes a state or an action:

EXERCISE 7.18

Use a preserving jar which contains about 10 cm of soil to which peat has been added in the proportion of two measures of soil to one of peat. Cover the top of the jar with muslin.
    You must keep the atmosphere moist, but be careful that no mould is allowed to grow as this quickly kills the animals. Should the muslin feel dry sprinkle it lightly with water. Slugs will eat carrot discs, which may be supplemented occasionally with pieces of potato and green food. When the food begins to decay it must be removed from the jar.

From *Form 5 Science: An Animal Study. Core Material*
(Wellington, New Zealand: Department of Education)

Complex Syntax

8.1 COMPLEX PHRASES AND CLAUSES

In Chapter 7 we looked at phrases that have a single level of embedding, that is, they have a single phrase as modifier, and we looked at sentences containing a single lexical verb. We can now put this knowledge to work by looking at more complex structures.

If we begin by looking at phrases, it is clear that the phrases embedded within phrases can, in turn, have phrases embedded within them. For example, in the phrase *the person on the seat within the theatre,* the PP *within the theatre* is telling

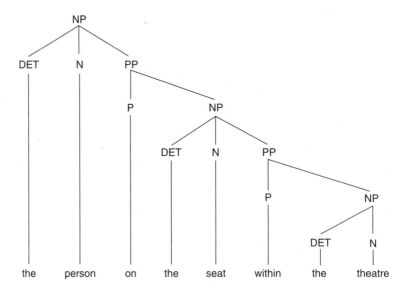

Figure 8.1

us where the seat is and so must be embedded in the NP which has *seat* as head, as follows:

the person [PPon [NPthe seat [PPwithin [NPthe theatre]]]]

The tree diagram would look like Figure 8.1

There is clearly no end to this process, as can be seen from the way one can embed possessive noun phrases within noun phrases, for example, *John's father's uncle's wife's mother's ... dog*. Because of the capacity of phrasal embedding to go on ad infinitum, this process is technically referred to as 'recursive', that is, having the property of being able to recur indefinitely.

Phrases have the same structure regardless of whether or not they are embedded. For the purpose of drawing tree diagrams, therefore, the crucial question for any embedded phrase is to ask what head the phrase modifies. An embedded modifier phrase will always modify the head of another phrase. Whatever head that is, the modifier phrase and the head it modifies will be dominated by the same node of the tree. In this regard, more deeply embedded phrases are no different from other phrases.

recursive

Draw tree diagrams for the following phrases:

EXERCISE 8.1

(a) the cottage by the edge of the lake

(b) my aunt's dog's lead

(c) Fred's family's old car in the city's museum

Having looked at what happens within complex phrases, we can now see what happens with more complex sentences. So far we have looked only at sentences which have a single lexical verb in their predicate.

Look at the following sentences:

(a) Sally hoped that Paul would meet her today.
(b) Gerry understood why the jury found him guilty.
(c) Horace cried after his dog died.

Find the lexical verbs in each sentence, and their subjects.

You will notice that these sentences have two lexical verbs each: (a) has *hoped* and *meet*; (b) has *understood* and *found*; (c) has *cried* and *died*. Each of these

clause

verbs has its own subject. Sally does the hoping, Paul does the meeting, Gerry understands, the jury finds, Horace cries, and the dog dies. So a sentence can have 'sentences' within it. Because of this, a distinction has traditionally been made between sentences and clauses. In a clause there is only one single lexical verb, while a sentence may consist of a number of clauses each with its own lexical verb. In the previous section, in order to keep things simple, we dealt with the structure of sentences where each contained only a single clause. Now we will look at multi-clause sentences.

Such sentences show that clauses as well as phrases may be embedded. But, as we saw in the previous section, not all clauses are embedded. This allows for a distinction to be made between clauses which are not embedded, usually called

main clause

'main clauses', and 'embedded clauses'.

Having just previously considered the relationship between heads which have phrases as modifiers, we can now look at the function of embedded clauses to see what grammatical roles they play.

Look at the following two structures, which each contain the same embedded clause. What function does this clause perform in each case?

(a)   Joanna knew [that Henry would come].

(b)   the expectation [that Henry would come]

Answer:

In (a) the embedded clause is an object since it is what Joanna knew. In (b) it is a modifier of *expectation,* which is the head of a noun phrase. So embedded clauses can both be modifiers of heads within phrases and play other major functional roles such as the object in clauses. We will look at both these situations.

First it has to be noted that, unlike embedded phrases, embedded clauses often change their grammatical structure in order to allow them to fit into a particular location in another clause or phrase. The simplest way to do that is for

subordinating conjunction complementizer

them to be introduced by a subordinating conjunction or complementizer such as *that.* For example, in the sentence *She decided* [*that* [*her bicycle was defective*]], the word *that* introduces the embedded clause.

There is a large number of subordinating conjunctions. Many of them introduce adverbial clauses of one kind or another. For example, in the sentence *John was improving* [*because* [*the doctor had seen him*]], there are two lexical verbs, *improve* and *see,* and therefore two clauses. The main clause is *John was improving.* A reason for John's getting better is given as part of the clause. That reason, *because the doctor had seen him,* is itself a clause, that is, it is an embedded clause within the main clause. The complementizer *because* tells us that the clause it introduces is a particular kind of adverbial, namely, one which gives a reason for something happening.

An embedded clause can also be the complement of a verb. For example, verbs such as *ask, know* and *say* often have whole clauses as their complements, as is shown in the following examples:

(a)   Bill knew [that [Freda was coming]].

(b)   Freda asked [whether [anyone knew the answer]].

(c)   Sophie asked [for [the teacher to explain the problem]].

Bill knew something, and what he knew is the object of the verb. So *that Freda was coming* is the object of *knew*.

Clauses can also be subjects. For example, consider the sentence [*That Bill leaves early*] *creates problems*. If you ask what it was that created problems, then the answer is *that Bill leaves early*. You can also see that it is a subject from the fact that the verb *creates* has a third person singular present inflection. This shows that subject clauses must be third person and singular as far as the verb is concerned. So *that Bill leaves early* is an embedded clause with its own lexical verb and introduced by a complementizer.

Clauses can also modify heads of phrases, as we saw earlier. Look, for example, at the following noun phrases:

(a)   the goat [which was tied up at the back fence]

(b)   the ferry [which you take to Harwich]

(c)   the cleaner [who comes every evening]

(d)   the night [that you went to Monaco]

In each case the bracketed clause clearly modifies the head noun, telling us more about it. In the case of clauses which modify nouns, these clauses are termed 'relative clauses'. However, clauses can also modify prepositions in prepositional phrases, and adjectives in adjective phrases, as the following examples show: **relative clause**

(a)   The cat was sleeping *in* [*what Freda had knitted*].

(b)   She seemed *quite astounded* [*that Fred played bridge*].

Sentences which contain embedded clauses are often called 'complex sentences'.   **complex sentence**

Now that we have looked at single and multi-clause sentences we need to know how to draw tree diagrams of them. It is clear, if we look at many embedded clauses, that the subordinating conjunction (or complementizer) is, in some sense, not part of the clause. For example, an embedded clause such as *that radios make a lot of noise* consists of a simple clause, *radios make a lot of noise*, introduced by the complementizer. For the purpose of this book, we will label the clause itself *S* and the clause which includes the complementizer *S'* an abbreviation for *S bar*. All embedded clauses are thus S bars. On their left they have complementizers like *for* or *that,* and on their right is the clause proper, S with its subject and predicate.

We can now set about drawing some tree diagrams of clauses and phrases which contain embedded clauses. Again, this is not difficult. Embedded clauses function just like embedded phrases. It is only their structure which is sometimes different from what it would be if they were main clauses. (We shall have more to say about these structural differences later in this chapter.) So if a clause modifies the head of a phrase, then it is telling you more about the head. For instance, in the phrase *the cat which lives with Nellie, which lives with Nellie* is telling you more about the cat and the embedded clause is therefore dominated by the same phrase category as its head, *cat,* namely, NP. We can use a triangle for constituents whose internal structure we do not wish to analyse in the tree diagram, as shown in Figure 8.2. There are complications that we are steering clear of by doing this, as will be evident to the eagle-eyed later in the chapter. Not only do complementizers fit to the left of the subject of the embedded clause but sometimes pronouns do as well. For example, in *[They knew [what Joanna saw.]* *what* is not a complementizer although it is in the same position as a complementizer would occupy if there was one. Advanced theories of syntax have ways of dealing with such facts which we will not pursue. But they do have the effect that there is more than one way of drawing the relevant the tree diagrams.

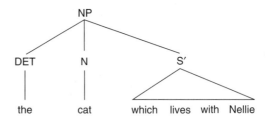

Figure 8.2

If an embedded clause is functioning as a subject, then it is, just like a phrasal subject, the answer to the question Who? or What? placed before the verb of the clause in which it is the subject. For example, in the sentence *What we did yesterday scared Tom,* if we ask 'What scared Tom?' then the answer is the embedded clause *what we did yesterday.* It is therefore the subject of the main clause, as shown in Figure 8.3.

If you are still finding problems with the drawing of tree diagrams, here are:

Some rules of thumb for doing tree diagrams

1. *Find the lexical verbs*
    For each lexical verb there will be one associated verb phrase and one associated clause. Therefore you know how many clauses there are in the sentence by counting the number of lexical verbs.

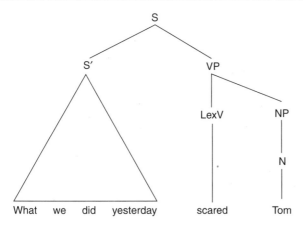

Figure 8.3

2. *Find the main clause*

To do this, ask yourself what the whole sentence would say at its most simple if it were to be put into a telegram or newspaper headline with one lexical verb. For example, the sentence *Three Spanish ballerinas murdered an impressive impresario in Morocco*, would be reduced to *Ballerinas murdered impresario*.

This telegram gives you the 'top' structure of the sentence by telling you who is doing what. That also gives you the head words of the main phrases. The phrase which has *ballerinas* as head is the subject. The phrase with *murdered* as head will be the verb phrase and the phrase with *impresario* as head will be the object.

So you can now draw this much of the diagram, as shown in Figure 8.4. The pieces left over from your telegram (if you got it right) will either belong with the head words you have already found or will be adverbials.

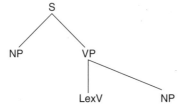

Figure 8.4

Three and *Spanish* belong with *ballerinas*; *an impressive* goes with *impresario*; and *in Morocco* is an adverbial. We know this because *three* and *Spanish* tell us more about the ballerinas, so *ballerinas* must be the head of these two modifiers; *an* and *impressive* both tell us more about the impresario, so *impresario* must be their head; and *in Morocco* is the place where the murdering of the impresario took place, so it is an adverbial of place.

3. *Start at the top and work down*
    Once you have worked out the main functions in the main clause you can fill
    in the 'top' of the structure as shown in Figure 8.5.

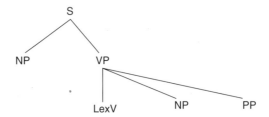

Figure 8.5

4. *Find embedded clauses*
    All the rest of the clauses you have found that are not the main clause can be
    treated in the same way. Since they are embedded they must either be modi-
    fiers of a head of phrase, or functioning as the whole of a subject, object,
    intensive complement or adverbial.
       To find out if an embedded clause is functioning as part of a phrase, ask
    yourself if it goes with the head word of a phrase, just as you would ask that
    about a phrasal modifier.

Now try to draw tree diagrams of a few simple examples for yourself.

EXERCISE 8.2   Draw tree diagrams of the following sentences.

    (a)   The red baroness crashed her plane into a haystack.

    (b)   Anybody can do that.

    (c)   The dog's kennel by the house looked untidy.

    (d)   She gave her father a watch.

8.1.1   SUBCATEGORIZATION OF HEADS OF PHRASE

Now that we have seen something of the structure of single- and multiple-clause
sentences, we can revisit a topic we looked at in Chapter 2 and do some revision.
In Chapter 2 we looked at grammatical sub-classes of words, which are established on the basis of how they fit with other words. For example, we saw that
proper nouns do not go with determiners. On that basis we established a sub-
category of nouns, namely, proper nouns (see Chapter 2.1.2). This analysis can
be extended. Categories of words, such as noun and verb, can be broken down
into sub-categories. One of the most important ways of doing this is in terms of

the complements which heads of phrase require. Because some verbs require complements to complete their meaning, we can set up sub-categories of verbs on the basis of the complements they require. We find that some verbs take direct objects and some do not. For example:

(a)   Jill slept.

(b)   *Jill slept the bed/Bill/the child.

Verbs that require objects are called 'transitive verbs'. Verbs that cannot take objects are called 'intransitive verbs'.   **transitive verbs**
intransitive verbs
    Other verbs have objects as an optional complement. For example:

(a)   The athlete jumped the hurdle.

(b)   The athlete jumped.

Some verbs take two objects: a direct and an indirect object. For example:

(a)   Jill gave her mother a treat.

(b)   *Jill gave her mother.

(c)   *Jill gave a treat.

A few verbs require the indirect object to be in the prepositional phrase form.

(a)   *The president donated Freda the trophy.

(b)   The president donated the trophy to Freda.

As we saw earlier, a verb like *put* must take both a direct object and a phrase or clause indicating location. Such a phrase would also be a complement in that it is a constituent which is required in order to complete the meaning of the verb. For example:

(a)   Jill put the book on the table.

(b)   *Jill put the book.

(c)   *Jill put on the table.

Put therefore belongs to another sub-category of verb.
    The verbs which take intensive complements form another sub-category. Those which take the intensive complement directly to their right include the lexical verbs *be, seem, appear* and *become*, as in:

(a)   Joanna became very ill.

(b)   Sean was quite bright.

(c)   Liz seemed terribly upset.

(Note that the verb *be* is a lexical verb here and not an auxiliary verb.) Those which require both an object and a following intensive complement form another sub-category. These include: *elect, appoint, nominate,* and *consider,* as in:

(a)   The voters elected Mr Bean president.

(b)   The Council appointed Mrs Bean national co-ordinator.

You can see that the verb has a central place in clause structure since the verb's sub-category determines what kinds of complement the clause will contain.

What sub-category a verb belongs to clearly depends on its meaning. It is in the nature of giving that there must be a giver, something given, and someone to whom it is given. It is in the nature of putting that something has to be put some-where. Meaning, as we saw earlier, is not independent of syntax. That relation-ship is demonstrated clearly here.

Sub-categorization is not restricted to verbs. Take a noun like *sister*. For some-one to be a sister there must be two people. You can only be a sister if there is someone else to be the sister of. So in a noun phrase such as *the sister of Bill, Bill* is in a very similar situation to the complement of a verb. In an adjective phrase such as *very wary of anteaters, anteaters* is a complement of *wary*. On the other hand, the adjective phrase *rather old* does not require the head, *old*, to have a complement. Someone can be old without any additional complementation. We might therefore want to say that all heads of phrase sub-categorize on the basis of the complements they take. Just to make the point again, let us look at preposi-tions. A preposition like *into* must have a complement, as is clear when it is left without one, as in **Jean walked into.*

The relationships of heads and their complements is illustrated further where a transitive verb has a derived form which is a noun. For example, *decide* requires a complement that can be either a noun phrase or a clause:

(a)   They decided the matter.

(b)   They decided that Freda should be president.

The noun derived from *decide* is *decision*, and it takes the same complements:

(a)   their decision on the question

(b)   their decision that Freda should be president

Our previous discussion suggests that the phrase *of the matter* and the clause *that Freda should be president* were modifiers of the head noun *decision*. You can see from the discussion above that some modifiers share important properties with complements.

Let us now look further at the ways verbs in one clause sub-categorize for their clausal complements. It appears that certain verbs sub-categorize for the comple-mentizer of the clause which is their complement. Look, for example, at a com-plex sentence such as *Max understood [that [Joanna would drive his sports-car]]*.

Here the lexical verb in the main clause is *understood.* It has as its complement a clause which has *that* as complementizer. By way of contrast, *understand* cannot take as its complement a clause with *for* as complementizer, as the following case shows, *Max understood [for [Joanna to drive his sportscar]]. So it is clear that, regardless of the clause which is the complement, the verbs are sensitive to the complementizer which introduces the complement clause.

In turn, complementizers themselves also belong to sub-categories. Their basis for sub-categorization requires us to look at tense.

Main clauses in English are always tensed. Tensed clauses are often termed 'finite clauses' and clauses without tense 'non-finite clauses'. Embedded clauses may be with or without tense. Look, for example, at the following bracketed embedded clause: *Joanna asked* [$_S$'*for* [$_S$*Nick to come*]]. In the place where we would expect the tense to be, we find the word *to.* This clause is therefore untensed. For the purpose of drawing tree diagrams we will regard this marker of the absence of tense as a modifier within the VP much as we would an auxiliary verb, but, as in the example in Figure 8.6, we will not give it a label itself. (Note that it is not a preposition when it is functioning as a marker showing that the clause is not tensed just as *for* is not a preposition when it is functioning as a complementizer.)

finite clause
non-finite clause

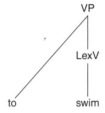

Figure 8.6

When we look at complementizers a clear pattern emerges. The complementizer *that* requires its following clause to have tense. In English *He knew that Freda had sat the exam* is grammatical but **He knew that Freda to sit the exam* is not. By contrast, *for* requires the following clause not to have tense, so that *He asked for Freda to sit the exam* is grammatical but **He asked for Freda had sat the exam* is not. Let us suppose that the clause is the complement of the complementizer. It seems that some complementizers require their following complement clauses to be tensed while others require them not to be tensed.

This suggests that there is a closer relationship between the head of a phrase and its complements than between a head and those phrases and clauses which function as other kinds of modifier. The way we have been drawing tree diagrams does not make this distinction clear. For the purposes of this book, we merely point this out and leave it to more advanced treatments of syntax to deal with it in detail.

We can now update the table at the end of Chapter 7.2 with some additional information. (You might like to look at the table again to refresh your memory.) As well as the structural units mentioned there as functioning in various ways in clauses, we now know that clauses can function as subject, complement and adverbial in other clauses. Clauses can also function as modifiers in phrases.

8.1.2 CO-ORDINATION

co-ordinating conjunction

One further process that makes phrases and clauses more complicated is the process of co-ordination. It uses words called co-ordinating conjunctions. Coordination involves the joining of similar units by the following conjunctions:

> *and*
>
> *(either) ... or*
>
> *(neither) ... nor.*

Co-ordination of clauses may also be by *but*. Any constituent in English can be joined to any other of the same kind by the first three conjunctions: *and*, *or* and *nor*. In most cases the conjuncts joined by a co-ordinating conjunction must belong to the same structural category so that co-ordination joins noun phrases to noun phrases, VPs to VPs, APs to APs, PPs to PPs. But sometimes the conjuncts can have the same function. For example, co-ordinating conjunctions can join units both of which are intensive complements but which have different structures. For instance, in the sentence *He was* [*fabulously wealthy*] *and* [*a target for kidnappers*], the two units joined by *and* are *fabulously wealthy* and *a target for kidnappers*. Although the first unit is an adjective phrase and the second is a noun phrase, that is, of different structure, both are intensive complements of the verb *is*.

EXERCISE 8.3

In the following sentences, bracket the structures that have been joined and say what kind of structures each pair is:

(a)   The man and the boy walked to town.

(b)   The singer sang at the concert and in the shower.

(c)   Gertrude whistled at boys and patted dogs.

(d)   Melissa ate chicken and Angela talked turkey.

(e)   Henry and Alfred walked, talked and fought in the park.

(f)   Neither Angela nor Melissa liked Brahms.

(g)   Gertrude either slurped or burped her soup.

(h)   Either the weather turned nasty or the opposition did.

(i)   The orchestra will play the Brahms or Angela's new concerto.

(j)   The orchestra neither played nor heard Angela's concerto.

There are some interesting observations to be made about the meaning of co-ordination. Put simply, *and* has a kind of additive meaning in that the phrases or clauses co-ordinated by it give the total set of the conjuncts added together. In Noah's Ark, for example, the animals were the sum total of elephants and kangaroos and pigs and wombats, etc. *Or* is disjunctive in that a set of phrases or clauses linked with *or* allows for only one of the conjuncts to be selected. In a cage in the zoo there might be elephants or kangaroos or pigs or wombats, etc., that is, only one of the set of conjuncts. Phrases or clauses co-ordinated with *nei-ther... nor* mean you can have none of the set of conjuncts, neither elephants, nor kangaroos, nor pigs, nor wombats, etc. The cage is empty.

However, consider the following sentences:

(a)   I crashed the car and drank too much.

(b)   I drank too much and crashed the car.

Is there any difference in meaning between these two sentences? Which one would you use if you were being interviewed by a traffic officer and attempting to escape the charge of drink-driving?

In English we frequently understand *and* as 'and then'. Actions that are joined by *and* are thought to have happened in the order in which they appear in the sentence. Consequently, we would choose the first sentence if we did not wish to incriminate ourselves. This point is made even more obvious by the following:

(a)   She mounted the horse and rode off into the sunset.

(b)   She rode off into the sunset and mounted the horse.

(c)   He opened the can and poured out the contents.

(d)   He poured out the contents and opened the can.

However, we do not always interpret *and* as *and then*. Sometimes the events or actions joined by *and* can occur in either order or at the same time:

(a)   She read the newspaper and ate breakfast.

(b)   She ate breakfast and read the newspaper.

(c)   He plays the flute and she plays the violin.

(d)   She plays the violin and he plays the flute.

What this shows is that there is a difference between the semantics of an expression, that is, its meaning as contained in the words and their structural configuration, and how that meaning is interpreted in context. *And* has a simple additive meaning but, in context, may be interpreted as having a chronological aspect. This again shows the distinction between semantics and pragmatics, which we mentioned in Chapter 3.1.7 when we looked at word connotations. That distinction is therefore relevant not only for the meanings of words but also for the meaning of syntax.

Earlier we said that sentences containing embedded clauses are often called complex sentences. Sentences which consist of co-ordinated clauses are known **compound sentence**   as 'compound sentences'.

APPLICATION

In the passage below, what impression do you get of the narrator who is telling the story, as a result of the author's frequent use of co-ordination?

> Curley's wife lay with a half-covering of yellow hay. And the meanness and the plannings and the discontent and the ache for attention were all gone from her face. She was very pretty and simple, and her face was sweet and young. Now her rouged cheeks and her reddened lips made her seem alive and sleeping very lightly.
>
> John Steinbeck, *Of Mice and Men*

Discussion

So much co-ordination makes the speaker seem very natural and simple, suggesting he or she is speaking, rather than writing. This is because, when speaking, people tend to use co-ordination in preference to embedding. This is particularly so when they are telling a story.

8.1.2.1   Diagramming compound and complex sentence structure

We can now update our procedures for drawing tree diagrams to include co-ordination. Tree diagrams indicate co-ordination by placing a co-ordinating conjunction between two or more structures which normally have the same syntactic category label, as shown in Figure 8.7. Their immediately dominating node, their

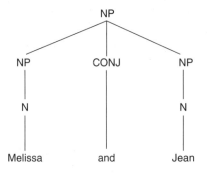

Figure 8.7

mother, also has that label. This is not an arbitrary decision. When two or more NPs are co-ordinated they can be pronominalized, showing that together they are also an NP. ***The fox and the hare*** *were solid friends.* ***They*** *had met years before.* When two singular noun phrases are co-ordinated with *and*, the resulting noun phrase is, of course, plural.

> When the coordinator is *or,* what pronoun does the 'top' NP take?

This is an interesting question. In *The coach will select Joan or Mary. Either would make a great captain, either* seems to act as the pronoun which has Joan or Mary as antecedent.

In the few cases we mentioned where the conjuncts have different structural labels, linguists are not sure what the dominating node should be.

Draw tree diagrams to show the structure of the following sentences, which contain co-ordinated and embedded clauses: **EXERCISE 8.4**

(a)   Jean knew that Tom and Jerry would come.

(b)   Sally asked for her father to sign the lease.

(c)   Ibrahim had seen that the birds had left their perches and were flying away.

(d)   The boy whom I admire has given the lady her present.

(e)   The people in the old house decided to call their son Jim.

(f)   James cooked tasty and cheap lasagne when Harry came to the flat.

(g)   The plane which the test pilot had flown had suddenly been put in a hangar because it was wet.

• •

Having now completed our discussion of the structure of clauses and complex sentences we can briefly look at sentences in speech. From the way we have presented them, it would appear that sentences are always syntactically well-formed. There are times, however, when they are not spoken in their complete form.

First, we can distinguish between sentences that are complete and sentences that are incomplete. In formal written English, sentences must normally be grammatically complete but when we speak, our sentences are often incomplete, **complete sentence** interrupted or broken off. If you listen carefully to a tape-recorded casual conversation you will hear many incomplete sentences. There are two reasons for **incomplete sentence** this. Sometimes speakers are interrupted and don't get to finish what they have to say. At other times a speaker realizes that they are saying not quite what they intended and interrupt themselves. Often it is impossible to work out exactly how the speaker would have completed such a sentence. Here is an example showing an italicized incomplete sentence. The speaker might have been going to say something like 'I never did get the hang of knitting', but aborts this sentence in favour of another:

I never di   I could never take to knitting ...

Crystal and Davy, *Investigating English Style*

major sentence
minor sentence

There is also another form of incompleteness where only part of the sentence is given but where we can be quite sure what the rest of it is. In such cases we make a distinction between major sentences, where everything is said, and minor sentences, where only a particular phrase is said but the rest can be filled in from the context. Minor sentences are often given in answer to a question, for example, *Where did you go yesterday? To town.* The major sentence would be *I went to town.*

APPLICATION

Writers occasionally use punctuation in ways which turn phrases into what look like minor sentences. If you were writing a formal essay, such punctuation would be marked as being ungrammatical, but, in the example below, it allows the writer to draw attention to a list of 'environmental hazards' by making each appear to be a sentence of its own rather than having them as phrases separated by commas:

In the country of the old and sick there are environmental hazards. Cautious days. Early nights. A silent, ageing life in which the anxiety of the invalid overrides the vitality of the untouched. A wariness, in case the untoward might go undetected. Sudden gratitude that turns bitterness into self-reproach.

Anita Brookner, *A Start in Life*

8.2   SYNTACTIC RELATEDNESS

8.2.1   YES/NO QUESTION FORMATION

So far it has seemed as if we have suggested that all that is needed to describe the syntax of English is to draw a tree diagram of each sentence and so show its syntactic structure. Sure enough this tells us what the syntactic constituents of the sentence are, and to what category each belongs, and how the constituents relate to each other. But one of the tests for phrases which we used in Chapter 7.1 rested on the assumption that phrases can move. If that is so then the movement involves a tree which represents the syntax of the sentence before movement took place and another representing the results of making the movement. These two trees specify a location from which the phrase is moved and another loca- **declarative** tion to which it is moved. **interrogative**

Look, for example, at the following pairs of statements (declaratives) and questions (interrogatives):

(1a)		John is	eating.
(1b)	Is	John	eating?
(2a)		Geraldine has	dined.
(2b)	Has	Geraldine	dined?
(3a)		Pauline might	come.
(3b)	Might	Pauline	come?

You will see that there is a syntactic relationship between the question and its related statement. The relationship lies in the fact that an auxiliary verb appears before the subject in the question, whereas in the statement the same auxiliary appears after the subject.

How do we know that it is the same auxiliary?

Look at the following parallel cases:

(a)   *Is John has eaten?

(b)   *Has John is eating?

(c)   *Might John has been eating?

Remember that we discovered in Chapter 7.1.6 that aspect auxiliaries select par- ticular forms of the following verb. *Have* requires the following verb to be in its perfect participle form, and *be* requires the following verb to be in the progres- sive participle form. If we look at the sets of data above, the auxiliary at the left of a question does not determine the inflection of the subject on its right. It isn't a verb. It *does* select the form of the auxiliary that is to the right of the subject. This suggests that the auxiliary verb at the front of a yes/no question has been moved **yes/no question** from an original position where it was next to the auxiliary verb whose form it is determining.

So let us suppose that, in general, it is possible that one tree diagram per sentence is not enough to represent all its syntactic properties. We may need two or more tree diagrams, where one tree diagram has a constituent moved from an original position, which we shall call its 'extraction site', into another position, which we shall call its 'landing site'.

extraction site
landing site

We can now look in a little more detail at the movement which we have just begun to explore.

Here is a complication in the data relating to questions. See if you can sort out the source of the complication:

(1a)	Ethne	writes letters.
(1b) Does	Ethne	write letters?
(2a)	Thomas	skates on thin ice.
(2b) Does	Thomas	skate on thin ice?

Three things are notable about these data. First, there is no auxiliary verb in the (a) forms, that is, in the declarative form. Secondly, the third person singular present inflection -s has moved in the (b) cases, that is, in the interrogative form, from the end of the lexical verb and into the left-of-subject position. Thirdly, in the interrogative form, the third person singular present inflection is attached to the auxiliary verb *do*, which was not present in the declarative form.

What sense can we make of this? The key is to recall that the tense inflection in English, if it is present, is attached to the *first* auxiliary verb if there are auxiliary verbs, and to the lexical verb only if there is no auxiliary. Forming interrogatives must therefore be performed by moving the tense inflection and any auxiliary it may be attached to.

We can show that this is so by moving an auxiliary which does not have an attached tense, as in the following cases:

(a)   *Been Joanna has   walking the dog?

(b)   *Have Joanna could   walked the dog?

What makes these cases ungrammatical is that we have moved an untensed auxiliary. Remember that the tensed auxiliary is always the first auxiliary.

So what happens when there is no auxiliary and when the tense is attached to the lexical verb? It is not possible in contemporary English to move the lexical verb and an attached tense, as we shall see later, so the inflection moves on its own. Clearly it is not possible to have a verb inflection unattached to a verb stem since they are bound morphemes, and so *do* comes along in a supporting role to allow the unattached tense to be attached to a verb stem. This should not surprise us when we recall the conditions under which *do* appears in statements, conditions which we explored in Chapter 7.1.6. There, too, *do* appeared only when there was no auxiliary present, and it also carried the tense inflection when the sentence contained a negative, as in:

John didn't like mutton.

or a heavy emphasis, as in:

Joanna **did** like Marmite.

On the basis of these facts we can think of the formation of yes/no questions as involving the movement of the tense inflection.

Notice something else which supports our exploration in Chapter 2.1.4 of the irregular forms of the tensed verbs. Tense does not have to be indicated by a suffix. We saw there that the past tense of *see* is *saw*, not *seed*. So what happens with yes/no questions?

Joanna   saw   the yacht.

Did Joanna   see   the yacht?

There right underneath *saw* is *see* and the past tense is now in a more regular form on the end of *do*.

We have also, and without setting out to do so, found a further test for the subject of a sentence. The tense which moves, moves over the subject from its right to its left, thus indicating the left- and right-hand ends of the subject by the tense's extraction and landing sites.

An interesting sidelight on this discussion is that we said that it was not possible to move the lexical verb and its attached tense to create yes/no questions in contemporary English. However, it was possible in earlier forms of English. In Shakespeare's time it was possible to ask the following questions:

(a)   Came you to London yesterday?

(b)   Liked not you the music?

By studying the grammar of a language in terms of rules such as the ones we have just looked at we can see how the grammar of a language has changed over time. We will look at some further examples of historical change in section 8.2.7.

8.2.2   *WH* QUESTIONS AND *WH* MOVEMENT

To support the theory that questions can be formed by moving constituents out of an extraction site and into a landing site we might look at other questions such as the following:

(a)   When is Marcia coming?

(b)   What has Marcel brought?

(c)   Where will we eat tomorrow?

The answers to these questions might be:

(a)   Marcia is coming tomorrow.

(b)   Marcel has brought the champagne.

(c)   We will eat in the bistro tomorrow.

or these answers might be shortened to phrases such as:

(a)   Tomorrow.

(b)   The champagne.

(c)   In the bistro.

wh **question**
interrogative
pronoun

These questions are called '*wh* questions' on account of their having a *wh* word, or interrogative pronoun, at their beginning.

What is the form of *wh* questions? Those with an eagle eye will already have noticed that all the *wh* questions above also show the effects of tense movement. We can test this by trying a sentence without an auxiliary, for example *Harry eats when?* The *wh* question form of this sentence is *When does Harry eat?* Indeed *wh* questions seem to require tense movement, as shown by the presence of *do,* which has come to support the moved and therefore 'orphaned' tense affix.

But what of the interrogative pronoun?

Examine the data below and see what you can find out about the interrogative pronoun:

(1a)   The cat has caught a bird.
(1b)   *The cat has caught.

(2a)   The plumber fixed the pipe.
(2b)   *The plumber fixed.

(3a)   The storm damaged several boats.
(3b)   *The storm damaged.

(4a)   *The cat was purring a bird.
(4b)   The cat was purring.

(5a)   *The plumber laughed the pipe.
(5b)   The plumber laughed.

(6a)   *Several days elapsed the week.
(6b)   Several days elapsed.

(7a)   What has the cat caught?
(7b)   Which bird has the cat caught?
(7c)   How many birds has the cat caught?

(8a)   *What has the cat caught the bird?
(8b)   *Which pipe has the plumber fixed something?

(9a)   *What was the cat purring?
(9b)   *What has the plumber laughed?
(9c)   *What did several days elapse?

This data set brings together the discussion we held earlier on sub-categories of verbs, and the idea that constituents can move. The ungrammatical examples in (1), (2) and (3) are ungrammatical because the verbs in them are transitive, that is, they require objects. The ungrammatical examples in (4), (5) and (6) are ungrammatical because the verbs in them require not to have objects. So much is familiar territory.

You might think that the cases in (7) should all be ungrammatical, because there is no object after the verb, and the cases in (8) should both be grammatical, because there *is* an object after the verb. Also the cases in (9) should all be grammatical because the verbs are intransitive, since none has an object after the verb. But these suppositions are incorrect; the cases in (7) are grammatical and those in (8) and (9) are ungrammatical.

Let us suppose that the *wh* words are the objects of the verb, as they appear to be from the meaning of the sentences and the answers that one would give to these questions. If we ask Who? or What? after the verb, then the answer is the *wh* word or phrase. For example, if we ask 'Who or what has the cat caught?', then the answer is *which bird*. That being the case, then the judgements as to whether or not the sentences are grammatical are as we would expect. The sentences in (7) all have objects, as they should. The sentences in (8) have two objects, the interrogative pronoun being one and the object after the verb being a second. Since the lexical verbs in these sentences require that they have one and only one object, then the sentences in (8) have an object too many and are thus ungrammatical. The questions in (9) have interrogative pronouns which are objects, but the verbs are intransitive, that is, they should not have objects. The questions are therefore ungrammatical.

So this reasoning again suggests that a movement has taken place, namely, that the interrogative pronouns have, in these cases, moved from object position after the lexical verb into a position on the far left of the clause. Let us suppose for the purposes of this book that the landing site for *wh* words is a similar slot to that occupied by complementizers, that is, a position to the left and outside the S but within the S'. So is this the only possible landing site?

Look at the following two sentences and determine the extraction site and landing site of the interrogative noun phrase in bold type:

(a) [$_S$John knew **which hat** [$_S$Mary had hoped [$_S$that [$_S$Arthur would wear.]]]]

(b) [$_S$ **Which hat** did [$_S$John know [$_S$that [$_S$Mary hoped [$_S$that [$_S$Arthur would wear?]]]]]]

In each of these two complex sentences *which hat* is the object of *wear*, and has been extracted from the object location immediately to the right of *wear* and moved not just to the left of its own clause but to the left of a higher clause, that is, a clause in which the clause of which it is a constituent is embedded. This can be seen clearly from the bracketing in the examples.

Having looked at where *wh* phrases may be moved to, we can now look at where they may be moved from. The examples we have used up to now show that objects can be questioned by interrogative pronouns which appear to have undergone movement from their underlying position on the immediate right of the lexical verb to a position on the extreme left, either of the clause in which they were originally contained, or of a clause in which that clause is embedded.

So is the object position the only extraction site from which *wh* words may be moved?

Which clause function has been questioned in each of the following *wh* questions?

(a) When is Freda joining the party?

(b) Where is the party being held?

(c) How are you going there?

(d) Why is Joanna holding a party?

(e)   What will Mary give Joanna for her birthday?

(f)   Who will drive the car?

(g)   What did Joanna become?

Answers:

As you will have worked out, (a), (b), (c) and (d) show that all the four kinds of adverbial (time, place, manner and reason) which we looked at in Chapter 7.2 can be questioned; (e) shows that indirect objects can be questioned; (f) shows that subjects can be questioned; (g) shows that intensive complements may be questioned.

Not all varieties of English work in quite this way. As we suggested in Chapter 1.7 syntax is also a source of variation. In some New Englishes, *wh* questions don't also involve tense movement. In the English spoken in India people might say, 'Where you would like to go?' In Malaysian English *wh* questions like this occur: *When he is coming?, Where the man is going?*

In conclusion, we have now seen that two important constructions in English, yes/no questions and *wh* questions, appear to be the result of constituent movement. Such movements take constituents from extraction sites and relocate them in landing sites.

APPLICATION

Examine the passage below and sort out the yes/no questions from the *wh* questions, and then see if there is anything odd about the way these questions are answered. There are two speakers: Sherlock Holmes, who is answering the questions, and Dr Watson, who is asking them. Holmes is the great detective and Watson his well-intentioned but rather bumbling friend.

'When I say, therefore, that Mycroft has better powers of observation than I, you may take it that I am speaking the exact and literal truth.'
'Is he your junior?'
'Seven years my senior.'
'How comes it that he is unknown?'
'Oh, he is very well known in his own circle.'
'Where, then?'
'Well, in the Diogenes Club, for example.'
I had never heard of this institution, and my face must have proclaimed as much, for Sherlock Holmes pulled out his watch.

Sir Arthur Conan Doyle, 'The Greek Interpreter'

Discussion

Watson asks three questions. The first is a yes/no question and the other two are *wh* questions. Holmes plays with Watson in answering them. To the first question, where Watson would expect a yes or no answer, Holmes gives the answer to a *wh* question. (Notice that it is a minor sentence, the kind of sentence that is often given in response to a *wh* question.) To the next *wh* question Holmes gives what is close to a yes/no answer. He also suggests that Watson has made a mistaken assumption in asking the question. Finally, Watson gets exasperated and asks a very short question, and is rewarded with a straight minor sentence answer to his *wh* question. Sherlock Holmes, being a great detective, is naturally a master in the art of asking questions. Here he appears to be showing up his friend's relative lack of skill in asking the appropriate kinds of questions.

8.2.3 RELATIVE CLAUSES AND *WH* MOVEMENT

relative pronoun

We can now return to the relative clause, a construction which we looked at in the previous section. You will recall that relative clauses are typically introduced by relative pronouns, and you can now see as well that the *wh* words which introduce relative clauses are a kind of pronoun. Look at a noun phrase such as *the man whom I met*. *Whom* has an antecedent and that antecedent is *the man*. Because words like *whom* introduce relative clauses and are pronouns, they are termed 'relative pronouns'. The following sentence, for example, contains two bracketed relative clauses and the two relative pronouns are in bold:

The man [**whom** Bill liked] slipped on the ice [**which** the cold temperatures had created].

These relative pronouns look suspiciously like the interrogative pronouns we have just examined. They too are *wh* pronouns. They also are at the far left of their own clauses, as the bracketing shows. Are they also moved? It would seem so. In the first relative clause the lexical verb is *like*, which is a transitive verb, that is, it requires an object. If we ask whom it was that Bill liked, then the object of *like* is clearly *whom*. The pronoun *whom* has *the man* as antecedent and Bill liked the man. That *whom* has the form of the object (*whom* as opposed to *who*) supports the view that it is the object. Similarly the second relative clause contains the lexical verb *create*. In this clause it looks as though *which* (the pronoun with *the ice* as antecedent) is the object of *create*, since the low temperatures had created the ice.

This shows that *wh* movement is involved not only in forming *wh* questions but also in the formation of relative clauses. But in relative clauses it is not associated with tense movement since relative clauses do not move their tense to the left of the subject, as you can see from the following ungrammatical case:

*The man [**whom** did Bill like] slipped on the ice [**which** had the low temperatures created].

So we have two rules, tense movement and *wh* movement, both of which are optional. That gives four possibilities. It is possible for neither to be used, giving us a plain statement in a main clause, or tense movement can be used on its own, giving us a yes/no question, or *wh* movement can be used on its own and that gives relative clauses, or both can be used, giving *wh* questions. In Indian English, what would be relative clause order in embedded clauses, is also used for *wh* questions in main clauses.

The rules we have been looking at which move constituents are often called 'transformations'.   **transformation**

We will now look at some well-known constructions of English, many of which can be seen as being formed by movement of constituents.

8.2.4 COMMANDS

Commands in English are structurally related to statements. For example:

Henry eats his porridge.

becomes, as a command,

Eat your porridge.

Commands are, as you can see, subjectless. They take a bare form of the verb, that is, without inflection, and the lexical verb can take no auxiliary verbs before it. For example, it is ungrammatical to order someone to *be driving the car tomorrow*. However, there is some evidence that commands do have a subject. We might be tempted to think that the subject in (b), above, is *Henry*. But that cannot be the case because, if it were, then the verb would be inflected for the third person singular present tense, that is, the command would be *Eats your porridge*.

However, if we add a tag question at the end of the command, as in *Eat the porridge, won't you?*, then the tag question on the end of the command suggests that the subject of the command is *you*, because other tag questions also contain a pronoun copy of the subject. For example, in the sentence *Martin ate his porridge, didn't he?*, *he* has *Martin* as its antecedent and *Martin* is the subject of the sentence.

The syntactic form of a command is termed the 'imperative' form. Why the   **imperative** subjects of imperative sentences are missing is an interesting question. Some linguists have proposed that this is a result of their having been deleted. The important fact for our purposes is that statements and commands are syntactically related.

<table>
<tr><td>

APPLICATION

Find the imperative sentences in the following advertisement. Why are they being used?

Come to life in Singapore and explore the fabulous 'Circle'. Take in the lyric isles of Tioman and Rawa. The virgin beaches and cool highlands across the causeway. Jewel-like Penang. Sensual Bali. Take home a million memories.

</td></tr>
</table>

Discussion

All the sentences in the advertisement are imperatives. (Do not be fooled by the stops.) The imperatives are used to persuade you to do what the advertiser wants you to do. (The persuasion is, however, not binding since the advertiser has no right to order us to do anything.)

8.2.5 PASSIVE

In Chapter 1 and elsewhere we have spoken about language being rule-governed. We can see this again with another syntactic construction of English, the passive.

passive

Let us start with familiar territory and look at the verb *occupy*. In the sense of 'to live in', *occupy* requires as object the kind of things that can be lived in and as subjects the kind of things that can live in such places. Abstract nouns cannot occupy anything literally and people can only occupy locations and not, for instance, psychological states, for example **Grizelda occupies anger.* Recall that passive sentences contain, as their last auxiliary verb, a form of the verb *be* or *get* followed by a perfect participle. If we look at a passive sentence, such as *The White House is occupied by the President,* it appears that the object of the verb has been moved into subject position since the basic situation is that someone is occupying somewhere. The logical subject – that is, in this example, the person occupying the White House – may be expressed by means of a prepositional phrase introduced by the preposition *by,* or it may be unexpressed.

logical subject

active

Passive sentences may be contrasted with the form they had before the movement of the object. That form is termed the 'active' form of the sentence. The active form of the above sentence would be *The President occupies the White House.* In the following examples, the (a) sentence is in the active form. The others are all in forms of the passive.

(a) Henry ate the porridge.

(b) The porridge was eaten by Henry.

(c) The porridge was eaten.

(d)   The porridge got eaten by Henry.

(e)   The porridge got eaten.

Whether you choose *be* or *get* in passives is a matter of social dialect or possibly of the degree of formality of your speech or writing. *Be* passives are often considered more correct or more formal than *get* passives. So this looks like a case of free variation in syntax.

In Chapter 7.2, when we were discussing the function of the subject, we saw that some sentences looked as though they had two subjects. One of these is the underlying or logical subject, the other is the surface subject, that is, the object which has been moved into subject position by movement.

Passives, where the logical subject is unexpressed – that is, where there is no prepositional phrase introduced with *by* containing the logical subject – are often used in political speech or writing when the speaker or writer does not wish to say who is responsible for something. For example, if an official says that the notes for a meeting have been mislaid, then that may be very convenient; and since the logical subject is unexpressed, no one can be blamed. Politicians and government officials are a good source of such sentences. It can be an interesting, informative, if somewhat time-consuming exercise to record a set of questions to political figures and their answers, for instance, from the proceedings of a broadcast legislature. There you will often find examples where unexpressed logical subjects are used as a tactic for evading responsibility or for not fully answering the question.

Pick out the lexical and auxiliary verbs in the following paragraphs. What is distinctive about the way auxiliary verbs and particularly passives have been used in this extract?

EXERCISE 8.5

This system of training is best suited to vigorous growing vines. Weaker vines would be more suitable on strong rootstock. A mature vigorous vineyard can be readily converted to GDC training in one or two growing seasons.

This trellising system is adaptable to mechanical harvesting by a new machine only recently developed. With this machine the wine grapes are shaken off the curtains by an impacting device and directed by shielding on to a conveyor which transfers them to a holding bin. The pivot bolt holding the T arms of the trellis permits the vine arms and suspended curtains of foliage to be vigorously shaken by the mechanical harvester.

An alternative T-arm arrangement may also be used. With this, the arms are of angle steel bolted to the posts to remain in a fixed position. A stay wire is stapled on top of the post and connects the T arms. This wire connection is formed into a vertical holding guide permitting the enclosed trellis wire carrying the crop to be shaken up and down without movement of the trellis posts and T arms.

F. Berrysmith, *Viticulture*

8.2.6 TAG QUESTIONS AND DIALECT

Earlier (section 8.2.4) we briefly mentioned tags. These come in a variety of forms, amongst which are the following:

(a)   Joanna can dance, can she?

(b)   Joanna can dance, can't she?

(c)   She can dance, can Joanna.

You might like to work out a set of rules which will give all three forms.

We could regard each of these as a realization of a tag, as allophones are realizations of phonemes. Which of these realizations gets chosen might therefore be a dialect feature. In the case of the tag realizations, (c) is used commonly in Yorkshire in England, as we said in Chapter 1.7, and is a feature of cricket commentaries on radio. This would be a typical example:

He's played well up to now, has Jones.

But in many parts of the word there are other tags. In New Zealand, *eh?* is a tag used more frequently by speakers with Maori ethnicity. In West African English, speakers tend to use *isn't it?* or *not so?* In some Asian communities in the UK, *innit?* has become a general tag. Here again it seems that syntax, no less than phonology and morphology, can provide variation which is a dialect indicator.

8.2.7 MAIN AND SUBORDINATE CLAUSES

In the previous section we drew a distinction between main clauses and embedded (or subordinate) clauses. This was a rather arbitrary decision at the time. We can now look at some syntactic movements which show that there is a clear syntactic difference between main clauses and subordinate clauses.

Each of the following pairs of sentences shows a structural movement. In some environments this movement is permitted and in others it is not permitted. What are the allowing and prohibiting environments?

(1a)   He has eaten his porridge.
(1b)   He has eaten his porridge, hasn't he?

(2a)   They could be coming.
(2b)   They could be coming, couldn't they?

(3a)   The old man whom he saw can't come.
(3b)   *The old man whom he saw, didn't he, can't come.

(4a)   I haven't been to see Roger when he is late.
(4b)   *I haven't been to see Roger when he is late, isn't he?

(5a)   The cathedral by the river which flows through Paris is Notre Dame.
(5b)   *The cathedral by the river which flows through Paris, doesn't it, is Notre Dame.

The movement, which we have earlier called a tag question, is permitted in main clauses but not in subordinate clauses. In (1) and (2) the tag is formed on the main clause. In (3) it is formed on a relative clause; in (4) on an adverbial clause, and in (5) again on a relative clause.

Just in case this might be an accident, look at the following movement data:

(1a)   John came in.
(1b)   In came John.

(2a)   The horse trotted down the road.
(2b)   Down the road trotted the horse.

(3a)   Henry strolled into the office.
(3b)   Into the office strolled Henry.

(4a)   The man left because John came in.
(4b)   *The man left because in came John.

(5a)   The man who was caught when the horse trotted down the road was Jim Anderson.
(5b)   *The man who was caught when down the road trotted the horse was Jim Anderson.

This inversion movement, like tag formation, appears to be sensitive to whether a clause is a main clause or an embedded clause because in (4) and (5) it has operated on embedded clauses and the results are ungrammatical.

We can now use these facts and the conclusions we have drawn from them to alter the definition of what constitutes a main clause.

Add the following data to your account of how movement is restricted within embedded clauses:

(a)   The boy shot a hare and Mary shot a partridge, didn't she?

(b)   John said, 'Mary shot a partridge, didn't she?'

(c)   *John said that Mary shot a partridge, didn't she?

(d)   The host clapped his hands and then in came Roger.

(e)   John said, 'Down the road trotted a horse.'

(f)   *John said that down the road trotted a horse.

It seems that (a) and (d) show that, as far as their behaviour with movement is concerned, co-ordinated main clauses are each main clauses; (b) and (e) show that the main clause in direct speech (speech in quotation marks) is also a main clause; but (c) and (f) show that the highest clause in indirect or reported speech (speech with its own complementizer and without quotation marks) is not a main clause.

Note that the process we have just used is one we have mentioned earlier when we were looking at the phonology of English. We are proposing hypotheses and testing them to see what the facts actually are. So the distinction between main and embedded clauses is not just an arbitrary one but is supported by particular ranges of syntactic facts. Those facts in turn allow for the definition of main clauses to be refined.

8.2.8   EMPTY CONSTITUENTS

There are a number of situations in which syntactic constituents appear to be missing. For example, in the imperative and passive we have already seen that a subject may be absent; in the case of imperatives *you* is understood to be the missing subject, while often in the passive a logical subject may go unexpressed, so that although the verb is one which requires someone to do something, that someone is not present in the syntax.

Let us look at still another way in which constituents may be empty. In a sentence like *Geraldine promised* [*to help her grandfather*] we have two clauses, the embedded one being *to help her grandfather*. However, this clause has no subject, that is, the position where a subject ought to be is empty. Nevertheless we do know who will be helping. It is Geraldine. This means that although the subject position is empty, it can be interpreted. This kind of empty position is rather like a pronoun in that it has an antecedent. Such empty positions are often called PRO, partly on account of their similarity to pronouns.

It is particularly obvious that there is an empty position when a complement is missing. We know that complements are obligatory. In a sentence such as *John asked*, with a missing complement, we know that there must be a question or request that John put to someone. For example, look at an exchange like this:

Speaker A: How was it you got permission to go on holiday?

Speaker B: John asked.

We know that John asked someone for permission for Speaker B to go on holiday. So the empty position is interpretable from the context. But the missing complement does not have a grammatical antecedent like a pronoun. Where constituents are 'missing' but interpretable from the context a process of ellipsis has taken place and the missing constituent is said to be 'ellipsed'. Minor sentences are therefore formed by ellipsis.   **ellipsis**

In the sentences below, find the antecedents for the empty positions, which are indicated by square brackets with nothing between them:

(a)   Joanna wanted [ ] to come.

(b)   Bill promised Joanna [ ] to come.

(c)   The dog was put [ ] in a kennel.

Answers:

In (a) the antecedent of the empty position is *Joanna*, who is the one who will come, that is, is the subject of come. In (b) *Bill* is the one who is coming, and in (c) *the dog* is the object of *put* but has been moved into subject position as a result of the passive construction.

The constructions we have looked at so far by no means exhaust all the cases of syntactic relatedness in English.

Look at the following sentence: *The waiter brought in the tea.* Then move its constituents into the same structural configurations as illustrated in the following examples:

(a)   The climbers brought the body down.

(b)   What the climbers brought down was the body.

(c)   The body was what the climbers brought down.

The fact that you almost certainly got the following answers:

(a)   The waiter brought the tea in.

(b)   What the waiter brought in was the tea.

(c)   The tea was what the waiter brought in.

means that these relationships are in the nature of rules which depend not on the words in a sentence but on its syntax. This again shows that syntax is a matter not just of phrase structure, that is, the tree diagram of a sentence, but also of relationships among tree diagrams.

8.2.9 GRAMMATICAL CHANGE

Just as vocabulary may vary in time and in geographic and social space, so can syntax as we saw with tags. Some syntactic constructions have become archaisms while others have evolved into different forms in different places. Translations of the Bible can provide interesting evidence for this. For example, in the four-teenth-century translation by John Wycliffe of one of the parables of Jesus is this passage (given here with modernized spelling and inflections):

> Therefore each man that hears these my words, and does them, shall be made like to a wise man, that has built his house on a stone. And rain fell down and floods came, and winds blew, and rushed into that house; and it fell not down, for it was founded on a stone.

You will see that some syntactic changes have taken place in the centuries between Wycliffe's English and ours. For us *these my words, like to a wise man* and *fell not down* are ungrammatical. However, these constructions are syntactically related to those of modern English and can be studied in much the same way as the relationships between active and passive. Let us take *fell not down* as an example. We saw earlier that when a lexical verb has no auxiliary before it and is preceded by a negative such as *not* then the 'dummy' verb *do* appears in order to carry the tense. Clearly this does not happen in Wycliffe's English. The question is, why not? One possible answer which uses some of the concepts we have just explored runs as follows.

Let us suppose that one of the facts of English syntax we need to explain is that, if a clause is tensed, then the tense is always attached to the first auxiliary verb whatever that auxiliary may be. We could explain this by supposing that tense starts out by itself and is later attached to verbs. That way the verb phrase is free to select any of the available auxiliaries and a lexical verb, and the tense will always attach to the leftmost verb stem available. Let us also suppose that the attachment takes place by the verb moving to attach itself to the tense rather than the tense attaching itself to the verb. (There are good syntactic reasons to suppose this, which need not concern us here.)

However, we have seen that there is an exception to this verb attachment process and that is when, in the case of yes/no questions without auxiliary verbs, the tense moves on its own to the left of the subject and is then provided with the dummy stem *do*.

This account not only explains why the first auxiliary in tensed clauses receives the tense; it also explains why there can be tenseless clauses. This is because the choice of whether or not a clause is tensed is made independently of what verbs there are in the clause.

If we look at what happens when *not* comes between the verbs and the tense, an interesting pattern is apparent in contemporary English.

Look at the following examples and see what you can discern about the attachment of the tense affix to verbs:

(a)   Joanna was not coming.

(b)   Joanna had not come.

(c)   The ball was not found.

(d)   Joanna did not find the ball.

It seems that the presence of *not* allows the auxiliary verbs to attach themselves to the tense affix, but it blocks the capacity of the lexical verb to attach itself. If there is only a lexical verb to the right of the tense and an intervening *not*, then *do* must be inserted so that there is a stem for the verb to attach to. This is the situation in contemporary English syntax.

But it seems that in Wycliffe's time the verb to the right of the tense and which moved leftward to attach itself to the tense affix could be either an auxiliary verb or a lexical verb. Hence the contrasting ways of saying the same thing: Wycliffe's *fell not down* and our *did not fall down*.

We might look at other related historical changes. Why can we say, *Didn't you come?* but not *Did not you come?* whereas in Shakespeare's time *Did not you come?* was grammatical? In Shakespeare's time the *do* was not necessarily emphatic in sentences like *Why man he does bestride the world like a Colossus*, but in our grammar *does* in the same sentence must have emphatic stress. How has this change come about?

If you give this some thought you can see that explanations for how syntactic configurations change through history may require reference both to theories of phrase structure and to theories of movement.

8.3   LEXICALIZED PHRASES AND CLAUSES

In Chapter 3 we saw how words can be coined by the rules of word formation and then lexicalized – that is, at some historical point they become vocabulary items in the lexicons of speakers and languages. Phrases and clauses can also be lexicalized. They are initially constructed according to the rules of syntax; however, sometimes a particular expression comes to be used in much the same way by a community of people in a wholly or partly frozen form. This means that the expression has come to be stored in the memory of a speaker or speakers. In other words, it has been lexicalized. Lexicalized syntactic constructions are of many varieties.

The most commonly recognized variety is the idiom. An idiom is usually   **idiom**
taken to be a syntactic constituent which has undergone semantic drift. In other words, it has acquired a new meaning in the way that words can also acquire new

meanings over time. Many idioms can also be understood in a compositional way but that is not how they are normally interpreted. In the United States, if one says, 'Give us a break' then one normally is talking of only oneself, that is, *us* is semantically odd, and the word *break* is metaphorical. It is also not really a request or command but an expression of mild annoyance, often at someone taking you for a fool. But that does not mean that the expression cannot be taken literally.

It is interesting to look at a dictionary of idioms and compare the compositional meaning of some of the idioms given with their idiomatic meaning. In many cases, the idiomatic meaning has come about through metaphorical extension of one or more of the words in the idiom. For example, the idiom *to hold the whip hand* has been metaphorically extended so that the whip hand is any kind of power, not just the power one gets from holding (and using) a whip. But for some idioms it is harder to imagine their source.

In Chapter 3 we looked at restricted collocations. These can be regarded also as lexicalized phrases. They are the usual way of saying things, for example, *start the car*, rather than *turn the car on*; and *catch the bus*, rather than *use the bus*; and *get on the bus*, rather than *get into the bus*. In each of these cases we can think of other ways of saying the same thing that native speakers just do not say. There is nothing grammatically the matter with *fetch the bus*. It's just not the way we say it. So this must be lexicalized, that is, the phrase must have an entry in the lexicon.

proverb

Proverbs are a third group of lexicalized syntactic constituents. They are usually a whole sentence in length and are used as a way of morally evaluating human actions and giving advice on what to do. For example, if one wishes to impress on a child the importance of having a clean house, and one comes from a religious family, one might say *Cleanliness is next to godliness*. If one wishes to get someone to do something quickly one might say *A stitch in time saves nine*. Proverbs can be used persuasively to attempt to get someone to do some cleaning or to act quickly, or to express approval for performing these actions. There are a great many English proverbs and looking at them gives a fair impression of the kinds of values people might draw on to justify their own or others' actions. They constitute a kind of folk morality. But the morality is not consistent, in that the proverb which justifies one course of action is often contradicted by another proverb which justifies the opposite course of action. See if you can think of pairs, like *Sufficient unto the day is the evil thereof* and *Never put off until tomorrow what you can do today*.

Since they incorporate folk morality, proverbs can serve as templates for subversive alternatives, such as *Do it unto others before they do it unto you, Never put off until tomorrow what can be put off until the day after*, or James Thurber's *Early to rise and early to bed makes a man healthy and wealthy and dead*. Such cases show that the people who make them up must be aware of the originals they are using as models.

formula

A fourth kind of lexicalized syntactic phrase is often termed a 'formula' or 'speech formula'. Formulae are used in many situations to facilitate social interaction, or just to facilitate speech itself. In English, if we wish to apologize for doing something wrong we might say *I'm sorry* or *I'm very sorry*, or *I apologize*, or *I do apologize*. Then there are legal apologies, '*I apologize unreservedly for any distress….'* These apologies are not original. We have memorized them for the purpose for which we are using them. Greetings are the same, as are leave-takings. We say *Hello. How are you? See you later. Good-bye.* In replying to a letter of resignation your employer may write, *Your resignation is accepted with regret.* We take these formulae from the lexicon, where we have them stored, and we store them along with the uses to which we put them. We know that *Hello* is a greeting and that *I apologize* is used when offering an apology. We also know that *I am apologetic* is not an apology. We also know that it is not done to write, *I am personally delighted with your resignation.* We can learn a great deal about ourselves as social animals by understanding how we use formulae. Look, for example, at the births, marriages and deaths notices in your local paper and the formulae that are used to announce these major life events. What do they tell you about social attitudes to such events?

Like lexicalized words, lexicalized syntactic constructions can drift not just in their semantics but in other aspects of their linguistic form. *Goodbye* was once *God be with you.* You can look at the *Oxford English Dictionary* for the history of some idioms. Most specialist dictionaries of idioms, however, do not have an etymology for their entries.

Since we have now reached an end of the exposition in this book it is appropriate for us, Scott Allan and Koenraad Kuiper, also to say goodbye. We hope you have enjoyed reading and using this book.

Further exercises •

Draw tree diagrams of the following phrases and clauses:

EXERCISE 8.6●

(a)   the man in the hut by the river
(b)   the coat which I bought in London
(c)   The policeman knew that the parson helped old soldiers.
(d)   That Harold did not appear annoyed the police.
(e)   They sang while the boat drifted down the river.

What complements can the following verbs take:

EXERCISE 8.7●

like, sob, clean, preserve, declare, drag, place, agree.

Consider the following text:

EXERCISE 8.8●●

Philip Swallow had been made and unmade by the system in precisely this way. He liked examinations, always did well in them. Finals had been, in many ways, the supreme moment of his life. He frequently dreamed that he was taking the examinations again, and these were happy dreams. Awake, he could without difficulty remember the questions he had elected to answer on every paper that hot, distant June. In the preceding months he had prepared himself with meticulous care, filling his mind with distilled knowledge, drop by drop, until, on the eve of the first paper (Old English Set Texts) it was almost brimming over.

David Lodge, *Changing Places*

In the above text, identify the following constructions:

(a)   a passive sentence,

(b)   a compound sentence where both conjuncts have the same subject,

(c)   a sentence where the subject and direct object refer to the same entity,

(d)   a noun phrase which contains two adjective phrases,

(e)   a noun phrase which contains a single adjective phrase and a prepositional phrase,

(f)   a prepositional phrase which contains an abstract noun,

(g)   an example of a verb phrase which contains a progressive participle,

(h)   an example of a verb phrase which contains a perfect participle.

EXERCISE 8.9•••

In his novel *Bleak House*, Dickens tells the story through two voices: that of the narrator and that of one of the characters, Esther Summerson. These voices 'sound' quite different. Can you identify the speaker in the following extracts and demonstrate by what characteristics of their syntax Dickens establishes the different 'styles' or 'sounds' of one voice which distinguish it from the other? Look, for example, at the use of major and minor sentences.

(a)   LONDON. Michaelmas term lately over, and the Lord Chancellor sitting in Lincoln's Inn Hall. Implacable November weather. ...

Smoke lowering down from chimney-pots, making a soft black drizzle with flakes of soot in it as big as full-grown snow-flakes – gone into mourning, one might imagine, for the death of the sun. Dogs undistinguishable in mire. Horses, scarcely better; splashed to their very blinkers. ...

Fog everywhere. Fog up the river, where it flows among green aits and meadows; fog down the river, where it rolls defiled among the tiers of shipping, and the waterside pollutions of a great (and dirty) city. Fog on the Essex marshes, fog on the Kentish heights.

(b)   I have a great deal of difficulty in beginning to write my portion of these pages, for I know I am not clever. I always knew that. I can remember, when I was a very little girl indeed, I used to say to my doll, when we were alone together, 'Now Dolly, I am not clever, you know very well, and you must be patient with me, like a dear!' And so she used to sit propped up in a great arm-chair, with her beautiful complexion and rosy lips, staring at me – or not so much at me, I think, as at nothing – while I busily stitched away, and told her every one of my secrets.

(c) She was such a sharp little lady, and used to sit with her hands folded in each other, looking s' very watchful while she talked to me, that perhaps I found that rather irksome. Or perhaps it was her being so upright and trim; though I don't think it was that, because I thought that quaintly pleasant.

(d) No. Words, sobs, and cries, are but air; and air is so shut in and shut out throughout the house in town, that sounds need be uttered trumpet-tongued indeed by my Lady in her chamber, to carry any faint vibration to Sir Leicester's ears; and yet this cry is in the house, going upward from a wild figure on its knees.

(e) It was in a state of dilapidation quite equal to our expectation. Two or three of the area railings were gone; the waterbutt was broken; the knocker was loose; the bell-handle had been pulled off a long time, to judge from the rusty state of the wire; and dirty footprints on the steps were the only signs of its being inhabited.

(f) DARKNESS rests upon Tom-all Alone's. Dilating and dilating since the sun went down last night, it has gradually swelled until it fills every void in the place.

Glossary...

Active The form of a sentence where the object comes immediately after the verb, and without the passive auxiliary *be* followed by the perfect participle; contrasts with **passive**.

Adverbial Usually comes towards the end of a clause. It tells how, when, where, and why. Adverbials are normally grammatically optional constituents but there can be obligatory adverbials, which function as complements of verbs such as *put*.

Agreement Agreement takes place where a morphosyntactic category of a head requires the selection of particular forms of words elsewhere in the phrase.

Antecedent The constituent which a pronoun 'stands for'.

Article Either *a* or *the*.

Aspect auxiliaries *Have*, which together with a perfect participle form of the following verb, indicates perfective aspect, and *be*, which together with a progressive participle form of the following verb, indicates progressive aspect.

Attributive adjective One which acts as a modifier before the head noun within the noun phrase.

Auxiliary verb Verbs which precede and modify a lexical verb.

Clause   Unit with the basic structure of a sentence (e.g. having a lexical verb), but which may be part of a compound or complex sentence.

Complement   A unit in the predicate which is required to be there by the lexical verb to complete the verb's meaning. Complements as a general class include objects and intensive complements.

Complementizer   *See* **Subordinating conjunction**.

Complete sentence   A sentence that has a subject and predicate.

Complex sentence   A sentence containing embedded clauses.

Compound sentence   A sentence consisting of two or more co-ordinated clauses.

Constituent   A grammatically well-formed syntactic component.

Co-ordinating conjunction   One of *and*, (*either*) ... *or*, (*neither*) ... *nor*. These conjunctions syntactically join constituents of the same syntactic category (or sometimes of the same function).

Declarative   Form of a statement.

Definite article   The word *the*.

Demonstratives   The set of determiners consisting of: *this, that, these, those*.

Determiners   Collectively the class of articles and demonstratives all function as determiners in noun phrases.

Direct object   The answer to the question *Who or what did/does* (*subject*) (*lexical verb*)? For example, if you want to know the object of the sentence *Marsha loves Harold*, you ask *Who or what does Marsha* love? Answer: *Harold*. So *Harold* is the direct object. If the sentence contains two objects, as in the case of *The committee sent Henry a letter*, then if we put the same question it becomes *Who or what did the committee send?* The answer is *a letter*. So *a letter* is the direct object.

Distal   The two determiners *that* and *those* are distal in that they indicate that the referent of the noun phrase in which they occur is to be regarded as more 'distant' than if *this* and *these* were used.

Distribution   Any syntactic constituent can fit in only a restricted range of syntactic environments. These are its distribution.

Dominance   The property of having syntactic constituents as parts of other constituents.

Ellipsis   The situation where a constituent is missing but interpretable from context.

Embedding   The process where either a phrase or a clause appears as part of another phrase or clause.

Extraction site The syntactic location from which a moved constituent has been extracted.

Finite clause A clause with a tensed verb.

Formula A lexicalized phrase or clause used for a particular social purpose.

Head The obligatory word, in a phrase, which determines the distributional properties of the phrase of which it is the head.

Idiom A lexicalized phrase which is semantically non-compositional.

Imperative A form of a sentence that is characteristically used as a command. It does not generally have a subject or normally an auxiliary verb. The lexical verb is not inflected.

Incomplete sentence A sentence that has been interrupted or is unfinished.

Indefinite article The word *a*.

Indirect object The answer to the question *To, or for whom or what, did/does (subject) (verb) (object)?* For example, if you want to know the indirect object of the sentence *Marsha gave Harold a book*, you ask *To, or for whom, did Marsha give a book?* Answer: *Harold.* So *Harold* is the indirect object.

Intensive complement A unit that follows a small group of verbs. It refers back to either the subject or object and introduces no new people or things into the clause.

Interrogative Form of a question.

Interrogative pronoun *Wh* pronoun which introduces a *wh* question.

Intransitive verb A verb that does not take complements.

Landing site The syntactic location which a moved constituent occupies after it has been moved.

Lexical verb The head of a verb phrase.

Logical subject The subject of the active form of a sentence.

Main clause The 'top' clause in a sentence, that is, highest in the tree diagram of the sentence, or a 'top' clause quoted in direct speech, or any co-ordinated 'top' clause in the sentence.

Major sentence A complete sentence with all its required phrases.

Manner adverbial One which indicates how the action takes place.

Minor sentence Part of a complete sentence, often given in answer to a *wh* question.

Modal auxiliary verb One of can, *could, shall, should, will, would, may, might* or *must.* If modal auxiliaries appear in a verb phrase they are the first unit in the phrase. Only one modal can appear in the verb phrase in most dialects of English.

Modifier   The function of a constituent of a phrase which is not the phrase's head.

Non-finite clause   One not bearing tense.

Noun phrase   A phrase that has a noun as its head.

Object   Units that immediately follow the verb and that are usually noun phrases. There are two kinds: **direct object** and **indirect object**.

Passive   The passive form of a sentence has two crucial properties: the object has been extracted and placed in subject position, and a form of *be* or *get* is in final auxiliary position followed by the perfect participle form of the lexical verb.

Passive auxiliary   The auxiliary verb *be* when it is followed by the perfect participle form of the lexical verb.

Perfective aspect   Indicated by the auxiliary verb *have* followed by a perfect participle. The perfective aspect indicates that the action of the lexical verb is completed relative to some point in time.

Phrase   The units intermediate between words and sentences in the structure of sentences. Phrases have heads, and all the constituents of a phrase belong together to make the phrase a syntactic unit.

Place adverbial   One which indicates where the action takes place.

Possessive noun phrase   These are noun phrase modifiers embedded in noun phrases, and occupy the same location as determiners. They have a possessive marker, *-'s* or *-s'*, attached.

Precedence   The syntactic property of having one constituent preceding another.

Predicate   A clause minus its subject.

Predicate adjective   An adjective or adjective phrase which is in the predicate, functioning as an intensive complement.

Prepositional phrase   Phrase that has a preposition as head.

Progressive aspect   Indicated by the auxiliary verb *be* followed by a progressive participle. The progressive aspect indicates that the action of the lexical verb is on-going at a particular point in time.

Pronoun   Single-word noun phrase which has an antecedent.

Proverb   A lexicalized phrase, or more normally a whole sentence, which is used to provide moral advice or morally to justify a course of action.

Proximal   The two determiners *this* and *these* are proximal in that they indicate that the referent of the noun phrase in which they occur is to be regarded as 'closer' than if *that* and *those* were used.

Quantifier   A category of words indicating quantity, such as *many, some, both* and *few*.

Reason adverbial   One which indicates why something took place.

Recursive   A process which has the capacity to go on infinitely many times has the property of being recursive, e.g. the embedding of phrases within phrases.

Relative clause   An embedded clause which functions as a modifier in noun phrases. Often introduced by a relative pronoun.

Relative pronoun   A *wh* pronoun which introduces a relative clause.

Subject   The noun phrase attached directly to S and followed by VP in the tree diagram of a sentence. It can be found by asking *Who?* or *What?* before the verb. In the sentence *Leisha breeds rabbits,* if we ask *Who or what breeds rabbits?* the answer is *Leisha* and that is the subject of the sentence.

Subordinating Conjunction   A word which is used to signal that a unit with the structure of a clause is embedded within a phrase or other clause.

Time adverbial   One which indicates when an event took place.

Transformation   A rule of syntactic movement.

Transitive verb   A verb that takes objects.

Verb phrase   A phrase containing a lexical verb as head.

***Wh* question**   Question which starts with a *wh* word, such as *how, when, who, what, which* etc.

Yes/no question   A question which takes 'yes' or 'no' for an answer.

Further reading. . . . .

Aarts, B., *English Syntax and Argumentation*, 3rd edn (Basingstoke: Palgrave Macmillan, 2008).

Baker, C. L., *English Syntax*, 2nd edn (Cambridge, MA: MIT Press, 1995).

Burton Roberts, N., *Analysing Sentences*, 2nd edn (London: Longman, 1997).

Fabb, N., *Sentence Structure* (London: Routledge, 1994).

Hurford, J. R., *Grammar: A Student's Guide* (Cambridge: Cambridge University Press, 1994).

Kim, J.-B. and Sells, P., *English Syntax: An Introduction* (Chicago: University of Chicago Press, 2008).

Kuiper, K., *Smooth Talkers: The Linguistic Performance of Auctioneers and Sportscasters* (Mahwah, NJ: Lawrence Erlbaum Associates, 1996).

Kuiper, K., *Formulaic Genres* (Basingstoke: Palgrave Macmillan, 2009).

Miller, J., *An Introduction to English Syntax* (Edinburgh: Edinburgh University Press, 2002).

Newby, M., *The Structure of English: A Handbook of English Grammar* (Cambridge: Cambridge University Press, 1987).

Tallerman, M. *Understanding Syntax*, 2nd edn (Oxford: Oxford University Press, 2005).

Wekker, H. and Haegeman, L., *A Modern Course in English Syntax* (London: Croom Helm, 1985).

Electronic resources •

http://www.palgrave.com/language/kuiperandallan/
This site provides electronic resources related to Part III of this book.

http://grammar.ccc.commnet.edu/grammar/
This site contains some useful quizzes and other resources on English grammar. (Not all the material is in line with the exposition in this book.)

http://englishgrammar101.com/
This is a traditional grammar site for secondary school grammar study in the USA.

http://www.euralex.org/bibweb/
http://kollokationen.bbaw.de/bib/index_de.html
These sites contain numerous references to work on the phrasal vocabulary.

Answers to Exercises

PART ONE

CHAPTER 2

2.1

rose, worm, night, storm, bed, joy, love, life.

2.2

modest, humble, threat'ning, white, bright.

2.3

heard, rise, turns, come, gone, arise, wasted.

2.4

witches, noun; *hopped,* verb; *in,* preposition; *red,* adjective; *drove,* verb; *gently,* adverb; *to,* preposition; *evening,* noun; *wines,* noun; *entertaining,* adjective.

2.5

LaserWriter, hard disk, built-in, read-only memory, download, random access memory.

2.6

Inflectional morphemes: singularitie̲s, neglectful, soil̲s, deliberation, sacrifice̲s, artificially.

Derivational morphemes: singul+*ar*+*iti*+es, neglect+*ful*, soils, deliberat+*ion*, sacrifices, artific+*ial*+*ly.*

309

Note: In the last two words you might want to make a case for *sacri-*, and *arti-*, to be derivational morphemes. But notice how few words they come with. Perhaps they are just bound stems such as *cran-* in *cranberry*. Perhaps they are not morphemes at all. The safest thing in many cases like this is to try and think of other words which have the same morpheme in them. If you cannot think of any other plausible cases, it is often clearer to follow your intuitions and say that these are not really morphemes.

2.7

Free	*Bound*	
	ation	
nation	pre	
post	post	Free if it is a thing you put in the ground; bound as in *postscript*.
angle	ible	
infra		
out		

2.8

Stems	*Affixes*
train	s
succeed	ed
light	er
determine	pre, ed
active	retro
confuse	ion, s
instruct	ion, al

2.9

(a)   clean: free, *-ing*: bound, *lady*: free; *anti-*: bound, *skid*: free, *-ing*: bound, *device*: free; *mushroom*: free; *nation*: free, *-hood*: bound; *deputy*: free, *-ize*: bound; *de-*: bound, *rail*: free, *-ment*: bound, *-s*: bound; *pre-*: bound, *destin*: free, *-ation*: bound; *inter-*: bound, *nation*: free, *-al*: bound, *-ize*: bound, *-ation*: bound.

(b)   *-ment*: affix, *involve*: stem; *-able*: affix, *support*: stem; *in-*: affix, *supportable*: stem; *sub-*: affix, *professorial*: stem; *-ial*: affix, *professor*: stem; *-or*: affix, *profess*: stem; *inter-*: affix, *subjectivity*: stem; *-ity*: affix, *subjective*: stem; *-ive*: affix, *subject*: stem; *sub-*: affix, *ject*: stem.

(c)   *-ful*: bound, derivational; *-ive*: bound, derivational; *-ary*: bound, derivational; *-ed*: bound, inflection; *thing*: free; *-es*: bound, inflection; *-al*: bound, derivational.

2.11

(a)

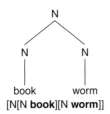

[N[N **book**][N **worm**]]

Figure 2.9

(b)

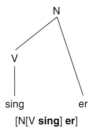

[N[V **sing**] er]

Figure 2.10

(c)

[V[**mis**[V **lay**]]]

Figure 2.11

(d)

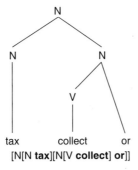

[N[N **tax**][N[V **collect**] **or**]]

Figure 2.12

(e)

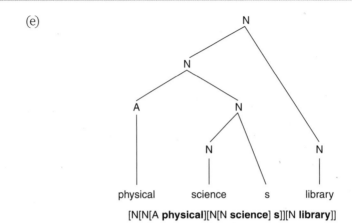

[N[N[A **physical**][N[N **science**] **s**]][N **library**]]

Figure 2.13

(f)

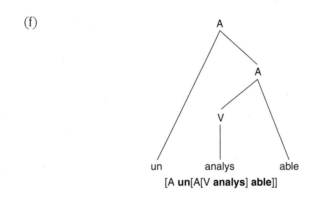

[A **un**[A[V **analys**] **able**]]

Figure 2.14

(g)

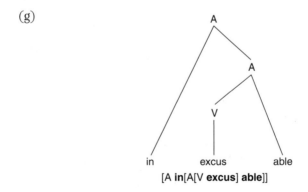

[A **in**[A[V **excus**] **able**]]

Figure 2.15

(h)

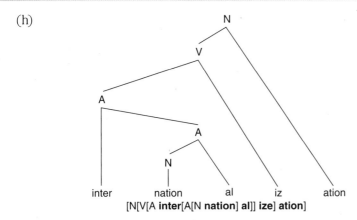

[N[V[A **inter**[A[N **nation**] **al**]] **ize**] **ation**]

Figure 2.16

2.12

old, adj; *by*, preposition; *of*, preposition; *seemed*, verb; *lost*, verb; *headlights*, noun.

2.13

derive, stem, free; *-ation*, affix, bound; *-al*, affix, bound, derivational; *head*, free; *strong*, free; *un-*, affix, bound, derivational; *likely*, stem, free; *locate*, stem, free; *-or*, affix, bound, derivational; *beacon*, stem, free; *-s*, affix, bound, inflectional.

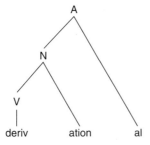

Figure 2.17

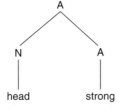

Figure 2.18

Figure 2.19

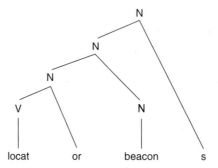

Figure 2.20

2.14

   (a)   [N[N peanut][N vendor]]

          [N[N[A new][N comer]] s]

   (b)   [N[V vend] *or*], i.e. *-or* attaches to a verb stem and creates a noun.
          [N[V come] *er*], i.e. *-er* attaches to a verb stem and creates a noun.
          [ADV[ADJ[N grace] *ful*] *ly*], i.e. *-ly* attaches to an adjective stem and creates an adverb while *-ful* attaches to a noun stem and creates an adjective.
          [ADV[ADJ[N/V marvell] *ous*] *ly*], i.e. *-ly* attaches to an adjective stem to create an adverb while *-ous* attaches to a verb (or maybe a noun) stem to create an adjective.
          (Note that you need to look at more words that take the *-ous* suffix to see whether it attaches to noun or verb stems or both.)
          [N[N rail] *ing*], i.e. *-ing* attaches to a noun stem to create a noun.
          [N[V hawk] *er*], i.e. *-er* attaches to a verb stem to create a noun.
          [ADJ[N sinew] *y*], i.e. *-y* attaches to a noun stem to create an adjective.

   (c)   new/come/er/s, marvell/ous/ly

   (d)   derivational suffixation

   (e)   *-ed* on *pleased, started* and *lifted* is a past tense suffix.
          -ing is a progressive participle suffix.

2.15

(a)   *sunlight* is a noun made up of noun + noun, *downstream* is an adverb made up of preposition + noun, *inshore* is an adverb made up of preposition + noun, *newborn* is an adjective made up of adjective + adjective (perfect participle), *dragonfly* is a noun made up of a noun + noun.

(b)   *un* D, *believ* F, *able* D, *dragon* F, *fli* F, *es* I.

(c)   In these words, *-ly* attaches to adjective stems and the derived words are manner adverbs.

(d)   *important*: *-ant* attaches to a noun and the derived word is an adjective; *wildness*: *-ness* attaches to an adjective stem (*wild*) and the derived word is a noun; *ecstatic*: *-ic* attaches to a noun stem (*ecstasy*) and the derived word is an adjective; *lightning*: *-ing* attaches to a verb stem (*lighten*) and the derived form is a noun.

(e)   *-s* is a plural inflection on noun sterns, whereas the *-ed* suffix is a past tense affix on verb stems.

(f)   These forms are irregular in that the regular past tense forms would be *swimmed* and *breaked*.

(g)   The word appears in the dictionary as a modifier of a noun, no longer just as the name of a person but as having to do with something the person did. This is half way to a proper noun conversion, which we find with a noun like *diesel*.

In the passage the word has been converted to a verb. This has also happened to the word *diesel* when it means 'to make the kind of sound typical of a diesel engine', as in *The car was dieseling*.

CHAPTER 3

3.1

(a)   Each sentence entails the other but not because either contains a word or expression which is synonymous with one in the other sentence.

(b)   Here the two-way entailments are the result of *hit* being synonymous with *struck*.

(c)   If your socks are scarlet it follows that they must be red but if they are red it doesn't follow that they are scarlet.

(d)   If you bought the tomatoes then you must have purchased them and if you purchased them then you must have bought them. This is because *buy* and *purchase* are synonyms.

(e) If your dog is bigger than my dog then my dog must be smaller than your dog, but this is not because any words or phrases in the two respective sentences are synonyms.

(f) If her dad likes you a lot then her father must too, and vice versa. This is because *dad* is an informal synonym for *father*.

(g) If Roger owns the pencil then it must belong to him, and vice versa. This is not because *own* and *belong to* are synonyms.

(h) If Ken almost shot his foot then he must nearly have shot his foot and vice versa, because *nearly* and *almost* are synonyms.

(i) If your neighbour owns a pistol then he or she must own a firearm but if they own a firearm it need not be a pistol.

In summary:
Reverse entailments: (a), (b), (d), (e), (f), (g), (h).
Reverse entailments resulting from synonymy: (b), (d), (f), (g).

3.2

Homonyms: (a), (d), (e).

3.4

(a) mammal, rodent, mouse

(b) structure, building, house, bungalow

(c) move, run, jog

(d) weapon, firearm, pistol, revolver

(e) person, relative, uncle

(f) beast, dog, hound, beagle

(g) take, steal, pilfer.

3.5

(a)

Figure 3.7

(b)

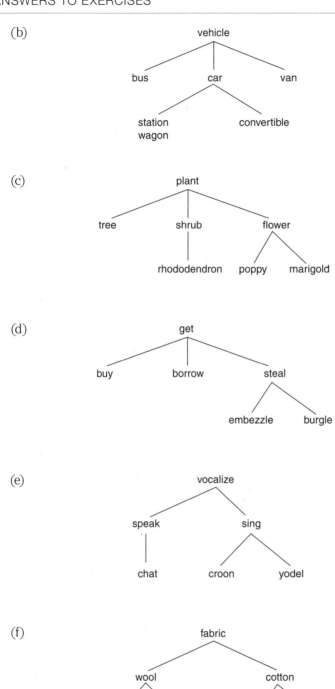

(c)

(d)

(e)

(f)

Figure 3.7 Continued

(g)

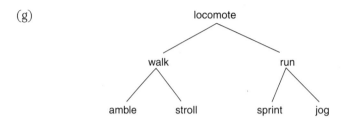

Figure 3.7 Continued

3.6

Entailments: (a), (b), (d), (f), (g), (i), (j), (k), (m).

Entailments resulting from hyponymy: (d), (i), (j), (k).

3.7

Some of the possible components are: metal vs fabric; twisted vs solid vs braided; relative cross-sectional diameter ranging from very thin through thin, medium, and thick.

3.8

Let us suppose that the significant semantic components of one's kin are whether they are male or female; whether they are the same generation as one-self or from one, two or three generations older, or one, two or three generations younger; and whether they are in a direct line of descent with oneself or at one or more removes from a direct line of descent. That gives the following semantic features:

(a)   male vs female;

(b)   same generation as self vs 1, 2, 3 generations older vs 1, 2, 3 generations younger;

(c)   direct line of descent vs 1, 2, 3 degrees of distance from direct line of descent.

Using these semantic features we can say that the senses of some of our kinship terms are:

Sister: female, same generation as self, same line of descent.
Aunt: female, 1 generation older than self, 1 degree of distance from direct line of descent.
Father: male, 1 generation older than self, direct line of descent.

3.10

Yacht was borrowed from Dutch, *curry* from Tamil, a language of southern India; *transfer* from Latin; and *pyjama* from Persian via Hindi (the same route as pyjamas themselves took from Persia to India to England).

3.11

Radar: radio detection and ranging; laser: light amplification by stimulated emission of radiation; IATA: International Air Transport Authority; NATO: North Atlantic Treaty Organization; quango, quasi non-governmental organization; AIDS: acquired immune deficiency syndrome; NASA: National Aeronautics and Space Administration; RAM: random access memory.

3.15

(a) yes, (b) yes, (c) no, (d) no, (e) yes, (f) yes, (g) no, (h) yes, (i) yes, (j) no, (k) yes, (1) no, (m) no.

(*Note*: some of these pairs may differ in their senses in different dialects. For example, in North America a silencer is what one puts on a gun but not under a car, whereas it can be both in the UK.)

3.16

(a), (j) antonyms; (b), (i) antonyms; (c), (e) converses; (d), (g) complementaries; (f), (h) complementaries.

3.17

(a)   deep, shallow

(b)   Both are often used metaphorically of human character.

(c)   buy, sell

(d)   legal, illegal

(e & f)   animal (superordinate), deer (hyponym)

(g)   deep, profound

(h)   One cannot use *profound* of physical objects like mineshafts so it is a synonym only of the metaphorical sense of *deep*.

(i)   buy, by

PART TWO

CHAPTER 4

4.1

But the real horror amongst spiders was more likely to be encountered in the lavatory itself. This was the redback. The redback is mainly black with a scarlet stripe where its spine would be if it were a vertebrate.

4.2

[wʌn əv ðə moust ɪntərestɪŋ θɪŋz əbaut ðə sɪks hedəd ɒmnɪkwɔːgz əv ðə plænət saigouswɒrəldɒŋ ɪn ðə staː sɪstəm əv grʌdniːvougəræktɪnæks ɪn ðə kɒnstəleiʃən əv gou ən ʌpset ənʌðə skræbəlbɔːd lez ai niːd ə njuː neim ɪz ðæt ðei hæv ounlɪ wʌn wɜːd tə stænd fə ɔːl fɔː hʌndrəd mɪljən naunz ædʒəktɪvz prepəzɪʃənz vɜːbz ənd ædvɜːbz]

Note: Not all dialects of English have exactly the same phoneme inventory or use it in exactly the same way. The transcriptions are those of the authors. We have aimed at a socially and regionally neutral form of British English.

4.3

	Voiced	Voiceless		Voiced	Voiceless
bacon		✓	cheese	✓	
salami	✓		cream	✓	
rice		✓	shrimp		✓
orange	✓		flour		✓
walnut	✓		grape		✓

4.4

*ca*b*in*, *c* is a stop and *b* is a stop
*ship*s, *sh* is a fricative and *p* is a stop
*than*ks, *th* is a fricative and *k* is a stop
*yach*t, *y* is an approximant and *t* is a stop
*ga*th*er*, *g* is a stop and *th* is a fricative
*d*rop, *d* is a stop

4.5

[p] is a voiceless labial stop

[g] is a voiced velar stop

[z] is a voiced alveolar fricative

[j] is a voiced palatal approximant

4.6

    (a)   busy, electricity, raising, pleasing

    (b)   link, unit, youth, write

    (c)   laugh, cuts, tough, bath

    (d)   fly, flow, through

4.7

(a)	voiced palatal approximant	[j]
(b)	high back vowel	[uː]
(c)	voiceless post-alveolar fricative	[ʃ]
(d)	voiced alveolar nasal stop	[n]
(e)	voiced labio-dental fricative	[v]
(f)	high front vowel	[iː]
(g)	voiced velar stop	[ŋ] [g]
(h)	voiceless dental fricative	[θ]
(i)	low front vowel	[æ]
(j)	voiced alveolar lateral approximant	[l]

4.8

If a redback bit you on the behind you were left with the problem of where to put the tourniquet and not long to think about it. Nor could you ask anyone to suck out the poison unless you knew them very well indeed.

He must have heard how boring they were since he never appeared. But it was not for want of having his name invoked. The whole faculty salivated *en masse* at the mere mention of him.

4.9

(a)	strength	[strengθ]	[streŋθ]
(b)	crime	[craim]	[kraim]
(c)	wishing	[wɪshɪŋ]	[wɪʃɪŋ]
(d)	wives	[waivs]	[waivz]
(e)	these	[θiːz]	[ðiːz]
(f)	hijacking	[haijækɪŋ]	[haidʒækɪŋ]
(g)	yellow	[jellou]	[jelou]
(h)	thesis	[ðiːsɪs]	[θiːsɪs]
(i)	extra	[extrə]	[ekstrə]
(j)	chop	[chɒp]	[tʃɒp]

4.10

(a)	eat	[eːt]	[iːt]
(b)	like	[liːk]	[lɑik]
(c)	shout	[ʃout]	[ʃaut]
(d)	open	[ɔːpən]	[oupən]
(e)	bait	[bɑit]	[beit]
(f)	equal	[ekwəl]	[iːkwəl]
(g)	aura	[aurə]	[ɔːrə]
(h)	bottle	[bɔːtəl]	[bɒtəl]
(i)	seize	[seiz]	[siːz]
(j)	tough	[tɔːf]	[tʌf]

4.11

Active articulator	Passive articulator	Place of articulation
Lower lip	Upper incisors	**Labio-dental**
Back of tongue	Soft palate	Velar
Front of tongue	**Hard palate**	Palatal
Tip of tongue	**Incisors**	Dental

4.12

	Phonetic description	Phonetic symbol	Example
(a)	voiceless labio-dental fricative	[f]	*fling*
(b)	voiced palatal approximant	[j]	*yes*
(c)	voiced post-alveolar affricate	[dʒ]	*John*
(d)	voiced dental fricative	[ð]	*this*
(e)	voiced alveolar lateral	[l]	*lot*
(f)	voiced velar nasal	[ŋ]	*long*
(g)	voiceless dental fricative	[θ]	*thing*
(h)	voiced alveolar approximant	[r]	*ring*

Note: You won't be able to find a word beginning with a voiced velar nasal.

4.13

(a)	[d]	voiced alveolar stop	*d*eep
(b)	[m]	voiced labial nasal	*m*ud
(c)	[uː]	high back vowel	*oo*ze
(d)	[f]	voiceless labio-dental fricative	*f*ine
(e)	[dʒ]	voiced post-alveolar affricate	*g*in
(f)	[æ]	low front vowel	*a*xe
(g)	[w]	voiced labio-velar approximant	*w*ine
(h)	[k]	voiceless velar stop	*c*ake
(i)	[r]	voiced alveolar approximant	*r*abbit
(j)	[e]	mid front vowel	*e*gg

4.14

(a) **Vowels**

/ɑustreiljə/	/ɑu/ should be /ɒ/ giving /ɒstreiljə/
/ʃælow/	/ow/ should be /ou/ giving /ʃælou/
/huːndrɪdz/	/uː/ should be /ʌ/ giving /hʌndrɪdz/

Consonants

/whɑit/	/wh/ should be /w/ giving /wɑit/
/juːs/	/j/ should be /dʒ/ giving /dʒuːs/
/swɪmɪng/	/ng/ should be /ŋ/ giving /swɪmɪŋ/
/puːls/	/s/ should be /z/ giving /puːlz/

(b) /koust/, /ɒstreiljə/, /hʌndrɪdz/

4.15

(a) **Consonants**

[whɑil]	[wh] should be [w] giving [wɑil]
[ɪncluːdɪŋ]	[c] should be [k] giving [ɪnkluːdɪŋ]
[sɪgəretts]	should have only one t

Vowels

[post]	[o] should be [ou] giving [poust]
[out]	[ou] should be [ɑu] giving [ɑut]

(b) [ænd] [ɪnkluːdɪŋ] [stæmpɪŋ]

(c) [ɒzlou]

4.16

[ai kɔːt ðɪs mɔːnɪŋ mɔːnɪŋz mɪnjən kɪŋdəm əv deiluits dɔːfɪn dæpəl dɔːn drɔːn fɔːlkən ɪn hɪz raidɪŋ əv ðə roulɪŋ levəl ʌndəniːθ hɪm stedɪ eə ænd straidɪŋ hai ðeə hau hiː rʌŋ ʌpɒn ðə rein əv ə wɪmplɪŋ wɪŋ]

[sou ai meid mai wei aut seiɪŋ gudbai tə tɒd ənd ælɪsn ənd suː ənd ɔːl ðiː ʌðə wʌndəfəl njuː frendz aid meid ənd stoul ə kæb nou nɒt lɪtrəlɪ ɪts ən ould estæblɪʃt njuː jɔːk kʌstəm wen juː siː ə lʌɡɪdʒ leidn trævlə heilɪŋ ə kæb juː ɒbstrʌkt hɪz pæsɪdʒ wail hiːz traiɪŋ tə hɔːl hɪz giə ənd dʒʌmp ɪntə ðə kæb əhed əv hɪm laːfɪŋ haːtɪlɪ əz juː duː sou]

[ðeə wəz trʌbl ouvə ðiː ɒrɪndʒəz ðə kʌstəmz ɒfisəz staːtəd aːskɪŋ kwestʃənz ənd meikɪŋ dɪfɪkʌltɪz pɜːhæps ðə rait mæn wɒzənt ɒn djuːtɪ ɔː hædnt biːn peid ɪnʌf ɪt siːmd ə lɒt əv fʌs ouvə ə kreit əv fruːt wɜː ðiː ɒrɪndʒəz stʌft wɪð drʌgz ɔː daimndz ɔː eksplouzɪvz fæntæstɪk ekspləneiʃnz prəpouzd ðemselvz mɔː redɪlɪ ðən aːnsəz]

CHAPTER 5

5.2

Xena has 6 oral stops [p t k b d ɡ].

All the voiced oral stops are between vowels. All the voiceless stops are elsewhere.

The voiced and voiceless pairs are in complementary distribution, are phonetically similar and are therefore allophones of one phoneme. There are therefore only three stop phonemes in Xena. When any one of them appears between vowels it becomes voiced.

5.3

All nasal consonants in Hercules appear to come directly before oral stops. [m] comes only before [p] and [b]. [n] comes only before [t] and [d]. [ŋ] comes only before [k] and [g]. Put differently, the bilabial nasal comes before bilabial stops, the alveolar nasal before alveolar stops and the velar nasal before velar stops. The nasals are therefore in complementary distribution and are possibly all allophones of one nasal phoneme. Their place of articulation is determined by the following stop.

5.4

Vowel length is influenced by the consonant following the vowel. If the following consonant is voiced, the vowel is longer than it is before unvoiced consonants. If we say that syllables ending in voiced consonants are long syllables and ones ending in unvoiced consonants are short syllables then long vowels are long in long syllables and half long in short syllables whereas short vowels are short in short syllables and half long in long syllables.

5.5

[l] occurs word-initially, before vowels and the palatal approximant.
[ɬ] occurs word-finally and before all consonants except the palatal approximant.

5.6

$$\begin{Bmatrix}[p]\\[t]\\[k]\end{Bmatrix} \to \begin{Bmatrix}[b]\\[d]\\[g]\end{Bmatrix} / V\_\_\_\_V$$

$$N(asal\ consonant) \to \begin{Bmatrix}[m] / \_\_\_\_[p\ b]\\[n] / \_\_\_\_[t\ d]\\[ŋ] / \_\_\_\_[k\ g]\end{Bmatrix}$$

$$\begin{Bmatrix}[V]\\[V\cdot]\end{Bmatrix} \to \begin{Bmatrix}[V\cdot]\\[V\colon]\end{Bmatrix}/ \_\_\_\_\ voiced\ C$$

$$/l/ \to [ɬ] / \_\_\_\_\#\qquad /l/ \to [ɬ] / \_\_\_\_all\ C\ except\ /j/$$

5.7

(a)	sip & tip	(b)	lip & nip	(c)	fine & vine
(d)	do & shoe	(e)	lease & liege	(f)	suck & sung
(g)	zoo & chew	(h)	pump & jump	(i)	link & mink
(j)	bead & bed	(k)	owe & are	(l)	pit & pot
(m)	gate & gut	(n)	now & gnaw	(o)	pet & pot
(p)	park & pick	(q)	bay & bough	(r)	beat & boat

5.8

The open o [ɔ] appears only before nasals. The closed o appears everywhere else. They are therefore in complementary distribution.

5.9

The second member of each pair is the negative of the first.

The prefixes are: *im, in, il,* and *ir.*

The form of each prefix is phonologically conditioned. The consonant of the prefix assimilates to the initial sound of the stem to which it is attached. In selecting one prefix to represent the underlying form, we look for the prefix with the widest distribution. *in* has the widest distribution. It occurs with /t/, /d/, and vowels.

5.10

There are three nasals in the data, [m n ŋ].

Only [m] and [n] are phonemic. Both occur in initial, intervocalic and preconsonantal positions. [ŋ] only occurs before the consonants [k] and [g]. The distribution of [m] and [n] suggests that they are phonemic, whereas the distribution of [ŋ] suggests that it is may be an allophone of [n].

$$/n/ \rightarrow [\eta] \ / \ \underline{\qquad} k, \qquad /n/ \rightarrow [\eta] \ / \ \underline{\qquad} g$$

5.11

The simplest approach to this problem is to identify the contexts in which the long vowels occur. There are two reasons for this. Firstly, the suggested rule takes the short vowels as underlying and derives the long vowels from the short ones. To identify the contexts in which the long vowels occur will provide the context section for the rule. Secondly, a cursory glance at the contexts for the long and short vowels suggests that the former occur in a more homogenous set of contexts than their short counterparts.

The conditioning factor must be what follows the vowel and not what precedes it. We can assume this from the fact that both long and short vowels can be preceded by the same elements. For example, both long and short /i/ can be preceded by /b/, /l/, and /h/.

The long vowels are followed by /v ð z r/ and # (a word boundary). The short vowels are never followed by any of these. Consequently, we can assume complementary distribution and proceed to writing the rule:

$$V \rightarrow V: \ / \ \underline{\qquad} \left\{ \begin{matrix} v \ \eth \ z \ r \\ \# \end{matrix} \right\}$$

The additional data look like minimal pairs, and therefore appear to contradict our previous assumption that the long and short vowels were allophones of a single phoneme. However, this contradiction is only apparent. If we consider these data, we can note that, if we remove the contraction and the past tense markers, then all the long vowels are in word final position (just as they were in the initial data set). Consequently, there are no minimal pairs in the data and our initial assumption and rule were correct. We simply apply the vowel lengthening rule before the past tense suffix is attached to the stem, or before the contraction.

An alternative would be to remove the word boundary from the rule and replace it with +, which is the symbol for a morpheme boundary.

5.12

Both [k] and [g] always occur before consonants and back vowels, while [tʃ] and [dʒ] occur only before front vowels.

5.13

The fricatives occur between vowels, and the stops elsewhere.

5.14

[s] occurs initially before vowels and before voiceless consonants.

[z] occurs before voiced consonants and between vowels.

5.15

/k/ → [tʃ] / ____/i/
/k/ → [tʃ] / ____/e/

/g/ → [dʒ] / ____/i/
/g/ → [dʒ] / ____/e/

/b/ → [β] / V____V
/g/ → [ɣ] / V____V

/d/ → [ð] / V____V

/s/ → [z] / ____Voiced Consonant
/s/ → [z] / V____V

5.16

There is no obvious answer to this problem. One possibility is that [ŋ] is an allophone of /n/, which appears only before [k] and [g] as a result of assimilation and that [g] is deleted word-finally in some words but not others. It may also be deleted after [n] and before vowels in some words but not others. On the other hand there look to be clear minimal pair cases such as *Ron* and *wrong*. Find as much data as you can to see if you can get a clear picture of what is going on.

CHAPTER 6

6.1 (a)

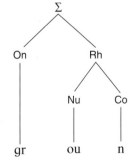

Figure 6.8

(b)

(c)

(d)

(e)

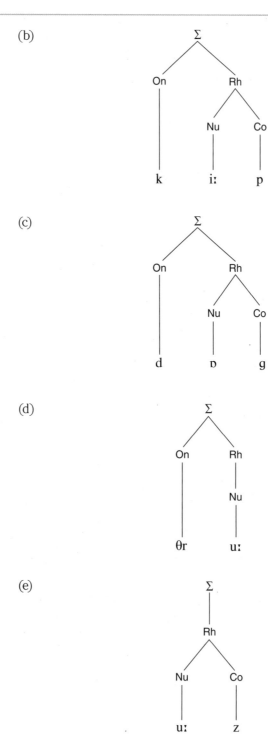

Figure 6.8 Continued

(f)

(g)

(h)

(i)

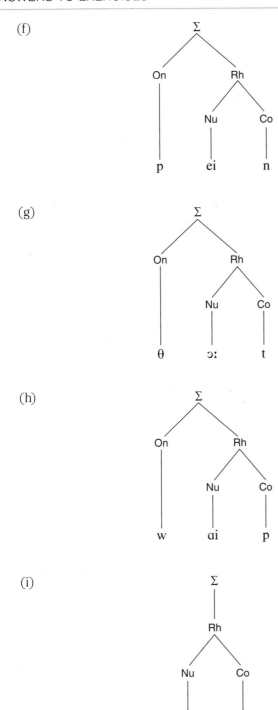

Figure 6.8 Continued

(j)

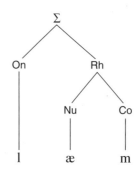

Figure 6.8   Continued

6.2

    (a)   'likely

    (b)   per'fection

    (c)   ˌinter'ference

    (d)   ˌso'lidify

    (e)   ˌsingle'handedly

6.3

    (a)   What was her ˊNAME?

    (b)   You did ˇWHAT?

    (c)   We had deˊCIDed | some time a ˊGO | that we would ˋWALK.

    (d)   By the time the team had reached the ˊTOP | the light was ˋFADing | and it was too late to des ˋCEND.

    (e)   Is there ˊREALly more to him | than meets the ˊEYE?

PART THREE

CHAPTER 7

7.1

    (a)   an ancient monument, fell down during the bombing, during the bombing

    (b)   several young Latvian artists, danced gracefully before the Empress, before the Empress

7.2

(a) elephant, (b) books, (c) women, (d) material, (e) thick, (f) pleasant, (g) delighted, (h) sitting, (i) bored, (j) delayed, (k) rhythms, (l) lovely, (m) in, (n) out, (o) above, (p) unimpressed, (q) eating.

7.3

(a) *out,* preposition; (b) *given,* verb; (c) *cycled,* verb; (d) *slowly,* adverb; (e) *large,* adjective; (f) *work,* noun; (g) *up,* preposition; (h) *correct,* adjective; (i) *silly,* adjective; (j) *beside,* preposition.

7.4

The head of *some very old cars* is the noun *cars*. It is modified by *some* and the adjective phrase *very old*, which contains the head adjective *old* modified by the degree adverb *very*.

The noun phrase *six plants in the shop* has the head *plants*. There are two modifiers of the head, the numeral *six* and the prepositional phrase *in the shop*. This phrase has *in* as head and that head is modified by the noun phrase *the shop*, whose head is *shop*. *Shop* is modified by *the*.

7.5

(a) head, *mare*; modifiers: *the, old, grey, down in the paddock*

(b) head, *uncle*; modifiers: *my, with the fish and chip shop*

(c) head, *bus drivers*; modifiers: *these, three, intelligent, I met yesterday*

(d) head, *person*; modifiers: *an, other, I don't know*

(e) head, *goblins*; modifiers: *six, in green*

7.6

Pronouns are in italics:

her: 3rd pers., fem., sing.; *it*: 3rd pers., neut., sing.; *I*: 1st pers., sing.; *them*: 3rd pers., plur.; *you*: 2nd pers., sing./plur.; *them*: 3rd pers., plur.; *He*: 3rd pers., masc., sing.; *she*: 3rd pers., fem., sing.

7.7

other, very hard, big, rather clumsy-looking, big, heavy, long, flat, big, expressionless, broken-nosed, surprising.

7.8

about, far down the beach, to where the surf was breaking, under a beach umbrella, towards her, down, on the white sand, with her back *to the land*, out *to sea*, above her, with white frills and tassels that swayed *in the breeze*, by the breeze *from the sea*, in proportion *to her long tapering back and narrow waist*, to Smith, on either side, from where Smith watched, above her, in green, up the sand, against the white froth and the blue *of the sky*, in the relative quiet *between breakers*, of music, among her things, about the beach towel *on which she sat*.

Discussion

The prepositional phrases are important in relating things, people, events to each other in time and space. Since the central aim of a description in words is giving a picture, such relating is very important.

You may also have noticed that many of the prepositional phrases have still other prepositional phrases embedded within them. Such embedded PPs are in italics above.

7.9

Noun phrases

(a)

Figure 7.18

(b)

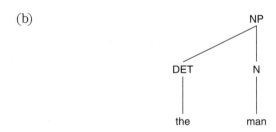

Figure 7.19

(c)

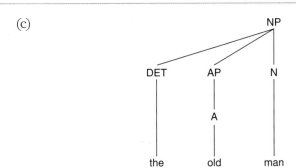

Figure 7.20

(d)

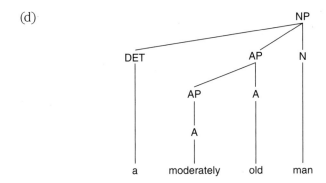

Figure 7.21

(e)

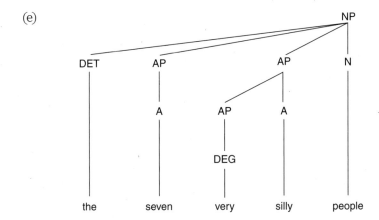

Figure 7.22

(f)

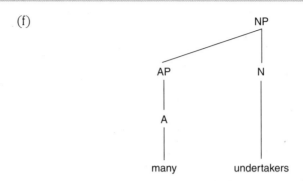

Figure 7.23

(g)

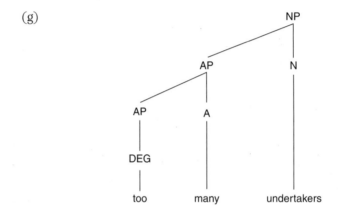

Figure 7.24

(h)

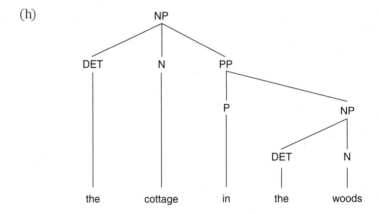

Figure 7.25

(i)

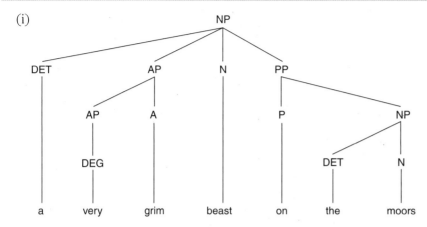

Figure 7.26

(j)

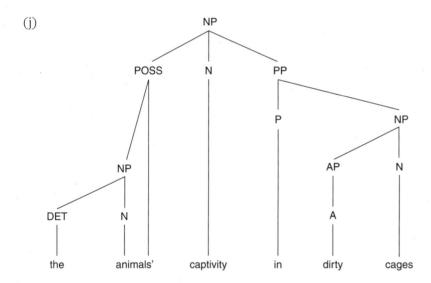

Figure 7.27

Prepositional phrases

(a)

Figure 7.28

(b)

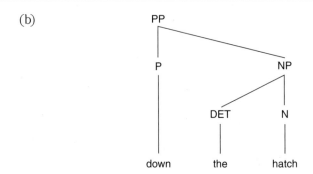

Figure 7.29

(c)

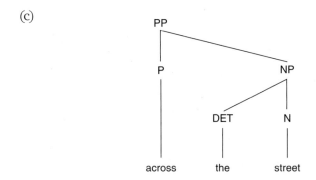

Figure 7.30

(d)

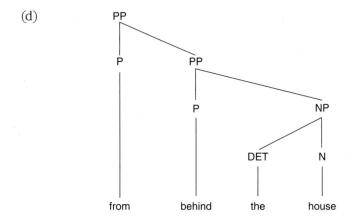

Figure 7.31

(e)

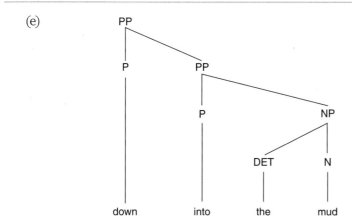

Figure 7.32

(f)

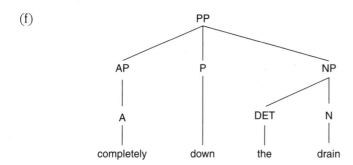

Figure 7.33

(g)

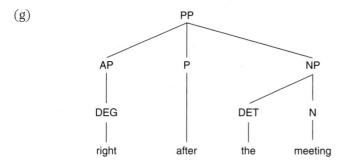

Figure 7.34

Adjective phrases

(a)

Figure 7.35

(b)

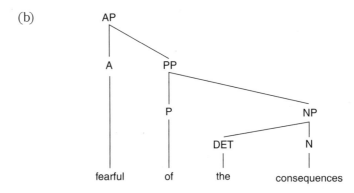

Figure 7.36

(c)

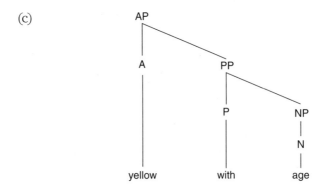

Figure 7.37

(d)

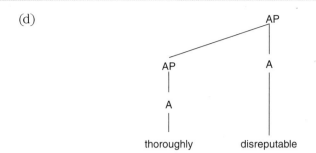

Figure 7.38

(e)

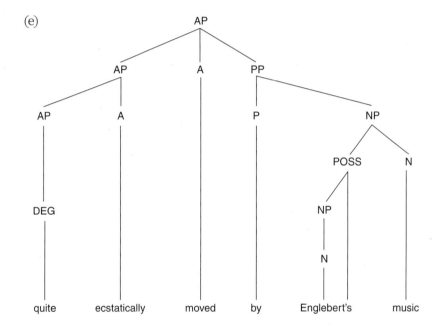

Figure 7.39

(f)

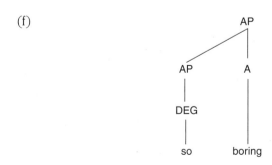

Figure 7.40

(g)

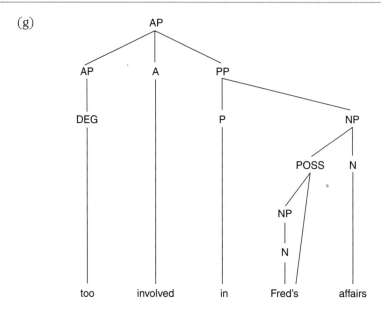

Figure 7.41

7.10

(a) B and C; (b) R, S and T; (c) B, C and D; (d) B, C, D, P, Q, R, S, T and X; (e) C; (f) B, C and D.

7.11

(a)

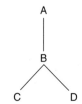

Figure 7.42

(b)

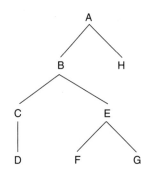

Figure 7.43

(c) $[_A[_BDE][_CF]$

(d) $[_A[_BDE][_CFGH]I]$

7.12

(a) Peter, (b) the greatest magician of all time, (c) three monkeys, (d) they,
(e) that Lionel saw the escape.

7.13

(a)

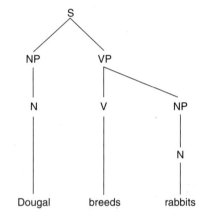

Figure 7.44

(b)

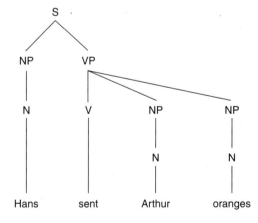

Figure 7.45

(c)

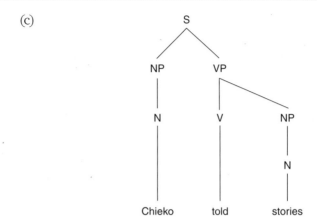

Figure 7.46

(d)

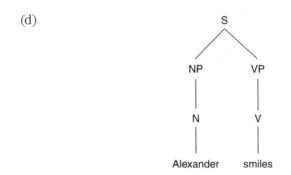

Figure 7.47

(e)

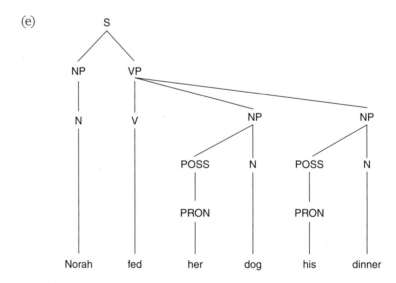

Figure 7.48

7.14

(a) *Freda* is an indirect object and *a bicycle* is a direct object.

(b) *a new camera* is a direct object.

(c) *her breakfast* is a direct object and *hot* is an intensive complement.

(d) *very shy* is an intensive complement.

(e) *Harriet* is a direct object and *the most valuable player* is an intensive complement.

7.15

(a) *Heather* is the subject, *the ferry* is the direct object, and *across to Istanbul* and *yesterday* are adverbials.

(b) *Isabelle* is the subject, *the lamp* is the direct object, and *lightly* is an adverbial.

(c) *Bricks* is the subject, *best* is an intensive complement, and *because they are heavy* is an adverbial.

(d) *Cotton fabrics* is the subject, *everyone* is the direct object, and *this season* is an adverbial.

(e) *Everyone* is the subject, *expensive presents* is the direct object, *to their friends* is the indirect object, and *this season* and *for Christmas* are both adverbials.

7.16

(a)

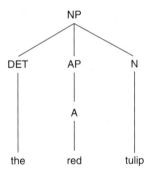

Figure 7.49

(b)

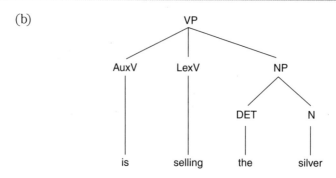

Figure 7.50

(c)

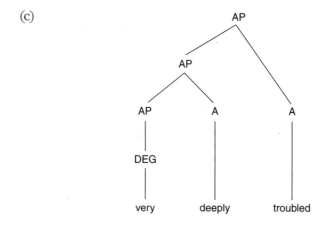

Figure 7.51

(d)

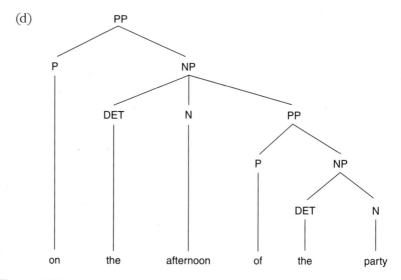

Figure 7.52

(e)

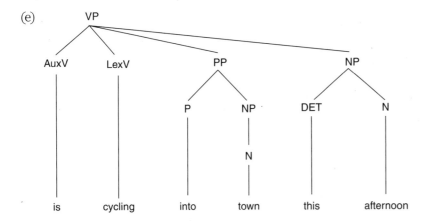

Figure 7.53

(f)

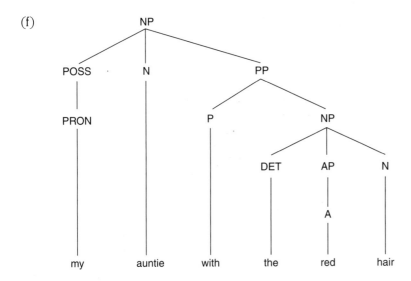

Figure 7.54

7.17

(a) We SUBJECT
gave him a raise PREDICATE
him INDIRECT OBJECT
a raise DIRECT OBJECT

(b) He SUBJECT
donated his stamp collection to the gallery PREDICATE
his stamp collection DIRECT OBJECT
to the gallery INDIRECT OBJECT

(c)   She   SUBJECT
       put the wombat in the alligator's cage   PREDICATE
       the wombat   DIRECT OBJECT
       in the alligator's cage   PLACE ADVERBIAL

(d)   Xavier   SUBJECT
       cried   PREDICATE

(e)   The key   SUBJECT
       opened the door   PREDICATE
       the door   DIRECT OBJECT

(f)   The alligator   SUBJECT
       ate its prey   PREDICATE
       its prey   DIRECT OBJECT

7.18

Use LEXV: ACTION a preserving jar which *contains* LEXV: STATE about 10 cm of soil to which peat *has* AUXV *been* AUXV *added* LEXV: ACTION in the proportion of two measures of soil to one of peat. *Cover* LEXV: ACTION the top of the jar with muslin.

You *must* AUXV *keep* LEXV: ACTION the atmosphere moist, but *be* LEXV: STATE careful that no mould *is* AUXV *allowed* LEXV: ACTION to *grow* LEXV: ACTION as this quickly *kills* LEXV: ACTION the animals. *Should* AUXV the muslin *feel* LEXV: ACTION dry *sprinkle* LEXV: ACTION it lightly with water. Slugs *will* AUXV *eat* LEXV: ACTION carrot discs, which *may* AUXV *be* AUXV *supplemented* LEXV: ACTION occasionally with pieces of potato and green food. When the food *begins* LEXV: ACTION to *decay* LEXV: ACTION it *must* AUXV *be* AUXV *removed* LEXV: ACTION from the jar.

8.1 (a)

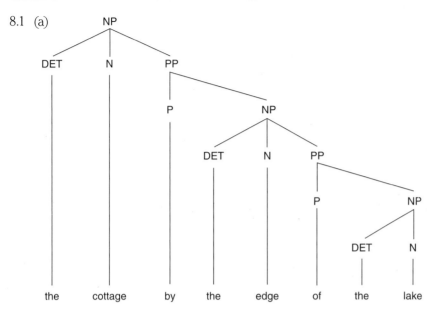

Figure 8.8

(b)

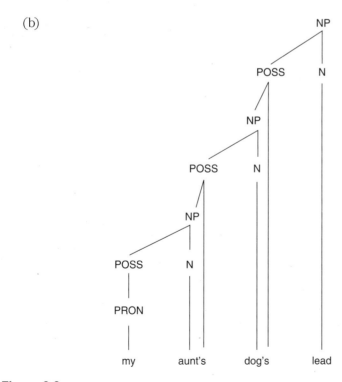

Figure 8.9

(c)

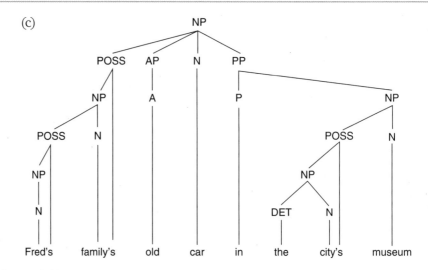

Fred's   family's   old   car   in   the   city's   museum

Figure 8.10

8.2 (a)

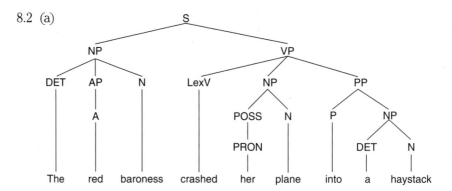

The   red   baroness   crashed   her   plane   into   a   haystack

Figure 8.11

(b)

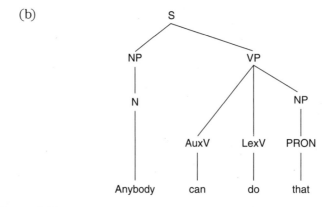

Anybody   can   do   that

Figure 8.12

(c)

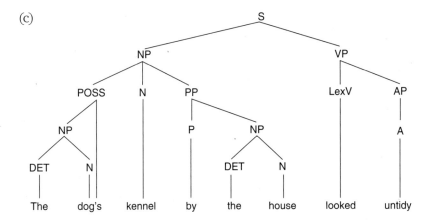

Figure 8.13

(d)

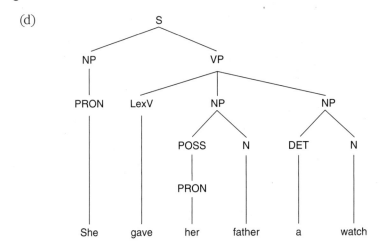

Figure 8.14

8.3

(a)   noun phrases

(b)   prepositional phrases

(c)   verb phrases

(d)   whole clauses

(e)   noun phrases and verb phrases

(f)   noun phrases

(g)   verb phrases

(h)   clauses

(i)   noun phrases

(j)   verbs

8.4 (a)

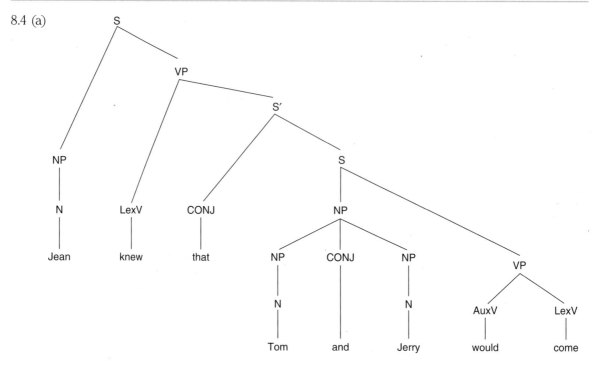

Figure 8.15

(b)

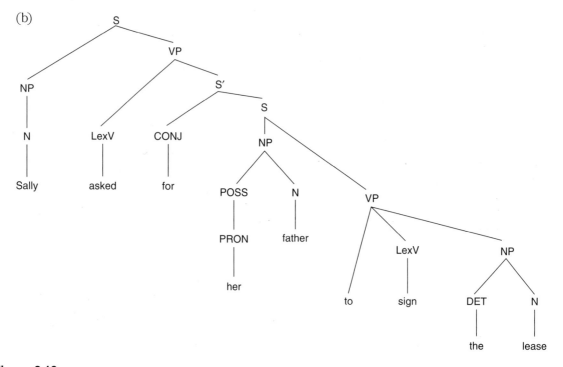

Figure 8.16

(c)

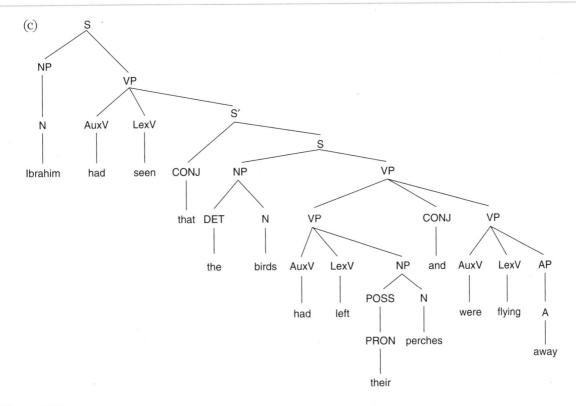

Figure 8.17

(d)

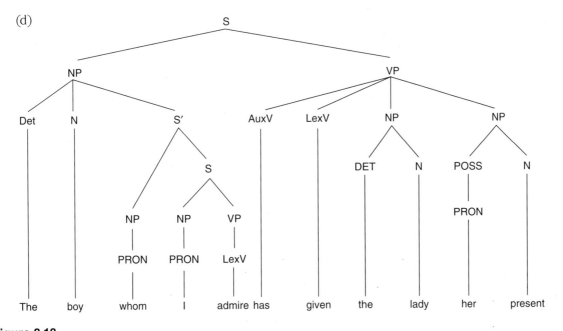

Figure 8.18

(e)

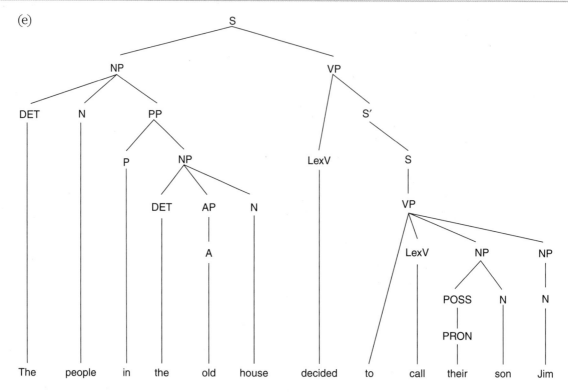

Figure 8.19

(f)

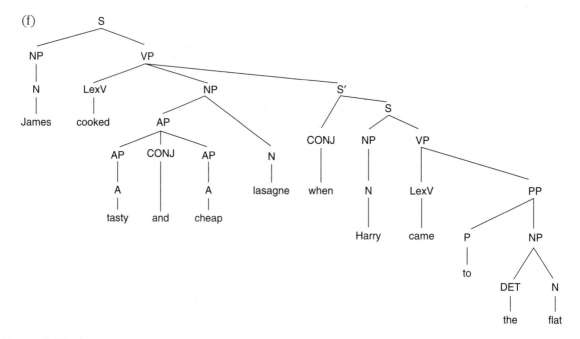

Figure 8.20

(g)

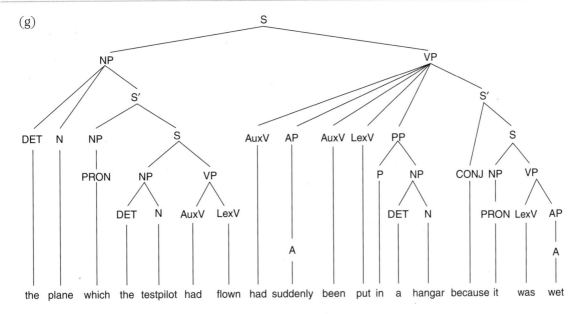

Figure 8.21

8.5

is suited, would be, can be converted, is, developed, are shaken, directed, transfers, holding, permits, to be shaken, may be used, are, bolted, to remain, is stapled, connects, is formed, permitting, carrying, to be shaken.

The auxiliary verb *be* in one or other of its forms is used a great deal, particularly to form passives. Passives are often found in technical writing such as this.

8.6 (a)

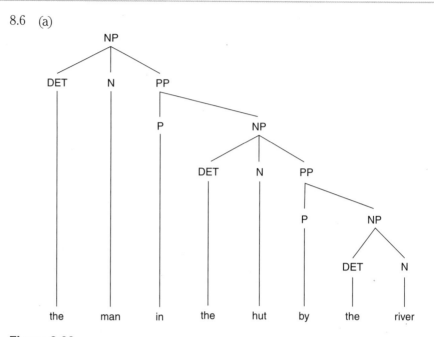

Figure 8.22

(b)

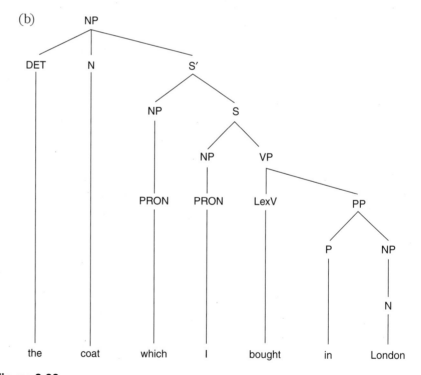

Figure 8.23

(c)

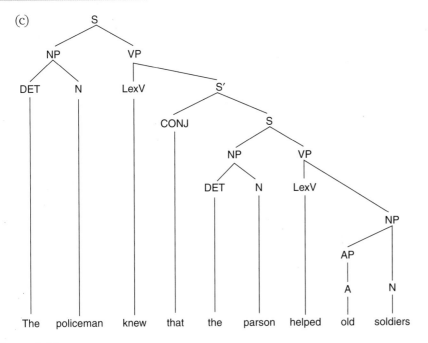

Figure 8.24

(d)

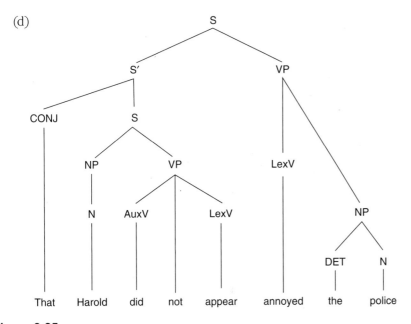

Figure 8.25

(e)

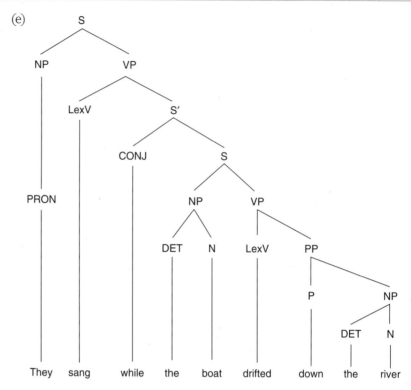

Figure 8.26

8.7

Like can take noun phrases and clauses as objects, e.g. *They liked games. They liked James to come.*

Sob does not typically take complements unless they are redundant, such as *He sobbed great sobs.*

Clean normally takes NPs as direct objects, e.g. *He cleaned the curtains.*

Preserve is a transitive verb which takes a direct object, as in *They preserved the old family customs.*

Declare takes clause complements with *that* as a complementizer, e.g. *They declared that the meeting was very dull.* It can also take an NP direct object followed by an intensive complement, e.g. *The Chair declared the meeting closed.*

Drag is transitive and therefore takes an object, as in *They dragged the chair.*

Place is like *put* in normally requiring both a direct object and a location, e.g. *They placed the chair on the carpet.*

Agree can be intransitive in sentences like *The partners agreed.* It can also take a clausal complement, e.g. *They agreed to come tomorrow. They agreed that Henry should be prosecuted.*

8.8

(a) Philip Swallow had been made and unmade by the system in precisely this way.

(b) He liked examinations, always did well in them.

(c) In the preceding months he had prepared himself with meticulous care.

(d) that, *hot distant* June

(e) the *supreme* moment *of his life*

(f) with meticulous *care*

(g) was *taking* the examinations again, OR
filling his mind with distilled knowledge, OR
it was almost *brimming* over

(h) had *been* made and unmade by the system in precisely this way, OR
had *been*, in many ways, the supreme moment of his life, OR
had *elected* to answer on every paper that hot, distant June, OR
he had *prepared* himself with meticulous care

Index